Preparation for IELTS Academic

IELTS Target 6.5

Teacher's Book

Chris Gough

Garnet
EDUCATION

Published by
Garnet Publishing Ltd
8 Southern Court
South Street
Reading RG1 4QS, UK

ISBN 978 1 90757 512 9

British Library Cataloguing-in-Publication Data
A catalogue record for this book is available from
the British Library.

Production
Project manager: Clare Chandler
Editorial: Clare Chandler, Sue Coll, Kate Kemp,
Karen Kinnair-Pugh
Design and layout: Neil Collier, Mike Hinks, Bob House
Audio recorded and produced by Silver Street Studios.

Printed and bound
in Lebanon by International Press: interpress@int-press.com

Acknowledgements
Page 90, text taken from Wikipedia,
    http://en.wikipedia.org/wiki/All_work_and_no_play_make
    s_Jack_a_dull_boy. Text has been modified and used
    under the CC-BA-SA 3.0 license,
    http://creativecommons.org/licenses/by-sa/3.0/legalcode.

Page 109, text taken from Wikipedia,
    http://en.wikipedia.org/wiki/Role_of_the_Catholic_Church
    _in_Western_civilization. Text has been modified and
    used under the CC-BA-SA 3.0 license,
    http://creativecommons.org/licenses/by-sa/3.0/legalcode.

Page 28, text taken from Wikipedia,
    http://en.wikipedia.org/wiki/Virgil. Text has been modified
    and used under the CC-BA-SA 3.0 license,
    http://creativecommons.org/licenses/by-sa/3.0/legalcode.

Pages 87–88, text taken from Wikipedia,
    http://en.wikipedia.org/wiki/My_Bed,
    http://en.wikipedia.org/wiki/Damien_Hirst,
    http://en.wikipedia.org/wiki/Ai_Weiwei. Text has been
    modified and used under the CC-BA-SA 3.0 license,
    http://creativecommons.org/licenses/by-sa/3.0/legalcode.

Page 198, text reproduced with kind permission of Terri
    Guillemets, www.quotegarden.com.

Page 218, text taken from Wikipedia,
    http://en.wikipedia.org/wiki/List_of_atheist_authors.
    Text has been modified and used under the
    CC-BA-SA 3.0 license,
    http://creativecommons.org/licenses/by-sa/3.0/legalcode.

Contents

Book map

Unit 1	Life and death
Speaking	exchanging personal information / talking about stages and events
Vocabulary	stages of life and life events
Listening	listening for gist
Reading	skimming for gist
Writing	different types of figure / describing figures

Unit 2	Nature or nurture
Speaking	nature or nurture? / talking about background and upbringing
Vocabulary	in the family
Listening	listening for specific information
Reading	scanning
Writing	understanding the task / deciding what to say / organizing your points

Unit 3	Boys and girls
Speaking	changing roles / agreeing and disagreeing
Vocabulary	characteristics
Listening	listening for paraphrased language
Reading	scanning for paraphrased language
Writing	interpreting and describing line graphs / dealing with more information / deciding what to include in your report / writing your report

Unit 4	Past and present
Speaking	memories / describing memories
Vocabulary	looking back / idioms
Listening	listening to label pictures and diagrams
Reading	making sure that information is given in a text
Writing	understanding the task / deciding what to say / writing a balanced composition

Unit 5	Work and play
Speaking	work hard and play hard / talking about your free time
Vocabulary	busy or free / prefixes / free time
Listening	listening to complete a summary
Reading	paragraphs and topic sentences
Writing	interpreting a simple bar chart / interpreting a simple pie chart / comparing and contrasting information

Unit 6	Home and away
Speaking	what are holidays for? / comparing and contrasting
Vocabulary	confusing words
Listening	maps and plans / noticing how information is repeated
Reading	using topic sentences to predict
Writing	organizing paragraphs and using topic sentences

Unit 7	Kill or cure
Speaking	lifestyle / giving yourself time to think
Vocabulary	health and fitness / health issues and minor accidents
Listening	listening to complete a table
Reading	unknown words and phrases in context / working out meaning from context
Writing	describing a flow chart

Introduction

How *IELTS Target 6.5* works

IELTS Target 6.5 is aimed at students who are currently at intermediate level (IELTS Target 5.0), but who want to achieve a score of 6.5 in the IELTS Academic exam. It is especially helpful for students who need support and guidance with some or all of the various tests that make up the exam. Carefully scaffolded tasks aim to orientate and prepare students, rather than throw them directly into challenging exam practice. Frequent reflective exercises encourage students to think about how they approached an exam task, why they performed well or not as well as they'd hoped, and how to go about performing better next time. The course aims to help students develop their all-round English, as well as prepare them specifically for the exam.

The course consists of 12 units and develops in terms of challenge, to take students from an intermediate level through to an advanced level. In the earlier units, language is graded and texts and recordings are simplified to guide students and give them confidence. By the end of the course, they will be tackling texts and working with language at the advanced level that they will deal with in the exam.

Each unit consists of five modules, which are briefly summarized below.

Speaking and Vocabulary

The focus is on speaking exam practice and preparing students for the type of interaction they can expect with the examiner. There is frequent practice of understanding and answering appropriately the type of questions the examiner is likely to ask. The vocabulary selected is the vocabulary students are most likely to need during the interview. Students are also encouraged to record and revise vocabulary that is particular to their own interests, and that they will need to remember in order to talk fluently about their life. There are frequent reflective exercises that allow them to assess their progress and talk about any concerns they may have.

IELTS Target 6.5 doesn't have a grammar syllabus. Grammar is dealt with mainly as revision, as it is assumed that students will be studying grammar on a general English course at the same time as they work through this course. Some major grammar points are dealt with a little more thoroughly, but, generally, the aim is to develop their ability to use grammatical structures to communicate or to recognize them when reading texts.

The *Grammar checks* in each unit focus attention on key grammar points as they arise. If students feel they need further practice with a particular grammar point, they should use an appropriate grammar resource in their own time or ask you to assist in the lesson.

The speaking part of each unit focuses attention on a key pronunciation point. Sometimes this involves practising difficult individual phonemes, and sometimes it involves working with features of connected speech, stress and intonation. These points are there to help improve pronunciation in the Speaking test.

Listening

The Listening Module is roughly divided into two sections. The first section aims to engage students in a topic, pre-teach key vocabulary and then focus on a key skill or particular IELTS exam technique. The second section aims to practise the skill or technique, and then encourage assessment and reflection. Each unit focuses on a different skill or technique, but those skills and techniques are revised as the course progresses. All listening tasks are just like those that students will tackle in the exam.

Reading

The Reading Module is designed like the Listening Module. Earlier units focus on a number of short texts and practise general reading skills, while later units deal with longer texts and provide practice with specific exam techniques.

Both the Listening and Reading Modules end with a focus on *Key vocabulary in context*. The aim here is to focus on the semi-formal vocabulary that students are likely to meet in the recordings and texts which make up the IELTS exam. Students are encouraged to select vocabulary from a text that they think will be particularly useful and that they should record and revise.

Writing

The Writing Module focuses equally on the two parts of the Academic Writing test. Each unit provides analysis of and practice with a particular writing skill or technique that is required for the exam. There is a focus on step-by-step guided writing, and there are model compositions and reports for all of the writing tasks.

Consolidation and Exam Practice

This is divided into two parts. The first part revises the speaking focus and vocabulary presented in the first module. Occasionally, a speaking skill will be developed and there might be a new focus. The second part practises listening, reading or writing skills under exam-type conditions. Each unit practises one skill – reading, listening or writing – so over the 12 units, each skill is practised four times.

Exam tips and Question-type tips

These tips occur all the way through the course. They are there to help students know how to approach the various tasks that make up the exam and to provide advice on how to go about getting the highest score possible in the exam. They also give advice that will help students improve their all-round level of general English.

Reviews

There is a review at the end of each of the three sections. The aim is not simply to revise language that has been learnt, but to reflect on what has been achieved and what subsequently most needs work. There are exercises that encourage students to revise vocabulary independently and to reflect on what is most useful to them personally.

Workbook

There are Workbook exercises for each of the first four modules in the Course Book units. You might complete these exercises in class if a teacher feels that they need further practice with a point, or complete them for homework. At this level, the aim is both to revise and develop. The speaking and vocabulary exercises in particular aim to develop and expand students' vocabulary, and often introduce language that will help to improve their general English, such as idioms and phrasal verbs. In the Course Book Reading Modules, direct reference is made to the Workbook exercises because the exercises specifically focus on the content of that particular module.

As students work through the course, they will learn more about the exam and what they have to do in each of the tests. By the end of the course, students will know everything about every part of the exam and what is expected of them. When they have finished this course, they will be ready to either sit the Academic exam or to take a short post-advanced course that will prepare them to achieve an even higher score in the exam.

1 Life and death

Speaking and Vocabulary

Objectives

- **To introduce students to the IELTS Speaking test, Part 1.**
- **To practise typical questions and answers related to the initial introductory stage of the interview.**
- **To present and practise vocabulary related to stages of life and life events.**

Give students two minutes to read the quotation and think. Give them a minute to discuss it in pairs, focusing on what it means and their reaction to it. Spend another two minutes discussing it as a class. Ask students if they think some people make things happen while many people just let things happen to them.

> *John Lennon was widely regarded as the most creative of the four Beatles. It is ironic that someone so successful admits to not being in control of what happened in his life.*

Speaking 1

Exercises A and B develop into short natural spoken exchanges.

A Students match questions and answers individually and then compare answers with a partner. Monitor to check progress. Do not give feedback as students will listen to check answers in Exercise C.

B Students match follow-up comments to exchanges individually and then compare answers with a partner. Monitor to check progress. Again, do not give feedback as students will listen to check answers in Exercise C.

C 🎧 Play the whole recording so that students can check answers and get a feel for the interaction. Then play the recording again, pausing briefly between each exchange. Deal with words and phrases that you think are unclear or that students ask about as you go.

Answers are not provided here as they are evident in the tapescript.

Tapescript 🎧 1 (1 min, 47 secs)

C Listen to the complete exchanges and check your answers.

1
Speaker 1: What's your name?
Speaker 2: Orlaith.
Speaker 1: That's pretty. It's Irish isn't it?

2
Speaker 1: Where are you from?
Speaker 2: Well, originally from Bangor.
Speaker 1: Sorry, is that in Wales or Ireland?

3
Speaker 1: What are you studying?
Speaker 2: Psychology.
Speaker 1: Oh how interesting? What do you want to do in the future?

4
Speaker 1: What do you do for a living?
Speaker 2: I'm in film production.

Speaker 1: Oh, how glamorous. I wish I could do something like that.

5

Speaker 1: Have you got brothers and sisters?

Speaker 2: No, I'm an only child.

Speaker 1: Are you? My family's huge. There are eight of us!

6

Speaker 1: Are you married?

Speaker 2: Not yet, but I am engaged.

Speaker 1: How lovely. Have you set a date?

7

Speaker 1: Have you got any children?

Speaker 2: Yes two, one of each.

Speaker 1: That's nice. What are their names?

8

Speaker 1: What do you do in your free time?

Speaker 2: I play golf most of the time.

Speaker 1: Do you? I play a bit myself now and again.

Pronunciation check

Write on the board *an apple*. Drill it, demanding natural production. Say it yourself, clearly producing the *n* at the beginning of the second word. Write on the board /ən'æpl/ and /ə'næpl/ and ask students which they hear. Refer students to the *Pronunciation check* and give them time to read and absorb the information and examples. Drill the examples, and then put students into pairs to practise – one should speak, the other should listen and provide feedback. Monitor and provide your own feedback. Allow the time necessary to make progress, though do not expect perfection.

D Students should write questions individually and then mingle to ask and answer the questions.

Vocabulary 1

The aim is to present vocabulary and to prepare for speaking practice later.

A Point out that items are in chronological order, so that students can follow them through logically. Make sure they understand the difference between a *stage* or *period* and a *single event* before they start the exercise.

Students should work in pairs so that they can discuss meaning as they go. They can check in a dictionary if neither in a pair knows the word or phrase.

Be prepared to spend sufficient time giving feedback. Students will want and need some clarification and will benefit from useful expansion.

Vocabulary suggestions

- *Infancy* is the period of being a very young child (up to about seven). A very young child is an *infant*.
- *Adolescence* is the period of changing from a child into an adult, typically 13–15. A person of this age is an *adolescent*.
- A *wedding* is an event – a marriage ceremony, and the celebrations that follow. Note that *marriage* can also be used for the moment a couple say their vows and exchange rings during the ceremony.
- *Pregnancy* is the period during which a woman carries a baby. A woman is *pregnant*.
- *Middle age* as a period is written as two words. The adjective *middle-aged* is hyphenated.
- *Retirement* is both a single event (the day she retired) and a stage (the time after you stop working). *Retire* is the verb. *Retired* as an adjective often comes before the noun – *a retired policeman*.
- We do not use an adjective *old-aged*. A person is *old* or *elderly*.

Answers:

infancy S   childhood S   changing school E
adolescence S   moving house E
leaving school E   leaving home E
graduating from university E   18th birthday E
starting work E   wedding E   marriage S
pregnancy S   birth of a child E   divorce E
middle age S   retirement E and S   old age S
funeral E

B Students should work in pairs, so that they can communicate and compare ideas as they go. Monitor to check interaction. Feedback is probably not necessary.

Answers:
a. leaving home   b. birth of a child
c. wedding   d. funeral   e. moving house
f. graduating from university

C Pronounce each of the key nouns for students, but do not explain meaning. Students can look up or discuss meaning with a partner as they match the nouns to the pictures.

They can compare answers with a partner and explain reasons for their choices. Check answers as feedback. Deal with any remaining uncertainties.

Answers:
Students' own answers.

D Students should work in pairs, using dictionaries if necessary. Check answers as feedback and refer back to the pictures to consolidate and expand. Ask questions such as *Who looks anxious in any of the pictures?*

Answers:
joyful / apprehensive / sad / excited / anxious / proud / fearful

Speaking 2

The aim is to personalize language learnt in the lesson so far and to provide Speaking test practice.

A Read the instructions for each step with students, so they know what they are doing and why. Then manage each step separately. Monitor during the interaction stage to assess performance and make a note of any points that could be shared as feedback. As feedback, choose two students to share ideas with the class.

Refer students to the Exam tip.

B Give students sufficient time to read the questions and check what they need to. Monitor to see what students are checking and clarify anything with the whole class if necessary.

C 🎧 Read the instructions and make sure students know what to do. Play the whole recording as students tick. Then play the recording again, pausing after each exchange to check answers. Ask students to explain their choices. Emphasize that the important thing is to sound interested and to try to give a full

answer. Some of the poorer answers do contain any grammatical errors, but that is not the principal consideration.

Answers:
1. B 2. A 3. B 4. B 5. A 6. B

Tapescript 🎧 2 (4 mins, 13 secs)

C **Listen to some students answering the questions in Exercise B. For each question tick the student that gives the better answer.**

Question 1 – Student A
Examiner: Where did you grow up?
Student: Grow up? Oh yes, in my country. Belgium.

Question 1 – Student B
Examiner: Where did you grow up?
Student: Well, I was born in a small town called Myshkin, but my family moved to St Petersburg when I was nine, so really I grew up there – in St Petersburg.

Question 2 – Student A
Examiner: What important decisions have you made recently?
Student: Mm, well I had to decide if I wanted to go to a university near my home city and stay living at home, or apply to a university in Rome and move there. I chose Rome.

Question 2 – Student B
Examiner: What important decisions have you made recently?
Student: Err, I don't know. Maybe to take my exams.

Question 3 – Student A
Examiner: Who influenced you as a child?
Student: Mm, my teachers.

Question 3 – Student B
Examiner: Who influenced you as a child?
Student: Sorry, influence? You mean like parents or teachers, or do you mean like people in sport or pop stars?
Examiner: You decide. Who had a big influence on your life when you were young?

Student: Well, lots of people - my parents and my older sister and some of my teachers. I guess my dance tutor influenced me a lot because I still dance, and I might do it professionally one day.

Question 4 – Student A

Examiner: Do you have regrets about any choices you've made?

Student: What is 'regrets'?

Examiner: I mean, do you feel you would like to change something in the past – make a different decision.

Student: No, everything is good. I'm happy.

Question 4 – Student B

Examiner: Do you have regrets about any choices you've made?

Student: Mm, that's a difficult question. I think everyone has some regrets, but I don't think you should look back. You must look forward in life and think about how you can be happy in the future.

Question 5 – Student A

Examiner: Tell me about a turning point in your life.

Student: *Turning point*? Do you mean an event that changed my life – made things different?

Examiner: Yes, exactly.

Student: Well, two years I finished a relationship. I was going to get married but really I was young – only 20. It was a very difficult decision to make, but I'm glad I made it. My life is very different and I feel freer.

Question 5 – Student B

Examiner: Tell me about a turning point in your life.

Student: *Turning point* is big thing in your life I guess. For me, it was get my first job.

Question 6 – Student A

Examiner: Do you ever worry about growing old?

Student: No, I'm young – too young to worry about being old.

Question 6 – Student B

Examiner: Do you ever worry about growing old?

Student: Mm, I don't really worry about it, but I don't look forward to it. I'm healthy and very active, and I see a lot of old people who don't have good health. I don't want to be an old person that can't do things.

D Both students in a pair should answer all the questions. Monitor to check performance, and make a note of anything that needs clarification at the end.

Grammar check

Students should find the grammar point in this first module straightforward. Read through the instructions and put them into pairs to answer the questions. Check answers orally.

Answers:

1. Present simple – general present time / permanent concept
2. Present continuous – specific present time – around now / temporary concept
3. Past simple – specific past time
4. Present perfect – unspecified past time – linking past to present / result of action in present

Watch out!

Draw attention and tell students that the boxes are a feature of each unit. They should look out for the boxes themselves as they work through the book. You can focus on examples of error in the boxes if you think a particular point needs to be made.

Listening

Objectives

- To introduce the concept of listening for gist (global comprehension).
- To practise listening for gist.
- To show that understanding gist facilitates understanding of specific information and detail.
- To introduce students to a range of IELTS listening tasks.

Listening 1

A The aim is to prepare students for the listening stage, rather than to provide extended speaking practice. Set a time limit of one minute to talk about the pictures. Monitor to check ideas. Feedback is not necessary.

B 🎧 Make sure students know what to do before they listen. Play the whole recording. Check answers without listening again. Students should discuss the process on the strength of one listening.

Answers:

1. c   2. d   3. b   4. a

> **Tapescript** 🎧 3 (3 mins, 18 secs)
>
> **B** Listen to four extracts and match them with the pictures. Write the number of the extract in the box.
>
> **Extract 1**
> **Woman 1:** So, does it really change your life as much as everybody warns you?
> **Woman 2:** Nobody can warn you – it turns your life upside down! You go from thinking about and looking after yourself, to thinking permanently about and looking after another little person. Life will never be the same again.
> **Woman 1:** Oh dear. Don't you get any time to yourself?
> **Woman 2:** Well, yes – at about 11 o'clock after the last feed – but then you're too tired to do anything.

Woman 1: Mm – but once they're at school it must get easier, surely.
Woman 2: Yes, I'm sure it does but that seems a long way off at the moment.

Extract 2
Voice: … it's an activity that unites the mind, body and spirit. The mind and the body become one and that's therapeutic. People become aware of body posture, alignment and how they move. The body becomes more flexible and it's possible to maintain relaxation even in a stressful atmosphere. People have more energy and are happier all-round with life.

Extract 3
Boy 1: So, have you thought about this 'People of the World' presentation we have to do yet?
Boy 2: Mm, I've thought about it. I can't say I've got any real ideas, though. I was thinking about doing something about the Egyptians – you know, I think their lives were very interesting.
Girl: No, you're supposed to talk about people that live now. As far as I know, Egyptians now live just like we do! It has to be a presentation about people whose lives are totally different from ours now.
Boy 2: Oh, I didn't realize that. So, something like the lives of Eskimos, you mean?
Boy 1: Or Aborigines, maybe.
Girl: Well, maybe …, but neither of those is very imaginative, is it? I'm not sure there are many Eskimos now, anyway.
Boy 2: Oh right – so what are you going to talk about then?
Girl: Well, I was thinking about Bedouins in the Sahara Desert. I can show some really good …

Extract 4
Voice: Okinawa is something of a phenomenon. It has a population of around a million people, but 900 of those are centenarians – that means they are 100 years old or more. That is four times the number of centenarians in most other parts of the world. What is perhaps even more

remarkable is that this seems to be the only place in the world where both men and women are equally likely to reach a hundred. Now, much of this is to do with Japanese lifestyle but there's much more to it …

C Students should complete sentences individually, and then compare answers with a partner and discuss. Go over answers and clarify where necessary.

Answers:
1. general idea / main idea
2. specific information / details
3. every word
4. specific information / details

D Discuss the first extract as a class. Ask:

- did you listen for ideas that you could predict from the pictures?
- did you hear any key words or phrases that helped?
- did the speakers' voices (stress and intonation) help?

Direct them towards whole phrases like, *it turns your life upside down!* and *looking after another little person*, as well as specific words like, *feed* and *school*. Note that, if students only pick out single key words, they are not really focusing on gist.

Put students into pairs to discuss the other three extracts. Monitor to check ideas, as lengthy feedback will not be beneficial. Elicit one or two key items for each extract. Answers are not provided as each extract contains several possibilities and students should decide for themselves which they hear.

Refer students to the Exam tip – note that the advice relates directly to the exercise that follows. Give them a minute to read it. Tell them to cover it and ask them what advice it gave.

E Read through the instructions with students. Students should look at the images and think individually for two minutes. Then they should discuss ideas with a partner. Monitor to check ideas, rather than conduct whole-class feedback.

F 🎧 Play the whole recording as students match. Play the recording again, pausing between each extract to check answers and elicit key language that provided answers.

Answers:
1. b   2. d   3. a   4. c

Tapescript 🎧 4 (2 mins, 7 secs)

F **Listen to the four extracts and match them with the images in Exercise E.**

Extract 1
Voice: … generally it's agreed that ultimately there are four main areas of life in which people look to find fulfilment. What is difficult – some might say impossible – is to find fulfilment in all of those areas at the same time. Now, let's start by …

Extract 2
Tutor: David, how's the project going? I … I sort of got the impression you weren't making much progress.
Student: Oh … it's fine, really. I was a bit stuck, but now I know which writer I want to write about, it's all going quite well.
Tutor: Oh, good. So, which writer have you chosen after all?
Student: Noel Coward. I'm going to write my project on Noel Coward.

Extract 3
Woman 1: Uh huh, yeah, but haven't you got the directions on the invitation?
Woman 2: Well, yes, but … but Steve threw it out. Once we'd told you we were coming … you know Steve.
Woman 1: Well, the church is in Argyll Road. It's really easy to find. Look, Sue and Tim are coming too. Why don't you give them a call and come up together? You can all share a taxi when you get off the train – then you won't get lost, will you?

Extract 4

Voice: … and they were very important. They were far more than places simply to wash. They were central to the community – places where people from all walks of life could meet to talk and relax, exercise or conduct business. The ruins of these magnificent …

Listing 2

A Note that the exercise here is designed to practise listening for gist; it is not a typical IELTS Listening test task. Though multiple-choice questions are common, they rarely assess the overall purpose of a recording like this.

Read the instructions with students and emphasize how important it is to use questions to make predictions about content. Look at the questions for Extract 1 as an example. Establish that students will hear a man and a woman discussing a domestic issue. Then give students sufficient time to discuss the other three extracts.

Students should look at the questions and think individually for two minutes. Then discuss ideas with a partner. Provide concise answers as feedback.

Answers:
Extract 2: Students will hear one speaker talking about life choices.
Extract 3: Students will hear several young speakers comparing or making choices.
Extract 4: Students will hear a lecturer talking about countries in the developing world.

B 🎧 Play the whole recording as students match. Check answers, explaining why any options chosen may be wrong.

Answers:
1. a   2. b   3. b   4. c

Tapescript 🎧 5 (3 mins, 39 secs)

B Listen to Extracts 1–4 and choose the correct summary a, b or c for each extract.

Extract 1

Man: Frankly, we just need somewhere bigger. We're bursting out at the seams here.

Woman: Well, yes, I agree. You know I do, but it's not that easy, is it? We'd have to pay a fortune for somewhere bigger round here.

Man: So, let's start looking further afield, then.

Woman: Haven't we already discussed that? I really don't want to uproot the kids. They're happy at school, and they've got so many good friends. We've got so many good friends. I don't want to start all over again.

Man: We won't have to. People would come and see us. The kids would get used to it pretty quickly. I grew up with a big garden – running around outside all the time. I want them to have that. I just think …

Extract 2

Voice: … you must also try to ensure a goal doesn't directly interfere with other aspects of life. If business travel is a frequent part of your schedule, or you're inclined to work 70 or 80 hours a week, it'll have a drastic effect on your personal relationships. The travel and long hours might result in poor health or family breakdown. In a nutshell, certain goals are mutually exclusive and are not compatible with other goals.

Extract 3

Female 1: So, have you decided yet?

Female 2: No, not yet. It's so difficult – too many choices. It's such a big decision too. It's going to affect the rest of our lives.

Male: Well, certainly the next four or five years.

Female 2: So, what about you Keith, I bet you know exactly what to do, don't you?

Male: No, not really. I'd love to go to Manchester, but that's only because I think it'll be such a great place to live. The course isn't supposed to be especially good. Then there's London. The courses are supposed to be the best, but I really don't want to live somewhere quite so huge.

Female 1: I think you should base your decision on what's best for your future. Not on where's a great place to live.

Female 2: No, I don't completely agree. I definitely don't want to study too close to home. I'd have to stay living at home with mum and dad – I don't really want that. But if I do move away, it's got to be to somewhere exciting. I'm not going to spend four years in some dull place just so I can say I've got a 2:1.

Extract 4

Voice: Almost all the world's shortest life expectancies occur in Africa where the AIDS epidemic, malnutrition, curable diseases and civil unrest continue to take a dreadful toll on human life. Of 29 countries where life expectancy at birth is 50 years or lower, 28 are in Africa. Afghanistan, a country ravaged by war, is the only other country in that list of 29. There life expectancy is 42 years. Of the 40 countries with the shortest life expectancy, 38 are in Africa.

Refer students to the Exam tip.

C 🎧 Read through the instructions with students and point out that this is a task they will see a lot during the course. Note that this first task of its type is fairly easy. Tell students they will hear the words they need to write as answers. Give them time to read all the sentences before you play the recording. Tell them not to answer from memory yet.

Play the recording again. Do not check answers as students will do so in Exercise D.

Tapescript 🎧 **6 (0 mins, 9 secs)**

C **Listen again and complete the sentences.**

[Play Track 5 again]

D Checking and reflecting on answers is a constant feature of the skills modules. Give students sufficient time to check and think about why they may have answered incorrectly before moving onto Exercise E.

Answers:
1. a garden
2. long hours
3. Manchester / London
4. 50 years

E Students may not be familiar with this type of reflective process. Explain that identifying what they are doing well and not so well is a very good way of focusing on what they can do better next time. In this first unit, you might like to work through the exercise as a whole class, asking various students to reflect. Later, they can work on these exercises individually or in pairs.

Key vocabulary in context

Sometimes it is necessary to pre-teach vocabulary and sometimes vocabulary is best learnt in context once it has been read or heard. This follow-up vocabulary work is a constant feature of the skills modules in this course. Tell students this before they begin the exercise. Students should complete the exercise individually and then compare answers with a partner. Check answers orally. Students may need some clarification and will benefit from useful expansion (see *Vocabulary suggestions* on next page for guidance). Note that *life expectancy* is a focus in the next module.

Answers:
1. way you live your life
2. long you are likely to live
3. satisfaction
4. there is some sort of problem
5. negative
6. changes dramatically

Vocabulary suggestions

• If you feel *fulfilled*, you feel satisfied.
• *Conflict* is similar to fighting – *conflict between rival gangs*.
• If you *interfere*, you become involved in something that is not your concern. The noun is *interference*.
• The *root* is the part of a plant or tree under the ground. If you are *uprooted*, there is sudden dramatic change in your situation (especially location).

Refer students to the Workbook exercises related to this module. Choose to work on them now or set them for homework.

Reading

Objectives

- To introduce the concept of skimming for gist (global comprehension).
- To practise skimming for gist – whole text and paragraphs.
- To show that understanding gist facilitates the understanding specific information and detail.
- To introduce students to a range of IELTS reading tasks.

Reading 1

The first part of the lesson introduces students to the concept of reading for gist. The second part practises the skill.

A The three items are the topics of the extracts that students will read. Give students two minutes to check them in a dictionary and then tell them to close their books. Ask:
- which phrase is related to babies dying?
- which phrase is related to how long you will probably live?
- which word means *living a long time*?

B Note that two of the phrases from Exercise A are consolidated here. Put students into pairs and give them three minutes to discuss the questions. Tell them they are not expected to know the answers, but should attempt to offer suggestions.

As feedback, answer the questions briefly as a whole class. Specific answers are not provided as they are too numerous, but during feedback try to introduce the following ideas that occur later in the lesson.

genetics / diet / lifestyle / exercise / poverty / standard of healthcare

C Read through the instructions with students. Remind them they worked through a similar task in the Listening Module. Make sure they understand they are headings of short texts they will read. Allow students sufficient time to read, think about and discuss each heading.

Students should read the headings and make predictions individually. Then compare answers with a partner.

Monitor to check understanding and also to make a note of which students you can ask for feedback. As feedback, choose one student to make a suggestion for each heading. Note that good answers will involve paraphrasing the heading.

Possible answers:
1. More babies die when families are very poor.
2. People with less money / worse jobs may die earlier.
3. People want to know why some people seem to live longer.

D Read through the instructions with students and make sure they know what to do. Explain that the words and phrases blocked out are those that make the task too easy if shown. Emphasize that they only have a 90 seconds – 30 seconds per extract – because the aim is not to read for detail. Impose a strict time limit.

Check answers before Exercise E as there is no point in students discussing why they made wrong matches.

Answers:
1. B   2. C   3. A

E The aim is for students to reflect on the process of skim reading. Read the instructions with them and put them into pairs. Tell them to be selective about what they highlight – there is no point in highlighting almost everything.

Monitor and check that students are highlighting logically. The ideal way to give feedback is to make an OHT or other visual medium of the text to show on the board and ask selected students to come and highlight parts of it. If you choose to elicit orally and write key phrases on the board, limit the number to two per extract, otherwise it will be time-consuming and potentially unclear.

F The aim is both to assess what students have finally understood and to provide some speaking practice. Students keep their summaries brief and use their own words. Monitor as they talk to check performance. Avoid a repetitive feedback stage.

G Tell students to cover the Exam tip. In pairs, ask students to recap on why skimming is an essential skill. Feedback is unnecessary as this will be covered in the Exam tip below.

Refer students to the Exam tip. Emphasize the fact that skimming for gist facilitates reading for detail. IELTS Reading tests do not provide gist tasks and it is essential that students learn to discipline themselves to read texts quickly for overall meaning before tackling questions.

Reading 2

In the second part of the reading modules, students are left to work more independently to practise exam type tasks. In this first unit, however, there is an introductory stage to prepare them and to facilitate their first attempt at reading a long challenging text.

A Conduct as a whole-class discussion. Give students a minute to look at the maps and pictures and then elicit ideas. Tell them that the theme of life expectancy and longevity is continued into this part of the lesson. Do not confirm or correct any suggestions for now.

B Give students a minute to read the paragraph and establish whether their predictions in Exercise A were accurate or not. Check the meaning and pronunciation of *phenomenon* at this point.

C Read through the instructions with students. Students should read the reasons and make predictions individually. Then compare answers with a partner. Conduct quick feedback to check which reasons most students believe to be most likely. Do not confirm their suggestions.

D Make sure students appreciate the task assesses their skimming skills. Tell them to read as quickly as possible to identify the four reasons. Check answers when the first five students have completed the task. Clarify by identifying the parts of the text that provide the answers. Ideally, highlight relevant lines on an OHT or other visual medium of the text shown on the board.

Answers:

1. ✓ … whole grain bread, beans, vegetables, fruit / … a plant-based intake, consisting of stir-fried vegetables, sweet potatoes, tofu and other soy-based fare. / … consume 20% fewer calories … / As in the other zones,

these people eat healthily. / Here, a traditional diet is tortillas, beans, rice, and a variety of fruits and vegetables.

2. ✓ … eat until you are 80% full. / These people never overindulge and …

4. ✓ For the majority of inhabitants, demanding physical labour is the norm. Even the elderly take pleasure and pride in completing their everyday chores.

6. ✓ They embrace *ikigai* – a purpose for living, … / … and here longevity may be connected with faith. / Adventists also take a weekly 24-hour break for the Sabbath to focus on God, …

Note that the text mentions consuming red wine. It does not mention anyone not smoking.

Refer students to the Exam tip at the end of the text.

E Students should now work independently to practise the skills they have focused on. The two tasks are typical exam tasks, and later in the course they will be taught how to approach them methodically. For now, they attempt the tasks as an early taste of exam practice. Set a time limit of ten minutes to complete both tasks.

Students should read instructions and answer questions for both tasks individually. They should check with you if they do not understand the instructions. Students then compare answers with a partner. Monitor to check how quickly students are working and whether some of their answers are correct. Help with instructions if necessary, but do not help with any questions. Do not check answers as students will do so in Exercise F.

F Checking and reflecting on answers is a constant feature of the skills modules. Give students sufficient time to check and think about why they may have answered incorrectly before moving onto Exercise G. Students might want to know why some of their answers were not correct. Going through all of them would be very time-consuming and it is best to tell them that they will learn more about how to do these tasks later.

Answers:

1. T 2. F 3. T 4. NG
5. C 6. E 7. B 8. A 9. F 10. D

G Students may not be familiar with this type of reflective process (they took this approach for the first time in the Listening Module). Remind them that identifying what they are doing well and not so well is a very good way of focusing on what they can do better next time. In this first unit, you might like to work through the exercise as a whole class, asking various students to reflect. Later, they can work on these exercises individually or in pairs.

H The aim is to provide some more, hopefully motivating, speaking practice. Students may well enjoy an extended debate, but you should have a time limit in mind. Conducting the discussion as pairwork will ensure that all students can contribute. If time is short, however, you may prefer to conduct it as a whole-class discussion to conclude the lesson.

Key vocabulary in context

Remind students that an effective way to learn and remember new vocabulary is to study it closely once it has been presented in context.

A Read through the instructions with students and make the first choice together as an example. Students should locate the words in the text to fully understand meaning. Students should then work individually, before comparing answers with a partner. Encourage them to look back and check each item in context as they go. As feedback, show an OHT or other visual medium of the exercise on the board and delete the option that is different from the others in each case. Explain why the deleted option is different if necessary.

Answers:
1. choice 2. common 3. moderation
4. sedentary 5. purpose

B Approach as A. Simply write the preposition against the number to check answers.

Answers:
1. in / with 2. to 3. of 4. to 5. of

Refer students to the Workbook exercises related to this module. Choose to work on them now or set up for homework.

Writing

Objectives

- **To familiarize students with the various figure types reported in Writing Task 1.**
- **To practise the basic features of report writing.**

The Writing Module in this unit concentrates on Writing Task 1. It presents the various figures that students interpret and describe data from.

Writing 1

Tell students to spend two minutes looking through the three pages of the Writing Module, so that they have a visual image of the various figures described in the Exam tip. Refer students to the Exam tip and give them time to read it. Do not explain what any of the figures are now, as students will be introduced to them one by one.

A Read the instructions with students and elicit the meaning of the phrase. Compare *developed* with *developing* and give examples of developed countries – the United States, Germany, etc.

Students should read the questions and think individually about what to say for two minutes. They can then discuss the questions with a partner. Get quick feedback, but do not allow a discussion to develop. It is not the aim.

Answers:
1. It has increased dramatically – better diets / medicine / less physical labour.
2. Most estimates fall between 78 and 82 years old.

B Refer students to Figure 1.

Students should read the instructions and answer the questions individually, before comparing answers with a partner.

Show an OHT or other visual medium of the graph on the board, or draw a very simple graph on the board, as students answer the questions. Use the board graph to identify the various features – vertical axis, horizontal axis and so on. Check answers orally, but write any key words on the board.

Note that if any students find it difficult to understand what the graph shows, you can use a copy of the graph on the board to explain.

Answers:
1. a line graph
2. ages 0–90 in ten-year blocks
3. years 1900–2010 in 20 year blocks
4. That life expectancy at birth increased dramatically between 1900 and 2000 – from about 48 to about 76. That life expectancy for somebody who was already 40 increased noticeably – from about 68 to about 79 over the period. That life expectancy for somebody who was already 70 increased very slightly over the period – from 79 to about 84.
5. Students' own answers.

C Work through as A. Answers are not provided here as they are provided in Figure 2.

D As you read the instructions with students, explain the two types of disease – *communicable* = passed from one human to another – *non-communicable* = not passed from one human to another.

Refer students to Figure 2.

Students should answer questions individually, and then compare answers with a partner. Check answers orally, but write any key words on the board.

Answers:
1. a pie chart
2. segments
3. That far more people die of communicable diseases in developing countries.
4. Students' own answers.

E Read the instructions with students and put them into pairs. Set a time limit of five minutes to write six causes. Tell them to think about question 2 as they write the causes. Monitor to check progress and make suggestions if necessary.

Get some quick feedback, but note that answers are provided in Figure 3.

F Work through as B, though give students a little more time to check items in their dictionaries. Advise them not to look up every word on the horizontal axis that they do not know.

Answers:
1. a bar graph / a bar chart
2. deaths per 100,000 inhabitants
3. various causes of death
4. The two bars on the left represent causes of death that are far more common than any other causes – the vertical axis covers a different range of figures.
5. That circulatory disease and heart disease are by far the most common causes. / That men are significantly more likely to die from circulatory disease, heart disease or in an accident.
6. Students' own answers.

G Work through as A and C. Note that students may need to guess the answers to these questions.

Get some quick feedback, but note that answers are provided in Figure 4.

H Refer students to Figure 4 and discuss.

I Check the meanings of the highlighted items with students. Demonstrate what *choke* means. Put them into pairs to answer the questions. Get some brief feedback.

J Work through as F, giving students a little more time to check items in their dictionaries.

Answers:
1. a flow chart
2. the process of dealing with a choking fit
3. to show the direction of the stages in the process
4. Students' own answers.

Writing 2

The aim of this part of the module is to give students a taste of report writing – not to practise one specific aspect.

A Read the instructions with students. Point out that the extracts are from various parts of a report – the opening line, the middle or part of the conclusion. Make an OHT or other visual medium of the extracts to show on the board and work through as an example. In Extract A, highlight *what action to take* and *what to do in both very severe and milder cases*. Point out that *mild* and *severe* are words that occur on the flow chart.

Students should complete the matching individually, and then compare answers with a partner. Go over answers in a similar way to the example with Extract A.

Answers:
A = Figure 5   B = Figure 3
C = Figure 1   D = Figure 4   E = Figure 2

B Students can either work in pairs or work individually and then compare ideas. They should decide. Monitor to check style and accuracy. Set a time limit of ten minutes. It is better to dedicate more time to practice than to conduct a feedback stage.

Writing task

The Writing tasks are found either in the Workbook or in the Exam Practice Module at the end of the unit. In this unit, the task is in the Workbook. Refer students to the Workbook exercise. Work through the stages of conducting the survey in class and set the report writing for homework.

Consolidation

Instructions are given for Speaking exercises when the procedure is not clear from instructions in the Course Book. Set the Vocabulary and Errors exercises either for individual completion and pairwork checking, or as pairwork when you feel immediate interaction is beneficial.

To correct errors in the final exercise, ask students to come and write the correct sentences on the board while other students offer help. You will need to write the corrections on the board to clarify.

Speaking

A Students will know answers from the first module of the unit or perhaps from having read about the IELTS exam or having spoken to people who have done it.

Answers:
1. 4–5 minutes
2. your name and where you are from

3. Students' own answers.
4. everyday life / home and family / school or college / job / hobbies and interests

B Answers:
1. Why   2. What   3. Where   4. How   5. Who
6. When

Vocabulary

A Answers:
life expectancy / infant mortality / mortality rate / lifestyle choices / household incomes / calorie intake

C 1. marriage   2. graduation   3. infancy
4. pregnancy   5. spiritual   6. Fulfilment

Errors

A Answers:
1. … There are seven of us.
2. That's a Scottish name, isn't it?
3. Have you made any important …
4. … interfere with my life.
5. Knowing what action to take can …
6. … the advantages of becoming older?

Exam Practice

Listening

Point out that students have not yet been introduced to, let alone practised, the various task types that occur in the Listening test. The aim of this Exam Practice Module is to consolidate what has been achieved in the unit and to give students a taste of exam practice. They should not expect to answer all questions correctly at this early stage.

Work through the two listening sections here as two completely separate exercises.

A Note once more that students will not have an introductory exercise like this when it comes to the actual exam. Students will not be told what each listening section is about. The aim here is to facilitate the process at this early stage.

Give students five minutes to brainstorm ideas and then get some feedback. Do not confirm or correct if you have read the tapescript in advance.

B Remind students of the importance of using the 30 seconds they have to read the questions effectively. Remind them that they have 30 seconds at the beginning of each section. Emphasize the need to read carefully and make predictions. Make sure they know to only read questions 1–12 that pertain to the first section.

Students should spend 30 seconds reading questions and making predictions individually, before comparing ideas with a partner.

Monitor to check ideas. At this stage, deal with any unknown words in the questions, but tell students that they will not be able to do this in the exam and that they will have to get used to not understanding some words in the questions. Feedback is unnecessary.

C 🎧 Play the whole recording. Check answers. You can decide if students should hear the recording to check why any answers were incorrect.

Answers:

1. a 2. a

The answers to questions 3–6 are in alphabetical order, but any order is fine as long as the correct four answers are chosen.

3. A 4. D 5. E 6. H

7. 100 8. 40 9. 8 10. swimming pool

11. sauna 12. online

Tapescript 🎧 7 (3 mins, 23 secs)

C **Listen and answer the questions.**

Tina: … you know how it is. I don't really feel unhappy about any particular thing, just generally a bit fed up. You know, everything's always the same – not much to look forward to.

Susan: Oh Tina, you've got so much to look forward to. It's the school holidays soon. You'll have a great time with the children – days out, down to the seaside, camping. You're off to Italy soon too, aren't you?

Tina: Yes, I know there are big things like that. I mean things every week

– every day. I think I just feel older … and a lot less healthy than I did. I never get any exercise and I'm eating far more than I ever did.

Susan: Well, I've told you to join the gym, haven't I?

Tina: Mm, I don't know if I'm really a gym kind of person. I haven't got the discipline to keep going – you know me – start things but never finish them. And it's all a bit isolated. I mean, it's not a very social thing to do, is it? Just going from one machine to the next for two or three hours.

Susan: Tina, that's absolute nonsense, and I think you know it is. Most people go to the gym because it is social. Everyone has a good chat before they exercise, and then they usually have a coffee afterwards. I've made some really good friends there. There are some women that spend more time nattering than they do on the machines.

Tina: Really? I thought gyms were full of really serious health fanatics. You know, women like stick insects that get all anxious if they even see a bar of chocolate and men with bulging muscles.

Susan: No. No. First of all, most women go on days when it's women only. The more serious ones go on the days when it's mixed. I think they like showing they're as fit as the men! Most of the women that go on the days I go just want to stay in shape. They're not really even trying to lose weight. They just don't want to put any more on!

Tina: Mm, isn't it very expensive? I heard it's about £300 a month or something.

Susan: £300!? Where did you hear that?

Tina: Well, how much is it then?

Susan: It depends. If you find it difficult to go regularly and you pay for each visit, then it works out a bit more.

I'm not really sure because I've got a membership card and I pay a monthly rate. I think it's £8 if you pay on the door – you still have to be a member though and that's £100 a year. You have to pay another £2 if you want to use the swimming pool and another £3 for the sauna.

Tina: Mm, it adds up then. That's £13 and if you go every week that's a lot.

Susan: That's why people pay a monthly rate. It's £40 a month and for that you can use whatever you like. I think you have to pay to use the squash courts, but I never do, so I don't worry about that. I go at least once a week and sometimes twice a week, so I make quite a big saving. You just pay the bill online too, so you don't have to mess around with cash at all.

Tina: Mm, I'm still not sure if it's me. I think going for a run or even playing tennis would be more up my street.

Susan: You just said that going to the gym wasn't very social. I can't see that you're going to make a huge number of friends running round the park by yourself. And, tennis – who are you going to play with? I bet you haven't picked up a racket for 15 years.

Tina: Yeah, OK, OK. I suppose I could think about it. What days do you …

D, E and F 🎧 Read the instructions for each exercise as a class. Each exercise will help students prepare for the second listening section. Make a few predictions quickly together as a class. Set a strict 30-second time limit to read questions 13–22.

Play the whole recording. Check answers. You can decide if students should hear the recording again to check why any answers were incorrect.

Discuss whether students are happy with the number of correct answers they achieved. Conclude by asking students what they think of some of the advice given in the second recording.

Answers:
13. one or two   14. motivate   15. exercise
16. distracted   17. focus and energy
18. essential / important   19. react to
20. in need   21. daily routine   22. the next

Tapescript 🎧 **8 (6 mins, 1 sec)**

F   Listen and answer the questions.

Voice: Now, let me start by asking a question. If you could just choose one or two habits to create and develop over the next few months – habits that would have the biggest impact on your life – what would they be? I'm often asked this question, because people are overwhelmed when it comes to positive life changes.

Now, over the years I've given advice to many people for many different reasons. I've helped people with career changes, I've helped people with relationships, I've helped people sort out their finances and I've helped people to stop smoking. All these people ask me what they should do to change their lives – how they should start seeing things and doing things differently. It's not an easy question to answer because everyone is different and everyone wants different things, but I'm going to talk about seven areas of behaviour – habits, if you like – that I think everyone needs to think about. These are habits that, if implemented, will change your life. The idea is to choose one or two of these habits and try to practise and develop them over a few months. Remember that the choices must be yours – no one should follow my advice as a set of rules. As Confucius said 'Men's natures are alike; it is their habits that separate them.'

So, first of all develop positive thinking. I mention this first as it's the keystone habit that will help you form the other habits. Of course, positive thinking by itself won't lead to success, but it certainly helps to motivate you to do the other things required. I learnt this when I gave up smoking – when I allowed myself to think negative thoughts, I would end up failing. When I learned how to squash negative thoughts and think positively instead, I succeeded.

The second habit is exercise. This may seem obvious and not especially life-changing, but it makes you feel better about yourself and more confident. That leads to success with other positive changes. It reinforces the positive thinking, as you need to think positively to sustain exercise. It relieves stress and gives you time to think. This leads to better mental well-being in your life overall.

Now, single-tasking – that's the opposite of multi-tasking. Why is it life-changing? Here are a couple of very good reasons. You'll be more effective with your tasks and you'll get more done. It's hard to achieve anything if you're constantly distracted by other things. You'll be less stressed and happier throughout your day.

Similarly, you should focus on one goal. Just as focusing on one task is more effective, so is focusing on one goal. While it might seem difficult, focusing on one goal at a time is the most efficient way of achieving it. When you try to take on many goals at once, you're spreading thin your focus and energy, and that means you're more likely to fail.

Habit five – eliminate the non-essential. First, identify the essential – the things in your life that are most important to you, that you love the most. Then eliminate everything else. This simplifies things and leaves you with the space to focus on what matters. This process works with anything – with your life in general, with work projects and with relationships. This will change your life because it will help you to simplify.

Now, the next habit may sound strange. It's kindness. Yes, kindness is a habit and it can be cultivated. Focus on it every day for a month and you'll see profound changes in your life. You'll feel better about yourself as a person. You'll see a change in the way people react to you. How do you develop a habit like this? First, make it a goal to do something kind each day. At the beginning of the day, figure out what your kind act will be and then do it. Then, each time you interact with someone, try to be friendly and compassionate. Finally, try to go beyond small kindnesses to bigger acts of

compassion – volunteering to help those in need and taking the initiative to relieve suffering.

And finally, daily routine. It's so simple, but creating a daily routine for yourself can make a big difference in your life. The best routines, I've found, come at the start and end of the day – both your workday and your day in general. That means, develop a routine for when you wake up, when you start work, when you finish your work and at the end of your evening. How will that change your life? It will help you have a great start to your day and finish your day by preparing for the next. It'll help you focus on what's important, not just what comes up. It'll help you make sure you get done all the things you want to get done. And that can mean a lot. Now, I'm going to go on to talk about how each habit can be …

Unit 1 Workbook answers

Vocabulary development

A 1. lifestyle = how you live your life / choices you make
2. life expectancy = how long you can expect to live
3. lifespan = how long somebody lives or how long something lasts
4. life-changing (usually before certain nouns *experience, moment, etc.*) = having a very dramatic effect

B 1. lifelong (very often before nouns *ambition, dream,* etc.) = lasting a lifetime / since earliest memory
2. a way of life = what is normal and routine
3. late in life = when the person is older than usual
4. a life sentence = a punishment that is life in prison (though it is normally anything from 15–30 years)
5. lifeline = something that saves you
6. life-threatening = a danger to life / potentially fatal

C 1. life goes on 2. that's life 3. life's too short
4. this is the life 5. not on your life

D 1. make 2. Doing 3. had 4. make 5. do
6. had 7. made

Listening

A 1. f 2. a 3. d 4. b

Tapescript 🎧 **9 (2 mins, 16 secs)**

A Listen to four extracts and write the number of each against the topic. There are two topics you will not hear about.

Extract 1

Voice: It could be that your life has changed and that when you first went into the line you're in, your situation was very different from what it is today. You may, for example, have been single then and now have a family. The crazy schedule or the frequent travel may not suit your new lifestyle. In this case, you should look for something more 'family friendly'.

Extract 2

Voice: Some people would say it's so they can live together, but many couples already do this without tying the knot. Having children might be a good reason, but again it can happen outside wedlock. Many couples claim that it's all about commitment and making things official, but that doesn't sound very romantic. Are these people just trying make it harder to walk away when the going gets tough? No – I think there's only one reason and that it's all about divinity. Couples must feel that something bigger than the two of them is bringing them together.

Extract 3

Voice: Most importantly it allows you to get your priorities right. Nobody on his or her deathbed ever said, 'I wish I could have spent more time in the office.' Life goes whizzing by, and we are usually so busy worrying about what's ahead that we have no time to enjoy what's here now. Wouldn't you love to have the time to do what you want to do, when you want to do it and say goodbye to the tyrannical boss that says you can't?

Extract 4

Voice: My husband and I decided long ago that we were perfectly happy with our lives, and that we just didn't need the burden of parenthood.

I remember watching a documentary about a couple in the southern states of the US or somewhere – they had 16 children. We just looked at each other and didn't need to say a word.

Tapescript 🎧 **10 (0 mins, 10 secs)**

C Listen again as you read the tapescript.

[Play Track 9 again]

Reading

B 3 is the correct summary

C 1. D 2. C 3. E 4. A

D 1. c 2. f 3. b 4. a 5. d 6. e

Writing task

See notes in the Course Book Writing Module.

2 Nature or nurture

Speaking and Vocabulary

Objectives

- **To introduce students to the IELTS Speaking test, Part 2.**
- **To practise typical interaction that takes place during the second part of the interview.**
- **To present and practise vocabulary related to upbringing.**

Give students two minutes to read the quotation and think. Give them a minute to discuss it in pairs, focusing on what it means and their reaction to it. Spend another two minutes discussing it as a class. Once students understand the motto, ask whether they believe it to be true or whether people can change fundamentally later in life for whatever reason.

The motto is widely attributed to Francis Xavier, the co-founder of the Jesuit Order. The original motto almost certainly carries the message that religious beliefs can easily be indoctrinated into a small child. It has come to be used to suggest that what happens to a child before he or she is seven years old shapes his or her personality in a way that cannot be reversed and that what happens after that has far less impact.

Speaking 1

The aim is to introduce the relatively heavy content of the unit through an initial channel which students will relate to and find interesting. Core vocabulary related to the theme is presented.

A Students will almost certainly know these celebrities, even if they do not know that they have all adopted children. However, they will probably know that at least one of the celebrities has adopted children and will be able to work out the connection. Students should answer the questions with a partner.

During feedback, students will probably be interested to know more about each situation. Elicit as much as possible, but fill in any gaps. The core words *adopt* and *adoption* will probably emerge at this stage. Point out the adjective is *adoptive*, and explain that we talk about *adoptive parents* and sometimes an *adoptive country – The United States is the adoptive home of many immigrants.*

Answers:
a. Nicole Kidman and Tom Cruise adopted Isabella in 1993 and Connor in 1995.
b. Madonna adopted two children from Malawi, David Banda in 2006 and Chifundo Mercy James in 2009.
c. Steven Spielberg has two adopted children, son Theo and daughter Mikaela George. Theo was originally adopted by Kate Capshaw, Spielberg's current partner, and later by Spielberg himself.

d. Angelina Jolie and Brad Pitt have three adopted children; Maddox Chivan, adopted in 2002 from Cambodia, Zahara Marley, adopted in 2005 from Ethiopia, and Pax Thien, adopted in 2007 from Vietnam.

B The aim is to present core vocabulary and to initiate the debate around what is inherited and what is learnt. Students may want to discuss the issue in some depth and it would be a good idea to have a clear time limit in mind. Note that discussing the issue in groups will allow more students to express an opinion. Avoid a situation whereby group discussion is brought to a close only for a lengthy whole-class debate to begin.

Students should check highlighted words in questions individually, using a dictionary. Then answer the questions in a group. Monitor to assist and to make a note of salient points that can be used during a feedback stage. Keep feedback brief, concentrating on clarifying uncertainties with vocabulary rather than reopening the debate. Choose one student from each of the three groups to give a summary of what his or her group concluded.

Answers:
Students' own answers.

Vocabulary 1

The aim is to present or consolidate a range of both exam-related and informal vocabulary and to prepare for the speaking practice that follows.

A Students should answer the questions in pairs as they check words and phrases in a dictionary when necessary. Choose individual students to answer the questions as feedback.

Answers:
1. *Real* implies *better* or *more valid*. The adoptive parents are ultimately the 'real parents'.
2. *Look like* is related to physical characteristics – *take after* to character and personality.
3. *Pick up* means *get* or *inherit* – *pass on to* means *give*.
4. *Your education* is related to your school and what you learnt there – *your upbringing* is related to what you learnt from your parents and what they intended to teach and show you – *your family background* is more related to the social class and financial status of your family and if the situation was stable.
5. Yes – the verbs are used differently, but have the same basic meaning in this context.

Vocabulary suggestions

- *Look like* and *take after* are inseparable phrasal verbs – you cannot *take somebody after*.
- *Pick up* and *pass on* are separable – you can *pass your good looks on to a son* or *pass on your good looks*.
- *Upbringing* is the noun of *bring up* (many phrasal verbs have noun forms like this).
- *Grow up* is sometimes rather crudely defined as *becoming an adult*. In the context of this unit, it really means *spend your formative years*. *I grew up in London – I lived in London for most of my childhood*.
- When *bring up* is used actively it means *teach and show*. When it is used passively, which is frequently the case, it means more or less the same as *grow up* – *I grew up in the country. / I was brought up in the country*. = I know all about country life. (See *Grammar check*.)

Pronunciation check

Write *educate* on the board and model it, emphasizing the stress on the first syllable. Then write *education* and model it with the stress on the third syllable. Ask students to give an example of a similar word group.

Refer students to the *Pronunciation check* and give them time to read and absorb. Make sure they look at the example words before you play the recording.

🎧 Play the recording and then check answers. Write each word on the board, emphasizing the shifting stress.

Answers:
1. b'iology / bio'logical
2. 'character / characte'ristics
3. 'parent / pa'rental

Show how the stressed syllable in *biology* is pronounced /ɒ/ and how the following syllable is pronounced weakly as /lə/. Then show how in *biological* the second syllable is pronounced weakly as /ə/ while the stressed syllable is now produced strongly.

Play the recording a second time. Drill all the words and then give students two minutes to practise in pairs.

B Students at this level will want to develop informal and idiomatic language they can use in conversation as well as more obviously exam-related vocabulary. The expressions here are common and fairly easy to use.

Students should spend two minutes reading the sentences individually, before discussing the rubric points in pairs. Monitor to assist and to identify which students can provide concise definitions during a feedback stage. Tell students to cover the exercise as you provide feedback, so that you can check retention. As well as simply asking them to explain expressions, ask guiding questions like, *Which two materials are compared to say that people are different?* and so on. If you have time, write the expressions on the board again with one key word missing – *It ... in the family* and so on.

Grammar check

The passive is generally looked at in purely grammatical terms, when, in fact, the very meaning of the verb often plays an important part in how it is used. *Educate*, for example is more likely to be used passively than actively. Of course, we can say *His parents educated him at home*, but *He was educated at/in* ... is a far more likely and predictable structure. Any students hoping to fully understand active and passive use should also appreciate which verbs are transitive and which are intransitive and why some verbs cannot be used passively.

If you do not think your students know *transitive* and *intransitive* as terms, start by giving them simple examples. *Hit* is a transitive verb – you must *hit somebody or something*. *Go* is an intransitive verb – you cannot *go something*. Develop the explanation by saying that somebody *can be hit by something* – a car, for example – but cannot *be gone by something* – it does not make sense.

Give students time to read and absorb the information and make sure they look at the examples in the *Watch out! box*.

Speaking 2

A The aim is specifically to practise the vocabulary acquired. Students should not converse simply using what they already knew before the lesson.

Students should spend three minutes individually planning what they will say, before exchanging information in pairs. Monitor and check retention and use of new language. Whole-class feedback is unnecessary.

B You can either read through the Exam tip and then look at the task cards or look at the task cards first, so that students better understand the Exam tip. Students will practise this process numerous times during the course and become very familiar with it.

Make sure students know who is A and who is B in their pair and then tell them to read their task card carefully. Check that everyone understands all the points on his or her card and knows what to do. Then stop them and tell them that they will listen to an example.

C 🎧 Read through the rubric with students and make sure they understand what they are listening for. Play the whole recording and give them time to compare thoughts with a partner before you check answers. Get some feedback and then play the recording again, pointing out elements of good and poor interview practice as you go.

Answers:
The first student performs better. She checks key words, clearly plans her answer, uses a rich range of vocabulary and is grammatically accurate. She responds appropriately and enthusiastically to the examiner's question.

The second student has not planned as well. He produces short, unlinked sentences and waits for the examiner to develop the conversation. His range of vocabulary and grammatical structure is fairly limited.

Tapescript 🎧 **12 (3 mins, 11 secs)**

C Before you start talking, listen to two students talking to the examiner. Which student do you think performs better? Why?

Speaker 1

Student: Can I just check something?

Examiner: Yes, of course.

Student: I know *look like* is about physical characteristics. Is *take after* more about personality and habits?

Examiner: Yes, that's right.

Student: OK – and your *upbringing* is how you are educated?

Examiner: Mm, not really educated – more about how your parents treat you and show you how to live.

Student: Yes, I understand.

Examiner: OK, are you ready, then?

Student: Yes, I want to talk about my friend Ivana. She looks like her mother – she has her eyes and her smile. They are both very pretty. I think so anyway. She takes after her father more, though. She's very ambitious and determined to do well – she always was like that. She's quite a serious person, like him, but also very friendly and kind. This is also what I want to say about how her upbringing affected her. She was brought up to be very confident and always had her parents' support. They wanted her to do well, but also to be happy. I remember she was always 'star of the week' even in primary school, and she did very well in all her exams. She was very cross if she didn't get a good grade for any school work. Now she's working as a journalist.

Sometimes I see her on TV doing some reports. It's no surprise that she's successful.

Examiner: So, do you still see her?

Student: Yes, but not so much like I did. She lives now in Moscow and that's …

Speaker 2

Student: OK, I want talk about Jay-Z. You know the rap guy?

Examiner: Yes, I think so – there are so many.

Student: He's married to Beyoncé.

Examiner: Oh, yes I know who you mean.

Student: He's from a poor background. I mean, he had a tough start in life …

Examiner: … in what way?

Student: Mm, I think his family was poor. Maybe his father was in prison.

Examiner: But, Jay-Z's very successful now?

Student: Yes, very successful. He's a musician and an actor. He's a kind of businessman. I think he's very clever.

Examiner: So, tell me how you feel about him.

Student: I feel good. I mean, I admire him. He worked very hard for everything what he has now.

Examiner: OK, so tell me a bit more about …

D Give students a minute to plan what to say. Tell them to make notes – not to write full sentences and then read them. Some students might prefer not to write down their ideas. You should not expect them to each talk for an unbroken two minutes yet, but they should talk for as long as possible. One student should talk and then the other, as this is what they do in the exam. Monitor closely so that you can identify what they do well and not so well. Later, you might like to record (perhaps on a camcorder) interview practice like this.

Listening

Objectives

- To introduce the concept of listening for specific information (names, dates, times, etc., – and key words in a formal lecture).
- To practise listening for specific information.
- To revise use of capital letters with real nouns.
- To encourage pre-listening prediction from questions and notes.

Listening 1

The aim is to familiarize students with the type of information that they frequently have to write as answers in gap-filling tasks, particularly in Section 1, and then to provide some practice.

A The aim is to prepare for the listening stage and motivate, rather than to provide extended speaking practice. Refer students to the picture. Check that they understand *primary school* in question 2.

Students should read the questions individually and think about answers. Then give them about three minutes to answer the questions in pairs.

As feedback, establish that this is a *nursery school* – most people say simply *nursery*. The American term *pre-school* is being used more in British English, but is still not common. *Kindergarten* is often erroneously used by non-native speakers. Get a show of hands as to who went to nursery and get two students to tell the class what they remember.

B Refer students to sentences a–l, give them a minute to read and ask them where the conversation they will hear takes place and what it is about. Read through questions 1–3 with the class and make sure they know what to do. Students should work in pairs to share knowledge and communicate as they go.

Monitor and assist, but do not confirm or correct answers as students will listen in a moment. As feedback, ask three or four students direct questions like, *Which gap requires a figure as an answer? Which gap requires a name?* and so on. You can check use of capitals when you check the answers in Exercise C.

C 🎧 Play the whole recording and then give students a couple of minutes to compare answers. Re-emphasize the need to use capital letters for some answers. Find out how many students have answers to all questions having listened only once, and who needs to listen again. Emphasize that they will have to become accustomed to listening to recordings only once.

Play the recording again as you check answers. Making an OHT or other visual medium of the sentences to show on the board will enable quick, concise feedback. Point out that:

- numbers can be written as figures or words – large numbers should be written as figures.
- dates can be written in various ways – writing simply the month and day is quickest.
- some names of people and most names of towns and streets will be spelt for them.
- they will hear phone numbers twice at least.

Go over each use of a capital letter, getting students to explain why they are used in each case.

Answers:
a. 3 / three days b. Anne c. 30 / thirty children
d. waiting list e. July 1 / 1st July f. Noah / Katie
g. Yeats h. three years i. 49 Southampton Street
j. her mobile / 07795 673453 k. 32 l. 26

Tapescript 🎧 **13 (3 mins, 31 secs)**

C Listen and fill in the missing information.

Mother: Oh, hello, is it OK to come in?

Manager: Yes, of course. Hi.

Mother: I'm only round the corner. I thought it would be easier to pop round than speak on the phone … It's bigger in here than I expected. It looks quite small from outside.

Manager: Yes, lots of people say that.

Mother: Anyway, I wanted some information. I'm hoping to go back to work very soon and I need to get some childcare sorted out. I think it'll only be three days a week, but we'll talk about that in a minute … I'm Anne, anyway.

Manager: Hi Anne, so how old is your … mm … do you have a boy or a girl?

Mother:	Both actually – twins. So, it's two spaces I'm hoping for.
Manager:	Goodness, I bet that's hard work. Mind you we've got 30 here so we know what's it like. Let's go through to the office. It's always terribly noisy out here.
Manager:	Right, that's better. Now, first of all, let me say that we don't actually have any spaces at the moment, but spaces do come up pretty frequently. We've only got one other child on the waiting list, so it's worth taking your details.
Mother:	And then you contact us as soon as there's a space?
Manager:	Exactly. So, when would you want them to start?
Mother:	At the beginning of July – that's about six weeks away.
Manager:	Well, that might be a good time. Lots of parents take children out over the summer. You know, brothers and sisters off school, family holidays and so on. Shall I put July the first?
Mother:	Yes.
Manager:	OK, and what are their names? Are they identical twins by the way, will we be able to tell them apart?
Mother:	No, don't worry, they're not. Actually, identical twins are always the same sex.
Manager:	Oh yes, I did know that.
Mother:	Noah's my little boy and Katie's my little girl.
Manager:	Noah, that's unusual. It's N-O-A-H, isn't it?
Mother:	Yes, that's right. It's not as unusual as it was actually. We know a couple of other Noahs now.
Manager:	And the family name?
Mother:	Oh yes, that's Yeats – Y-E-A-T-S.
Manager:	And how old are they?
Mother:	They're two years and ten months – so coming up for three very soon. Are most of the children around that age?

Manager:	Mm, they'll be a bit younger than most of the others, but we've got a few of that age. And you said you live round the corner.
Mother:	Yes, Southampton Street, number 49.
Manager:	Oh, I know Southampton Street. My auntie lives there. It's one of the nicest streets round here.
Mother:	Yes, we like it anyway.
Manager:	Mm, oh yes, phone numbers.
Mother:	I'll just give you the mobile number. Then you can call any time. It's 07795 673453.
Manager:	07795 673453.
Mother:	That's it.
Manager:	OK, so why don't I show you round and you can ask questions as we go.
Mother:	Yes, OK. Can I just check prices first, though? I'm told it's £32 a day. Is there any reduction if they do three days?
Manager:	No, I'm afraid there's only a reduction if they do a full week – all five days. However, there is a slight reduction if you have two children in the nursery. It'd be £26 a day each. I know it's not much but it all helps. Anyway, shall we take a little tour and then we'll go over any details once you've decided what you think. I'll make us a cup of …

Refer students to the Exam tip. Give them a moment to read and absorb.

Listening 2

The practice part of the lesson is a little more demanding than the first. Students listen to a talk rather than a conversation. Specific information includes key words and phrases as well as names, numbers and so on. Note that the preparation phase is designed to orientate and motivate students and to facilitate listening practice at this early stage of the course – they will not be prepared in this way in the exam. Note also that the second part of the lesson develops the theme of the first and recycles key language.

A The main aim is to prepare for the listening stage, rather than to provide extended speaking practice. Though students should be encouraged to develop a conversation, you may like to have a clear time limit in mind. Note that discussing the questions in pairs will give more opportunity for more students to contribute. Avoid a situation whereby the pair discussion is brought to a close only for a lengthy whole-class debate to begin.

Students should look at the pictures, read the questions and think for two minutes individually, then answer the questions in pairs. Monitor to assist and to make a note of points that can be used during a feedback stage. Keep feedback brief. Establish that the pictures show identical and non-identical twins and that, as they learnt earlier, identical twins are always the same sex. Choose one student to give feedback on each of the questions 3–5.

Refer students to the Exam tip and give them a moment to read and absorb. Tell them to cover it and select one student to summarize the advice.

B Remind students that they will not be told what the topic of each section is in the actual Listening test, and that using the questions (1–13) to make predictions is essential. Remind them they get only 30 seconds to read the questions, but give them a minute now.

Make a few predictions together as a class. Ask students if they think that *fraternal* means the same as *non-identical*, if they think the answer to question 3 will be a percentage and what is required for question 4, for example.

C 🎧 Read through the instructions with students and then refer them to the Question-type tip at the bottom of the notes. Ask them how many words is a maximum for this particular task.

Play the whole recording as students complete the task. Do not check answers as students will do so in Exercise D.

Tapescript 🎧 14 (5 mins, 1 sec)

C Listen and complete the notes a student made.

Voice: Well, we've been looking at various aspects of genetics, and this morning I want to talk specifically about twins. Some of you were asking about twins last week and particularly about how environment or nurture affected their development.

First of all, I want to establish the fact that there are two and possibly even three types of twins. I'm sure everyone has heard the term *identical twins*. The scientific term is actually *monozygotic twins*. Now, people assume that with identical twins it's all about appearance – that they look exactly the same. Now, that might be the case, but the important thing is actually how they form. Identical twins form when a single fertilized egg splits into two. *Non-identical twins* form when two eggs are fertilized separately. Twins that are not identical are usually called *fraternal twins*, though the scientific term here is actually *dizygotic*.

Around a third of twins are identical – two-thirds are fraternal. So, fraternal, or non-identical twins, are quite a lot more common than identical twins. Now, I mentioned a possible third category, but not very much is known about this yet. Some twins might be hybrid or half-identical. This may happen when an unfertilized egg splits into two and the two parts are then fertilized separately. I'm not going to say much about this today – I don't know much! – but there's a very good website where you can find out more. That's www.humangenetics.com. Human genetics is all one word. Take a look.

OK, some facts about the two types of twins. Firstly, identical twins are always the same gender – two boys or two girls, and they have the same blood group. Fraternal twins can be the same gender or a boy and a girl. They often have the same blood group, but not necessarily. Now, perhaps most importantly, identical twins share 100% of their genetic markers – fraternal twins share around 50%. So, it's clear that identical twins are more likely to be the same in many ways – not simply the way they look.

Now, before I talk about how twins can be very similar or what might cause them to be different, I'm going to mention another difference between the two types of twins – the reason that they are born as twins in the first place. We know that fraternal twins are more common when women have babies later in life – perhaps after 35 years of age. We also know that fertility treatment can increase the likelihood of twins. With identical twins, this doesn't seem to be the case at all. There are no known causes for identical twinning.

So, are identical twins the same in every way? No, they're not. They're probably very similar, but it's a question of nature and nurture. There are all sorts of factors and influences that determine how a person grows up and it's no different for twins. Even before birth, in the womb, twins can develop differently. It is common that one twin has a better connection to the placenta and this will mean he or she will grow bigger. Identical twins can often be slightly different heights and weights. Recent research suggests that although identical twins are born with many identical genetic characteristics, as they age and spend more time apart, these similarities diverge. Twins develop their own personalities and follow different interests. It is likely that identical twins even deliberately try to establish individual identities as they grow up. It is not known yet whether certain identical genes actually disappear as twins age, or whether external influences play a bigger part in determining individuality.

Now, this research has been carried out at a cancer research centre and this is important. It might be that the genetic make-up which makes identical twins so similar is also related to the development of disease like cancer and conditions such as autism.

But, to get back to similarities and differences – I like one comparison I've seen that compares twins to cakes cooked from the same or different recipes. Two cakes cooked from the same recipe are more likely to be very similar than two cakes cooked from two different recipes. The two cakes from the same recipe will be very similar, but not exactly the same. Various external influences will mean that each cake has something slightly different about it. Another way to look at this is to think about your own face. Both sides of your face come from the same DNA, but they are not exactly the same – they're not a mirror image of each other. All sorts of factors and experiences in life mean that one side of your face is almost certainly a little different, and in some cases very different, from the other side.

D Checking and reflecting on answers is a constant feature of the skills modules. Give students sufficient time to check and think about why they may have answered incorrectly before moving onto E.

Answers:
1. into two   2. two eggs   3. ⅓ / a third
4. humangenetics   5. blood group
6. (about) 50%   7. 35 (years old)
8. height and weight   9. personalities
10. identity   11. cancer   12. cakes
13. a face / your face

E Students will by now be a little more familiar with this type of reflective process, but note the statements are not the same as in the previous unit. Remind them that identifying what they are doing well and not doing so well is a very good way of focusing on what they can do better next time. Allow students time to reflect and complete the exercise and then ask them if they are happy with the number of correct answers.

Key vocabulary in context

Students will know some of the nouns without looking back at the text, while others may be quite new.

Students should complete the exercise individually and then compare answers with a partner. Write answers on the board. Students may need some clarification.

Answers:
1. difference   2. treatment   3. similarity
4. likelihood   5. development
6. connection   7. fertility   8. individuality

Refer students to the Workbook exercises related to this module. Choose to work on them now or set up for homework.

Reading

Objectives

- To introduce the concept of scanning (reading for specific information).
- To practise scanning a text for specific information.
- To introduce students to further examples of IELTS Reading tasks.

Reading 1

The first part of the lesson introduces students to the concept of scanning a text. The second part practises the skill. Students read two related texts, the second of which is longer and more challenging. The overall theme of the first two modules is developed and core language recycled.

A Pronounce the two key words again for students and drill them if necessary. Point out that the appeal of the phrase is the fact that the two words are opposites in terms of meaning, but very similar in the way they look and sound. Students should answer the question in pairs.

Monitor to make a note of who can provide an answer as feedback. During feedback, recycle core vocabulary. Establish that *nature* is all about what you *inherit* – what is *passed on* through *genes / genetically*. Nurture is all about *upbringing* – what is learnt or *picked up* through experience.

B The aim is to reintroduce the concept of skimming from the last unit, and to demonstrate that skimming a text before scanning for specific information is an essential step.

Read through the instructions with students and then make sure they read the three summary options before they read the text. Check that students understand everything in each option – point out the use of *shape* as a verb and check that *open to debate* is clear. Either set a time limit, or tell students you will check the answer when the first three students have one.

Students should read and choose a summary option individually, before comparing their choice with a partner.

Answers:
3 is the correct summary

C You can decide whether to set both exercises or to do one at a time. Students should read and answer questions individually, before comparing their answers with a partner. Write the answers on the board for clarity.

Answers:
1. (dazzling) blue eyes / (your) blue eyes
2. physical characteristics   3. France
4. NG   5. F   6. T

Refer students to the Question-type tip and read through each part with them, referring back to the exercises they have just completed. Point out that they were told to use a maximum of three words for the short answers so, *your dazzling blue eyes*, is not an option. Point out how language in the question is reworded – not the same as language in the text – *inherited* and *acquired* are used in the text, *pass on* is used in the question. Students will look in-depth at paraphrasing later in the course. Point out that the third option of NG makes the second task more challenging than a straightforward T/F exercise, which they may be more accustomed to. Again, they will look in-depth at strategies for tackling this question type later in the course.

D Tell students to cover the Exam tip before they answer the questions. They should then answer the questions in pairs. Check answers quickly.

Answers:
1. skimming for B and scanning for C
2. scanning
3. because so many questions involve locating specific information

Refer students to the Exam tip and give them time to read and absorb.

Reading 2

The text is fairly challenging and students should begin to understand that they will not have time to read every word (or line) of a text, nor do they need to in order to answer questions. Note that the preparation phase is designed to facilitate reading practice at this early stage of the course – students will not be prepared in this way in the exam.

A The aim is to pre-teach core vocabulary from the passage and to facilitate the reading process. Grouping the items into the two categories should help them appreciate that the text further explores the *nature or nurture* theme. Note that the vocabulary items are flexible and fairly high frequency, so will be useful to learn and remember. Students are expected to already know some of the items.

Students should categorize each item individually, using a dictionary if necessary. Then they can compare answers with a partner. During a feedback stage, spend some time on clarification and useful expansion of language.

Vocabulary suggestions

- *Condition* as a verb is likely to be passive. If somebody is *conditioned*, he or she behaves in a way that they have been shown to – they do not think about what they are doing. *Conditioning* as a noun is fundamental to the nature or nurture debate.
- *Modify* means *change*.
- *Innate* and *inborn* are more or less synonymous and mean existing since birth.
- Your *temperament* is similar to your personality, but refers more to basic emotions – a tendency to be happy, rather than unhappy or to get angry easily, for example.
- *Mould* as a verb has the same meaning as *shape*. A *mould* (noun) is used to reproduce products in a factory – the products are all exactly the same.

Answers:
conditioning (NU) / modify and control behaviour (NU) / innate (NA) / inborn (NA) / inherited temperament (NA) / moulding (NU)

B Make sure students read all the ideas before they skim the text. Note that, although they will not be required to order information like this in an exam task, they will be required to match ideas to paragraphs.

Students should complete the exercise individually and then compare answers with a partner. Showing an OHT or other visual medium of the sentences on the board will enable quick, concise feedback.

Answers:
3 – a description of research that proved that nature was also important in human development
1 – the fact that, historically, scientists have disagreed about roles of nature and nurture
4 – the suggestion that nurture affects nature and nature affects nurture
2 – a description of research that supported the nurture theory

C Students are now left to their own devices to practise the skills they have focused on. The two tasks are typical exam tasks, and students will be given plenty of practice with each type, and be taught how to approach them methodically. Set a time limit of 12 minutes (a minute for each question) to complete both tasks.

Students should read instructions and answer questions for both tasks individually. They can check with you if they do not understand the instructions. They can then compare answers with a partner. Monitor to check how quickly students are working and whether some of their answers are correct. Help with instructions if necessary, but do not help with any questions. Do not check answers, as students will do so in Exercise D.

D Checking and reflecting on answers is a constant feature of the skills modules. Give students sufficient time to check and think about why they may have answered incorrectly before moving onto E. Students might want to know why some of their answers were not correct. Explaining some points may be necessary and beneficial, but going through all of them will be very time-consuming. It is best to tell students that they will learn more about how to do these tasks and that their scores will improve.

Answers:
1. a pendulum   2. earlier behaviourists
3. a reward   4. 133   5. temperament / temperamental style
6. T   7. NG   8. F   9. F   10. T   11. NG   12. F

E Students will, by now, be more familiar with this type of reflective process, but note the statements are not the same as in the previous unit. Remind them that identifying what they are doing well and not doing so well is a very good way of focusing on what they can do better next time. Allow students time to reflect and complete the exercise and then ask them if they are happy with the number of correct answers.

F The aim is to conclude the lesson rather than develop an extended debate. You will know whether your students will enjoy and benefit from an extended pair or group discussion, or whether a quick whole-class discussion will suffice. Whatever approach you take, encourage students to use core language learnt in the module.

Key vocabulary in context

Remind students that an effective way to learn and remember new vocabulary is to study it closely once it has been presented in context. Note that, in this case, the aim is to practise the skill of understanding new words and phrases in context as well as actually learning the selected words and phrases. Students should complete the exercise individually, and then compare answers with a partner. Write answers on the board for clarity and deal with any remaining uncertainties. Point out root words where relevant – *pioneer*, *complex*, *mature*, etc.

Answers:
1. pioneering 2. controversial
3. straightforward 4. punished 5. complexity
6. unique 7. correlate 8. isolated 9. maturity

Refer students to the Workbook exercises related to this module. Choose to work on them now or set up for homework.

Writing

Objectives

- **To introduce students to a typical IELTS Writing Task 2.**
- **To understand Writing Task 2 instructions.**
- **To make students aware of the fundamental question of composition content.**
- **To introduce students to the basic principles of composition organization.**

The Writing Module in this unit concentrates on Writing Task 2. The aim is to start addressing the fundamental issues of understanding the task, knowing what to say and organizing ideas, so that they are easy to follow even if not perfectly expressed.

Writing 1

The first part of the lesson focuses on reading instructions and understanding the task.

A Refer students to the Writing task and give them two minutes to read in silence. Do not assist in any way or explain any unknown language at this point.

B Give students two minutes to read, think and choose options before comparing thoughts in pairs. Monitor to listen to suggestions, but do not offer assistance or advice. Read aloud the four options, getting a show of hands for each. Reassure them that they will become familiar with Writing task instructions and will learn words and phrases frequently used.

C There is no specific task here. Showing an OHT or other visual medium of the instructions on the board will be the best way of drawing attention to the features and ensuring that the process has benefit.

Give students two minutes to read and absorb. Show them a copy on the board with the student's notes covered or erased. Ask why each feature was highlighted and elicit the notes the student made. Point out the distinction between the items highlighted in yellow and purple. Those in yellow are specific to this task, those in purple are fixed features used for all Writing tasks.

Refer students to the Exam tip and give them a moment to read and absorb. Reassure them that vocabulary used in Writing task instructions will never be unnecessarily difficult or advanced. At their level, they will almost always know the words and phrases used and should be able to understand anything they do not know from the context.

Writing 2

The aim now is to tackle a problem that is often underestimated – whether students actually know what to say about the issue, regardless of the fact they have to do it in a foreign language. Younger students, especially, have simply never thought about the issues that are typically the subject of Writing Task 2. It is often a good idea to ask students if they could answer the question in their own language. They often admit that they would not be able to. Students will need extensive guidance and practice, and will need to learn that simple ideas are perfectly acceptable – nobody is expecting them to solve a complex social issue!

A Give students two minutes to read, think and choose an option before comparing thoughts in pairs. Monitor to listen to interaction. Read aloud the three options, getting a show of hands for each. Note that, since the issue has been the focus of the unit up to this point, they may well feel they have more to say than they would about a random fresh topic. It may be worth pointing this out.

Refer them to the Exam tip, and then expand on it by giving them some of the advice outlined above.

B Read through the instructions with students and then elicit an example on the board to get the ball rolling. Refer back to the recording in the Listening Module and write up, *Twins develop their own personalities and follow different interests*. Point out that this suggests experience and outside influence do play a significant role. Set a time limit of six minutes, but be prepared to cut that short if students struggle. The stage that follows will provide more guidance and direction.

Monitor and assist with ideas. If two pairs have different points listed, but have nothing more to say, put them together to share ideas. Keep feedback fairly brief, getting a couple of points that support each side of the argument up on the board. Avoid feeding points of your own – students will hear concrete points in the exercise that follows.

C 🎧 The aim is to demonstrate how students should go about addressing a Writing task like this. They should focus on how the two students approach the task, how they use the task instructions and how they decide what to include and what not to include.

Make sure students understand exactly what they are going to listen to and tell them to read the questions carefully first. Use the picture to set the scene. Play the whole recording.

Students should listen and answer questions in note form – they should not attempt to write more than is necessary as they listen. Then they can compare answers with a partner.

Go over the answers – most can be dealt with orally, but some will need to be written on the board. It is probably best not to play the recording at this point as students will hear it again when comparing the conversation with the composition later.

Answers:
1. the female student
2. he's not an expert
3. you don't need to be an expert
4. it doesn't answer the question
5. saying that it isn't true
6. both
7. checks the instructions again
8. Children of aggressive or violent people will also be aggressive and violent.
9. similarities and differences within their families / cousins who are twins
10. the conclusion

Tapescript 🎧 **15 (3 mins, 50 secs)**

C **Listen to some British students discussing the Writing task and answer the questions below.**

Male: What do you think about this composition then, Denise?

Female: Mm, I think it's easier to do because we've been discussing the topic this week. There's quite a lot to say about it.

Male: Really? I think it's quite difficult. I'm not a scientist, so I don't know whether nature or life experience is the bigger influence.

Female: But you don't have to be an expert on the topic. You need to show that you understand what the debate is about and then make some relevant points. You can balance your argument if you don't have a strong opinion.

Male: So, I guess we should write about the history of the debate. You know, when the debate started and what different scientists have

Female: believed at various times in the past.

Female: Mm, I'm not sure about that. It doesn't really answer the question. You could write pages about that too. First of all, we need to look at the statement and think about whether it's obviously true or whether it's there to be challenged. You know, whether the statement invites us to say that we don't really agree.

Male: So, what do you think of the statement?

Female: Well, it says that recent research shows that the characteristics we inherit are more important than what we experience as we go through life. I don't think that's true. What we've read this week does suggest that more may be passed on through our genes than was previously believed, but nobody's saying that we inherit everything. I mean, what we experience is still a hugely important factor.

Male: So, you think disagree with the statement – say that life experience is more important?

Female: Not necessarily. I would say that environment and nurture is very important, but that the really important thing is the interaction between what's inherited and what's then learnt or experienced.

Male: OK, but we have to give reasons and say something about our personal experience. Shall we mention something about studies with twins?

Female: Yes, good idea. Mentioning twins is a good argument to support the idea that genetics is important.

Male: And also that nurture's important. Twins are not exactly the same. Should we compare what's definitely inherited, like eye colour, with what is probably influenced by environment, like our tastes and interests?

Female: Mm, maybe – let me check the instructions again. Mm, the instructions say characteristics that have an influence on our personality. I don't think we need to mention physical characteristics at all. We could say something about why it's worrying to accept that our personalities are determined only by our genes. I mean, if that's the case, surely the children of aggressive or violent people will also be aggressive and violent. The nature only theory suggests that we are prisoners – we have no control over who we become.

Male: OK, but we have to write 250 words. We won't be able to say everything. I don't know what I can say that's related to my own experience. I mean, I don't know any twins.

Female: I don't think that matters. You can say that you and your brother are very similar or very different, or that you're different from your father because you had a different education – something like that, anyway. I suppose I'm lucky because my cousins are twins.

Male: That's OK for you then. I must say I still find this part of the task a bit difficult.

Female: So, how do you think the composition should be concluded?

Male: Well, from what we've discussed that part should be easy now. We have to say that nature and nurture interact and that one is not more important than the other.

Female: OK, are you ready to start writing a rough plan then?

D The aim now is to present a model composition, but more importantly to show how the planning process facilitated the writing process. Make sure students answer the question properly in order to appreciate this.

Students should read the composition carefully and note the obvious point that was discussed, but not included in the composition. They can then compare thoughts in pairs.

Answers:

The obvious point not included is the one about violent people passing on their characteristics.

E 🎧 Make sure students know what to do before you play the recording again. Pause at appropriate moments to emphasize the point being made and to allow students time to identify the relevant part of the composition.

Providing feedback on this task is not straightforward. You could play the recording a third time, highlighting the various points in a composition on an OHT or other visual medium on the board. However, this would be time-consuming and potentially rather repetitive. It is probably best for students to simply benefit from the process without necessarily checking each specific part of the task.

> **Tapescript** 🎧 **16 (0 mins, 14 secs)**
>
> **E   Listen to the students in Exercise C again. Highlight the points in the composition as you hear them.**
>
> [Play Track 15 again]

F Students will focus in depth on the various ways a discursive composition can be approached. The aim now is to get them thinking retrospectively about how this one was approached.

Students should read the options and make their choice individually, before comparing their answer with a partner. Establish together that the approach adopted was option 2.

Writing 3

Another aspect of discursive composition writing that students find particularly challenging is organizing their ideas logically and cohesively. They will often have a series of points they want to make, but struggle to effectively organize them so their train of thought is easy to follow. During the course, there will be rigorous focus on composition planning and

organizing. For now, students are introduced to the concept by retrospectively studying the composition they have worked on.

A Students should complete the task individually and then compare answers in pairs. Write the correct order on the board for clarity.

Answers:

2 – She says that she understands why some people would believe the statement to be true.
5 – She summarizes what she believes to begin the conclusion.
6 – She ends by making a powerful point that she hopes will make people agree with her.
3 – She gives evidence to support the fact that she does agree with the statement.
1 – She shows that she understands the statement and topic generally – by expanding on the statement.
4 – She provides an example from her own experience to support her opinion.

Refer students to the Exam tip and give them time to read and absorb.

Writing task

The Writing tasks are found either in the Workbook or in the Exam Practice Module at the end of the unit. In this unit, the task is in the Workbook.

Note that, in this unit, it would be a good idea to complete the Exam Practice Module before attempting the Writing task. The text discusses the topic and introduces points that students might want to include in their composition.

A At this early stage of the course, students will produce better compositions if they have some time to prepare and compare thoughts with other students.

Give students time to read the task instructions and check any words and phrases they need to. Note that, if they work through the Exam Practice Module first, they will be familiar with the items *sibling* and *only child*, and understand more about the concept of *social skills*. Give them two minutes to think and looks at points 1–3.

B You will know how much preparation and peer assistance your students will benefit from.

Students can either discuss ideas in pairs or small groups. You may feel that some students would prefer to go straight onto tackling the task.

C   You may choose to set most of the Writing tasks for homework, particularly Writing Task 2, for which students need 40 minutes. It would be a good idea to occasionally set a task within class time so that you can check they spend the right amount of time on it and you can monitor to check development. If they do work at home, encourage them to be strict with time limits – they will not benefit from over-planning or spending longer than they are allowed writing.

When students have completed the task, they should compare it with the model composition on page 263. The model is reproduced below.

If you collect students' compositions to mark, use the process to get an idea of what they are capable of and give general feedback. Correcting everything they write early on will not be very motivating. At this stage, you may be still be correcting most of what they write.

Model composition:

In many parts of the world the number of families with only one child is increasing. I read that, in China, it is the norm for families to have only one child due to government policies. In the USA and Europe, couples are choosing to have one child more for economic and financial reasons. Now, more than ever, it is essential that there is debate about whether children with brothers and sisters have advantages over those who do not.

Many people assume that children with brothers and sisters are happier because they see them playing together and interacting. They feel that they naturally learn important social skills that are essential to succeeding in life. On the other hand, people assume that an only child spends a lot of time playing alone and will fail to develop in a way that will help them achieve success. It is argued that parents are either busy, so leave only children to entertain themselves, or devote too much time to only children making them self-centred and spoilt.

Personally, I think that there are some practical disadvantages to being an only child, but not the huge social disadvantages suggested. Teenagers often need a sibling to talk to about personal

issues that they do not want to share with parents. However, it could be that only children develop closer relationships with school friends or cousins to compensate. I do think that, later in life, an only child will have an additional burden in terms of looking after ageing parents.

In conclusion, I would say that despite the practical considerations, I do not think that children with siblings have huge advantages, especially since it is becoming so much more common to be an only child. I have three close friends without siblings and although they sometimes say that they would like a brother or sister, they are perfectly well-adjusted and not spoilt. I also have friends with siblings who they do not get on well with. They do not feel that they have any advantages.

Consolidation

Instructions are given for Speaking exercises when the procedure is not clear from instructions in the Course Book. Set the Vocabulary and Errors exercises either for individual completion and pairwork checking, or as pairwork when you feel immediate interaction is beneficial.

To correct errors in the final exercise, ask students to come and write the correct sentences on the board while other students offer help. You will need to write the corrections on the board to clarify.

Speaking

A   Students will know answers from the first module of the unit or perhaps from having read about the IELTS exam or having spoken to people who have done it.

Answers:
1. 3–4 minutes
2. a task card
3. think about the topic for a minute and make notes if you wish to
4. the meaning of words and phrases on the task card
5. whether you answer the questions or not / fluency – ability to talk without too many

pauses / vocabulary range / grammatical accuracy / clear pronunciation (individual sounds / rhythm and stress / intonation)

B 🎧 The aim is to practise checking words and phrases on the task card. Whether or not students already know *siblings* will probably depend on whether or not you have already worked through the Exam Practice Module.

Give students two minutes to look at both task cards. Make sure they know they are going to listen to students who are unsure about some of the words on their card. They should highlight or underline the words on the cards as they listen. Play the recording and check answers. It would be beneficial for students to read the tapescript as they listen to the recording again.

Answers:
Student A – siblings
Student B – siblings / only child

Tapescript 🎧 17 (1 min, 27 secs)

B Look at the cards and then listen to two students doing the exam. Which words do they check?

Speaker 1

Student: I just need to check a few words on the card before I make my notes? Is that OK?

Examiner: Yes, please do.

Student: This word *siblings* – I guess it means brothers and sisters. Is that right?

Examiner: Yes, that's what it means.

Student: So, when it says *a large family*, it means with lots of brothers and sisters?

Examiner: Yes. Now, are you ready? You have a minute to plan what you want to say and make notes.

Speaker 2

Student: I want to make sure I understand a couple of words before I begin making my notes.

Examiner: Yes, OK, what do you need to check?

Student: Well, I guess it's clear from the context – *an only child* is a child with no brothers and sisters.

Examiner: Yes, exactly.

Student: OK, and *siblings* are brothers or sisters, then? I don't know this word.

Examiner: Yes, it's not a very common word. It's used in academic language more. But, yes, it means brothers or sisters.

Student: Thank you. I'll start making my notes.

C Work through as with the same exercise in the Speaking Module.

Vocabulary

A Students have learnt all of these phrasal verbs, but have not yet looked at them as phrasal verbs.

Answers:
1. looks like   2. pass on   3. takes after
4. grew up   5. brought up   6. picked up

Note that 4 could also be … *was brought up*. Pointing this out will illustrate the point that *grow up* and *be brought up* have more or less the same basic meaning.

Grammar check

Start by referring students to the *Watch out!* box. They will innately appreciate that the first example looks unnatural – the *Grammar check* will explain why. You can ask them to explain why the second example is a mistake. It is probably best for students to read the *Grammar check* quietly to themselves. They are unlikely to absorb the information if it is read to them. Emphasize the advice in the penultimate line.

B **Answers:**
bio'logical / be'haviour / pa'rental / sig'nificance / 'likelihood / ma'turity / com'plexity / individu'ality (*individuality*, with seven syllables carries secondary stress on the third syllable – indi'vidu,ality)

B Mark the main stress on these words.
Then listen and check.

biological
behaviour
parental
significance
likelihood
maturity
complexity
individuality

Errors

A Answers:
1. ... runs in our ...
2. can't tell Mark and ...
3. ... follow in my grandfather's ...
4. ... chalk and cheese ...

Exam Practice

Reading

Point out that students have not yet been introduced to, let alone practised, the various task types that occur in the Reading test. The aim of this Exam Practice Module is to consolidate what has been achieved in the unit, and to give students a taste of exam practice. They should not expect to answer all questions correctly at this early stage.

A Remember that students will not have a preparation stage in the exam. The aim here is to orientate them towards the topic, to motivate and to facilitate reading practice at this early stage. They will also benefit from the speaking practice as they set their own gist reading task.

Students should spend five minutes looking at the pictures, reading the questions and planning answers individually. They can then answer the questions in pairs.

Note that, if you have chosen to work through this Exam Practice Module as a prelude to the Writing task and before the Consolidation

Module, you will have to pre-teach *siblings* and perhaps *only child*.

Though students should be encouraged to develop a conversation, you may like to have a clear time limit in mind. Give them eight minutes (two minutes per question) before you get some quick feedback. You are likely to have a few only children in the class and they may well want to express an opinion. Try to get a general *yes/no* consensus for questions 2–4. You do not need to confirm answers or give your own opinion. Students read the text to check ideas in B.

B Students should skim read the text highlighting points they discussed in A individually. They can then compare what they have highlighted with the same partner they worked with in A. As feedback, ask a couple of students if the passage confirmed what they discussed previously before moving on to the practice.

C The passage is fairly long and there are more questions than students will be set for one passage in the exam. Although students have already skimmed, they will need another 15 minutes, or slightly more, to complete the tasks.

You can decide whether students should compare answers before you give feedback. Write answers on the board for clarity or provide students with a copy of the answer key.

Answers:
1. one-child policy 2. smaller families
3. India 4. 88% 5. 88% 6. 80%
7. d 8. c 9. b 10. a
11. b 12. c (in either order)
13. a 14. c (in either order)
15. ageing parents 16. family home
17. sandwich generation 18. Depression

Conclude the lesson by asking any only children in the class if they agree with the passage.

Unit 2 Workbook answers

Vocabulary development

A **A** make / affect / determine / influence / shape

B show / demonstrate / illustrate / prove / confirm

The verbs in **A** all mean *change* or *cause to change*, the verbs in **B** all mean *show*.

B 1. influential   2. illustrations   3. proof   4. effect   5. confirmation   6. demonstration

C 1. Family members have a similar physical characteristic or habit.
2. You can not detect a difference between them.
3. They are very different.
4. I'm going to do something my father has done (usually the same job / career).

D 1. black   2. water   3. peas   4. eye   5. cat

Listening

A 1. 42   2. 273   3. 07783 961224   4. 11,000   5. 7,845   6. 210,000

Tapescript 🎧 19 (2 mins, 25 secs)

A Listen and write the numbers you hear in the extracts.

Extract 1
Man: So, how old did you say you were?
Woman: I don't think I did.
Man: Oh, didn't you? Is it a secret then?
Woman: No, of course not.
Man: Well?
Woman: I'm 42.

Extract 2
Client: Right, so how much do I owe in total?
Salesperson: Mm, let me see – altogether that's £273.
Client: Oh, I didn't think it was quite that much.

Extract 3
Receptionist: You'll need to give me your phone number – a mobile number ideally.

Man: OK, I never remember my mobile number. Just let me check. Yes, here we are. It's 07783 961224.
Receptionist: Sorry, I got the first part. Can you say the last three numbers again?
Man: Um, I'll say it all again a bit more slowly. 07783 961224.

Extract 4
Guide: … the town looks quite small – I think that's because the centre's very compact – but, in fact, the population is close to 11,000. Of course, numbers are swelled in the summer when …

Extract 5
Teacher: So, you've had the time I set. Who has the answer?
Boy: Mm, I think I've got it. Is it 7,845?
Teacher: What do the rest of you think? Anyone else got that answer? No? Well, it's the right answer. Well done, Geoffrey Clarke.

Extract 6
Voice: … and now house prices. For the third month running, prices have risen. The average price of a house in the UK is now £210,000. That's the highest figure since March last year. Economists say it's too early to say whether this looks like a continuing trend.

B 1. August 27 / 27th August
2. February 3 / 3rd February
3. October 16 / 16th October
4. December 10 / 10th December
5. May 12 / 12th May
6. January 22 / 22nd January

Tapescript 🎧 20 (2 mins, 12 secs)

B Listen and write the dates you hear in the extracts. Write only the month and a figure.

Extract 1
Man: There's a bank holiday soon, isn't there?
Woman: Yeah, at the end of August. The 27th, I think.

Extract 2

Woman: Greg, when do these documents need to be back by? I don't need to do them today, do I?

Man: Oh, no, not at all. The ones you're working on are due back by Thursday next week. That's the 3rd of February.

Woman: Oh, that's a relief.

Extract 3

Woman 1: Are you free next Saturday?

Woman 2: Um, I think so, why?

Woman 1: Well, I was thinking about making dinner for a few people. I'd love you and Mark to come along.

Woman 2: Let me check. Oh no, I'm not free. That's the 16th of October. It's my cousin's wedding. Goodness, I'd completely forgotten. Sorry.

Extract 4

Man 1: I've just been checking the football fixtures.

Man 2: Oh, yeah?

Man 1: United play Liverpool on December the 10th. That's Justin's birthday. Do you think I'd get tickets?

Man 2: Mm, difficult. You know how quickly tickets go for that game. Let me know if you do get some, though. I'd fancy going to that one with you.

Extract 5

Woman: Hey, come and check this out. Look, if we go on the 12th, it's cheaper. We can fly into Prague for £95 each.

Man: Wow, that's good. Do you definitely want to go in May, though? People say it's really amazing in April.

Woman: No, I'm too busy in April.

Man: OK, May the 12th then, book them up.

Extract 6

Voice: ... now that brings us to a very important date. January the 22nd 2005. That was the day that the gallery first opened to the public after several years as a ...

C 1. name: Christine Howell

    address: 57 Belle View Gardens
                       Maidstone, Kent
                       MD6 8QP

2. name of hotel: Rose Hill

    address: 72 Elm Lane
                       Winchester
                       Hampshire

Tapescript 🎧 21 (1 min, 59 secs)

C   Listen and write the names and addresses you hear in the extracts.

Extract 1

Travel Agent: ... so would you like to go ahead and make a booking.

Woman: Yes, I think so.

Travel Agent: OK, I'll need some details. First, can you give me your name?

Woman: Yes. It's Christine Howell.

Travel Agent: Is that Christine with an *h*?

Woman: Yes, C-H-R-I-S-tine. Howell is H-O-W-E-double L.

Travel Agent: OK, and your address with a postcode.

Woman: It's 57 Belle View Gardens. That's B-E-double L, E and then *view* as a separate word. Belle View Gardens, Maidstone, Kent.

Travel Agent: Sorry, Maidstone? Is that M-A-I-D-stone?

Woman: Yes, that's right.

Travel Agent: And Kent is K-E-N-T?

Woman: Yep.

Travel Agent: OK, and a postcode?

Woman: MD6 8QP

Travel Agent: OK, thanks and now, could you tell me ...

Extract 2

Jim: Hello?

Craig: Hi, Jim. It's Craig.

Jim: Oh, hi Craig.

Craig: I'm just phoning to check the address of the guest house again before we set off. I'm not sure if I've got it quite right.

Jim: Wait a moment. I'll go and get it. ... OK, ready? It's called Rose Hill. That's two words – *rose* and then

Reading

B a. 2 – events
b. 4 – the behaviourist model
c. 1 – the twins
d. 6 – female only children
e. 5 – certain aspects of our personalities
f. 3 – trauma in early life

Writing

B 1. Siblings, especially those of similar age,
frequently fight over small matters.
2. Everything we experience, even what we
completely forget, shapes who we later
become.
3. Adopted children, except those placed at a
very young age, frequently have irregular
sleeping habits.
4. Single parents, particularly those with more
than one child, need a support network of
family and friends.

Writing task

See notes in the Course Book Writing Module.

3 Boys and girls

Unit overview

The third unit presents language related to an overall theme of *male/female equality, typical male/female behaviour* and the *roles of men and women in society*. Language from Unit 2 related to *nature or nurture* is integrated and recycled. Students are presented with, and practise, specific tasks from the Speaking, Listening, Reading and Writing tests that make up the IELTS exam.

Speaking and Vocabulary

Objectives

- To introduce students to the IELTS Speaking test, Part 3.
- To practise typical interaction that takes place during the third part of the interview.
- To present and practise vocabulary related to temperament and typical behaviour.

Give students two minutes to read the graffiti and think. Give them a minute to discuss it in pairs, focusing on what it means and their reaction to it. Spend another two minutes discussing it as a class. Make sure students appreciate the two meanings of *simple* – *uncomplicated* and *stupid*. Once students understand the message, ask whether they think it is intended to be purely humorous or whether there is some truth in it.

'The simple things in life' is a typical expression that refers to pleasures which are uncomplicated and usually free rather than material possessions – a walk in the country, for example. Simple can also mean stupid. The message is ultimately saying that women are more intelligent and sophisticated than men.

Speaking 1

The aim is to introduce the overall theme of *male/female differences* and *change (or not) in society*.

A   The images are chosen to be perhaps stereotypically non-stereotypical – men doing what is more commonly associated with women and women doing what is more commonly associated with men. They are chosen to reflect changing norms in the workplace, in education and in leisure-time activities. Emphasize that the time you give students to prepare should be spent thinking about a reaction to each image – simply saying that the pictures show how society has changed is not enough.

Students may want to discuss the issue in some depth, so have a clear time limit in mind. Note that discussing the issue in groups will give more students the opportunity to contribute. Avoid a situation whereby a group discussion is brought to a close only for a lengthy whole-class debate to begin.

Monitor to make a note of salient points that can be shared during a feedback stage. Make sure feedback is focused, taking the opportunity to introduce key vocabulary rather than simply reopening the debate. Ask students if they think behaviour shown is *normal* or *natural*, and if any of the people are behaving in an unusually *masculine* or *feminine* way.

B   The aim is both to provide some typical interview Part 3 interaction and to prepare for the vocabulary work in the next part of the lesson.

Some preparation time is essential here. Students will not be able to express a sensible opinion spontaneously. Encourage them to make a few notes during the time they are given to think and prepare. Discourage students from making comments to be provocative – it may stimulate debate, but not very authentic debate.

Monitor to assist with key vocabulary and to make a note of interesting points that can be used in feedback. Keep feedback brief, getting one example as an answer to each question from different students.

Vocabulary 1

A The aim is to present or revise the vocabulary. Students should not start discussing the statements at this point. (See Speaking 2A.) Students can work on the exercise in pairs, but there is likely to be quite a lot of dictionary work and some may prefer to work individually. Monitor to assist and check pronunciation. If any words are being mispronounced regularly, stop the activity to model and drill them.

Going over each word or phrase as feedback will be time-consuming, repetitive and probably not very beneficial. It is better to ask students if they want to you to clarify anything. Alternatively, tell students to cover the exercise and ask them to remember some of the items. You can decide when students would benefit from any expansion – checking the noun or verb of an adjective or eliciting an opposite, for example – but a few suggestions are made below.

Vocabulary suggestions

- *Sensitive* and *sensible* are easily confused. Point out that *sensible* is a related more to the first statement – it means *logical* and *rational*.
- *Thoughtful* means *considerate* – not *intelligent*. Phoning a friend to ask how an interview went is *thoughtful*.
- You can be *hurt* physically or emotionally. A *hurtful* comment is a comment that makes somebody feel bad.
- *Vain* has only one syllable so the assumed comparative form is *vainer*. However, there are some one-syllable words that sound slightly strange with ~*er* on the end, and many native speakers would say *more vain*.

Speaking 2

The aim is to use the rather controversial statements in the previous exercise to focus on and practise ways of agreeing and disagreeing.

A Students will have thought about what they agree and disagree with as they completed the vocabulary work. Make sure they understand how to mark the statements and give them five minutes to complete the task. Tell them they will need to explain choices in the next part of the lesson and they should think carefully.

B Read the instructions with students and give them a further three minutes to think and prepare. Put them into groups of three (or four, with two males and two females in each). The discussion could go on indefinitely, so set a time limit of around 15 minutes. Tell groups to select statements they want to discuss if they feel they will not have time for all of them.

Monitor to assist, if necessary. Make a note of any particular comments a student could share with the class as feedback. For a change, as feedback, ask three students to choose statements and turn them into questions to ask you, for example, *Do you think men are more competitive than women?* Take the opportunity to give them some natural listening practice – they will be interested to hear your opinions too. Avoid a feedback stage that simply repeats the discussion stage.

C The aim is to consolidate language from the previous part of the lesson and to provide some authentic listening practice. Language of agreeing and disagreeing is developed and students are prepared to agree and disagree again using more sophisticated structures.

Make sure students know what they are listening for and play the whole recording. Students can go over answers with a partner before you check them. If there are uncertainties, play the recording again, pausing after each conversation to check answers.

Answers:
Conversation 1: 6 / Conversation 2: 13 / Conversation 3: 9

C Listen to some native speakers and decide which statement they are discussing. Write the number of the statement for each answer.

Conversation 1

Male: So, what do you think of this statement?

Female: Mm, it's difficult. Of course, it's ridiculous to say simply that this is true, but perhaps there's some truth in it. Some women obviously want to win and beat an opponent – there wouldn't be female sporting heroes if not. But, I think generally men are more obsessed with outdoing each other. Women want to succeed and do well, but don't worry so much about beating other people. I mean, if you said to most women, would you rather score 80% and be top of the class or score 90% but finish third, they would choose the latter – you know they want to do as well as possible. I think most men would choose the former. It's being better than someone else that matters. You know, they just can't bear the thought of other people scoring higher than they do.

Male: Oh, come on! You don't really think …

Conversation 2

Female: This is the statement that I disagree with most strongly. It's just nonsense.

Male: Yes, I thought you might not like this one. You must admit that there are still more men in positions of power, though.

Female: Yes, of course – that's because they don't give women a chance. When women are in positions of power they do just as well, if not better, than men. Women can manage other people without being competitive and overbearing. Frankly, I didn't really like Margaret Thatcher, but surely she proved that a woman can be a figurehead.

Male: Mm, I'm not sure she was a typical woman, though.

Female: Why not? What makes me really angry is attitudes like this in the workplace. There are still men who say they don't feel comfortable with a female boss or supervisor. There are women everywhere that could be much higher up the career ladder if only they were given the opportunity.

Conversation 3

Female: So, my guess is that you think this is true.

Male: Yes, absolutely true. The thing that drives me crazy about my wife is her inability to make choices – or at least her inability to stick to the choices she makes.

Female: That's because men just act on the first thought that comes into their head. Women need to consider all the pros and cons.

Male: Pros and cons! How can it take an hour to decide if a pair of shoes is the right pair of shoes? I mean, if I see a pair of shoes I like, I buy them. If I don't like them, I don't buy them. Why should it be more complicated than that?

Female: Yes, but then a week later you regret having spent so much on a pair of shoes you didn't really need.

D 🎧 Give students a moment to read the sentences before playing the recording. Play the whole recording as students fill the gaps and then again, pausing after each sentence to check answers. Do not explain the grammar point before students look at the *Grammar check*.

Answers:
See tapescript for Track 23.

Tapescript 🎧 23 (0 mins, 30 secs)

D Listen and complete these sentences from the conversations.

1 It's being better than someone else that matters.
2 What makes me really angry is attitudes like this in the workplace.
3 The thing that drives me crazy about my wife is her inability to make choices.

Grammar check

The grammar point may be new to students and there is a practice exercise to consolidate within the *Grammar check* this time. Tell them to read the information, but not to start the exercise yet. Give them time to read and absorb. Read each of the conventional sentences aloud and then each of the cleft sentences, demonstrating the emphatic stress and intonation that gives the structure its real purpose. Set the practice exercise.

• Students work individually to write the cleft sentences.
• Students compare sentences with a partner.
🎧 Play the whole recording to check answers. Then play the recording again and write each sentence on the board for clarity. Making an OHT or other visual medium of the sentences that you can reveal one by one on the board will be more efficient.

Answers:
See tapescript below.

Tapescript 🎧 24 (0 mins, 57 secs)
Grammar check

Listen and check your answers.

1 It's men who think they are more intelligent than women that make me furious.
What makes me furious is men who think they are more intelligent than women.
The thing that makes me furious is men who think they are more intelligent than women.
2 It's the time women need to get ready that drives me crazy.
What drives me crazy is the amount of time women need to get ready.
The thing that drives me crazy is the amount of time women need to get ready.

Pronunciation check

The pronunciation focus here is simply an extension of the grammar point. Note that the grammatical structure has no real meaning unless pronunciation is appropriate – the real message is carried in the stress and intonation. Make students aware of this.
🎧 Play the whole recording allowing students simply to listen and absorb. Then play the recording again, pausing after each sentence to drill. Finally, allow students sufficient time to practise saying the sentences in pairs. Monitor and give feedback.

Tapescript 🎧 25 (1 min, 23 secs)
Pronunciation check

Listen to all the emphatic sentences from Exercise D and the *Grammar check*.

1 It's being better than someone else that matters.
2 What makes me really angry is attitudes like this in the workplace.
3 The thing that drives me crazy about my wife is her inability to make choices.
4 It's men who think they are more intelligent than women that make me furious.
5 What makes me furious is men who think they are more intelligent than women.
6 The thing that makes me furious is men who think they are more intelligent than women.
7 It's the time women need to get ready that drives me crazy.
8 What drives me crazy is the time women need to get ready.
9 The thing that drives me crazy is the time women need to get ready.

E The aim now is to provide further Speaking test practice and to practise the newly acquired grammar point, if and when appropriate. Make sure students understand that they should not try to force the emphatic sentences and end up using them unnaturally.

Note that a robust discussion of each point could mean the whole stage lasting up to 30 minutes. Either tell pairs to choose questions to discuss or set a time limit for each question – two or three minutes perhaps.

Students should spend five minutes reading the questions, thinking and preparing answers individually. They should then answer the questions in pairs or groups of three. Monitor to check overall performance and particularly retention and use of language learnt in the lesson. As feedback, you could simply get a *yes/no* answer for questions 2–6. Tell students that the Listening and Reading Modules will develop the theme and that they will have further opportunity to discuss the issues.

Refer students to the Exam tip. Tell them to cover it and ask them what advice it gave.

Listening

Objectives

- **To introduce the concept of listening for paraphrased language.**
- **To practise listening for paraphrased language.**
- **To familiarize students with further examples of IELTS Listening task types.**

The overall theme of the Listening Module is *women in sport*. The Speaking and Vocabulary Module touched on this aspect of *male/female equality*, so it should be fairly straightforward to orientate students towards the topic.

You could start the lesson by asking the class who some of their favourite sporting characters are – do not say *sportsmen* or *women*. It is likely that the majority of names mentioned will be male. Point this out and ask them, *What about women in sport?* Ask some of the female students if they enjoy sport and if they do, whether they prefer men's or women's sport.

Listening 1

It may be obvious to some students that the listening tasks will not simply involve listening to sentences or extracts that they can see in front of them on the page. However, it is likely that many students will think that they will hear language as it is written in questions and that they will simply have to tick options or fill in missing words. It is essential that

students understand what paraphrasing means, and how language in tasks is paraphrased. Note that this aspect of exam practice applies to the Reading test as well as the Listening test.

A The principal aim is to prepare for the listening stage and motivate students towards the theme, rather than to provide extended speaking practice. Set a time limit of six minutes (two minutes for each question).

Students should spend three minutes reading the questions and thinking about answers individually, and then another six minutes answering the questions in pairs.

Use feedback to elicit examples and suggest a few of your own, preparing students for information they will learn from the recording. Students may suggest that women are competing with men in some sports already. Note that the final question might be more interesting to discuss once students have listened to the recording – *Will women ever play against men at football?*.

B Refer students to the pictures and develop the discussion from A. Conduct as a whole-class discussion as a change from pairwork. Check that students know the sports – *motor racing, golf, darts* and *horse racing*. If students know any of the names (Michelle Wie is most likely), write them on the board. Do not feed them information otherwise. Decide together whether women really are competing with men at the very highest level in each sport shown.

C 🎧 The aim is to provide an opportunity to listen for gist before the challenging gap-fill task that follows. Note that, although students will not be able to listen more than once in the exam, neither will they be required to fill gaps in eight sentences in a single task. Understanding the general idea of the four extracts should enable students to complete the task.

Tell students that they will not hear the sports mentioned and will need to listen for clues and key words and phrases. Play the whole recording and check answers immediately. Do not play the recording a second time for this exercise.

Answers:
1. d   2. c   3. a   4. b

C **Listen to four extracts and match them with the pictures.**

Extract 1

Voice: There has not previously been a female jockey quite like Hayley Turner. In 2005, she became only the fourth woman in history to ride out her claim. This meant she could compete equally with male jockeys. In that year, she also became the first female Champion Apprentice. She is the first female jockey to have ridden a hundred winners in a season and is now considered to be one of the best jockeys in the country. Her determination and self-discipline have made her not just an exceptional female jockey, but an exceptional jockey. She is as strong and tactically aware as any male and is respected in the profession as the equal of any of her peers.

Extract 2

Voice: The idea that men and women should compete on a level playing field has been discussed in relation to many sports. In major sports like football and tennis, the physical difference between male and female competitors is usually put forward as a reason for this not being possible. Here, however, no such physical difference is in any way relevant and surely there is nothing that should prevent women competing alongside men. It seems strange that most male players are against equality and believe that women should continue to play in their own competitions.

Extract 3

Voice: In 2009, Danica Patrick raced at the Indianapolis 500, where she finished third behind winner Helio Castroneves and second-place Dan Wheldon. This was her best finish in five attempts in the race, one place better than her 2005 finish, and a new record high finish for a female driver. Despite all her success however, there are many who feel that she will not be suited to racing Formula 1, and there is still much prejudice that she will have to overcome.

Extract 4

Voice: The main argument against women succeeding in men's events has always been physical strength. Women simply can't hit the ball as far. When the ladies world number, one Annika Sorenstam, was invited to play in a major men's event in 2003, she missed the cut by five shots and was stunned by the experience. She later admitted that it had been much tougher than she had expected and that she was looking forward to going back to play where she belonged. Michelle Wie might be the woman to challenge the theory. At six foot and one inch, she can hit the ball as far as almost any male, and commentators all over the world have agreed that she has the potential to be as good as any male player.

D 🎧 Remember that the aim now is to present the concept of paraphrasing – not to provide exam practice. Help students to understand as much of the context before they listen as possible.

Read the instructions carefully with them. Point out the instruction to use only two words for each answer – they will need to get used to checking this each time they do a task of this type. Give them longer than usual to read through the sentences. Point out that the names of a female jockey, a female racing driver and two female golfers are mentioned in the sentences. Do not, however, explain the meaning of *rode out her claim* – most native speakers would not know this expression so tell them you do not know it. You can ask them what they think it means from the context later.

Play the recording, pausing for a moment between each extract to give students time to write. Give them two minutes to check answers in pairs before you write them on the board as feedback.

Answers:
1. male jockeys   2. 100 / a hundred   3. physical difference   4. male players   5. female driver
6. Formula 1   7. much tougher   8. 6 feet / six feet

C **Listen again and complete the sentences. There are two sentences for each extract.**

[Play Track 26 again]

E The aim is for students to work out for themselves that language on the recording is paraphrased in the written sentences. Students should read carefully and answer the questions individually before discussing their answers in pairs. Check their answers quickly before referring them to the Exam tip.

Answers:

1. yes   2. no

Refer students to the Exam tip and then tell them to cover it. Ask one students to explain the point made in his or her own words. If that student is not clear, ask another.

F 🎧 Refer students to the relevant tapescript and then play the recording through again as students listen and notice paraphrased language.

Alternatively, adopt a more rigorous approach. Show an OHT or other visual medium of the tapescript on the board. Play the recording, pausing after the gapped sentences to compare language use. For example, pause at the end of the line, *This meant she could compete equally with male jockeys* and point out the written sentence, *She could ride against male jockeys as an equal.* Emphasize that the part written as an answer is the same – it is the language around it that is different. This may seem obvious, but it will help students enormously.

> **Tapescript** 🎧 **28 (0 mins, 15 secs)**
>
> **F** Listen again as you read the tapescript. Notice examples of paraphrased language as you read.
>
> [Play Track 26 again]

Listening 2

The recording for the practice part of the lesson is a little longer, but students do not have to write as many answers – the first four are multiple choice. Point out that multiple-choice tasks also require the comprehension of paraphrased language – they will not hear one of the options as it is written!

A 🎧 There is no fresh preparation stage this time – the theme of the first part of the lesson is developed. Point out that in the exam they will

not even be given a line of rubric, as they are here, to say what they are going to listen to.

Emphasize the need to use the questions to make predictions. Remind them that they get only 30 seconds to read the questions, but give them a minute now – longer if you feel your students need it.

Play the whole recording as students complete the task. Do not check answers as students will do so in Exercise B.

> **Tapescript** 🎧 **29 (5 mins, 12 secs)**
>
> **A** **You will hear a talk given to students studying gender studies about women in sport. Listen and answer the questions.**
>
> **Voice:** … so I think we can say that despite some marvellous progress, it is still very difficult for women to succeed in the male-dominated world of sport. To actually compete against men in the same competitions is even more difficult, and women face an enormous amount of chauvinism and prejudice. Let me use horse racing as an example. For over 100 years women have been involved in horse racing as very successful owners and trainers, and for nearly 50 years as jockeys. It is still the case, though, that girls are used as exercise riders before the races and then snubbed when it comes to the racing. Even top female jockeys, who have done everything to prove that they are the equals of men, are not given the best rides and at meetings will regularly have two or three fewer rides than their male peers. The older generation of men who wield power still believe that a woman jockey will never win the very biggest races, like the Derby or the Grand National. Personally, I believe that they will soon be proved totally wrong.
>
> Now, of course it is true that men are generally physically bigger and stronger than women, and it's understandable that people feel that women will never compete with men at the highest level in contact sports, like football or basketball. People are afraid that women are not as robust as men and will get injured, or that men will refrain from playing as aggressively as they might against other men and that that would compromise the game.

There are others who feel that it is inappropriate for males and females to be in such close physical contact. My feeling is that at younger ages, girls should play against boys if they are good enough. Football, for example, isn't only about strength and speed. There are many smaller players who rely on skill and positional awareness. If girls prove they are the equals of boys, they should continue playing as long as they are able to compete. I don't think there should be archaic rules that prevent girls from competing with boys once they reach a particular age.

Now, games like tennis and golf are interesting. These are not contact sports and there are fewer arguments to support the theory that men and women should not compete together. As women's tennis progresses, the difference between how hard players hit the ball becomes smaller and smaller. As long ago as the 1970s Billie Jean King, a former ladies Wimbledon champion, proved that women could beat men when she triumphed over a former male Wimbledon champion, Bobby Riggs, in a special showdown match. Not only did she win, but she won in straight sets. Riggs may have been past his best at the time, but it was a moment that women all over the world enjoyed. The world's best lady golfer, Annika Sorenstam, had a less successful time when she was invited to play in a major men's event in 2003. She found it all far more challenging than she had expected and failed to make it through to the main competition when she missed the cut by five strokes. When Michelle Wie burst onto the scenes a few years ago, everyone believed that we had found a woman who was tall and powerful enough to be the equal of any male golfer. Professional male golfers claimed that she was as good as any young male player they had ever seen. Unfortunately, it doesn't seem to have worked out, and Wie is still to fulfil that promise. Who knows how long we will have to wait for a true female champion in a male-dominated sport.

One important thing we have to consider is whether it would always be an advantage for women to compete against men at the very highest level anyway. In tennis for example. It is generally accepted that Serena Williams, the women's world number one, would be rated at around 50th or 60th in the world if she were competing constantly against men. She would probably qualify through the earlier stages of the big events, beating male opponents as she did so, but she would find it very difficult to reach the semi-finals or even the quarter finals. Now, we have to ask, would the best women players rather be big fish in a smaller pond or small fish in a very big pond? Williams certainly would be nowhere near as famous and would have accumulated a tiny percentage of her prize money had she been playing with men all these years. Perhaps we should be fighting for all women's sport to be taken as seriously as men's sport, rather than driving towards actually competing with men. Women's tennis is probably now as popular as men's tennis – I know I'd rather watch women play any day. We need other sports to be viewed in the same way.

So anyway, to conclude, I think it's fair to say there's still a long way to go, and if schools continue to allow girls to play basketball with the net a little lower or score two points instead of one each time they make a run in baseball, girls will still be seen as somehow inferior. What I think is important is …

B Checking and reflecting on answers is a constant feature of the skills modules. Give students sufficient time to check and think about why they may have answered incorrectly before moving onto C. You can decide if it would be beneficial to play the recording again, but avoid doing so simply to check individual students' wrong answers.

Answers:
Key phrases from the recording that provide answers are given with the multiple-choice answers.
1. b (the male-dominated world of sport / women face enormous chauvinism and prejudice)
2. a (girls are used as exercise riders before the races)
3. a (women are not as robust as men and will get injured)

4. c (Football ... isn't only about strength and speed ... smaller players who rely on skill and positional awareness)
5. hit the ball
6. male
7. successful
8. promise
9. big events
10. prize money
11. seriously

C   Students will by now be more familiar with this type of reflective process. Here, the aim is to focus specifically on the point they have been practising. Remind them that identifying what they are doing well and not doing so well is a very good way of focusing on what they can do better next time. Allow students time to reflect and complete the exercise and then ask them if they are happy with the number of correct answers.

D   Make sure students focus on whether anything they have learnt in the lesson has changed their opinion, rather than repeat what they discussed at the beginning of the lesson. Once students are in their groups, tell them to spend three minutes individually noting two key points they want to make. Write on the board, *Women's world number one tennis player would be ranked only around 60th best player if competing with men* and say that this was a point that stuck in your mind. They should note similar key points.

Set a time limit of five minutes for the discussion and then get quick feedback from each group.

Key vocabulary in context

Tell students to look only at the nouns in the sentences. Ask whether they are familiar or if they heard the words used on the recording. Ideally, students should identify the words in the tapescripts for Listening 1 and 2, and check their meaning in context rather than use dictionaries. If you have already made an OHT or other visual medium of the tapescripts, highlight the words on the board. Make sure students understand what they have to do – move words from one sentence to another.

Students should complete the exercise individually and then compare answers with a partner. Select students to read the corrected

sentences as feedback or write them on the board. Check pronunciation and drill words if necessary.

Answers:
1. If you have awareness of something, you know about it and understand it.
2. If you show promise or potential, you are likely to develop and achieve something in the future.
3. If there is prejudice, people believe something that is unreasonable, often based on dislike or fear.

Refer students to the Workbook exercises related to this module. Choose to work on them now, or set up for homework.

Reading

Objectives

- **To apply the concept of paraphrasing to the Reading test.**
- **To practise identifying and understanding paraphrased language.**
- **To familiarize students with further examples of IELTS reading task types.**

The overall aim is to apply what was learnt about paraphrasing in the Listening Module to reading skills while it is still fresh in students' minds. As with the Listening Module, the first part of this module focuses on establishing what paraphrasing is and the second part on practising it.

The overall theme of *gender equality* moves from sport into the workplace, but a noticeable amount of core language is recycled.

Reading 1

A   Tell students to cover the text on the page – it is important that they don't see any figures. Refer them to the box of professions, and check that they know what each is and how to pronounce it. Read the rubric through with students and make sure they understand what they are predicting. Give an example if necessary, *I think about 35% of lawyers in the USA are female.*

Students should agree on a predicted percentage for each profession in pairs. Get a rough whole-class prediction for each profession and write it on the board.

B Tell students that the extracts are fairly challenging and that, for now, they are simply reading to check their predictions. Tell them to skim each extract quickly to establish which profession it is about and to the scan for the percentage. Tell them to ignore the highlighted lines – they do not relate to this exercise. Set a time limit of two minutes (30 seconds for each percentage).

Though the percentages are clear in the text, write the answers below on the board for clarity and ask students if they are surprised.

Answers:
engineers – 20% / lawyers – 25% / pilots – 6% / surgeons – 5%

C Point out that parts of the text are highlighted, and that students will need to read these parts carefully to answer the questions. Tell them to read the questions first so they know what they are looking for. Though students should concentrate on the highlighted parts, they will need to read the whole extracts to understand properly. Set a time limit of four minutes (one minute per question).

As you check answers, point out obvious examples of paraphrasing. Students will easily have identified the link between *talking dolls* and *children's toys*, but *closely guarded world* will probably need clarification.

Answers:
1. B   2. D   3. A   4. C

Refer students to the Exam tip and give them a moment to read and absorb.

D The aim now is to apply what has just been learnt. The task is the same as the previous one, but without the highlighting to guide them. At this stage, give students the time they need to do the task properly rather than set a time limit – tell them they will need to practise and do it more quickly later.

Students should complete the task individually, before comparing answers with a partner. Give feedback as in C, but write the key part of the text that provides the answer on the board too. Highlighting the key lines on an OHT or other visual medium on the board will be more efficient.

Answers:
1. B (… 'a lack of accommodation for women for child-bearing responsibilities …')
2. D (… does not guarantee a traditionally feminine approach to …)
3. A (… little general public understanding of what engineers do. / Engineering … thought of as a vocational option rather than an academic one.)
4. C (Cultural and gender stereotypes still dictate to what most young girls aspire to.)

Reading 2

The passage for the practice part of the lesson is longer, and students should be reminded that they will neither be able to nor need to read every word. They have already practised both task types, which should make them feel a little more confident. There is a short preparation stage, but students are largely left to their own devices.

A The aim is to link the two parts of the lesson together and further orientate students towards the concept of inequality at work.

Students should spend three minutes reading the questions, thinking and preparing answers. They then answer the questions in pairs.

As students do not read to check ideas discussed on this occasion, take the opportunity to use a feedback stage to pre-teach a few key points from the passage. Elicit reasons and write them in note form on the board.

Possible answers:
- They are conditioned not to go into some professions.
- They face discrimination. / There is a dominant male culture.
- There is a lack of accommodation for child-bearing (having children).
- There is a lack of mentoring (guidance and development).
- They are not given enough responsibility.

- They have lower salaries / are paid less money for doing the same job as men.
- They are overworked.
- They are less likely to be promoted to higher positions.
- They are considered 'too old' earlier than men are.

B Before you leave students to work independently, read the line of instruction and the heading of the passage with them. Make sure they understand that the passage focuses on women in academic medicine – point out that reading passages in the exam frequently have a very specific/narrow area of focus like this. Revise the meaning of *stereotype*, and check that they understand that *keep* here means *stop*.

Set a time limit of 15 minutes (approximately a minute for each question) to complete both tasks. Advise them to skim the passage in about three minutes and then read the questions carefully before reading again to locate information. Monitor at the beginning of the process, and if anyone is still reading the text for the first time after five minutes, tell them that that is too long to be reading without a specific focus.

C Checking and reflecting on answers is a constant feature of the skills modules. Give students sufficient time to check and think about why they may have answered incorrectly before moving onto D.

Students might want to know why some of their answers were not correct. Explaining some points may be necessary and beneficial, but going through all of them will be very time-consuming. It is best to tell students that they will learn more about how to do these tasks and that their scores will improve.

If you do want to identify the specific parts of the passage that provide answers to questions in the first task, make an OHT or other visual medium of the passage and highlight those parts on the board.

Answers:
1. D   2. F   3. E   4. I   5. A   6. C
7. T   8. F   9. NG   10. T   11. T   12. F
13. NG   14. F

D Students will now be more familiar with this type of reflective process, but note the statements are not the same as in previous units and there are more of them this time. Remind students that identifying what they are doing well and not doing so well is a very good way of focusing on what they can do better next time. Allow students time to reflect and complete the exercise and then ask them if they are happy with the number of correct answers.

E The aim is to conclude the lesson rather than develop an extended debate. You will know whether your students will enjoy and benefit from an extended pair or group discussion, or whether a quick whole-class discussion will suffice. Whatever approach you take, encourage students to use core language learnt in the module.

Grammar check

Students have already studied the passive and should be fairly confident with it anyway. The aim here is to raise their awareness of its use in the passages they will read for the exam. Tell them to read the first line of information and then refer them to the exercise.
- Students complete the exercise individually.
- Students compare answers in pairs.
- Students discuss why the passive is used in each example in pairs.

Write answers on the board for clarity and make sure answers given orally for the final task are clear.

Answers:
1. are offered (what happens is more important than who did something – the agent is not expressed)
2. were developed (the agent is placed at the end of the sentence for dramatic effect)
3. being given (what happens is more important than who did something – the agent is not expressed)
4. be expected (the agent is somebody in authority – there is no need to express it)

Key vocabulary in context

Remind students that an effective way to learn and remember new vocabulary is to study it closely once it has been presented in context.

A Note that, in this case, the aim is to practise the skill of understanding new words and phrases in context as well as actually learning the selected words and phrases. Discourage dictionary use for this exercise.

Students should complete the exercise individually, before comparing answers with a partner. Answers can be given orally, but must be clear. Alternatively, delete the wrong option on a copy made on the board. When answers have been checked, tell students to cover the exercise. Read out the correct definitions as they shout out the newly acquired key word.

Answers (correct options):
1. some people are treated better than others
2. gets in the way of something
3. somebody doing the same thing
4. very little
5. experienced people who give advice
6. is especially good
7. look after and help it succeed
8. is not good enough

B Students can complete the exercise in pairs. Write answers on the board for clarity.

Answers:
1. aspire to   2. combined with   3. emphasis on
4. on the part of

Refer students to the Workbook exercises related to this module. Choose to work on them now or set up for homework.

Writing

Objectives

- **To present and practise reports based on data shown in line graphs.**
- **To understand and describe more than one source of information.**
- **To practise deciding what to include and not include in a report.**

The Writing Module in this unit concentrates on Writing Task 1. The aim is to focus specifically on describing line graphs, but also to present language typical of descriptions of all figures presented in the first Writing task.

Writing 1

The aim is to start with a very simple figure, containing very little information and to present or revise some core vocabulary. Note that students will never see a figure showing as little information as this in an exam task.

A Students guessed percentages in the previous lesson and setting up the task should be straightforward. Make sure they cover the figure and then give them three minutes to read and agree on predictions.

You can get a consensus class prediction for each line of information, or refer students to the graph to check ideas.

B Though the graph makes the percentages clear, write the answer key on the board for clarity and find out which pair were closest to a correct prediction in each case.

Answers:
1. 1948 – 32% of women worked
2. 2009 – 60% of women worked
3. Between 1948 and 2009 – percentage increased by 100%

C Either set as pairwork with a one-minute time limit or discuss briefly as a whole class. If possible, find the information yourself online before the lesson so that you can give the correct percentage increase.

D These are the core verbs that students will need to describe trends. They are frequently used to describe line and bar graphs, but also to describe differences between two pie charts. You will know whether or not your students already know the verbs and how much teaching will be necessary here.

Refer students to the box of verbs and point out that they are all past simple forms. Say each verb aloud for students to absorb the pronunciation. Tell them they have two minutes to check any verbs they are uncertain of in a dictionary. Then give them another minute to read the instructions and tick the appropriate verbs. They can compare answers with a partner before you check.

Go through the verbs, drawing a simple line for each (see below). Establish that *increased*, *rose* and *grew* should have been ticked. Write the irregular forms *rise / risen*, *fall / fallen* and *grow / grown*.

increased /   decreased \   rose /   fell \
grew /   dropped \   remained steady —
fluctuated ~~~

E Pronounce the two verbs and give students a moment to choose. Establish that *doubled* is the correct option and that *trebled* means increased by three times.

Writing 2

Refer students to the Exam tip as an introduction to the next part of the lesson. Tell them to read it and then look at the line graph that follows to appreciate the point. Clarify the meaning of *compare* and *contrast* and point out that there will always be noticeable differences to describe – they will not see a bar graph with all the bars at the same height, for example!

A Students should spend three minutes studying the graph, thinking and planning how to explain what it compares. They should then talk in pairs about what the graph shows. There is no need to provide feedback as the graph heading and key clarify what the graph compares.

B Tell students to spend two minutes reading the task instructions and checking that they now fully understand what the graph compares. Then refer them to questions 1–8.

Students should spend three minutes reading the questions and thinking about answers. They then answer the questions in pairs. Select students to ask each question as feedback.

Answers:
1. You must look at the graph carefully, check you understand what it shows and plan.
2. You should show that you understand what the figure shows.
3. You identify information that stands out and that will be interesting to a reader.
4. No.

5. Yes – report writing is standard and predictable. It is not creative writing.
6. Yes – it should be as easy to follow as possible.
7. It is not always necessary to end a report for Writing Task 1 with a separate conclusion, though you should find a way of concluding what you have described.
8. He or she will check that you have:
   - answered all parts of the question using the required number of words
   - described information accurately
   - organized your report and linked ideas logically
   - used a range of vocabulary and structure typical of report writing
   - used grammatical structures correctly and appropriately
   - spelt accurately
   - punctuated appropriately

Refer students to the Exam tip and give them time to read and absorb.

C Students will feel far more confident about their report writing if they know how to start. Writing the first line of a report might seem straightforward, but there are a number of mistakes that students can make – most frequently, simply repeating what is written for them in the instructions. Make sure they appreciate that ALL of these opening lines are inappropriate – they are not choosing one.

Students should spend two minutes (30 seconds per sentence) reading and identifying a problem with each sentence, before comparing thoughts with a partner. Monitor to check ideas and to make a note of who can help give concise feedback. Give clear, concise explanations orally.

Answers:
1. It is copied direct from the task instructions. It does not show that the student understands the graph.
2. It explains only what one small part of the graph shows.
3. It attempts to give a reason for changes shown – this is not necessary, especially in the opening line.
4. It attempts to give far too much information about what the whole graph shows.

Refer students to the Exam tip and give them time to read and absorb.

D Students may find this difficult the first time they do it and they should work in pairs to share ideas. Point out that the first opening line in C is probably the least inappropriate and that they need to expand on the first line of the task instructions to show they understand the information. Ultimately, they will learn from seeing as many examples as possible.

Set a time limit of three minutes and monitor to assist and offer support. Make a note of any sentences that should be shared with the class as feedback. There is no one perfect opening line and you could choose two or three to write on the board, though be sure they are appropriate. If in doubt, use the model suggested.

Possible answers:
Model opening lines (three options):
The line graph shows what percentage of women in four different age groups were in full-time employment in the United States between 1948 and 2009.

The line graph shows that the percentage of women of working age in employment in the United States increased between 1948 and 1998, but fell slightly between 1998 and 2009.

The line graph shows that the percentage of US women in full-time employment in most age groups increased noticeably between 1948 and 2009.

Writing 3

Students frequently find it difficult to know what information to put in their report. They understand the graph, but fail to see information that stands out and can easily be compared and contrasted. They often think they should try to describe everything the graph shows – clearly not possible in 150 words – and either write too much or run out of time. In theory, no marks are deducted for failing to notice obvious data, but examiners are bound to compare reports with others they have marked and notice when relevant data is ignored at the expense of uninteresting data that makes the whole report seem rather dull. Students need to learn how to identify relevant data and get used to spending an appropriate part of the 20 minutes, choosing what to say.

A Make sure students continue to look at the first version of the graph and not the version with the comments on. It might be best to set up this exercise orally or by writing instructions on the board.

Students should work in pairs. Remind them that they need to identify enough data to write 150 words – advise them that that will probably mean five or six separate pieces. Set a time limit of six minutes, but tell them they will have to get used to doing this part of the task more quickly.

Show an OHT or other visual medium of the graph on the board. As feedback, get three or four students to come to the board, identify the part of the graph they want to describe and say why. You can tell them if they have selected data well, but there is no need to advise them yourself. The exercise that follows provides further guidance.

B Refer students to the second version of the graph and explain that a student (doing the same task as they are) has made comments to prepare to write a report.

Students should spend three minutes studying the comments and comparing them with their own ideas. They can then compare thoughts with the partner they worked with on A. Feedback is unnecessary.

Writing 4

The aim is to give further practice understanding graph data, and at the same time to develop vocabulary by introducing nouns and adverbs.

Once again, you will know how much of the vocabulary your students already know and how much will need checking and consolidating. There is no need to pre-teach anything as the graph contextualizes the target words and phrases. Note that the task itself is fairly easy and students can concentrate on the meaning of the target lexis. For now, point out the grammar of the highlighted items – *you know these verbs and now these adverbs are added; you know 'rise' and 'fall' as verbs – here they are nouns with new adjectives describing them.*

A Students should work individually to study the graph and complete the sentences, before comparing answers with a partner. Show an

OHT or other visual medium of the graph on the board to check the dates and give feedback. Deal with any uncertainties as you go.

Answers:
1. 1948   2. 1978   3. 1998 (approx)
4. 1956   5. 2009

Grammar check

The *Grammar check* serves as a quick check between Exercises A and B. Refer students to it, and give them three minutes to read and absorb. Tell them to look back and study the sentences in A as examples. Note that B now practises the point made.

B Students should work individually to complete the exercise before comparing answers with a partner.

As feedback, either write the answers on the board or show a copy of the answer key below.

Answers:
1. a sharp increase / increased sharply
2. a steady decrease / decreased steadily
3. a noticeable rise / rose noticeably
4. a dramatic fall / fell dramatically
5. a slight drop / dropped slightly
6. decreased gradually / a gradual decrease
7. increased sharply / a sharp increase
8. rose slightly / a slight rise
9. fell steadily / a steady fall
10. dropped dramatically / a dramatic drop

C The aim is to conclude the lesson with students seeing a model report that describes the graph they have been working on – they will work on a fresh figure for their own writing task. The fact that they have to complete the model means that they must re-engage with the figure and practise using some of the key language they have learnt.

Students should work in pairs, so that they can communicate and compare ideas as they go. Monitor as they work and assist when necessary. Point out any inappropriate gap-filling, so that it can be corrected before you reveal the model.

As feedback, refer students to the model report on pages 263–264. The report is reproduced opposite.

Model report:

The line graph shows that the percentage of women of working age in employment in the United States increased between 1948 and 1998, but fell slightly between 1998 and 2009. The percentage of women over 65 working changed very little.

In 1948, there were more women aged 16–24 working than women of any other age. However, the percentage of young women working did not increase for 20 years. In contrast, the percentage of women aged 25–54 in work rose sharply in that period. The percentage of women aged 16–24 in work rose dramatically between 1966 and 1978, but fluctuated between 1978 and 2009.

Between 1998 and 2009, the percentage of women under 54 working fell slightly. However, the percentage of women aged 55–65 working rose once again. In the last two or three years shown, there was a slight rise in the percentage of women over 65 in work. The percentage of older women working continues to rise while the percentage of younger women falls.

Writing task

The Writing tasks are found either in the Workbook or in the Exam Practice Module at the end of the unit. In this unit, the task is in the Exam Practice Module, and the teacher's notes for it can be found in the notes for that module.

Consolidation

Instructions are given for Speaking exercises when the procedure is not clear from instructions in the Course Book. Set the Vocabulary and Errors exercises either for individual completion and pairwork checking, or as pairwork when you feel immediate interaction is beneficial.

To correct errors in the final exercise, ask students to come and write the correct sentences on the board while other students offer help. You will need to write the corrections on the board to clarify.

Speaking

A Students can answer the questions using information they have learnt in the first three units of the course.

Answers:

1. In Part 3, the examiner will expand the topic discussed in Part 2. He or she will ask you to express your opinion on related topics.
2. In the first part, questions are about your personal situation. In the second, they require an opinion on more general topics and social issues. In the third part, they will ask you to express your opinion on related topics. The topics will be more abstract.
3. No.
4. You should spend some time thinking about your answer.
5. You should ask what it means.
6. whether or not you answer the question / vocabulary range / grammatical accuracy / pronunciation – individual phonemes; rhythm and stress and intonation

B The aim is to refocus students in preparation for C. They can just think individually for a moment or quickly remind themselves of possible answers in pairs. You may prefer to conduct this as a quick whole-class discussion.

C 🎧 Read through the rubric with students and make sure they know what to do. Play the whole recording. You can pause after each speaker during the next exercise. Check answers, but do not confirm or correct answers yet.

Answers:
Speaker 1 ✗ / Speaker 2 ✗ / Speaker 3 ✓ / Speaker 4 ✓

Tapescript 🎧 **30 (2 mins, 36 secs)**

C Listen to some students answering the question. Mark each speaker (✓) for a good answer or (✗) for not a good answer.

Speaker 1

Examiner: How have traditional male and female roles changed in your country in the last 20 years?

Student: Um, you mean the roles of the men and the women? Well, I was only born 21 years ago so I don't know much about 20 years ago. I think maybe the women work more nowadays – I mean they have jobs.

Speaker 2

Examiner: How have traditional male and female roles changed in your country in the last 20 years?

Student: Um, yes, I think they change a lot. Twenty years is a long time and I think life for everyone, life changes very much. I think Italy maybe changes more than other countries in 20 years. Can you ask me again, what did you ask about the males and females?

Speaker 3

Examiner: How have traditional male and female roles changed in your country in the last 20 years?

Student: Mm, it's a big question. Some people think in my country it is still the womens in kitchen but it is not so true – at least not for younger generation. Womans now, they work so hard like the men – sometimes they earn more money than the men. Also, now it is usual to see more girls out in town together – you know, before the girls go out in the night only with boys.

Speaker 4

Examiner: How have traditional male and female roles changed in your country in the last 20 years?

Student: Well, I think in France not so much has changed in 20 years – maybe in 50 years. I think women have gone to work, even when they have children, for a long time now, but I guess it's the kind of jobs they do that has changed. I know a friend whose mother is the big breadwinner – you know, she makes the money. She works in advertising or PR or something like that. Her father does most of the work around the house. I think

> maybe 20 years ago men in this situation would feel quite threatened.

D 🎧 Play the recording again, pausing briefly after each speaker. Students listen and make brief notes to support the view expressed in Exercise C. Some may want to change their answer in Exercise C. They can then compare notes with a partner.

As feedback, play the recording a third time, making sure it is clear why answers are considered good or poor. Emphasize that answers are poor if the student appears to be disinterested or fails to answer the question, not because of grammatical inaccuracy. The third speaker gives a good answer even though there are grammatical inaccuracies and he used wrong words.

Tapescript 🎧 **31 (0 mins, 11 secs)**

D **Listen again and make notes about each speaker's answer.**

[Play Track 30 again]

Vocabulary

A Answers:
  1. leadership   2. assumptions   3. approval
  4. responsibilities   5. decisive   6. criticism

B Answers:
  The words that should be deleted from each line:
  1. emotional   2. dearth
  3. determined   4. aspiring
  5. criteria   6. foster

C Answers:
  1. all competitors start in an equal position / the rules are the same for everyone
  2. too old
  3. not fitting in / in a situation that is unfamiliar / attempting to fulfil a role that you are not suited for
  4. confusing information

Errors

A Answers:
  1. The thing that …   2. Being given …
  3. … are expected …   4. emphasis on …
  5. … aspire to …   6. … rose steadily …

Exam Practice

Writing

The line graph that is the subject of the Writing task is similar to the one that students have been working with and is in some ways simpler in that there are only two sources of data to describe. The topic, however, is fresh, and at this stage students will need some preparation in terms of orientating towards the theme and identifying information that stands out.

A The aim is to introduce the general topic of the graph – students will not need to write about the causes of heart disease as part of the task. Refer students to the picture and then either set as pairwork as suggested in the rubric, or as a quick whole-class brainstorm. Write suggestions on the board.

Possible answers:
smoking / high fat diet – especially cholesterol and saturated fats / lack of exercise / obesity / having high blood pressure (sometimes itself caused by behaviour above) / stress / heredity

B The aim now is to focus students' minds on the more specific topic of the graph – comparing heart disease among men and women.

Students should spend two minutes individually predicting answers, before comparing answers with a partner or in small groups. Reveal the answers before looking at the graph.

Answers:
1. heart disease 2. men 3. more
4. Women 5. men

C Remind students of the importance of making sure they understand what the graph shows before they do anything else. Tell them to cover the task instructions and to look only at the figure.

Give them three minutes to study and absorb the information before comparing ideas with a partner. There is no need to orally check comprehension as the task instructions clarify.

D Refer students to the instructions and work through in the same way as with the preparation stage (A) in the Writing Module. Monitor and assist if necessary. Check that students are planning to include the right information before they start writing.

E While you may feel it is more practical to set discursive compositions (Writing Task 2) for homework, you will probably plan to do more report writing tasks in classroom time. Taking into account the time students have already spent preparing, they should need only 15 minutes to write the report and it will be best done while ideas are fresh in their minds.

If they do work at home, encourage them to be strict with time limits – they will not benefit from spending longer than they are allowed on the tasks. When students have completed the task, they should compare it with the model report on page 264. The model is reproduced below.

If you collect students' reports to mark, use the process to get an idea of what they are capable of and give general feedback. Correcting everything they write early on will not be motivating. At this stage, you may be still be correcting most of what they write.

Model report:

The graph shows that between 1979 and 2008, the number of deaths from heart disease in the United States decreased for both men and women.

In 1979, more men died from heart disease than women. Over the next few years, numbers of deaths fluctuated slightly for both genders, but by 1986 the number for women was higher.

Between 1986 and 2008, the number of deaths for men decreased fairly steadily, though the fall was sharper between 1988 and 1991 and there was a slight increase between 1991 and 1995. Since 1995, numbers for men have been steadily declining. Over the same period, the number of deaths for women fluctuated, but dropped significantly.

Between 1985 and 1990, there was a sharp fall in the number of deaths for women, but in 1991 the number began to rise once more and did so until 2000, when numbers reached a peak. Since 2000, numbers for women fell noticeably, but in 2008 were still 24,000 higher than for men.

Unit 3 Workbook answers

Vocabulary development

A 1. thoughtful   2. logically
    3. competitive   4. cautious
    5. decisive   6. leadership
    7. sensitive   8. protective

B and C (Likely/more conventional answers.)
    1. She / her / his
    2. his / him OR her / her
    3. His / him
    4. He / his (macho behaviour)
    5. She / her / She / her
    6. He / his

E 1. ladylike (*feminine* is possible)
    2. boyish
    3. macho (*manly* is possible)
    4. girly
    5. womanly

F 1. Behave in a masculine way – brave and tough.
    2. It'll help him grow up.
    3. This behaviour is typical of macho boys and men.
    4. She enjoys things that boys more often enjoy.
    5. He's neurotic.

Listening

A 1. c (Many of the most successful and influential owners have been women … almost all of the biggest races in the United States have been won by a horse owned by a woman.)
2. b (… top owners do not think twice about placing their best horses in a yard under a woman's charge.)

3. c

4. b (... she took the 1991 Belmont on Colonial Affair.)

5. a (Note that *don't get the limelight* means 'are not noticed')

Tapescript 🎧 **32 (2 mins, 11 secs)**

A Listen to a talk about women in horse racing and choose the correct answer a, b or c.

Voice: Though it is traditionally considered a male-dominated sport, women have always played an important role in horse racing at every level.

Many of the most successful and influential owners have been women and, at some time or another, almost all of the biggest races in the United States have been won by a horse owned by a woman. There have also been many exceptional women trainers. At one time, a female trainer was something of a rarity. These days they are commonplace and the top owners do not think twice about placing their best horses in a yard under a woman's charge.

Female jockeys really appeared on the scene in the late 60s when Diane Crump became the first woman jockey to ride in one of the bigger races in America. Around that time, Barbara Jo Rubin was the first female jockey to win a race, and then Tuesdee Testa was the first woman rider to win a race at a major American race course.

The most successful woman jockey of all, certainly in the States, is surely Julie Krone. She is the all-time leading female jockey and was the first to win a classic when she took the 1991 Belmont on Colonial Affair. In 2002, after coming out of retirement, she was successful once again, becoming the first woman to win a Grade 1 race in California.

Apart from the women in racing who make history, we must also take a moment to say something about the girls who don't get the limelight. Horse racing couldn't survive without the grooms, the exercise riders and the pony girls that do the hard work every day for little financial reward.

Reading

A 1. B   2. A   3. C   4. D
       5. T   6. F   7. NG   8. NG

Writing

A 1. remained constant
       2. increased dramatically / soared
       3. reached a peak
       4. increased steadily
       5. increased slightly
       6. fluctuated
       7. increased gradually

B
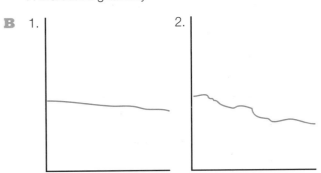

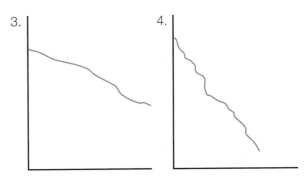

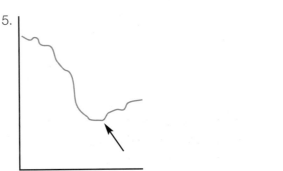

C

present simple	past simple	present perfect
rise	fell	have / has risen
		have / has fallen

4 Past and present

Speaking and Vocabulary

Objectives

- To practise talking about memories of past events.
- To practise interaction typical of the IELTS Speaking test, Part 2.
- To present and practise vocabulary related to memories.

Give students two minutes to read the quote and think. Give them a minute to discuss it in pairs, focusing on what it means and their reaction to it. Spend another two minutes discussing it as a class.

Cherokee Indians are the original residents of southeast America. The Cherokees were displaced from their ancestral homeland in Oklahoma in the 1800s along the Trail of Tears. Today, descendants of the Cherokee Indians live scattered throughout the original homelands. There are many traditional Cherokee legends, fairytales and proverbs. A proverb is a simple saying popularly known and repeated, which expresses a truth, based on common sense or the practical experience of humanity. They are often metaphorical. This Cherokee proverb can be best explained as, don't dwell on the past and let yesterday affect what you do today – live in the moment.

Speaking 1

The aim is to introduce the relatively complex concept of *nostalgia* explored in the Listening and Reading Modules through a simple initial channel which allows students to personalize the topic.

A Start by listing the five senses on the board – sight, hearing, smell, taste and touch. Then write *memories* on the board and get a quick consensus as to which sense students most associate with memories. Avoid starting a lengthy discussion at this point.

Students should spend three minutes reading the questions, thinking and planning answers individually. They can then answer the question in pairs.

Set a time limit of six minutes (two minutes for each question) for the discussion stage. Monitor and make a note of interesting points that could be used as feedback. Make sure feedback is focused, checking each question with one or two students rather than simply repeating points already made. Perhaps introduce the word *nostalgia* at this point if it relates naturally to a point made.

B Work through the steps as instructed in the Course Book. Set an overall time limit of ten minutes. Monitor to assist and to make a note of interesting points that could be used as feedback. As feedback, choose different students to say something about each picture – for example, *So, who wants to say something about picture a?*

c 🎧 The aim is to provide listening practice, consolidate what students have been discussing, and to introduce some of the core vocabulary from the next stage.

Make sure students know what they are doing and play the recording right through as students match each speaker with a picture. Check answers before they listen again to make notes.

Answers:
1. c   2. f   3. b   4. e

Play the recording again, pausing after each speaker.

Students should make notes as they listen and then compare notes with a partner. Monitor to check some of the notes. Then, refer students to the tapescript and play the recording once more as they absorb and check vocabulary. If they ask about key vocabulary now, tell them that they will focus on it in the next part of the lesson.

Tapescript 🎧 33 (1 min, 45 secs)

C   Listen to people talking about the pictures. Match each speaker with a picture.

Speaker 1

Voice: Pictures like this make me feel really nostalgic. I always loved this time of year when I was a kid. You know, freezing outside, but lovely and warm indoors. We had an open fire so it was really cosy. I remember looking out my bedroom window and seeing a white carpet outside. There was something wonderful about being the first person to walk on it.

Speaker 2

Voice: Mm, this picture doesn't bring back very fond memories, I'm afraid. I wasn't happy around this time. You know, when all the other kids were cool and had boyfriends or girlfriends and I didn't. My dad wouldn't let me wear what my friends were wearing. I felt like a bit of an outsider.

Speaker 3

Voice: I like to think I can remember the first few years at primary school, but I'm not sure I can. I think I might have just heard my mum talking about it. I remember I had a teacher called Mrs Craig. She was lovely, but I can't really recall which year it was or exactly how old I was.

Speaker 4

Voice: Actually this picture really takes me back. I'll never forget lying there trying to get to sleep. I used to have bad dreams and I remember waking up in the night. I hated the shadows that the moon made and the faces of some of my toys in the dark. My mum tucked me into bed every night, but she wouldn't lie with me.

Vocabulary 1

A Tell students to study how the words and phrases are used in context in the tapescript, and to only use a dictionary to confirm and consolidate.

Students should spend five minutes working through the task individually and then compare answers with a partner.

Monitor to assist and check pronunciation. If any words are being mispronounced regularly, stop the activity to model and drill them. Be prepared to spend sufficient time giving feedback. Students will want and need some clarification and will benefit from useful expansion. Vocabulary suggestions are given below with the answer.

Answers:
1. T – but, *remember* does not necessarily mean the same as *don't forget*. Emphasize that *remember* has two meanings (often looked at grammatically – see *Grammar check*) – *remember doing something* means *look back and call to mind*, *remember to do something* means *don't forget / fulfil a duty*.
2. F – *remember doing something* means *recall*. *Remember to do something does* not.
3. F – if one thing reminds you of another, the two things are similar. Point out also that you can *remind somebody to do something* – tell them not to forget.
4. T – point out that *recollection* is rather literary and is less common in spoken language. The most frequent spoken expression is *I have no recollection of …* and means *I don't remember it at all*.
5. F – when you *reminisce*, you think back about happy times.

6. T – emphasize that the noun and verb are the same.

7. F – *fond memories* are happy memories. Point out that the collocation is fixed and very common.

8. T – point out that the noun is *nostalgia*. (The meaning is dealt with in more depth later in the unit.)

B Students at this level will want to develop informal and idiomatic language that they can use in conversation, as well as more obviously exam-related vocabulary. The expressions here are common and fairly easy to use.

Note that these items might be termed *multi-word verbs* rather than *phrasal verbs* since their meaning is fairly literal and clear from the two parts. Though most are likely to be new to students, they should be able to work out the answers logically.

Students should complete the task individually, using a dictionary if necessary. They can compare answers with a partner. Monitor to check comprehension and assist. Go over answers, dealing with any uncertainties. Once students know the correct verb in each sentence, the meaning should be clear from the context. Note that *go back* (in both sentences) is the most idiomatic of the items and may need clarification. Point out that *You're going back ...* is a fixed expression and means *that's a long time ago. Go back a long way* is also fixed and means *have been friends a long time.*

Answers:

1. look 2. take 3. going 4. brings 5. go

The *Grammar check* and related *Pronunciation check* are more rigorous in this module than has been the case previously. There is practice as well as analysis, and you will need to dedicate around 30 minutes to this part of the lesson.

Grammar check

Give students time to read the first part of the *Grammar check* and study the examples. Then put them in pairs to discuss. Monitor and assist – it may well be easier to clarify the point with individuals than with the whole class. Emphasize

that *remember* or *not forget* + verb~*ing* means *look back*, while *remember* or *not forget* + infinitive means *fulfil a duty*. Point out the structure *remember* + subject + verb~*ing* – *I remember my father washing his car every Saturday* – as this may help comprehension. Give examples of *remember* and *forget* + infinitive that refer to the future also – *I must remember to phone my mum this evening* – as this will help students see that this form doesn't have to refer to the past as with the other form. Note that, if all students speak the same first language, translation might help, especially if there are two verbs instead of the one in English.

Deal with *I wish* and *If only* by asking concept questions. Write the first two examples on the board and then ask, *Does the speaker have enough money? What does he/she want? Is this probably going to happen?* and *Is the speaker young or old? How does he/she feel about that? Is it possible to change this situation?* Then write the second two examples and ask similar questions – *Did the speaker take the job? How does he/she feel about that now? Can he/she change the situation?* And *Was the speaker driving slowly or fast? What do you think happened? What does the speaker regret?*

Refer students to the *Watch out!* box, and this time get them to correct all the examples, working in pairs.

Answers:
I remember going to school in shorts.
Oh no, I forgot to turn off the lights.
If only I hadn't lost my passport.

Pronunciation check

The pronunciation focus here is once again an extension of the grammar point (related to *I wish* and *If only*). Make students aware that the grammatical structure has no real meaning unless pronunciation is appropriate – much of the message is carried in the stress and intonation.

🎧 Work through the task methodically, one part at a time. Tell students they will hear sentences they must write. Play only the example and write it on the board. Play the recording, pausing after each sentence for students to write. Play the recording again as you write the sentences on the board (see tapescript for answers).

Students will now listen to the sentences and mark the most heavily stressed syllables. Look at the example together. Model the sentence yourself if helpful. Play the whole recording allowing students simply to listen and absorb. Then play the recording again, pausing after each sentence as students mark the stressed syllables. Check answers by playing the recording as you underline the stressed syllables on the board. Allow students sufficient time to practise saying the sentences in pairs. Monitor and give feedback.

Answers:
Example: I <u>wish</u> I wasn't so <u>busy</u> all the time.
1. I <u>wish</u> I was a bit <u>taller</u>.
2. If <u>only</u> I lived a bit <u>closer</u> to the school.
3. I <u>wish</u> I hadn't <u>told</u> you now.
4. If <u>only</u> I'd <u>listened</u> to what she <u>said</u>.

Give students three minutes to think about some regrets they have (emphasize that they should not talk about anything that is private or upsets them). Give them another two minutes to plan how they want to express those regrets using the target language. Then give them a final two minutes to exchange ideas in pairs. Conclude by getting a few students to share ideas with the class.

Tapescript 🎧 **34 (0 mins, 56 secs)**
Pronunciation check

Listen and write the sentences you hear. Underline the syllables that are most heavily stressed.
   Example: I <u>wish</u> I wasn't so <u>busy</u> all the time.
   1 I wish I was a bit taller.
   2 If only I lived a bit closer to the school.
   3 I wish I hadn't told you now.
   4 If only I'd listened to what she said.
Listen again as you check the tapescript. Practise saying all the sentences with a partner. Then talk about your own life using *I wish* **and** *If only*.

Vocabulary 2

Students at this level will want to develop idiomatic language as well as more obviously exam-related vocabulary.

A Students probably won't know the idioms, but should be able to apply what they do already know and some logic to the task. If you are teaching in a monolingual environment, you will know if the idioms translate into the students' first language. They should complete the task individually, using a dictionary to check isolated words if necessary. They can then compare answers with a partner. Check that gaps are filled correctly, but do not discuss meaning at this point (see B).

Answers:
1. clock 2. milk 3. kick 4. regret

B You can either conduct this as pairwork or as a whole-class discussion. If students work in pairs, tell them to cover the task, and as feedback give definitions to see if they remember the idioms – for example, *Which idiom means I'm angry with myself?*

Answers:
1. Go back – have the opportunity to do things differently.
2. Don't waste time regretting what cannot be put right.
3. I'm angry with myself.
4. You will regret this decision later in life.

Speaking 2

A and B Work through the process as you have done previously (see Unit 2 Speaking 2B). Tell students that if they are unsure of a word on their task card, they should check it with their partner when he or she is playing the examiner's role as part of the interview, and not beforehand.

Tell students if you feel that their performance in Part 2 of the Speaking test is improving.

Listening

Objectives

- **To practise listening in order to label pictures and diagrams.**
- **To practise listening to a talk with specialist content and specialist vocabulary.**

The overall theme of the Listening Module is *old-fashioned machines and devices*, and *how machines and devices have changed*. The theme of *nostalgia* is developed, and language from the first module is recycled and extended.

Listening 1

Students will probably feel less confident about listening when the topic is something they do not know much about, especially if they fear there will be specific vocabulary they do not know related to the topic. Students need to understand that they will have to listen to (and read about) topics that are new to them, but that they will not be tested on what they have learnt about the topic, or on specialist words and phrases. The topic is purely a vehicle for language. You may like to explain that certain topics are not the focus of exam tasks because they may favour students who know more about them already.

A The principal aim is to prepare for the listening stage and motivate students towards the theme rather than to provide extended speaking practice. Set a time limit of six minutes (two minutes for each question).

Note that, depending on the age of your students, some of the items in the pictures may be seen simply as old-fashioned and no longer used, though it is hoped most will bring back a few memories and create a mood of nostalgia.

As feedback, write the name of each object on the board (students will probably want to know) and get a general consensus as to which bring back memories and why. Avoid long explanations about what each item was for as it will negate the listening exercise that follows.

Answers:
a. a record player
b. a space hopper
c. Space Invaders
d. a typewriter
e. a telephone
f. a Game Boy
g. a Rubik's cube
h. a Walkman

B 🎧 Point out that students will hear five of the eight objects described, not all of them. Tell them that they will not hear the actual names of the objects, but will need to listen for clues and key words and phrases. Play the whole recording as students match each speaker with an object and then again, pausing after each speaker to check answers. Tell students to read and study the tapescript later in their own time and notice how language they learnt in the first module is used in context.

Answers:
1. h 2. g 3. c 4. b 5. f

Tapescript 🎧 **35 (2 mins, 4 secs)**

B **Listen to some people talking about some of the objects. Match each speaker with an object.**

Speaker 1
Voice: I guess this look's pretty old-fashioned to you, but back in the 80s everyone wanted one of these. Before they came along, the only way you could listen to music when you were out was to carry a huge tape recorder around. I can't believe people used to do that. Anyway, these were kind of like an iPod, but you could only play tapes and wear a very silly looking pair of headphones.

Speaker 2
Voice: These were all the rage when I was a kid. I remember getting told off at school for playing with one instead of listening to the teacher. When they first came out, the kids who could solve the puzzle – I mean get all the colours in the right place – were thought of as really smart. Then, once they'd been around for a while, everyone learnt the trick. You know, there was a technique and when you knew that, you could do it. I guess that took away

the fun really. You never see them nowadays – I guess everyone plays computer games instead.

Speaker 3

Voice: Oh yes, this takes me back a bit. I guess this was like the first really popular computer game. First, the game was on machines in amusement arcades and bars. People used to spend hours sitting there shooting these little aliens instead of talking to their friends – the shape of things to come, I guess. Then you could buy hand-held versions of the game you could play at home. It looks so dated now, but I think it still looks fun.

Speaker 4

Voice: You know, I think kids still have these now but they're not so popular. I guess now there are fun centres and kids parks everywhere – who wants to bounce around on a big bag of air? I had one just like this one in the picture – I don't know if they were all orange, but I seem to remember most of them were.

Speaker 5

Voice: I remember I had one of these when I was ... oh, about seven or eight. I think they were the first hand-held computer games that everyone had. They were the first time any of us had heard of *Nintendo* too – probably the first time we realized all our technology would come from Japan in the future! I remember the huge START and SELECT buttons – it all seems so dated so soon.

c 🎧 The aim is to develop the theme and to start focusing on the exam listening task.

Focus students' attention on the pictures and read the instructions with them. Make sure they understand that they will hear a father and a daughter speaking about an old record player and a typewriter. Ask them to guess where the conversation will take place, and why. Ask them who they think will do most of the explaining. It would be best not to pronounce each of the words as students should get used to listening for key words like this without having previously heard them.

Play the whole recording as students label the diagrams and then again, pausing at appropriate points to check answers. Students can compare answers after the first listening if they choose to. Find out how many correct answers most students achieved.

Answers:
1. e 2. b 3. d 4. f 5. a 6. c

Tapescript 🎧 **36 (3 mins, 50 secs)**

c Listen to a father talking to his daughter about two more of the objects in the pictures. Match the words 1–6 below with the letters a–f on the diagram.

Father: Hey, look at this. I haven't seen this for ages. I'd forgotten it was up here.

Daughter: Is that a record player? Goodness, it looks ancient.

Father: It is ancient. This was my first one – I had this when I was about 12 years old. I bet you don't even know how it works, do you?

Daughter: Well, I know DJs have pretty much the same thing now – a bit more modern, of course. I've never actually looked at one properly, though.

Father: Well, it's pretty simple really. Here, let me find a record and show you. ... Ah, here we are – they're a bit dusty. You know, we only had records when I was a kid – no iPods or MP3s.

Daughter: Not even CDs?

Father: Not even CDs. Anyway, this is the turntable. You put the record on here – see how the hole in the middle of the record fits over this little knob in the middle of the turntable? Then you moved the arm across.

Daughter: The arm?

Father: Yeah, the arm. This long bit here. You move it across until it's over the part of the record you want to listen to – usually the beginning, I mean the first track. You could play any part of the record you wanted, though – that's why I always preferred records to tapes. This little sharp bit on the end of the arm is the stylus – it's like a little needle point that goes into the grooves in the record and plays the music – don't ask me how.

Daughter: It looks very sharp. Didn't it scratch the records?

Father: No, not if you were … Well, actually, yes it did. If you didn't position the arm properly, the stylus slipped and scratched your records to bits. In fact, all my records were scratched. Ah, here. Now, this is mum's old typewriter. It's a bit dusty too.

Daughter: Aren't these old typewriters valuable now? You should sell it instead of leaving it up here.

Father: Actually, I was going to give it to you to do your homework on.

Daughter: Oh, ha ha. It's quite a lovely thing, though, isn't it? I can't imagine actually using it though.

Father: Well, if you look at it properly, you'll see it's not much different to a PC. I mean, the basics are in the same place – certainly the keyboard part anyway. We used to call it the keytop. Look – all the letters and numbers are in more or less the same place as they are on a PC now – see the space bar down here too?

Daughter: Oh yes. What about all this up at the top, though?

Father: This whole top part is the carriage. There's a roller here, look, and that's where you feed the paper in. These clips hold the paper in place. The carriage moves along as you type and when you're at the end of a line, it shifts back to the beginning again.

Daughter: So the keys actually physically jumped up and hit the paper – amazing. Did you have to keep putting ink on the keys, then?

Father: What? No, of course not. Look, just below the carriage here, there's a ribbon. The ribbon was full of ink and the keys hit the ribbon against the paper. You had to replace the ribbon every so often – just like you replace the cartridge now if you've got a printer. I wish I could show you it working properly. Shall we take it down and see if we can get it working?

D 🎧 Don't say anything about how this exercise is different from C (students must write words they hear rather than match) as they will think about that later as part of the reflective exercise.

Make sure students understand that this is a continuation of the conversation and give them time to look at the diagram before they listen. Play the recording. Work through as with C. Write answers on the board for clarity.

Answers:
1. dial 2. handset 3. microphone 4. receiver

Check the number of correct answers again and ask whether anyone heard the word, but spelt it incorrectly. Point out that no marks will be given for incorrectly spelt answers.

Tapescript 🎧 37 (1 min, 39 secs)

D Now listen to the father and daughter talking about an old telephone. Fill in the missing information on the diagram.

Daughter: Hey, I like this phone. Can't we have an old-style one like this?

Father: Mm, they're not very practical – you can't walk around with them, you know. I guess you've never used a phone with a conventional handset like this, have you?

Daughter: What do you mean?

Father: I mean the phone downstairs doesn't have a handset and most of the time you use your mobile anyway. Grandma's got a phone a bit like this, but I doubt you've ever answered it.

Daughter:	No, I haven't. So, when you say the handset, you mean this part that you pick up?
Father:	Yeah, we always used to call it the receiver, but in fact that's not correct. The receiver is actually the part of the handset that you listen to – the part that the other person's voice comes out of. It receives the message.
Daughter:	So what's the other end called? I mean the part you speak into?
Father:	That's the microphone.
Daughter:	Oh, I guess that makes sense.
Father:	So what do you think of the dial then? Can you imagine dialling numbers instead of just touching the keypad?
Daughter:	The dial's this round bit on the front, right? I guess you put your fingers in the number you want and turn the dial?
Father:	Exactly, the trouble was, though, that if you didn't turn the dial right round far enough, the phone didn't read that number. You were always getting wrong numbers.
Daughter:	Mm, but that's no different from not touching the number on the keypad hard enough.
Father:	True.

E Students will be more used to reflecting on tasks in this way by now. They should answer the questions in pairs. Go over answers with them before referring them to the Exam tip.

Answers:

1. Study the diagram carefully, and then the words if any are given. Make predictions, but do not make assumptions.
2. Either match words to parts of the diagram or write words into spaces on a diagram.
3. No.
4. No correct answer – but point out that C involved matching, while D involved writing words.

Refer students to the Exam tip and give them time to read and absorb.

Listening 2

A The recording for the practice part of the lesson is longer, but is divided into parts to facilitate comprehension. Students are not given a fresh preparation stage, even though the topic of the talk is new, and they will find this listening practice the most challenging so far. Note also that they have three different task types to tackle.

Read the instructions with them (though you may like to point out once again that in the exam, they will not be given a line of rubric like this) and that they have a little longer than they will have in the exam to look at the diagrams and questions (two minutes). Make sure they appreciate that Figure 1 relates to questions 4–8 and Figure 2 to questions 9–12. Questions 1–3 relate to the introduction to the talk and they don't need to look at the diagrams during that part of the recording. Point out that answers here can be in any order, though they will hear the points in the order in which they appear.

Play the whole recording as students complete the task. Don't check answers as students will do so in Exercise B.

Tapescript 🎧 38 (8 mins, 34 secs)

A **You will hear three parts of a talk about the history of the bicycle. Listen and answer the questions.**

Voice: Bicycles were introduced in the 19th century and now number around one billion worldwide. Amazingly, that is twice as many as motor cars. They're the principal means of transportation in many regions. Bicycles also provide a popular form of recreation for many, if not most, people and have been adapted for such uses as children's toys, adult fitness, military and police applications, courier services and bicycle racing as a sport. The basic shape and configuration of a typical upright bicycle has changed little since the first chain-driven model was developed around 1885. However, many details have been improved, especially since the advent of modern materials and computer-aided design. The invention of the bicycle has had an enormous impact on society, both in terms of culture and of advancing modern industrial methods. Several components that played a key role in the development of motor vehicles were originally invented for the bicycle.

(Pause between parts)

Now these bicycles, which I'm sure you have all seen before, were known by a number of names – *high wheeler* and *high wheel roller* were commonly used, but you'll probably recognize them as *penny-farthings*. They were, of course, noted for the huge front wheel and much smaller back wheel. The name penny-farthing actually wasn't used until they were almost defunct. The term originated when people noticed that the design resembled two coins of the day, a penny and a much smaller farthing, laid side by side.

Now, let me say something about the design and features of this type of bicycle. Let me find the slide – here we are. Now the obvious feature is the much larger front wheel and that was there, of course, to enable much higher speeds. There were no gears back then and the pedals were welded directly to the hub in the centre of the front wheel. You see here how the relatively small pedals are attached to the hub. Each turn of the pedals took the rider further than the same turn would with a conventionally sized front wheel. The larger wheel also made for a more comfortable ride as the rider was high above the cobbled stones that were typical of the day.

Another important feature of the penny-farthing was the steel frame. Most bicycles had previously had a wooden frame. Steel was much stronger and meant more support and comfort for the rider. Around the same time, rubber tyres were introduced. It seems unthinkable now, but before rubber tyres, bicycles simply had wooden or metal wheels and were often known as *bone-shakers* because they literally shook the rider's bones.

OK, so we know the penny-farthing had two wheels of very different sizes and from the picture, you can see that the rider was seated in the saddle pretty much over the front wheel – we've already said that pedals were fixed to the front wheel hub. This meant that it was often difficult for the rider to mount the bicycle – I mean get on the bicycle to ride it. You can

see here that later designs had what was called a mounting step – a step that the rider could use to mount the bicycle.

Now, one final thing about the design. You see here the shape of the handlebars? Because the front wheel was so big, the rider's knees came up and were very close to the handlebars. Often riders' knees would hit the handlebars, especially if they were riding fast. This led to the design of what was called moustache handlebars – handlebars shaped like a moustache. The rider's knees could pass comfortably below the bars as he, or she for that matter, rode along.

Now, accidents. The height of the saddle and the …

(Pause between parts)

So, to bring us up to date. You'll probably all know about modern bicycles so I'm not going to go into great detail – it wouldn't be very interesting. What I would like to point out is some of the improvements that have been made and some of the details that have been made possible by technology.

As we said, the basic design has changed very little. I know the penny-farthing looked very different, but it was still ultimately two wheels attached to a frame and in fact, the period of the high wheeler was rather unique. The bicycles that came before that were actually shaped more like modern bicycles of today.

The first thing I want to point out is the cogset, which on a typical mountain or racing bicycle is now amazingly advanced. For years, bicycles had just one gear. The rider often had to push the bicycle up a steep hill. When gears were first introduced, there were usually three and later five gears. You can see here, that the whole chain assembly, with the larger front derailleur by the pedals and the smaller back derailleur attached to the hub of the back wheel, looks very much like a bicycle of 50 years ago. But the cogset might now be made up of anything between 10 and 30 cogs, allowing the rider to choose that number of gears. Even the average cyclist can now take on the steepest hill! Another feature that makes pedalling so much easier now is the fact that the saddle height can be adjusted.

Under the saddle here is the seat post. This is the part of the frame that can be adjusted, so that the rider is at exactly the right height – this feature is on every bicycle now, from a child's first bike to an expensive racing bike.

Now, safety. We said that there were frequent accidents on the high wheelers we looked at earlier. Modern bicycles are so much safer – safer all the time in fact – and of course, serious riders wear plenty of protection anyway. On the diagram here, you can see there is a shock absorber. This is at the top of the fork above the front wheel. If there is impact, the shock absorber compresses and literally takes the shock. These are featured on all motor vehicles as well as bicycles.

Finally, I want to mention spokes. Some people ask why bicycle wheels have spokes and you probably wonder why I mention them now, since bicycle wheels have had spokes since their conception. Well, the wheels have spokes because a solid wheel would be so heavy that the bicycle would be impossible to ride. With advanced materials, some racing bicycles do now have solid wheels, but certainly not the majority. What has changed over the years is the shape of the spokes. At one time spokes were made of wood, so had no tension or compression. For many years, spokes were designed to be …

B Checking and reflecting on answers is a constant feature of the skills modules and they will now more be accustomed to this process. Give students sufficient time to check and think about why they may have answered incorrectly before moving onto C. You can decide if it would be beneficial to play the recording again, but avoid doing so simply to check individual students' wrong answers.

Answers:
1. B (They're the principal means of transportation in many regions.) 2. C (… have been adapted for such uses as children's toys, adult fitness, military and police applications …, etc.)
3. E (… been improved, especially since the advent of modern materials and computer-aided design.)
4. hub 5. steel 6. rubber 7. mounting step

8. moustache
9. c 10. d 11. b 12. a

C Students will by now be more familiar with this type of reflective process. Note here that the questions relate directly to the task type they have just practised. Remind them that identifying what they are doing well and not doing so well is a very good way of focusing on what they can do better next time. Allow students time to reflect and complete the task and then ask them if they are happy with the number of correct answers.

Key vocabulary in context

Previously, students have been more directed with the post-listening vocabulary exercises. This is the first time they will discuss the meaning of items in such depth and they will need a little longer.

Students should spend four minutes (30 seconds for each word) checking the words in context individually. They should then spend another four minutes discussing them in pairs. Monitor and assist by pronouncing words for students and drilling when necessary. Make a note of which students can give accurate definitions during feedback. As feedback, you could tell students to cover the exercise and then read out definitions as students shout out the words – for example, *Which adjective means 'no longer in use'?*

Answers:
recreation – activities done for pleasure / to keep fit (Note that *recreation* is uncountable.)
advent – introduction of something new
components – parts which make up a whole
defunct – no longer in use
assembly – group of parts that when joined form one unit
adjusted – changed slightly (especially in terms of position)
compresses – pressed tightly / squeezed together
tension – degree to which something (rope/muscle, etc.) is pulled tight

Refer students to the Workbook exercises related to this module. Choose to work on them now or set up for homework.

Reading

Objectives

- **To increase awareness that information must be identified and not guessed or assumed.**
- **To practise checking that information is given.**
- **To provide further practice with the common IELTS Reading task types.**

The overall aim is to teach more in-depth strategies for approaching the most common reading tasks, especially in terms of identifying exactly where information is given in a passage and checking that questions are answered confidently and not guessed.

The overall theme of *past and present* is developed and the previously touched on topic of *nostalgia* is explored in depth.

Reading 1

A The principal aim is to prepare for the reading content of both passages rather than to provide extended speaking practice. The final question especially aims to start students thinking about something that is addressed in the passages and they will probably find it difficult to answer.

Though students should be encouraged to develop a conversation, you should have a clear time limit in mind (two minutes for each question). Note that discussing the questions in pairs will give more opportunity for more students to contribute. Avoid a situation whereby pair discussion is brought to a close only for a lengthy whole-class debate to begin.

Start by writing *nostalgia* and *nostalgic* on the board and ask if anyone feels they can give a good definition. Note that this is the first question to be discussed as pairwork, so don't go into detail at this point.

Students should read the questions, think and plan answers individually. They can then answer the questions in pairs. Monitor and make a note of interesting points to get or give brief feedback. You may prefer to skip a feedback stage completely here, telling students that the questions will be answered in the passages later in the lesson.

B The aim is to further prepare students for the first passage and to set a gist reading task. Suggest that students use a pencil, so that they can easily change answers when they read to check.

Students should read the points and order them individually, before comparing the order in pairs. Monitor to check ideas. Feedback is unnecessary.

C Make sure students understand they are skimming to check their answers to B. They will read the passage in much greater depth in a moment. Set a strict time limit of one and a half minutes. Check answers, asking for quick explanations lifted from the passage like, *So, who might benefit from nostalgia?* and so on. Ask students if their original answers to B were correct.

Answers:

3 give examples of who might benefit from nostalgia
1 define nostalgia and give some examples of what makes people feel nostalgic
2 explain why feeling nostalgic might be beneficial

D and E 🎧 This part of the lesson is designed to look like exam practice, but it is really preparation for the practice stage later. Students work with two familiar tasks and are guided towards identifying information that provides an answer rather than guessing or assuming. They listen to students discussing answers to the two tasks and learn how to dismiss wrong answers and explain why correct answers are correct.

Students work through the two tasks individually as they would exam practice. Do not set a time limit here – students will only benefit from the analysis and guidance if they have completed the tasks themselves first. Move on when most students have completed the two tasks. Students can spend a minute or two checking answers, but do not confirm or correct.

Explain that students will hear two students (a male and a female) discussing all the answers to the two tasks. For each question, one student gives a correct answer and the other a wrong answer – they must decide which.

Be prepared to work through the process methodically, playing the recording, or parts of the recording a number of times for students to fully benefit. They should listen as they read the tapescript at some point.

Ask students why they think one student is correct and why the other is wrong. Once all the answers are clear, play the recording once more as students read the tapescript. Check how many questions students got correct themselves initially.

Answers:
Exercise D:
1. a   2. b   3. c
4. NG   5. F   6. T   7. T   8. NG

Exercise E:
1. M   2. F   3. F   4. M   5. F   6. M   7. M   8. F

Tapescript 🎧 **39 (5 mins, 37 secs)**

E   **Before you check the answers to Exercise D, listen to some students talking about them. Which student gives the correct answer to each question? Write (M) male or (F) female.**

Male: OK, I've got my answers. Shall we compare?

Female: Hang on a moment. I'm still thinking about number three and number seven.

Male: Yes, I thought number three was quite tricky – but also number eight – I'm not sure about number eight.

Female: OK, well, let's compare, then. Number one, I think the answer is *c*. The text mentions children's bricks and catapults and I think that activities like these always make you feel nostalgic.

Male: Mm, I don't think so. Those are just examples of nostalgia. The text says, the 'tiniest trigger'. I'm not sure about trigger, but tiniest means smallest. My guess is that trigger means make something happen – like the trigger on a gun. I think *a* is the right answer.

Female: Mm, OK. What about number two, then?

Male: Well, it's definitely not *c*. The text says nothing about the future. I think it's *a* – the extract is all about memories.

Female: No. The extract is about memories, but this part says we are frequently told to live for the moment. That means that people are led to believe they should think about now. The answer is *b*. I'm quite confident about this one.

Male: OK, I see what you mean – perhaps you're right.

Female: OK, number three – we both thought this one was difficult. There are a couple of words I don't know. I think the answer is *c*. I think reliving 'high school glories' means thinking about proud moments – you know, what he succeeded in. I don't really know glories, though, so I'm working it out from the context.

Male: No, I don't think so. The student is struggling, so he finds something difficult. He thinks back to something that was also difficult at school. I'm not sure, but my answer is *b*.

Female: Well, we'll just have to disagree. We're not agreeing on many answers!

Male: No. Well, what about number four, then? I prefer these true, false, not given exercises.

Female: My answer is *true*. Everyone does feel nostalgic about school lunches. Now, there are even restaurants that serve food which people liked at school.

Male: Maybe, but that doesn't mean it's the right answer. The extract just gives thinking about school lunches as an example of nostalgia – I mean, what makes one person feel nostalgic. It certainly doesn't say that everyone reminisces about school lunches. No, I think the answer is *NG*.

Female: Mm, yes – you might be right. Let's go on to number five.

Male: I think the answer here is *NG*. The extract doesn't say anything about this.

Female: I disagree. The extract says, 'even for the least sentimental of us'. That line provides the answer. It's saying that people who are not especially sentimental – that is, not especially sensitive or emotional – are also affected by nostalgia. My answer is *false*.

Male: OK, and number six? I think this one's *true*.

Female: Mm, I'm not sure that the information is actually given. I've put *NG*.

Male: No, the information is definitely given. It says that thinking about the past for half an hour can make you feel better about your current situation. That means how you live now.

Female: So, you think that 'contemplating' means thinking about?

Male: Well, yes, I think so – anyway, I'm pretty sure the answer is *true*.

Female: Well, for number seven, I don't know the answer. I've put *not given* because I can't say that it definitely is given.

Male: I've put *true*. I think an 'antidote' is something that relieves or cures an illness – you know, a kind of opposite to something. Having nice memories is a kind of cure to sadness.

Female: OK, maybe you're right.

Male: So, what about the last one? This one is difficult. I've put *true*. I think that the extract is saying that people who don't think about the past are like leaves blown in the wind. They have no roots.

Female: Mm, I think that's the idea, but it doesn't actually state that these people are all directionless. It says that 'nostalgia can motivate people'. It's one of those statements that are a bit misleading. I think when there are

modal verbs like *can* or *might*, the answer is often *NG*.

Male: OK, let's check the answers.

Refer students to the Exam tip and give them time to read and absorb.

Reading 2

The passage for the practice part of the lesson is longer and more challenging and students should be reminded that they will neither be able to, nor need to, read every word. There are also more questions for one passage than there will be in the actual exam – they need to practise what they have been focusing on.

To facilitate the process, there is a short preparation stage, but students are largely left to their own devices.

A The aim is to prepare students for some of the ideas explored in the passage, not to pre-teach the words and phrases in the box. Note however, that pre-teaching *self-esteem, neurological disorder* and *sequel* will be helpful.

Put students into pairs to discuss each item – tell them to simply move on if they have no idea why an item should be mentioned. Monitor and check ideas, assisting and explaining when appropriate. If you feel your students will cope with the passage and should practise with a minimum of preparation, skip a feedback stage and tell students they will be able to check as they read (see B). If, on the other hand, you feel your students will struggle with the passage, go over answers, telling them in advance why each item is mentioned (see answers below).

Answers:
a spell in hospital or prison – is an example of a bad memory
a record collection – music reminds people of the past / brings back happy memories
the Greek language – the word *nostalgia* is from Greek
a neurological disorder – at one time, nostalgia was said to be a neurological disorder
self-esteem – reminiscing is believed to improve self-esteem
film sequels – people expect a sequel of a film to bring back happy memories of the first film
advertising – exploits nostalgia to sell products

B Set a time limit of 15 minutes (pretty much a minute for each question) to complete all tasks. If nobody has finished in that time, give them another five minutes. Advise them to skim the passage in about three minutes and then read the questions carefully before reading again to locate information. Remind them that answers to questions 9–16 will be found in order in the passage and that that will help them to know roughly in which part of the passage to look for information. Monitor at the beginning of the process, and if anyone is still reading the text for the first time after five minutes, tell them that that is too long to be reading without a specific focus.

C Checking and reflecting on answers is a constant feature of the skills modules. Give students sufficient time to check and think about why they may have answered incorrectly.

Checking why each answer is correct will be time-consuming, but given the specific focus of the module – checking that information is given – it would be worth giving some rigorous feedback. To identify the specific parts of the passage that provide answers, show an OHT or other visual medium of the passage and highlight those parts on the board as you go over answers (see answers below).

Answers:

1. D (All of the second half of Paragraph D.)
2. H (The idea that things were 'better in the good old days' is generally a myth + explanation in rest of paragraph.)
3. B (... feeling nostalgic about generally painful schooldays, a job they loathed or even a spell in hospital or prison.)
4. G (All of Paragraph G.)
5. F (Most of our days are filled with routine activities with no significance, like travelling to and from work or shopping for groceries.)
6. T (There is not yet a great deal of scientific literature on nostalgia.)
7. NG (Smell and touch are the senses that tend to most readily prompt nostalgia, perhaps.)
8. NG (Research suggests that a negative memory can evoke feelings of nostalgia as long as the period or situation to which the feeling relates was eventually overcome.)
9. F (... record collections ... are full of songs ... listened to more for old times' sake than

for their timeless quality.)
10. b (The brain is an incredibly energy-intensive organ, ...)
11. c (... that incapacitated sufferers through intense homesickness)

Note that 12–14 can be in any order.

12. A (... improves mood, increases self-esteem, ...)
13. B (... strengthens social bonds)
14. D (... gives meaning to life)
15. c (those recollections have always been viewed through rose-coloured spectacles)
16. b (Because we tend to focus on fond memories, we edit out what we do not want to remember.)

D Students will now be more familiar with this type of reflective process. Point out this time that they should focus on point 3 especially. Remind them that identifying what they are doing well and not doing so well is a very good way of focusing on what they can do better next time. Allow students time to reflect and complete the exercise and then ask them if they are happy with the number of correct answers.

E The aim is to conclude the lesson rather than develop an extended debate. You will know whether your students will enjoy and benefit from an extended pair or group discussion or whether a quick whole-class discussion will suffice. Whatever approach you take, encourage students to use core language learnt in the module.

Key vocabulary in context

Remind students that an effective way to learn and remember new vocabulary is to study it closely once it has been presented in context.

A The task is the same as the one in the Reading Module in the previous unit, so students will know what to do. Note that the aim is to practise the skill of understanding new words and phrases in context, as well as actually learning the selected words and phrases. Discourage dictionary use for this exercise.

Students should complete the exercise individually and then compare answers with a partner. Answers can be given orally, but must be clear. Alternatively, delete the wrong option on an OHT or other visual medium of the exercise shown on the board. When answers have been checked, tell students to cover the exercise. Read out the correct definitions as they shout out the newly acquired key word.

Answers:
1. the most important part of it
2. brings the emotion out
3. hate it
4. use and benefit from it
5. wrongly believe to be true

Vocabulary suggestions

- Students will recognize the more common adjective *essential*.

- Compare *evoke* and *provoke* – both useful IELTS words. *Evoke* means *cause an emotion to surface*, while *provoke* means *deliberately try to make a negative emotion surface.*

- Pronounce and drill *myth* and point out the unusual spelling. Give an example of a myth that your students will relate to.

B Students can complete the exercise in pairs. Write answers on the board for clarity. Ensure that the meaning of *serve as* is clear. One thing serves as another – it plays that role.

Answers:
1. with   2. between   3. as

Refer students to the Workbook exercises related to this module. Choose to work on them now or set up for homework.

Writing

Objectives

- To present students with further examples of IELTS Writing Task 2.
- To give further practice understanding Writing Task 2 instructions and appreciating what is required.
- To give further practice and increase confidence in terms of knowing what to say.
- To present and practise writing a balanced composition.

The Writing Module in this unit concentrates on Writing Task 2. The aim is to revise and develop the fundamental issues addressed in Unit 2 – understanding the task, knowing what to say and organizing ideas. Note that *understanding the task* now means appreciating what is required in an answer rather than simply understanding the instructions.

Writing 1

By devising their own writing tasks, students should develop more of an awareness of what is required when answering.

A The principal aim is to prepare for the writing focus rather than to provide extended speaking practice. Though students should be encouraged to develop a conversation, you may like to have a clear time limit in mind (three minutes for each question, perhaps). Note that the conversation will develop with more focus as students discuss ideas in B.

Discussing the questions in pairs will give more opportunity for more students to contribute. Avoid a situation whereby pair discussion is brought to a close only for a lengthy whole-class debate to begin.

Students should spend three minutes looking at the pictures, thinking and planning answers individually. They should the spend six minutes answering the questions in pairs. Monitor to check that students are discussing points that will help them tackle B. Give assistance and prompt when necessary. Make a note of observations that will be useful during feedback. Keep feedback brief and concise and use it to make sure that students have the basic idea to take into B.

Possible answers:
1. School children frequently access computers rather than read or write with pen and paper.
2. There is far more traffic on the streets.
3. Children eat more fast food. / Families eat meals together less frequently.

Students can briefly say if the changes have made life better or not.

B The aim is to increase awareness, not for students to competently write task instructions. Tell them to look back at previous Task 2 instructions and use them as a model. Set a time limit of nine minutes (three minutes for each set of instructions). Alternatively, divide the class into three groups and tell pairs in each group to write instructions for one pair of pictures only.

Monitor to check ideas and give students feedback as they work. A whole-class feedback stage is unnecessary as students can compare their ideas with the instructions they will see in the next part of the lesson.

C The matching task is obviously very easy and the real aim is for students to compare these instructions with those that they have just devised. Set a time limit of three minutes and tell students they will read them again more carefully in a moment.

D Tell students to read more carefully now and to apply what they learnt about reading instructions in the last unit. Tell them not to use dictionaries for any unknown words – they can discuss with them with a partner in a moment.

Students should spend six minutes (two minutes per task) reading, thinking and planning answers individually, before answering the questions in pairs.

As feedback, get a consensus as to which tasks are most and least popular and why. Deal with any vocabulary now, if necessary.

Writing 2

Students have already discussed that knowing what to say can be an issue, and the aim is to address that once again.

A Make sure students know what to do and set a time limit of five minutes.

B Students can mingle to find other students to work with for each step. Have a time limit in mind, but allow them sufficient time to compare.

C 🎧 The aim is to give students further guidance on how to go about planning what to say when tackling a discursive task. The fact that they listen to people talking about the issues should hopefully motivate them more than simply reading a list of possible points. Note that the three/four points made about each issue will provide all, or at least most, of the content

needed for each composition. Play the whole recording as students complete the exercise and then again as you check answers.

Answers:
1. B 2. A 3. C 4. A 5. B 6. C 7. B 8. A
9. C 10. B

Tapescript 🎧 40 (4 mins, 0 secs)

C **Listen to some people talking about the topics in the three tasks. Match each speaker with one of the tasks A, B or C.**

Speaker 1
Voice: Well, I don't really see how anyone can complain about using them at work. They do everything in a tenth of the time it used to take. I can't imagine people going back to typewriters and waiting three days for a letter to arrive.

Speaker 2
Voice: Actually, I think this has a lot to do with women going out to work. I know I won't be popular saying this, but it's obvious. If women are out all day, they don't have time to cook proper meals. The kids come in from school and get a meal out of the freezer or grab something from a takeaway.

Speaker 3
Voice: They've just got to improve public transport. People use their cars because they're so much more comfortable than buses and the underground. They can listen to music or the news on the radio and they travel door-to-door. Even if the journey takes a bit longer, people feel it's more convenient and often safer too.

Speaker 4
Voice: I'm not sure it really is that big a problem. There might be some kids who only eat burgers and pizzas, but not the ones I know. Mine eat as much in the way of fruit and vegetables as I did and I'm pretty sure most of their friends do too. I think the media just make up these issues to scare people.

Speaker 5
Voice: Mm, I do think that a lot of people spend too long online these days. What with the gossip pages, chat rooms and shopping sites, they're never away from the screen. I'm

sure it's affecting the way people relate to one another. Nobody actually talks anymore and what they look at has no real cultural value.

Speaker 6

Voice: I think there should be some sort of incentive to share journeys and pick up passengers. It doesn't make sense for so many individuals to sit there in their metal box. When we come in on the motorway, we can't believe the number of vehicles coming past us the other way with just the driver.

Speaker 7

Voice: Well, like all things, there are pros and cons, but surely the pros outweigh the cons. I mean, they're just sophisticated machines and frankly, we've always lived with machines. I guess we rely on them a bit too much – if anything suddenly made them all crash, we'd be in trouble, but that's unlikely. I do worry about what my kids look at on the Internet, but that's my only real concern.

Speaker 8

Voice: When I was a lad, we used to nag our parents to take us to McDonald's or Burger King, but it wasn't all the time. Nowadays, there are so many different chains all selling more or less the same thing – they're everywhere and I'm sure a lot of teenagers live on that junk.

Speaker 9

Voice: I think they have to have some kind of city centre ban – you know, stop people driving into the centre or at least charge them if they do. They have to make it so that people don't want to drive – so that driving actually becomes inconvenient. Only then will people walk or take the bus.

Speaker 10

Voice: It does worry me a bit when I think about how far things could go. Would we ever need to leave the house? I mean, we could all end up sitting there all day and all night tuned into some fantasy world where we can be whoever we want, and to be doing whatever we want. Who wants real life if that's possible?

D The purpose of reading the tapescript is to clarify the points that the speakers made. Ask students if they want to listen to the recording again as they read or just read to absorb.

Writing 3

In Unit 2, students saw how a student disagreed with the statement in this type of writing task. The aim now is to show students how they can balance and express both sides of an argument. The exercise also addresses the issue of whether students know what to say about the issue in the first place. They are presented with another approach to brainstorming and making notes.

A Make sure students understand which task they are now focusing on and give them a moment to read the task instructions again if necessary. Focus attention onto the student's notebook and run through the column headings with them. It would be more efficient to show an OHT or other visual medium of the notebook on the board. That way, you can add notes during a feedback stage for B.

Make sure that students understand what the + and – signs mean and then go through the notes, expanding and explaining where necessary, for example, *Children at school can learn about the world – and all sorts of other subjects very easily, if a computer crashes, it breaks down and a lot of important information can be lost*.

B Give students time to copy the table, making sure there is plenty of room to add notes. Students should work in pairs so that they can communicate and share ideas as they go. As feedback, add students' suggestions to the columns on the board in note form.

Refer students to the Exam tip and then tell them to cover it. Ask one student to explain the advice given.

C Make sure students do not look ahead at the composition. Make sure they know what to do – establish what the first stage is together as a class if you like. Suggest that they use a pencil so that they can easily change the order when they read the model later.

Students should read and order the stages individually, before comparing their order with a partner. Then, they should read the model composition to check their answers, though you can check their ideas first quickly if you think it will be of benefit.

D Give students time to read and check the order and generally absorb the content of the model.

While they are doing so, bring up an OHT or other visual medium of the answers below on the board. Clarifying the order of stages together will reinforce and hopefully encourage students to adopt the same approach in the practice part of the lesson. Note that, although the argument could be organized and staged differently, this approach is a good model to learn.

Answers:
4 – Describe the benefits of having computers at home.
1 – Show that you understand the question and introduce the argument.
3 – Describe the disadvantages of using computers at work and at school.
6 – Express your own opinion and conclude the argument.
5 – Describe the disadvantages of having computers at home.
2 – Describe the benefits of using computers at work and at school.

E Since clearly the model is a good model, the aim is to draw attention to elements of good discursive composition writing. Students can compare thoughts in pairs as suggested or in small groups. Start by giving a couple of examples – *I like the way the student keeps things simple* and *I like the way he expands the task instructions in the introductory paragraph and uses a rhetorical question to get the reader thinking.*

Set a time limit of three minutes and then get some feedback.

Writing task

The Writing tasks are found either in the Workbook or in the Exam Practice Module at the end of the unit. In this unit, the task is in the Workbook. In this case, there is the advantage that students have, to an extent, already prepared for the task, as they discussed the issue and read the task instructions in the Writing Module.

A Even if you choose to set the Writing task for homework, it would be best to work through the preparation part of the task in class time. Work through the stages as instructed in the Workbook, setting realistic time limits for each. Students can compare ideas between the stages.

B You may choose to set Writing Task 2 (for which students need 40 minutes) for homework. It would be a good idea to occasionally set a task within class time so you can check they spend the right amount of time on it and you can monitor to check development. If they do work at home, encourage them to be strict with time limits – they will not benefit from over-planning or spending longer than they are allowed writing.

Set a time limit of 25 minutes for the writing part of the task this time – students will have spent at least 15 minutes planning and organizing ideas.

When students have completed the task, they should compare it with the relevant model composition on pages 264 and 265. The models are reproduced on the next page.

If you collect students' compositions to mark, concentrate on what has been the focus of the Writing Module – balancing an argument and organizing points logically. You will want to start correcting more of the content, but remember that correcting every sentence will not be motivating. You may still be correcting most of what they write.

Model compositions:

Task A
There are stories in the media these days about the number of people who are overweight or even obese. This applies not only to adults – children too are less healthy and are putting on weight. The blame for this is usually attached to the amount of fast food that young people eat and the fact that families eat pre-cooked food that has a lot of fat and little goodness.

I have to say that I can't really say how much of a problem this is. I don't know how healthily people ate 20 years ago and my own diet now is a healthy balance. My friends and I go to fast-food restaurants occasionally but no more than my parents did.

I must admit that I see more and more fast-food places in my town and they are very popular. I suppose, in some families, the diet is less healthy too. Women work more now and perhaps don't have time to cook meals with fresh ingredients every day. It is convenient to eat frozen food. Nevertheless, I can't say that I see more overweight people, and young people I know play sports and stay fit.

There is a lot that could be done if this really is a problem. Fast-food restaurants are now encouraged to have healthier options like vegetarian burgers and salad and this is a good start. Supermarkets could have campaigns to convince people to buy fresh products and they could make fresh meat and fish less expensive. Most importantly, parents must show their children how to eat well.

Task C
If you go to any big city and even most towns now, the first thing you notice is the amount of traffic.

At certain times, there is terrible congestion and people are sitting in cars going nowhere. Apart from the number of cars on the road and the ridiculous number parked along every street, the pollution caused by all this traffic is a huge concern.

It is clear that governments must discuss the issue and then take action that will reduce the number of cars. At the moment, it seems they are putting the interests of the car manufacturers first. If the situation is allowed to continue, cities will simply be car parks and nobody will be able to breathe the air. Already, people wear masks.

The first step is to improve public transport. Underground systems need to be modern and safe, and buses should be more comfortable and less crowded. This could be achieved by having more buses and more bus routes. There should be a ban on cars in the city centre or high parking charges that could pay for public transport. In some cities, there is a charge to drive in the centre now. People could be encouraged to use bicycles more too. There are cycle lanes in all cities, but roads can still be dangerous.

All in all, I think people will only stop using cars when it is not convenient anymore or they cannot afford to do it. Personally, I think the only way to reduce the number of cars is to offer some tax deduction or other financial incentive to people who do not use them.

Consolidation

Instructions are given for Speaking exercises when the procedure is not clear from instructions in the Course Book. Set Vocabulary and Errors exercises either for individual completion and pairwork checking, or as pairwork when you feel immediate interaction is beneficial.

To correct errors in the final exercise, ask students to come and write the correct sentences on the board while other students offer help. You will need to write the corrections on the board to clarify.

Speaking

A and B 🎧 Students have now practised all parts of the Speaking test and will know enough to complete the extract. Note that the aim is to revise the advice – not to listen for difficult words. They should work individually and then compare answers before you play the recording to check answers. Once answers have been checked, tell them to cover the extract and revise the advice given.

Answers:
See highlighted words in the tapescript for Track 41.

Tapescript 🎧 **41 (0 mins, 46 secs)**

B Listen and check your answers.

Voice: When you are speaking with the examiner, he or she will listen and make a note of the vocabulary you use. However, you shouldn't worry about this. You can only use words and phrases you know and you shouldn't try to impress the examiner. If you try too hard to use words and phrases that you don't really know, you'll use them incorrectly or inappropriately and you won't sound natural. At the same time, you don't want your language to be too simple. After the interview, you might regret that you didn't use a word or phrase that you know was right for the situation. Listen to what the examiner says and think for a moment before you speak.

C Read through the instructions with students and make sure they appreciate that the idea is to replace wording that is too simple or slightly inappropriate with more precise, well-chosen vocabulary.

Students should spend four minutes (one minute per interaction) completing the task individually, before comparing their alternative vocabulary with a partner. Monitor to check ideas as they work, but use the recording in Exercise D to check answers formally.

D 🎧 Play the whole recording and then play it again, pausing between exchanges to check answers. Write the key words and phrases on the board for clarity.

Answers:
See highlighted words and phrases in the tapescript for Track 42.

Tapescript 🎧 42 (1 min, 6 secs)

D **Listen to the same students using the more appropriate words and phrases. Check your ideas.**

1

| Examiner: | Would you say that you were happy at school? |
| Student: | Yes, I have some very good memories of school. |

2

| Examiner: | What was your favourite time of year as a child? |
| Student: | Winter. When it's winter now, I always feel nostalgic. I mean, it takes me back to my childhood. |

3

| Examiner: | Is there a danger that people end up living in the past? |
| Student: | Mm, I don't think so. Everyone likes to sit and reminisce occasionally. |

4

| Examiner: | Do you have regrets about leaving university so early? |
| Student: | Oh yes. Now I wish I had my degree. If only I could turn back the clock. |

E Read through the instructions with students and make sure they appreciate that the aim is to choose vocabulary carefully. Show students questions 1–5 opposite on an OHT or other

visual medium. Give them five minutes to think and plan answers. Tell them to look back to the relevant part of the Course Book unit if they want to find and check specific words and phrases.

Once students start answering questions 1–5 in pairs, monitor closely to check performance and to make a note of answers that you want students to share with the class as feedback.

1. Can you remember anything about life before you went to school?
2. Tell me about a friend that you used to have that you no longer know.
3. Do you have any regrets about the choices you made related to studies or work?
4. Are there any annual events that make you feel nostalgic?
5. Is there a period in your life that you reminisce about especially?

Vocabulary

A **Answers:**
1. inequality   2. recollections   3. adaptation
4. unfulfilled   5. strengthen

B 🎧 **Answers:**
reco'llection   remi'nisce   a'ssociate (v)
associ'ation   funda'mental   spon'taneously

Tapescript 🎧 43 (0 mins, 34 secs)

B **Mark the main stress on these words. Then listen and check. Practise saying the words.**

recollection
reminisce
associate
association
fundamental
spontaneously

Errors

Answers:
1. … forget driving …
2. … remembered to phone …
3. I wish I had more …
4. If only I hadn't listened …
5. … regret taking …
6. … no use worrying …

Exam Practice

Listening

The Exam Practice Module aims to practise the skills practised in the Listening Module – labelling diagrams.

A Note once more that students will not have an introductory exercise like this when it comes to the actual exam, nor will they be told what each Listening section is about. The aim here is to facilitate the listening process and to motivate students to do as well as possible in the tasks. Note that the lead-in serves to link the two listening tasks and prepare students for both.

You may feel the best approach here is to conduct a quick whole-class discussion, but remember that discussing the questions in pairs will give more opportunity for more students to contribute. Keep to a time a limit of five minutes, whether you opt for pairwork or a whole-class discussion.

Keep feedback brief and try to take the opportunity to pre-teach any key vocabulary.

Possible answers:

1. They provide shelter. / They have walls. / They have roofs. / They are built with wood. / They have entrances – doors.
2. the shape, size, number of windows and doors / the range of materials – glass, metal, etc., used to build modern house / ability to retain warmth or keep out the cold

B 🎧 Remind students that they have 30 seconds at the beginning of each section of the listening. Tell them that the talk is divided into two distinct sections with a total of 16 questions and that they have two minutes to read all the questions and make predictions. That is twice the time they will be allowed in the exam.

Play the whole recording. Then check answers. You can decide if students should hear the recording again to check why any answers were incorrect. If you do play the recording again, pause after each talk, checking the answers as you go.

Answers:

1. c   2. a   3. b
4. c   5. e   6. b   7. a   8. d

9. information   10. visitors   11. other buildings
12. motion detector   13. external systems
14. security panels   15. master control
16. multimedia connection

Tapescript 🎧 44 (7 mins, 26 secs)

B **You will hear two parts of a talk about houses. Listen and answer the questions.**

Voice: OK, so, here we are. Can you see the image on the screen clearly enough at the back? … Oh good, OK then. Now, it's difficult to say exactly when houses like these were built because it probably happened at different times in different places. We talk about the Stone Age, but that lasted much longer in some parts of the world than in others. Houses like these may not have existed until what we call the Iron Age in many parts.

Anyway, the important thing is that during the Neolithic – or modern Stone Age – era, the way people lived changed dramatically. Before that, during the Palaeolithic era, people were nomadic. They moved from place to place and didn't really have houses at all – at least not permanent ones. They may have slept in caves or built very primitive shelters, but they didn't build houses. During the Neolithic era, people started to build houses. The growth of agriculture meant that people grew crops and kept their own animals. They no longer moved around hunting and gathering. For the first time, people wanted to settle and have a base.

Some houses from this period were rectangular, but the better preserved houses, those probably dating from a slightly later time, were usually round – like this one. These houses were made from stones or mud bricks, depending on where they were. In this picture, you can see that the walls were built with flint, a hard stone that was also used at the time for making tools. The stone or flint walls were then coated with plaster. At that time, plaster would have been little more than mud or clay, but it would have kept the rain out. The roofs were made from mud or sticks and grass. Doorways were sometimes at ground level as is usual now, but here you can see that sometimes they were actually cut into the roof and that there were ladders on either side of the roof for access. This would have been practised presumably to protect the inhabitants from large wild animals that couldn't climb. Inside the homes, strong wooden beams that were driven into the ground supported the roof. In the centre of most houses like this was a hearth. This was to keep people warm at night mainly, but may have been used for cooking too. Usually, these were little more than a fire made within a circle of stones, but later they were more like a primitive oven.

Some houses from this period had two separate rooms within. One of these would have been …

… I'm going to bring us right up to date now and talk about *smart houses*. I'm sure most of you will have heard the term smart house, but you might not know that much about what that means – unless you already live in one, of course. A smart house is a house that has a highly advanced automatic system. This can operate lighting, temperature control, security devices, window and door operations, multimedia and communication and potentially a host of other functions. *Smart* here means *intelligent* – the house is intelligent because it can monitor daily life within its walls and appears to make decisions. Not long ago, this would have sounded like something from a sci-fi movie, but now it's all very much reality.

In a smart house, the systems within the house are connected and can pass information to each other. So, for example, the security alarm can turn the lights on or off. You can also operate the systems from outside the house. You can turn on the heating so that the house is warm when you return. You can open and close curtains and turn on lights so that people think you are at home. The system can call your mobile to tell you you've have had a visitor or received mail and you can let visitors into your house if you want to. What's more, the systems could be connected to other buildings. The security system could be connected to the police station so that it alerts the police if you have an intruder. The fridge could be linked to the local supermarket so that it can order products, which will be waiting for you when you get home.

So, let's look at this house in the diagram. First of all, as the family arrives home, they activate the systems inside the house from inside the car – if they haven't already done so previously, of course. Above the garage here, there's a motion detector. This will detect any movement outside the house, whether it's an approaching vehicle or a person. When you are inside the house, you will know that you have a visitor well before they arrive. Outside the house, you can see that there are various external systems. External systems can check and maintain the temperature and cleanliness of a swimming pool or irrigate the garden, for example. Now, as you come round the front door here, there are security panels in the entrance area. These would be more sophisticated than conventional alarms – panels like these have an alarm, but also digital cameras and mechanisms for activating locks.

Now, inside the house, there would be various areas where parts of the system would function from. In this house, the master control is downstairs on the ground floor – the master control is the central part of the system – rather like a server to a system of computers. Upstairs, at the top of the house is the multimedia connection. This connects all the other systems to television screens and smaller computer screens around the house. In this house, the telephone connection is in a different location, but, of course, that could also be part of the multimedia apparatus in another house.

OK, now, down in the kitchen – personally, I think some of the kitchen features are the most interesting to talk about. Take the fridge, for example …

Unit 4 Workbook answers

Vocabulary development

A a. memorable / unforgettable b. memorize
  c. regrettable d. forgetful e. reminder

C 1. housed 2. schooled 3. mirrors
  4. shipped 5. eyeing / eying

D 1. vaguely 2. clearly 3. widely 4. deeply
  5. freely

E 1. temporarily   2. occasionally
   3. it must be done urgently / very quickly
   4. to make time go by more quickly
   5. it is inevitable   6. at the crucial moment

Listening

A a map = 3 / a graph = 6 / a process = 1 /
   an appliance = 2 / a building = 4 / the human
   body = 5

Tapescript 🎧 45 (2 mins, 59 secs)

A **Listen and match each extract to a type of
   diagram below. Write the number of the
   extract in the space.**

Extract 1

Voice: The glass is cut into what we call gobs,
which are individual pieces fired down into the
forming machine. In a matter of seconds, the
glass is pressed and blown into shape inside a
mould. It emerges as a brand new glass bottle
or jar. Each container is rigorously checked in
a series of quality controls.

Extract 2

Voice: The thermostat takes all the guesswork
out of ironing. The user can preset the exact
required temperature on the dial depending on
the fabric being ironed. He or she can be
confident that the correct heat is being
maintained and that there is no risk of burning.
A heat-sensitive contact cuts the supply as
soon as a selected temperature is reached.
When the iron cools, the current is resumed.

Extract 3

Voice: Brighton is a city on the south coast. It
has many attractions that young visitors can
enjoy. It's more or less directly south of
London and is about an hour by train.
Eastbourne and Hastings are smaller seaside
resorts to the east of Brighton. Hastings is the
larger of the two and has more in the way of
leisure facilities. Another seaside town – this
time further west in Dorset – is Bournemouth.
Bournemouth is a large town popular with
holidaymakers …

Extract 4

Voice: Early dwellings in Pompeii were built
around an atrium, a large open main hall.

There was usually a small opening in the
ceiling, the compluvium, through which light
and air were filtered. The impluvium was a hole
in the floor which collected rainwater when it
entered through the compluvium.

Extract 5

Voice: There are four chambers, two superior
atria and two inferior ventricles. The atria are
the receiving chambers and the ventricles are
the discharging chambers. The right ventricle
discharges into the lungs to oxygenate the
blood. The left ventricle discharges blood that
circulates around the rest of the body via the
aorta.

Extract 6

Voice: The biggest leap in the number of
female smokers was between 1992 and 1993
when 30,000 more women smoked. By 1993,
there were more female than male smokers.
For three years, the number of women
smoking remained fairly constant, but then
between 1996 and 1997, there was another
increase.

Reading

A 2 is good advice.

B The passage says that nostalgia <u>can</u> motivate
   people and make them feel they are rooted, i.e.,
   give them a sense of direction (not be blown
   around by the vagaries of everyday life). However,
   the passage does not actually say that people
   who do not indulge in nostalgia are directionless.

C Extract A: 1. NG 2. NG 3. F
   Extract B: 1. F 2. NG 3. T

Writing

A and B **Model answers:**

*Computers are everywhere <u>nowdays</u>. Everyone
uses a computer at work and children are using
them increasingly at school. Computers are
used in shops and hospitals and to drive trains.
Most <u>familys</u> have a computer in home and
perhaps a laptop too. So, do we rely for
computers too much and is that having a
<u>negitive</u> effect in how we live? Many people think
the answer is 'yes'.*

*At the workplace, computers do everything
quickly and <u>effisiently</u>. It is difficult to imagine going
back to pen and paper. E-mailing is more
convenient than making phone calls. In schools,
children can learn with interesting interactive
programmes about the world and its history.
However, all this could mean that people
<u>comunicate</u> less. In offices, people stare to a
screen instead of talking to each other and, at
school, children work less in groups to solve
problems.*

C   Model answers:

*People love having a computer at home. They
can find the information online immediately and
use the Internet for shop and <u>order</u> holidays.
Young people enjoy to play computer games and
making friends in chat rooms. However, there are
disadvantages here too. Families communicate
less and perhaps do not go out so often. Some
Internet sites are <u>uncomfortable</u> for children and
parents have to check that they are safe.*

*<u>Individually</u>, I think the advantages far
<u>overbalance</u> the disadvantages. Computers are
making life more convenient and enjoyable.
Information is at our fingertips instead of having
to search through books. Of course, people
should not sit at a computer all day every day,
whether at work, at school or at home, but as
long as they are used <u>sensitively</u>, computers
should be seeing as a great benefit.*

Writing task

See notes in the Course Book Writing Module.

Review 1

Speaking and Vocabulary

A Give students three or four minutes to discuss and then go over answers as a class.

Answers:
1. three / Part 1 – 4–5 minutes / Part 2 – 3–4 minutes / Part 3 – 4–5 minutes
2. In Part 1, the examiner asks questions and invites students to talk about their own life. In Part 2, the examiner will give the student a task card and the student will talk about the topic on the card for about two minutes. The examiner will ask one or two round-up questions. In Part 3, the examiner will ask the student more abstract questions and ask for the student's opinion about issues related to the topic on the card in Part 2.

B Give students six minutes to read the comments and decide what they agree with most. Tell them to tick three comments even if they agree with most of them. You can discuss the comments as a whole class or tell students to talk in pairs. This should take about ten minutes.

C Give students four or five minutes to write their own comments and then another three or four to talk about them.

D Give students a moment to look at the mind map and then read through the headings with them. Start by telling them not to look back at the Course Book units to see what they have retained. After five minutes, allow them to look back, adding words and phrases from the unit. Encourage them to do this in order to store new language rather than simply fulfil a task.

Listening

A Students should complete the exercise in pairs and share knowledge as they go. Students will need to use their own knowledge to answer some questions. Answers can be checked orally, but make sure they are clear.

Answers:
1. four   2. 40   3. two / social   4. one person
5. education   6. academic   7. challenging / fourth

B Students should discuss this from memory – the aim is to see what they have absorbed. Looking back at the units and listing the task types will be of little benefit.

C Suggest that students read all questions, think and answer individually and then compare ideas with a partner. Give them around eight minutes to read and make choices, and another six or seven to discuss them.

Note that pairwork gives everyone the opportunity to talk about their strengths and weaknesses – a quick whole-class feedback stage will not allow that. The benefit here is in identifying strengths and weaknesses and discussing them. No solutions can be offered to each student individually right now.

Reading

A Make sure students understand the task and give them five minutes to complete it individually. Then they can check answers quickly with a partner before you go over them.

Answers:
In the IELTS Academic Reading test, there are three texts that gradually become more challenging in terms of content and density of language. In total, there are 40 questions to answer in an hour. The texts come from books and articles in newspapers, magazines and journals and are academic in nature. The language used in the texts is generally fairly formal.

B Work through as with Listening, Exercise B on page 89.

C Students should talk in pairs. Monitor to make a note of concise definitions that can be shared during a feedback stage. Check answers orally.

Answers:
skim – read quickly for global comprehension / general meaning
gist – general meaning / global comprehension
scan – read quickly to locate specific information
prediction – guessing what information will be given before you read
vocabulary in context – understanding new words and phrases from other words and phrases around the unknown word
paraphrasing – saying the same or nearly the same thing using different words

D Give students five minutes to reflect and then get some feedback from the class.

Writing

A Students should answer the questions in pairs. Give them about ten minutes and then check answers orally. You might like to suggest that they answer questions 1–6, check answers, and then discuss points 7 and 8 separately.

Answers:
1. line graph / bar chart / pie chart / flow chart / diagram
2. a discursive composition
3. 150
4. 250
5. one hour
6. No – about 20 minutes for the first task and 40 for the second

B Give students around six or seven minutes to read and make their choices and then a moment to compare answers with a partner. Get some class feedback and provide the answer below.

Answers:
1 and 4 are the most important points.

C Work through as with Reading, Exercise D.

What next?

You might like to tell students to read this at home. You can check by asking questions or by having a brief feedback session at the beginning of the next lesson. If there is time to read it in class, it would be better to read through one section at a time and get some feedback rather than reading it right through in one go.

5 Work and play

Speaking and Vocabulary

Objectives

- **To practise talking about personal situations – work / leisure balance.**
- **To practise interaction typical of the IELTS Speaking test, Part 1.**
- **To present and practise vocabulary related to being busy and having free time.**

The aim of the first module is to concentrate once again on the first part of the Speaking test, during which students are most likely to personalize and give information about their own lives.

Start with books closed and write the proverb on the board with *play* blanked out. Elicit the missing word – students should be able to make sensible guesses even if they have never seen the proverb before. Once the proverb is complete, ask them to explain what it means – they can talk in pairs for a minute, focusing on what it means and their reaction to it. Spend another two minutes discussing it as a class.

Go on to discuss what a proverb is – a short, well-known saying that offers advice. Tell students that there are many proverbs in English and give them another example – such as, *You can't teach an old dog new tricks*. Point out that proverbs are rather predictable and people know them, but do not necessarily use them often. When people do use them, they often only say the first part of the proverb, knowing that the person listening can finish it, *Well,* *you know what they say about all work and no play, don't you?*

> *'All work and no play makes Jack a dull boy'* is one of the best-known English proverbs. It means that somebody who works constantly and takes no time to rest, enjoy life or socialize becomes both bored and boring. Though the spirit of the proverb had been expressed previously, the modern saying first appeared in James Howell's *Proverbs in English, Italian, French and Spanish in 1659.*

Vocabulary 1

The aim is to present students with new vocabulary they can use in the speaking exercises as the lesson develops. Note that the focus is mainly on informal phrases and expressions that most frequently occur in spoken English.

A Give students four minutes to complete the exercise individually, using a dictionary to check individual words within expressions – *rush, steam*, etc., if necessary. Advise them not to try to find the complete expressions in a dictionary as they will discuss them in a moment. Check the answers quickly, but do not discuss meaning yet.

Answers:
1. B 2. F 3. B 4. B 5. F 6. F 7. B 8. F

B Give students another four minutes to discuss the new vocabulary. Encourage them to find concise definitions that paraphrase the expressions and to translate them as closely as possible when appropriate.

As feedback, tell students to cover the exercise and read out definitions as they shout out the new words and expressions. Use the definitions in the Vocabulary suggestions below.

Vocabulary suggestions

- *Hectic* means *very busy*, but describes a situation and not a person – *It was a hectic morning*. NOT *I was hectic*.
- *Chill out* means *relax – forget about worries*. *Chill* is related to being cool, not hot and tense.
- If you're *on the go*, you're very busy – engaged with something.
- If you're *rushed off your feet*, you're extremely busy – you have more to do than you can manage. *Rush* or *be in a rush* means *move quickly* or *do things quickly*.
- Having your hair tied up implies that you are in some way controlled or restrained. If you *let your hair down*, you untie it and let it hang free. This implies that you have fun and forget your responsibilities for a while.
- When a kettle boils or an engine overheats, it *lets off steam* – it releases steam. If a person *lets off steam*, he or she releases energy or emotion that has been restrained.
- *Non-stop* means constant. It usually has a negative connotation. It can be used attributively or predicatively – *non-stop phone calls* or *the phone calls were non-stop.*
- You recharge a mobile phone when the battery runs out. If you *recharge your batteries*, you re-energize – you take a break in order to go back to a job with more energy and motivation.

Speaking 1

The aim is for students to practise using the newly acquired vocabulary, but also to start personalizing.

A Make sure students appreciate that the aim is to contrast *work time* and *play time* and to use some of the vocabulary they have just learnt. They should not simply describe what they can see in the pictures.

Students should spend four minutes looking at the pictures, thinking and planning what to say individually. Then compare ideas with a partner.

Monitor to check ideas and use of appropriate lexis. Prompt students to say more if you feel they have not really identified anything of interest. As feedback, choose one student to briefly describe each picture.

Possible answers:
a. Girl in office – She's clearly overworked. / She's stressed. / It's been a hectic day. / It's been non-stop.
b. Group in café – They're letting off steam at the end of a hectic day. / It's common for office people to go for a drink after work to relax, etc.
c. People on train – People are working longer hours. / Working hours are extending into travel time. / People work on laptops instead of read the newspaper or talk. / They're on the go all day.
d. Group bowling – They're letting off steam. / They're recharging their batteries. / They're letting their hair down.

B Students should spend five minutes reading the questions, thinking and planning answers individually. Then discuss the questions in pairs or groups of three.

Get some feedback, but try to avoid simply repeating the discussion that students have just had. Develop and conclude the points – *So, who is happy with the balance they have between study time and free time? Who thinks they spend too many hours each week studying?*, etc. Conclude the exercise by getting a consensus as to whether students feel that in the modern world, people have more free time, or whether they are actually spending more time doing things they have to do.

Vocabulary 2

The aim is to use the context and the vocabulary that has already been learnt to focus on an important language feature. Note that the aim is to increase awareness of affixes (especially prefixes in this case) rather than to learn the specific words presented.

A Make sure students understand what a *prefix* is – contrast with *suffix* if you think it will be helpful. Students should work in pairs on the exercise so that they can communicate and compare knowledge as they go. Note that explaining what a prefix means can be difficult even if it is perfectly well-understood. Monitor to assist and prompt.

As feedback, check comprehension by asking questions – *Which prefix has a general meaning of 'do something again' or 'repeat something'? Which prefix has a general meaning of 'not enough'?* and so on. Clarify and give additional examples where appropriate, though avoid examples that occur in the exercise that follows.

Answers:

1. The prefix has the effect of saying that something does not happen – if phone calls are *non-stop*, they do not stop. A *non-believer* is a person who does not believe.

2. The prefix has the general meaning of *do again*.

3. *Over* has a general meaning of excess or *too much*. *Under* has a general meaning of *not enough*.

4. The prefix has a general meaning of *against / in opposition to* – *anti-government forces* are forces in opposition to the government. It can also simply mean the opposite – *anticlockwise*.

5. The prefix has the general meaning *the opposite* and can imply achieving the opposite of what is desired. Note that, in American English, *anticlockwise* is *counterclockwise*.

6. The prefix has the general meaning of *reversing something* or *taking something away*.

B Students will learn affixes best by seeing examples. They should work individually to complete the task and then compare answers. Write answers on the board for clarity.

Answers:

1. destabilize the economy
2. overloaded with work
3. a non-smoker
4. relive the past
5. counteract negative effects
6. take antibiotics

Pronunciation check

Write *more potatoes* on the board and drill it. Then write *more apples* and drill that, too. Write the first phrase phonetically on the board /mɔːpəteɪtəʊz/. Then write the second phrase, but without the intruding *r* /mɔːæplz/. Say the phrase, clearly pronouncing the intruding *r* several times and elicit the sound students hear. Add it to the phrase on the board /mɔːræplz/ and explain how this happens naturally in rapid speech.

🎧 Play the recording and listen to the examples together. Give students time to read the information and absorb. Play the second part of the recording. Allow students to work on the task together. They should say the words aloud to each other. Play the recording, pausing between the phrases to check the answers.

Answers:

1. intrusion of /j/
2. intrusion of /r/
3. intrusion of /w/

Give students three minutes to practise saying all the phrases with a partner. Monitor to check improvement.

Tapescript 🎧 46 (0 mins, 39 secs)
Pronunciation check

Listen to these examples.

1 outdoor activities
2 on the go all day
3 crazy about

Decide which sound intrudes in the following phrases and where. Then listen and check.

1 stay indoors
2 better option
3 two others

The aim of the second half of the lesson is to develop language related to *free-time interests*. This is one of the topics most likely to be discussed in the first part of the interview (see Exam tip at bottom of Course Book page 71).

Vocabulary 3

A The aim is more to learn the category headings, and to get students thinking about how they might organize their free-time interests into various categories, rather than to add a long list of new words and phrases to each column. That said, students will enjoy and benefit from finding words and phrases related specifically to their own interests. Either set a time limit of six minutes (a minute for each column) or tell students to add two new items to each column.

Start by clarifying the meaning of the column headings, using the examples. Check pronunciation and drill when necessary. Point out that most of these words are flexible – we can talk about *outdoor activities* or *outdoor pursuits* – but that there are collocations that are more likely – we don't say a *social pursuit*, for example. Explain that a *hobby* or *pastime* is an area of interest that involves time commitment and usually some knowledge of a subject – most people don't talk about sports as hobbies.

Students can work in pairs to communicate and compare knowledge as they go, though some may prefer to work individually first. As they work, copy or bring up an OHT or other visual medium of the table on the board and, as feedback, add a limited number of examples to each column.

B At the level they are now at, students should be able to express the same idea in a number of different ways and they should certainly be able to understand the various ways that another person may talk about the same thing. Go through the sentences with students, asking whether or not they recognize the highlighted expressions – do not check any missing prepositions yet.

Students should work individually and then check answers in pairs. As feedback, tell students to cover the exercise and read out the

verbs, adjectives and nouns as they shout out the dependent preposition. Tell students they will practise using the expressions later. Clarify that *look forward to* is different from the other phrases in that it applies only to something planned in the future.

Answers:
1. in 2. on 3. about 4. from 5. to

Speaking 2

A 🎧 Make sure students understand that there are clues to the missing words in the sentences. The missing words are parts of fixed expressions or collocate frequently with other words.

Students should spend two minutes attempting to complete the exercise individually and then compare ideas with a partner. Play the recording to check answers. Pause after each sentence the first time you play it. Write the full phrases below on the board for clarity.

Answers:
1. spend your free time
2. free-time activities
3. taken up any hobbies
4. an active social life

Tapescript 🎧 47 (0 mins, 36 secs)

A **Guess the missing word in each of these examiner's questions. Then listen and check.**

1 Examiner: So, how do you spend your free time?

2 Examiner: Tell me about the free-time activities you enjoy.

3 Examiner: Have you taken up any hobbies in the last few years?

4 Examiner: Do you have a very active social life?

B 🎧 The aim now is to further develop the students' range of vocabulary with some more advanced informal expressions. Note that these expressions are aimed at the stronger students in the class – you may feel that weaker students already have enough new lexis to cope with.

Give students a moment to read the sentences, but don't expect them to make any predictions – the expressions will almost certainly be new to them. Play the whole recording, and then give students a minute to discuss answers in pairs. Play the recording again, pausing after the key expressions to check answers. Explain their meaning in greater depth if necessary and write the full expressions on the board for clarity. Play the recording one more time as students read the tapescript – it is always a good idea for them to fully absorb the interview interaction.

Answers:

1. I'm really into …
2. … my passion is …
3. … a health fanatic …
4. … a party animal …

Tapescript 🎧 **48 (2 mins, 9 secs)**

B **Listen to some students answering the questions. Complete the sentences below with ONE word in each space.**

1

Examiner: So, how do you spend your free time?

Student: Mm, in different ways. I'm really into painting so I spend a lot of my time in my studio or out painting in the countryside. Sometimes I just like spending time with friends – you know, having a drink or a meal out together.

2

Examiner: Tell me about the free-time activities you enjoy.

Student: Well, I like to keep fit. I go running and I go to the gym two or three times a week. I guess my passion is martial arts. I do karate and judo. I'm pretty good at that – I have a black belt in karate. It's not all exercise and sport, though. I go to the cinema a lot and I like other things that most people like, you know.

3

Examiner: Have you taken up any hobbies in the last few years?

Student: Um, yes, I have. I started doing yoga about nine months ago. I like to look after myself and yoga's very healthy. I stopped eating meat at that time too. I suppose I'm a bit of a health fanatic really. Apart from that, I'm very keen on music. I play violin and I'm in an orchestra – just an amateur one – but I really love it.

4

Examiner: Do you have a very active social life?

Student: Oh, I wouldn't say that. To tell the truth, I quite like staying in these days. I never was a party animal. I enjoy getting some takeaway food and watching a good movie on TV.

C Drill the questions so that students feel confident with the pronunciation. Give them four minutes to plan answers and then allow them time to ask and answer in pairs. Monitor to gauge performance and especially to check that students are using the newly acquired lexis. A feedback stage is unnecessary.

Refer students to the Exam tip and give them time to read and absorb.

Grammar check

Write on the board, *I look forward to play golf*. Ask students to identify the mistake and to explain why it is often made. Write on the board *I like going to the dentist every year*. Ask students why the sentence sounds rather strange and correct it. Check the difference between *like doing* and *like to do*. Emphasize that nobody actually enjoys the experience of going to the dentist. Finally, write *I spend most of time to work in my office*. Once again, elicit the mistake and correct it. Refer students to the *Grammar check* and the *Watch out!* box and give them time to read and absorb.

Listening

Objectives

- **To introduce students to a typical Listening test, Section 3.**
- **To practise listening in order to complete a summary.**

The aim of this Listening Module is to introduce students to, and practise listening to, a number of speakers engaged in a discussion (see the Exam tip on page 72 of the Course Book). The overall theme is one that your students should relate to – *the question of how hard they work and whether other people appreciate that*. In this Listening Module, the first conversation serves as the topic of the first and second parts of the lesson.

Listening 1

The aim of the first part of the lesson is to introduce the topic, the concept of listening to a number of speakers and the task type.

A The principal aim is to prepare for the listening stage and motivate students towards the theme rather than to provide extended speaking practice.

Set a time limit of ten minutes. Students should spend two minutes looking at the pictures and planning what to say individually. Then, they should spend eight minutes discussing student life in pairs.

Monitor to check ideas and the fluency of interaction and to make a note of interesting points that could be shared during feedback. Keep feedback brief and concise, perhaps checking key words like *demonstration* or *protest*, but avoid feeding too much information and negating the first listening task that follows.

B 🎧 The purpose of allowing students to listen to the recording right through with a gist task is twofold. Firstly, it is a good idea to present them with a conversation with a number of speakers without a difficult accompanying task, and secondly, to help them understand the basic context so that they can better benefit from practising the summary completion task that follows.

Make sure students understand that they must listen for clues, key words and phrases and tick each picture as they hear the students mention that aspect of student life during their conversation. Tell them that they can tick a picture more than once. Play the whole recording as students tick the pictures. As feedback, simply ask how many ticks they made – do not play the recording to check answers as that would mean students becoming too familiar with the conversation before the summary practice. You can monitor as students work to check they are ticking at the right time.

Tapescript 🎧 **49 (3 mins, 8 secs)**

B **Listen to some students talking and tick each picture as you hear it mentioned.**

Female 1: Have you read the stories in the newspapers recently about how hard, or should I say how little, students work?

Male 1: Mm, I saw something about it. I didn't really pay much attention.

Male 2: I haven't heard anything. What have they been saying?

Female 1: Oh, you know, the usual thing about students going to one or two lectures a week and then spending the rest of their time sitting around drinking coffee and smoking or going out to wild parties.

Female 2: It makes me really cross when I hear stories like that. They just say these things to sell their rags. I don't think they even believe any of it's true themselves.

Male 2: Yeah, but you do sit around drinking coffee all day. You never go to your lectures.

Female 2: Oh, ha ha! Seriously, I think I work as hard as most people that have a full-time job. I have eight lectures a week and then at least two assignments. The lectures take up 12 hours and then the assignments anything from another six to ten hours, once I've done all the research.

Male 1: Yeah, I think in the past students had things a bit easier. You know, they had bigger grants and they didn't have to worry about being in debt at the end of their course. Most students I know have to do a part-time job now on top of all the study.

Female 1: That's right. I mean, I do around 20 hours of study and then work another 15. That's pretty much a full-time job. I usually work Saturday lunchtime too. I have to say, I'm exhausted most of the time.

Male 2: Ah yes, but the average person doesn't see studying as real work. You'd have a job to convince Joe Public that you're doing a full-time job.

Female 1: I didn't say I was doing a full-time job. I just said that I work a lot of hours in a week.

Male 2: No, you said that …

Male 1: OK guys, calm down.

Female 2: So, do you really think we do more work than students did in the past?

Male 1: Well, like I said, I think they had it a bit easier. My dad talks about when he was a student and it's all about how many bands he went to see and how many parties there were. I wish I had enough money to go and see some bands!

Female 1: Yeah, I get the impression that my mum spent most of her time at university discussing politics or going on protest marches. I'm amazed she actually finished her degree!

Male 1: I have to say that I do worry about the amount of debt I'll accumulate. I worked out that I might owe around 10 or 12 thousand pounds by the time I've finished. I'll spend the first ten years of my working life paying it back.

Male 2: Yeah, but you're going to be a lawyer, aren't you? You'll be able to pay that much back in a couple of months.

Male 1: Oh, very funny. I wish you'd take a conversation seriously for once. I don't know why they've reduced the grants we get. I mean, it's not like families are all suddenly richer. My parents can't afford to give me lots of extra spending money. It's just not fair.

Female 2: No, that's true, but hey, look at the time. We're sitting round here chatting and we should be getting ready. It's Tina's party tonight, isn't it?

C Normally, you would set the gist task before students listen, but here, check retrospectively what they understood – there are enough references to the main topic to make the task simple. Give them a minute to read the options and make a choice and then establish the correct statement.

Answer:
option 3

Refer students to the Exam tip and give them time to read and absorb. Ask students if they found listening to more than two speakers more challenging.

D Do not introduce students to the idea of completing a summary before they start the exercise – the Question-type tip immediately after the exercise reflects on the nature of the task.

Make sure students understand that they will only listen to the first part of the conversation again. Give them time to read through the summary (a little longer than they will get in the exam) so that they know what to listen for. Point out that they might need to listen and absorb and then write answers into the spaces when the recording has finished. Play the whole recording and then give students two minutes to compare answers in pairs. Do not check any answers yet (see E).

D Listen to the first part of the conversation again and complete the summary.

Female 1:	Have you read the stories in the newspapers recently about how hard, or should I say how little, students work?
Male 1:	Mm, I saw something about it. I didn't really pay much attention.
Male 2:	I haven't heard anything. What have they been saying?
Female 1:	Oh, you know, the usual thing about students going to one or two lectures a week and then spending the rest of their time sitting around drinking coffee and smoking or going out to wild parties.
Female 2:	It makes me really cross when I hear stories like that. They just say these things to sell their rags. I don't think they even believe any of it's true themselves.
Male 2:	Yeah, but you do sit around drinking coffee all day. You never go to your lectures.

Refer students to the Question-type tip and give them time to read and absorb. Tell them to cover the tip and together as a class, go over the points made. Ask them if they feel that completing a summary is in any way easier or more difficult than completing notes or sentences.

E and F Read through the instructions with students, pointing out that the student's answers are wrong for various reasons.

Students should spend two minutes reading and analyzing the errors individually, before discussing the errors in pairs. As feedback, write the correct answers on the board as students explain them, or show an OHT or other visual medium of the summary on the board and get students to come up and write the corrections and explain each mistake. To conclude, check whether or not students made any of the same mistakes themselves.

Answers:
1. stories (spelling mistake)
2. lectures (too many words used)
3. sitting around (too many words / words not used in recording)
4. to sell (answer grammatically wrong / words not used in recording)
5. true (word (*truth*) not used in recording)

Listening 2

A Read through the instructions with students, emphasizing how important it is to do this. Point out that having already listened to the recording, they will understand the summary more quickly and be able to make better predictions. Remind them that in the exam they will have only 30 seconds for each section and that there will be more than just the summary completion task to look at. Give them a minute to read and think.

B 🎧 Play the whole recording as students complete the summary. Give them longer to compare answers before they check the answer key this time – the overall module aim is to check that answers fit and that possible mistakes are rigorously checked.

B Listen to the complete conversation again and complete the summary.

[Play Track 50 again]

C Checking and reflecting on answers is a constant feature of the skills modules. Give students sufficient time to check and think about why any answers were incorrect before moving onto D. You can decide if it would be beneficial to play the recording again, but avoid doing so simply to check individual students' wrong answers.

Answers:
1. grants 2. in debt 3. public 4. parties
5. bands 6. politics 7. paying back
8. reduced

Check the average number of correct answers, and ask whether anyone made any of the mistakes highlighted earlier. Ask whether anyone heard a word, but spelt it incorrectly. Remind them that no marks will be given for incorrectly spelt answers.

D Students will be more used to reflecting on tasks in this way by now. Note that here, once more, statements relate directly to the particular task type they have practised. They should answer the questions in pairs.

Key vocabulary in context

Encourage students to attempt to complete the exercise without checking the tapescript first. They can work in pairs to pool resources. Tell them to check the tapescript if they really don't know an answer. As feedback, tell students to cover the exercise and then read out noun phrases as students shout out the verbs.

Answers:

1. pay attention
2. get the impression that
3. do research
4. take something seriously

Refer students to the Workbook exercises related to this module. Choose to work on them now or set up for homework.

Reading

Objectives

- **To introduce or revise the concept of a topic sentence.**
- **To raise awareness of the purpose of paragraphs and topic sentences.**
- **To practise using topic sentences effectively to improve reading efficiency.**
- **To provide further practice with the common IELTS Reading task types.**

Although students do not have to actually identify topic sentences in an IELTS task, topic sentences are frequently mentioned in both reading and writing IELTS practice. Appreciating how topic sentences introduce the main point of a paragraph and facilitate the reading process is an essential skill.

In this Reading Module, students will complete exercises that increase awareness of how topic sentences function (non-exam tasks) and exam practice exercises that involve exploiting topic sentences.

It is not assumed that at this level, students understand the concept of using paragraphs to divide a text into manageable, logically organized chunks.

The theme of *work/leisure balance* introduced in the first module is developed in this module. Students work with two closely related passages.

Reading 1

The first part of the lesson refers to the *first* sentence of a paragraph rather than the *topic* sentence. The Exam tip then retrospectively tells students that these first sentences are called *topic sentences*. You should avoid referring to topic sentences in this part of the lesson if possible. You may well have students in the class who have learnt about topic sentences previously and if they bring the term up, you will need to decide how to deal with it.

A The principal aim is to prepare for the reading content in both passages rather than to provide extended speaking practice. Though students should be encouraged to develop a conversation, you may like to have a clear time limit in mind (two minutes for each question, perhaps). Note that discussing the questions in groups will give more opportunity for more students to contribute. Avoid a situation whereby group discussions are brought to a close only for a lengthy whole-class debate to begin.

Students should read the questions, think and plan answers individually. Note that you may need to clarify the meaning of *relieving stress* in question 4. They then answer the questions in pairs or groups of three. Monitor and make a note of interesting points that can be shared during a feedback stage. Keep feedback brief – try to avoid a repetition of the discussion that has already been had – but take the opportunity to orientate students towards some of the ideas in the passages, *Do any countries have a reduced working week? What are the consequences of overwork? What are good ways of relieving stress? – taking proper breaks, going on holiday,* etc.

B Make an OHT or other visual medium of the exercise that can be shown on the board. That way, you can focus attention on each step and make sure students are not tempted to look forward to the passage. It is important that this preparation stage is rigorously managed to ensure that students fully benefit – you will need to dedicate around 25 minutes of the lesson to it.

Read the first part of the instructions and refer students to sentences a–e. Then read the second part of the instructions and refer students to questions 1–3. Read questions 1–3 with them one at a time, emphasizing that questions 1–2 require them to think about the content and organization of the whole article, while question 3 requires them to focus on the content of each paragraph, i.e., working with each first sentence individually. Note that answering question 3 will mean organizing ideas probably already mentioned to answer question 2.

Students should spend five minutes reading, understanding the sentences and thinking individually. Check any key words with them, but avoid explaining text content in doing so. Students should then spend another five minutes looking at the questions, thinking and planning what to say. Finally, they should spend six minutes (two minutes for each question) comparing ideas.

Getting and giving feedback on the exercise will not be straightforward, but it is important. Simply telling students to read the passage to confirm ideas will not tell you what they have learnt or whether the process has been beneficial. Go through the questions, building up simply expressed ideas on the board together. Try to elicit as much from the class as possible, but feed ideas when necessary. Use the ideas in the key below.

Possible answers:
1. The text will be organized as follows:
   Paragraph 1: how and why people are feeling overworked
   Paragraph 2: the effects / consequences of overwork
   Paragraph 3: the biggest cause of overwork
   Paragraph 4: those most likely to overwork
   Paragraph 5: solutions

2. People are not necessarily happier. / People worry about money. / There are associated concerns – health, drinking, etc. / There are other ways of relieving stress – exercise, yoga, etc.
3. Organize points above into the appropriate paragraph and add:
   Paragraph 1: Society puts people under pressure. / People feel that they must compete.
   Paragraph 2: There are associated concerns – health, drinking, etc.
   Paragraph 3: People worry about money. / People feel that they don't earn enough. / Friends earn more money.
   Paragraph 4: They don't spend enough time with the family.
   Paragraph 5: There are other ways of relieving stress – exercise, yoga, etc. / People need to re-energize.

C Make sure students appreciate that they are reading to check and consolidate what they learnt from Exercise B. They should not find the passage demanding, having prepared so robustly, but give them five minutes to read and absorb.

D The aim is to check global comprehension and to refocus attention on what each paragraph contained. There is no need to check the comprehension of detailed information unless students ask specific questions. If you have a copy of the sentences on the board, tell them to close books and focus back on the board. Give them three minutes.

Monitor to check what has been achieved. Another feedback stage is unnecessary.

Refer students to the Exam tip – obviously a particularly relevant tip on this occasion – and give them time to read and absorb. Tell them to cover it and then ask one student to explain a topic sentence and another to explain a supporting sentence. You may even decide to put them back into pairs to make sure everyone checks this.

Reading 2

A Although students should now be more independent when working on the practice part of the skills modules, the important thing here is to consolidate and practise using topic sentences. The first task aims to do that.

Give students five minutes to read the topic sentences – make sure they appreciate they are not in the correct order – and to make predictions about the content of that paragraph. Ask them which sentence they think will introduce the first paragraph and which two will introduce the last two paragraphs. If they predict those correctly, ask them in which order they will be in. Do not confirm or correct any suggestions.

Students should spend seven minutes reading the passage and matching individually. Then, they should spend another three minutes checking and explaining answers in pairs. Check answers before moving onto the exam practice tasks.

Answers:
1. C 2. E 3. F 4. A 5. G 6. B 7. D

Refer students to the Exam tip at the end of the passage and give them time to read and absorb. Tell them they will talk later about how they feel learning about topic sentences has developed their reading skills.

B Students should now be left to work independently through the practice tasks. However, it would be a good idea to tell them to look at the first task (questions 1–6) and then to read the Question-type tip that follows. They have seen this task previously, but have not been given guidance strategies. Note that working on a paragraph-matching task like this should drum home the benefits of understanding topic sentences.

Point out that having to read the topic sentences separately from the rest of the text may be inconvenient, but that having done so much preparation work should compensate.

Set a time limit of 12 minutes (but give them three more if necessary), pointing out that they have already read the passage for overall meaning. Remind them that answers to questions 7–14 will be found in order in the passage and that that will help them to know roughly in which part of the passage to look for information.

C Checking and reflecting on answers is a constant feature of the skills modules. Give students sufficient time to check and think about why they may have answered incorrectly.

Students might want to know why some of their answers were not correct. Explaining some points may be necessary and beneficial, but going through all of them will be very time-consuming. It is best to tell students that they will learn more about how to do these tasks and that their scores will improve.

If you do want to identify the specific parts of the passage that provide answers to any questions, make an OHT or other visual medium of the passage and highlight those parts on the board.

Answers:
1. ii 2. vii 3. i 4. vi 5. ix 6. iv
(Note that 7–10 can be in any order)
7. A 8. B 9. E 10. F
11. T 12. NG 13. T 14. F

D Students will now be more familiar with this type of reflective process. Point out that all points are related to exploiting topic sentences this time. Remind them that identifying what they are doing well and not doing so well is a very good way of focusing on what they can do better next time. Allow students time to reflect and complete the exercise, and then ask them if they are happy with the number of correct answers.

Key vocabulary in context

Remind students that an effective way to learn and remember new vocabulary is to study it closely once it has been presented in context.

The aim is more to increase students' awareness of compound nouns than to learn these compounds specifically, though most of them are fairly high frequency and useful. Note that matching ten items with another ten items is quite challenging and students will probably need some assistance as they go.

Start by asking students to give you an example of a compound noun. Ask them how it should be written on the board – as one word, as two words or as a hyphenated word. Refer them to text in the *Key vocabulary in context* box and give them a moment to read and absorb.

A and B Tell students that all the compound nouns are in the passage and then see who can find an example first. Write that compound on the board, having agreed how it should be written. Point out that B deals with the meaning of the compounds, so they should find the matches and think quickly about the meaning from the context in A.

Students should work in pairs so that they can communicate and pool resources as they go. Either write the compounds on the board for clarity or highlight them on an OHT or other visual medium of the passage on the board. Note that doing the latter will help you deal with meaning in context more efficiently in B.

Answers:
health care / voicemail / turnover / backlog / stress levels / cutbacks / burnout / lay-offs / workload / well-being

C Point out that the first two items are compound adjectives. Give students a minute and a half to discuss, and then go over answers orally.

Answers:
hand-held = held in the hand – usually describing a device of some kind
short-term = temporary (contrast with *long-term*, meaning more permanent)
ill effects = negative consequences

Refer students to the Workbook exercises related to this module. Choose to work on them now or set up for homework.

Writing

Objectives

- **To present and practise language typically used to describe bar charts and pie charts.**
- **To practise writing reports based on data shown in bar charts and pie charts.**
- **To compare and contrast information from more than one source.**

The Writing Module in this unit concentrates on Writing Task 1. The aim is to focus on the type of language typically used to describe both bar charts and pie charts and there is a fairly robust emphasis on grammatical form.

Writing 1

The first part of the lesson focuses on understanding and describing data shown in a bar chart and on revising and consolidating comparative and superlative forms.

A The principal aim is to prepare for the writing focus rather than to provide extended speaking practice. Have a clear time limit in mind (two minutes for each question, perhaps). You may prefer to conduct the lead-in as a quick whole-class discussion, but remember that will mean far fewer students contributing.

Make sure students cover the graph – you may prefer to show the questions on the board with books closed so that students are not tempted to look ahead to the graph.

If students talk in pairs, give them a minute to read and think before they are expected to express ideas. Get some quick feedback, but do not confirm students' suggestions nor feed any information yourself (see B). It is quite likely that students will have heard about people in Japan or Korea working long hours, so expect the discussion to centre on that.

B The aim of the tasks is really to focus attention and motivate students to compare information once they fully understand the graph. They may not be able to guess the missing countries, but when they know the answers, they should be able to express a reaction. Give students a moment to look at the graph and read the instructions. Set a time limit of three minutes to answer the question and guess the missing countries.

Check question 1 orally and write the missing countries on the board for clarity. You may choose to show an OHT or other visual medium of the graph on the board so that the language in D can be checked or explained later, in which case, the missing countries can be filled in.

Answers:
1. It shows the number of hours worked in a year, going up in blocks of 500 from 0 to 2,500 per year.
2. (From top down) Mexico / Greece / Czech Republic / Germany

C Conduct as a quick whole-class discussion. There is no need to discuss each country – just information they find surprising. Students will probably be surprised to see Mexico so high. It would be expected that students would not be surprised to see South Korea so high, though they might have expected Japan to be even higher. It will be interesting to hear what they think about countries like France, the Netherlands and Germany being so low.

D The aim is not simply to present or revise comparative and superlative forms, but to practise using them in the context of report writing. Students may find the exercise itself fairly easy, but they need to absorb the sentences and practise using the structures.

Students complete the task individually, before checking answers in pairs. If you have an OHT or other visual medium of the bar chart on the board, refer to this as you check answers. Allow selected students to read the full sentences, but make sure answers are clear.

Answers:
1. far more   2. fewer   3. less   4. the fewest
5. The highest   6. The lowest   7. as many
8. nearly as

Grammar check

There is quite a lot of information, but it is divided into chunks and easy to absorb. Tell students to read each chunk and then check that all is clear. They should compare the information given with examples in the exercise they have just worked on. There should be no need for you to give further explanation, but you may need to clarify anything if it is not clear.

Note that it is becoming more and more common for native speakers of English to use *less* and *amount* with countable nouns. You do not need to confuse students with this information, but be aware that there may be examples that contradict the rules given.

Watch out!

Use the *Watch out!* box here to check what students have taken in. Give them two minutes to work in pairs to correct the errors. Write the corrections on the board for clarity.

Answers:
People work fewer hours.
People work far fewer hours.
The number of hours worked is high.
Fewer hours are worked in Japan than in South Korea.
People do not work as many hours in Sweden as they do in Mexico.

E Set a time limit of six minutes or tell students to write one sentence using one of the items from D. They can either work individually and then compare sentences, or work together to communicate and pool resources as they go. Monitor and check work rather than going through a feedback stage that can only be repetitious. Students will not necessarily benefit from seeing sentences that other pairs have written, unless the structures really do still need clarifying.

Writing 2

The second part of the lesson focuses on understanding and describing data shown in a pie chart, and on revising and consolidating language used to express amounts and percentages.

A The aim is to prepare students to understand information shown in the pie chart, especially to elicit some of the vocabulary used in the answer key. Start with books closed and the instructions written on the board so that students do not look ahead. Set a time limit of four minutes and monitor to check and assist when necessary.

Use feedback to check key words and phrases that are likely to be new – *sickness, disability, exhaustion, accidental injury*, and so on. Students may well suggest *maternity leave*, which is fine, though not included in the data shown in the figure. Do not feel that you must pre-teach all items as these can easily be dealt with as students look at the chart. Ask students to predict what the most common reasons are, but do not confirm suggestions.

B Give students three minutes and tell them to use the time to fully understand what the figure shows, compare data with what they discussed in A and to check any words and phrases they are unsure of.

When the three minutes is up, check that they understand the items in the answer key, pronouncing them and drilling if appropriate. Explain that *jury service* (being one of the 12 members of the public who sit in court and decide on a guilty / not guilty verdict) is an obligation in many countries – you can discuss whether it is in your country or the countries from which students come. You can also discuss the regulations on taking time off work with or without a doctor's certificate.

C Make sure students know what to do – work through the first sentence as an example if you think it is necessary. Point out that they will have to work out some of the answers.

Students should complete the task individually, before checking answers in pairs. As feedback, select students to read the complete sentences aloud. Check their pronunciation and drill key words and phrases if necessary. Show an OHT or other visual medium of the pie chart on the board and refer to it as you check answers. This will facilitate the clarification of the key words and phrases.

Answers:
1. c 2. a 3. c 4. d 5. b

Grammar check

Give students a moment to read and absorb the information. If you are teaching a monolingual group and the same thing applies in the first language, point that out as a quick means of retention.

D If you have not already done so, point out that there are three ways to express the same idea. Students will know how to express percentages and fractions, but may not be so familiar with the third option. Look at the example together and then give them time to write the remaining phrases.

As feedback, select students to come up and write answers on the board. Point out that they will also hear *out of* used instead of *in*, especially when higher percentages are expressed – *nine out of ten people.*

Answers:
2. one in four / one out of four
3. three in four / three out of four
4. nine in ten / nine out of ten

Writing 3

Refer students to the Exam tip and give them a moment to read and absorb.

A Students should spend two minutes studying the bar chart individually and then discuss what the chart shows with the partner. Monitor and check comprehension. Feedback is unnecessary as the task instruction clarifies what the graph shows.

B Remember that the initial difficulty for students is deciding what information to put in their report – identifying data that stands out and can easily be compared and contrasted (see notes for Writing 3 in Unit 3).

Give students a minute to study the task instructions. Making an OHT or other visual medium of the bar chart to show on the board will enable you to refer to it as you check they understand the task properly.

Tell them to cover the model report in Exercise C while they complete steps 1–4. Set a time limit of ten minutes to work through the whole exercise. Monitor and assist where necessary. Make a note of particularly good sentences that students could share with the class during a feedback stage. Choose one opening sentence and three more sentences that students can come and write on the board. Note that students simply reading out their sentences will probably not be very clear.

C Students should spend three minutes reading the model report and identifying weaknesses individually. They can then compare thoughts with a partner. Get some feedback and establish that the report is too short, that it is not very well organized, that the writer wrongly gives a reason for some information and some parts are expressed in rather an informal way.

D Refer students to the model report on page 265 and give them the time they need to read and absorb the improvements. The model report is reproduced here.

Model report:

The bar chart shows the differences in the percentage of time that men and women in various age groups take off work in the United Kingdom because they are sick.

The first thing to say is that women take more time off work than men in every age group. Women between 25 and 34 are more likely to take time off work than anyone else. They take 3.1% of time off, while men in this age group take only 2.2%.

Younger employees take off more time than older employees. In fact, workers over 60 take less time off than anyone else. In this age group, however, there is the biggest difference between the time taken off by men and women. Men over 60 take only 1.5% of work time off sick, while women take 2.1%.

All in all, it seems that the older employees are, the less time they take off sick.

E and F Work through as with Exercises A and B.

G Students should complete the task individually and then compare answers with a partner. As feedback, refer students to the model report on page 265. Alternatively, show an OHT or other visual medium of the gapped report on the board and complete it as you elicit answers from students. The model report is reproduced below.

Model report:

The pie charts show the various reasons why men and women take time off work as percentages. Although there are similarities, there are some noticeable differences too.

The most common reason for absence for both men and women is a short period of sickness. Nearly two thirds of time taken off by men is due to this, while for women it is just over half. Time taken off for more serious illness is about the same for men and women.

Women are more likely to take time off to care for a child or older relative. At 17%, this is the second most common reason for women to be absent. Caring for another person accounts for only 5% of time taken off by men.

Absence due to long-term disability or stress is similarly likely for both men and women as is a visit to the doctor or dentist. Men, however, are more than twice as likely to take time off due to accidental injury.

H You may feel that this exercise and the one that follows do not have a linguistic purpose. Remember, though, that the first thing students have to do is understand the figure, and designing a figure themselves will be a very useful process.

Students should think about the questions individually for a minute, before discussing them with a partner. Tell them that any data shown in a pie chart could also be shown on a simple bar chart. When data is compared in two pie charts, it can be shown, perhaps more effectively, on one bar chart. Information shown on a bar chart cannot always be shown on a pie chart. Bar charts do not always show data that totals 100%, as a pie chart is designed to do. The information shown on the bar chart in this Writing Module could not be shown on a pie chart.

I Students should work in pairs to draw the bar chart. Set a time limit of five minutes. Monitor and assist and perhaps choose a chart that could be shown to the class as a good model.

Writing task

The Writing tasks are found either in the Workbook or in the Exam Practice Module at the end of the unit. In this unit, the task is in the Workbook.

The topic of the chart is new, though it is a topic they should readily relate to. Students will need some preparation in terms of orientating them towards the theme and identifying information that stands out.

A Remind students of the importance of making sure they understand what the graph shows before they do anything else. Tell them to cover the task instructions and to look only at the figure. Give them three minutes to study and absorb the information before comparing ideas with a partner. You may need to check the meaning of *DIY – Do-It-Yourself*. There is no need to orally check comprehension as the task instructions will clarify, but you may feel that a quick feedback stage will be motivating – ask students if there is any data they find surprising.

B Refer students to the Writing task instructions and give them time to read and absorb.

Even if you decide to set the Writing task for homework, students will benefit from discussing what information to include and planning in pairs first. You can decide if they are to write their opening and concluding lines together or individually later.

Once they start writing their reports, take into account the time already spent preparing. They should need only 15 minutes. If they write the report at home, tell them to be strict with a time limit – they will not benefit from spending longer on the task than they will have when it comes to the exam.

When students have completed the task, they should compare it with the model report on page 265. The model is reproduced below.

If you collect students' reports to mark, concentrate on the selection of information and how well planned and organized reports are. Check that they have used appropriate structures to compare and contrast and that they have absorbed what was learnt in the module.

Model report:

The bar chart shows how different percentages of people in different age groups enjoyed a number of selected free-time activities in the United Kingdom in 2011.

The most common activity – watching TV – and the least common activity – arts and crafts – were more or less equally popular with all age groups, though a slightly higher percentage of older people enjoyed watching TV. Shopping was another activity equally popular with all age groups.

There were noticeable differences in the popularity of most other activities. Sport/exercise was significantly less common among the over 65s, while reading was slightly more popular. Fewer people in the youngest age group read frequently. DIY was mainly enjoyed by people in the middle age groups, but very little by younger people.

The biggest variation was in playing computer games. While only 10% of over 65s enjoyed playing computer games, almost half of all 16–24s participated.

Consolidation

Instructions are given for Speaking exercises when the procedure is not clear from instructions in the Course Book. Set Vocabulary and Errors exercises either for individual completion and pairwork checking, or as pairwork when you feel immediate interaction is beneficial.

To correct errors in the final exercise, ask students to come and write the correct sentences on the board while other students offer help. You will need to write the corrections on the board to clarify.

Speaking

Refer students to the Exam tip and give them time to read and absorb. This is an important feature of spoken English – perhaps most languages – but one that is generally not practised enough.

A Make an OHT or other visual medium of the exercise to show on the board. Focus attention on the first sentence and read it aloud naturally. As a whole class, decide which of the follow-up comments is appropriate and then model the whole utterance two or three times. Students can work through the rest of the exercise in pairs.

B 🎧 Play the whole recording as students check answers, and then again, pausing to drill.

Answers:
See tapescript for Track 52.

B Listen and check your answers.

1 I get a lot of pleasure from cycling. It helps me think.
2 I probably work harder than I should. I'm on the go all day.
3 I usually go dancing somewhere at the weekend. I really need to let my hair down.
4 To tell you the truth, I like staying in more than going out these days. I've never really been a party animal.
5 Frankly, I'm thinking about looking for a new job. I'm overworked and underpaid where I am.

C Give students sufficient time to practise the sentences in pairs.

Vocabulary

A, B and C Students should complete each exercise individually, and then explain answers to a partner.

Answers:

Exercise A:
1. enthusiasm   2. underpaid   3. guidance
4. temptation   5. replenish   6. lay-offs

Exercise B:
1. on   2. about   3. to   4. into   5. under
6. of   7. of   8. in

Exercise C:
1. very busy   2. release energy
3. somebody very keen on keeping fit and healthy
4. a very informal word for the public

Errors

Answers:

1. to swimming	2. listening to music
3. fewer friends	4. the number of people
5. Far fewer men	6. take it too seriously

Exam Practice

Reading

Since the aim is to practise exploiting topic sentences, there is a more robust preparation stage to the Exam Practice Module in this unit.

A Remember that students will not have a preparation stage when it comes to the exam. The aim here is to orientate them towards the topic, to motivate and to facilitate the practice with topic sentences.

Students should spend three minutes reading the options and choosing the correct summary individually. Then, they should compare their answer with a partner. Provide the answer so that students can concentrate on the exercises that follow before they skim the passage.

Answer:
1 is the correct summary

B You may feel the best approach here is to conduct a quick whole-class discussion, but remember that discussing the questions in pairs will give more students more opportunity to contribute (particularly with question 3). Keep to a time limit of six minutes, whether you opt for pairwork or a whole-class discussion.

Keep feedback brief – get a show of hands for the first question and select one student to tell the class about their memories of nursery school for question 2. Avoid opening an extended class debate for question 3 – stronger students will dominate and it would be better conducted as pairwork.

C Select a student to remind the class of what a topic sentence is and its purpose.

Make sure students spend enough time reading the topic sentences and thinking before they exchange ideas with a partner. Tell them that if they really do not know what additional information a paragraph will include, they should say so. The aim is not to make wild guesses – it is to use the topic sentence to draw logical conclusions.

A feedback stage, during which you check ideas and give some guidance, will be beneficial. Avoid feeding information from the passage if students do not have their own ideas, though.

Possible answers:

Paragraph B:
Children should play / pretend more. Children should not be conditioned too early.
Paragraph C:
(As above – it is important to point out that the same basic point is often repeated in a passage, using different supporting information.)
Paragraph E:
They should talk to their children / play with their children / respond to their child's interests.
Paragraph F:
A lot of TV and online entertainment is educational.

D The aim here is to specifically pre-teach one word, a relatively new word that students may not be familiar with. Point out that there may occasionally be a glossary at the end of an exam passage with a word like this explained.

Students can answer the questions in pairs. Explain orally.

Answers:

1. education / entertainment
2. toys that are supposed to educate
3. because the balance between education and having fun is the central theme

E The passage is fairly long and there are a number of questions – perhaps more questions than will be set for one passage in the exam. Set a time limit of three minutes to read and discuss the questions in Exercise F.

F Although students have been prepared for the passage, they will need another 15 minutes or slightly more to complete the tasks. You can decide whether they should compare answers before you give feedback. Write answers on the board for clarity or provide students with a copy of the answer key.

Students might want to know why some of their answers were not correct. Explaining some points may be necessary and beneficial, but going through all of them will be very time-consuming. It is best to tell students that they will learn more about how to do these tasks and that their scores will improve.

If you do want to identify the specific parts of the passage that provide answers to any questions, make an OHT or other visual medium of the passage and highlight those parts on the board.

Answers:

1. iv 2. i 3. vii 4. vi 5. ii 6. ix 7. b 8. b
9. c 10. a 11. online 12. control it
13. media-literate 14. in common

G The aim is to conclude the lesson rather than develop an extended debate. You will know whether your students will enjoy and benefit from an extended pair or group discussion, or whether a quick whole-class discussion will suffice. Whatever approach you take, encourage students to use core language learnt in the module.

Unit 5 Workbook answers

Vocabulary development

A 1. understaffed 2. overcharged 3. relocate
4. anti-virus 5. overambitious
6. non-profit-making 7. underachieved
8. re-examine 9. dehumanizes

B 1. go 2. hair 3. feet 4. steam 5. batteries

C 1. very busy 2. very busy 3. just about coping
4. work very hard 5. relax

D turnover = money coming in and going out of a business
burnout = exhaustion
cutbacks = reductions
lay-offs = redundancies / people losing their jobs

E 1. d 2. b 3. e 4. a 5. c

Listening

A 1. free time 2. public holidays 3. characters
4. animals 5. celebrities 6. Hunting
7. business

A Listen to a talk about the Romans and how they liked to enjoy their free time. Complete the summary below using NO MORE THAN TWO WORDS for each answer.

Voice: Now, the Romans knew all about work and play, especially play! One of the things we associate with Ancient Rome now is the fact that they loved their free time and that they invented all sorts of ways of filling it. The poet Juvenal was famous for saying that the people of Rome only demanded two things from their rulers – bread and circuses. Both were needed for life – people needed to eat to sustain the body and to visit the circus for pleasure.

To start with, the Romans were frequent visitors to the theatre and, for them, the theatre encompassed everything from traditional plays to chariot racing. The Romans only staged plays on days that were public holidays – but since there were something like 200 days of public holiday in Ancient Rome, there were plenty of opportunities to stage productions! Plays were noisy and people would shout and join in with the story. As in Greek theatre, the actors often wore masks to show that they were good or bad characters, and the whole atmosphere was more like a pantomime than the civilized notion of theatre we have today.

The amphitheatres were huge and here, of course, the Romans staged their games. I'm sure everyone's seen the film *Gladiator* and knows how sensational and sometimes terrifying these games could be. Thousands of spectators came to see specially trained slaves and prisoners – gladiators – fight each other to the death. Sometimes they fought wild animals like lions and bears. At the end of the shows, the crowd decided if the combatants should live or die. Some gladiators became famous and could demand huge sums of money – rather like boxers or footballers today. Chariot racing was another popular form of entertainment and the men who drove the chariots were also celebrities.

Societies, of course, had previously hunted for food, but wealthy Romans hunted for sport. They even tried to make hunting more enjoyable by introducing new species of animal, like deer, into the countries they occupied.

For total relaxation, the Romans went to bath houses. The ruins of Roman baths can still be found in many parts of the world that were once in the Roman Empire. The Romans would spend all day at the baths, exercising before bathing and then swimming afterwards. The baths were important meeting places and were where wealthy Romans conducted business as they bathed.

Reading

A A. 3 B. 5 C. 1 D. 2 E. 4

B 1. iv 2. v 3. i 4. vi 5. ii

Writing

A If students have difficulty identifying the errors, show them this version (either as an OHT or other visual medium on the board or on a handout) – they can then concentrate on correcting the errors.

Model report:

The bar chart shows the differences of the percentage of time that men and women in various age groups take off work in the United Kingdom because they are sick.

The first thing for saying is that women take much time off work than men in every age group. Women between 25 and 34 are more likely to take time off work than anyone else. They take 3.1% of time off when men in this age group take only 2.2%.

Younger employees take more time off than older employees. In effect, workers over 60 take less time off than someone else. In this age group, however, there is the biggest difference between the time took off by men and women. Men over 60 take only 1.5% of work time off sick, while women take 2.1%.

All in all, it seems that the older are employees, the less time they take off sick.

Writing task

See notes in the Course Book Writing Module.

6 Home and away

Unit overview

The sixth unit presents language related to an overall theme of *travel and tourism*. There is less noticeable recycling of language from previous units here, but there is clear recycling of language from one module to another within the unit. Students are presented with, and practise, specific tasks from the Speaking, Listening, Reading and Writing tests that make up the IELTS exam.

Speaking and Vocabulary

Objectives

- To practise talking about holidays (recent and past events).
- To practise interaction typical of the IELTS Speaking test, Parts 1 and 2.
- To clarify the meaning of a number of frequently confused words.
- To practise explaining when you do not know the appropriate word.
- To present and practise typical spoken phrases for comparing and contrasting.

The first module presents a range of spoken language features revolving around the general theme of *travel*. The aim is to prepare students for the content of the unit, and to practise exchanging personal information that can be typical of both the first and second parts of the Speaking test.

Start with books closed and write the quotation on the board with *page* blanked out. Elicit the missing word – students should be able to make sensible guesses even if they have never seen the quotation before. Once the quotation is complete, ask them to explain what it means – they can talk in pairs for a minute, focusing on what it means and their reaction to it. Spend another two minutes discussing it as a class.

St Augustine was a Latin-speaking philosopher and theologian who lived in the Roman Africa Province of Hippo (present-day Annaba, Algeria). His writings were very influential in the development of Western Christianity. The quotation can be best explained as: those who do not travel, experience only a tiny percentage of what the world has to offer.

Speaking 1

The aim is to provide the opportunity for students to exchange information about recent and past events revolving around *travel*. The assumption is that most of the vocabulary presented will be known and will need checking rather than fresh presentation.

Start the lesson with books closed. Write the question *What are holidays for?* on the board and brainstorm ideas. Students should suggest that the purpose of taking a holiday is to relax, escape daily routine and have fun, but also to learn and experience new cultures.

A Students should spend a minute reading and thinking as suggested in the exercise instructions. Then discuss the questions in groups of three. Use a feedback stage to check retention of vocabulary and clarify any remaining uncertainties.

Vocabulary suggestions

- *Get away* means *escape* both literally and metaphorically.
- *Abroad* is an adverb – not an adjective. People *go, travel, move* or *live abroad* – you cannot say *an abroad holiday*.
- *Unwind* was not presented in the last unit as an alternative to *relax*. Use the opportunity now to revise *chill out* and *recharge batteries*. If you *wind something up*, there is an implication of tension – if it *unwinds*, it releases that tension.
- *A package holiday* is often referred to as *a package deal* – where everything is included in the one price – or simply *package*.
- *Travelling independently* means buying the components of a holiday separately – perhaps finding a hotel when you arrive.
- *A resort* is a place typically visited by holidaymakers – perhaps a place that only really exists for that purpose. We tend to apply *resort* to towns by the sea rather than cities – Prague is popular *holiday destination*, but it is not a resort.
- Explorers *beat a track* through a forest – they create a path that others will follow. A destination that is *off the beaten track* is not yet popular with large numbers of tourists. Note that there is no phrase '*on the beaten track*'.

B Run through the holiday types together as a class, checking anything unclear. Give examples when appropriate – *Disneyland is a huge theme park. / Cruises are popular in the Caribbean or on the Nile.*

Set a time limit of five minutes, but tell students to answer the third question in a single word or phrase – C will allow them to expand.

Be selective during feedback – avoid repeating the discussions they have just had. Get a general consensus as to who likes camping, for example, and then ask one student to explain why people go camping.

C At this level, students should not simply ask and answer a series of questions – they should not form questions from the prompts. Tell them to spend a minute thinking about their last holiday or one taken recently. They should then use the prompts to plan what they want to tell a partner

about that holiday – they do not need to give information relating to every prompt.

Once they start exchanging information, they should ask spontaneous questions. Monitor to check fluency, range of vocabulary and accuracy with past forms.

As feedback, get students to ask you questions about your last holiday. Tell them to guess where you went from your answers – give them more revealing clues as you go.

Vocabulary 1

A The aim is as much to increase awareness of easily confused words as it is to learn these specific word pairs. Point out that there are easily confused pairs of words related to any topic.

Start by writing the example words *travel* and *journey* on the board. Ask students if they confuse these words and then select one student to explain the difference. If the explanation is not very clear, select another student. Refer students to the example explanation in the book to check.

Give them four minutes (30 seconds per word pair) to complete the exercise in pairs.

A feedback stage could be very time-consuming and is likely to be a repetition of what has just been discussed. It will be more efficient to simply give them quick explanations yourself or to show an OHT or other visual medium of the answers below on the board.

Answers:
1. holiday = time when not working or studying / time spent away from home visiting a new place
   festival = special occasion that people celebrate / event with music and other entertainment
2. travel / journey (see example in the Course Book)
3. journey = movement from one specific place to another (usually A to B)
   tour = a journey that involves stopping at a number of destinations
   (A tour is a journey – a journey is not necessarily a tour.)

4. trip = informal word for journey, short holiday
   or *excursion*
   excursion = organized visit to a specific place
   of interest (a holiday / school excursion)
   (An excursion is a trip – a trip is not
   necessarily an excursion.)
5. adventure = exciting experience
   expedition = organized journey to an
   unknown or difficult-to-reach location
6. sights = places / buildings / monuments that
   people want to see
   sites = specific locations of events (the site of
   the Battle of Waterloo)
7. reach a destination (no preposition) – the
   implication is the journey is over
   arrive at a destination = the implication is that
   you are now where you intended to be
8. gift = present – probably bought for another
   person
   souvenir = something that reminds you of a
   place you visited
   (A souvenir may be bought as a gift – not all
   gifts are souvenirs.)

B 🎧 Start with books closed and tell students they
will hear two short interview exchanges. Play the
recording through once, and then ask students
what difficulty each speaker had. Establish that
there were specific words they didn't know.
Check whether students think the students on
the recording dealt with the difficulty well.

Refer students to the exercise in the book and
give them a moment to read the gapped
sentences. Tell them not to attempt to
remember the answers – they will listen again.
Play the recording, pausing between the
exchanges for students to write the answer.
Note that, since *souvenir* was defined in the
previous exercise, it should not be too difficult
now. Give students a moment to compare
answers before you check them.

Write answers on the board for clarity and check
that *souvenir* is the defined word in sentence 1.
Since students are now going to practise similar
exchanges, it would be a good idea to play the
recording once more as they read the tapescript.

Answers:
1. ' … little presents that remind you of the place.'
2. transfer

Tapescript 🎧 **54 (0 mins, 53 secs)**

B **Listen to two students speaking in the
    exam and write answers to the questions.**

1
   Examiner: So, what do you especially like
   about being on holiday?
   Student: Actually, I like shopping more than
   anything else. Wherever I go,
   there's always something to buy
   and I love buying … mm … you
   know, little presents that remind
   you of the place.

2
   Examiner: Wow, Egypt. Did you stay in
   Cairo?
   Student: Yes, we were in Cairo for three
   nights and then we had a … erm …
   to Luxor, I mean we moved down to
   Luxor. They took a group of us from
   Cairo to Luxor in a coach.

C Make sure students understand the instructions
   and look at the additional example provided.
   Give them a couple of minutes to think and plan.
   Note that some students might find it difficult to
   think of something they do not know the correct
   word for, in which case they can describe an
   aspect of travel which their partner has to guess.
   Once students start talking, monitor and make a
   note of good examples that could be shared
   with the rest of the class.

Speaking 2

The aim is to revise and consolidate the language
practised in the Writing Module of the last unit
and transfer it to spoken interaction. Note that
pronunciation now plays a much more important part.

A 🎧 Read the instructions with students and
   then give them a moment to look at the
   sentences before they listen. You could ask
   them to predict words in advance, but do not
   confirm or correct. Play the whole recording as
   students write answers. Then play it again,
   pausing between sentences to check answers
   and clarify meaning. Though students will check
   the tapescript in a moment, writing the answers
   on the board will help to consolidate and aid

retention. As you check answers, ask concept questions, such as *Did the speaker expect New York to be good? Was it good? So, why was the speaker surprised? Did the speaker like Paris? Was she happy? Why not?*

Answers:
1. even   2. quite   3. far   4. nearly

Tapescript 🎧 **55 (1 min, 28 secs)**

A   **Listen to some more students talking with an examiner. Complete the sentences below with ONE WORD ONLY in each space.**

1

Examiner: So, was New York all you hoped it would be?

Student: Oh, it was even better than I hoped it would be. There's something new around every corner. Have you been there yourself?

2

Examiner: So, tell me about Paris, then.

Student: Well, Paris wasn't quite as nice as I thought it would be. I mean, it is nice, but I was expecting more. Maybe I heard too much before I went. Barcelona, on the other hand …

3

Examiner: So, what was the highlight of your tour?

Student: I think the highlight was Prague. I didn't know very much about Prague before I came to Europe and I wasn't very interested to see it. However, it was far more beautiful than I imagined. I want to go back there again one day.

4

Examiner: Did you like Hong Kong? I never know if it really appeals to me.

Student: Oh yes, it was very exciting and not nearly as polluted as I expected. I heard it was impossible to breathe there, but actually …

Grammar check

The *Grammar check* revises points dealt with in the Writing Module of the previous unit, so students should not need much additional assistance now. You may need to clarify exactly when we use *even* – if you are teaching a monolingual class, translation might be the most effective approach. Give students time to read and absorb.

Pronunciation check

On this occasion, the *Pronunciation check* simply develops the grammar point. Make students aware that much of the message is carried in the stress and intonation – without stress, and with flat intonation, the grammar has little meaning.

🎧 Play the whole recording, allowing students simply to listen and absorb. Then play the recording again, as they read the tapescript. Finally, play it a third time, pausing appropriately to drill. Allow students sufficient time to practise saying the sentences and then to practise the complete exchanges in pairs. Monitor and give feedback.

Tapescript 🎧 **56 (0 mins, 17 secs)**
Pronunciation check

Listen again to the exchanges in Exercise A. Notice how the modifying verbs are stressed to make the message clear.

[Play Track 55 again]

B   Read through the instructions and all the steps methodically with students, checking that they know what to do for each step. Then go back and set them up for the first two steps again. Point out that they should choose places that they really liked and others they were a little disappointed by. Have a time limit of about five minutes in mind.

Once students have exchanged lists and are ready to interact, monitor to check performance. Make a note of particularly successful exchanges that could be shared with the class as feedback.

C   Work through the process as you have done previously (see Unit 2, Speaking 2B), though

---

note that this time there is only one card and students are to mingle rather than talk in pairs. There is no vocabulary on the task card that students will need to check.

Tell students if you feel that their performance in Part 2 of the Speaking test is improving.

Listening

Objectives

- **To practise listening to information related to maps and plans.**
- **To further practise listening for specific information.**
- **To show students how key information is often repeated to help with spelling.**

The aim of the Listening Module is to familiarize students with typical tasks involving maps and plans, and to expose them to different types of recording with different registers and functions.

Note that, in the exam, it is unlikely that students will have to answer more than five or six questions working with a map or plan. A map or plan completion task will be one of three or four tasks that assess comprehension of a whole recording.

Listening 1

The first part of the lesson introduces the concept of listening to complete a map or plan and orientates students towards the kind of conversations they are likely to hear.

A Students will be more accustomed to making predictions about what they will listen to by now and they should understand the purpose of this lead-in exercise.

Students should spend a minute looking at the maps and plans and making predictions individually. Then, they compare thoughts with a partner. As feedback, elicit a couple of ideas for each diagram. Assist and prompt with suggestions, but do not feed any information that will help too much with the listening tasks.

Possible answers:
a – places / names of landmarks / names of islands
b – names of hotels
c – buildings / names of buildings in a town square

B 🎧 Make sure students understand that the first time they listen they are simply matching the maps to the extracts and not filling anything in. Play the whole recording. When you check answers, you can also check the function or purpose of each extract – *Where is the first conversation taking place? Who is the man speaking in the second extract?*, etc.

Answers:
1. b   2. c   3. a

Tapescript 🎧 **57 (5 mins, 44 secs)**

B   **Listen and match the extracts with the maps and plans.**

Extract 1

Customer 1: We've looked at the brochure and frankly all the hotels look quite nice. We've picked out a few that we'd like to know a bit more about. Do you have a map or a plan of the area so you can show where exactly each hotel is? They all say 'walking distance' to the beach and so on, but then they would, wouldn't they?

Travel agent: Yes, I've got a map and a more detailed plan of the harbour area. Let me see … OK, here it is. Now, which hotels are you looking at?

Customer 2: Can you tell us about this one first – *Las Gaviotas*. It looks really nice.

Travel agent: Yes, I like that one. *Las Gaviotas* means *The Seagulls*. I've stayed there myself and it's lovely. It's here … not right on the beach, but very close. Frankly, the hotels right on the beach can be a bit noisy. I mean, the noise from the beach bars and restaurants at night. *Las Gaviotas* is between the beach and the old village.

Customer 1: So, how far is that to walk to the beach?

Travel agent: Oh, less than five minutes. Really – maybe three or four minutes.

Customer 2: And about the same into the old village?

Travel agent: Less – about two minutes. You really do have the best of both worlds with this hotel. Now, which is the second one you wanted to know …

Extract 2

Voice: Right, so here we are in the main square. You can look round by yourselves in a moment, but first let me tell you something about the buildings and monuments around us – you'll enjoy looking round far more if you know what you're looking at. There's plenty more information in the guide book too. Right, first of all, this statue right beside us is Thomas Mendelssohn. He was the founder of the children's hospital, which we will visit later. He was responsible for many other projects and developments in the town and he's a very important figure. The statue was erected in 1954.

OK, to our left, at the end of the square, is the museum. I'll show you round the museum a little bit later, but you can have a quick look now if you like. Incidentally, just behind the museum is Thomas Mendelssohn's office. He worked there for almost all of the time he was resident in the town. You can get to it through a little lane by the side of the museum. At the other end of the square – to our right, that is – is the library. It's fairly modern compared with some of the buildings in the square, but worth having a look at. The old library was badly damaged by fire in the 1960s and it was decided that building a new one was better than trying to rebuild the old one. Next to the library is the town's oldest pub. Luckily, that wasn't damaged in the fire. I don't know if you can read it from here, but it's called Den Glade. Perhaps that would be a good place to meet again after you've had a look round.

Extract 3

Voice: There are a number of sites and features in the northern tip of the country and they can all be visited in a day – certainly if you're driving, anyway. I wouldn't want to rely on the buses up there! There are four islands off the coast of the northern tip and all of them are interesting. You can get to three of them by boat and the biggest is connected to the mainland by a road bridge. The island just to the north of that one – so the island off the west coast to the north – is the home of an important bird sanctuary. The island is called Mowbray and there are boats every two hours that will take you there in about ten minutes. It's a very peaceful place. Now, on the other side of the tip – so off the east coast – are two more islands. You can't get to the smaller island, but you can admire it from the mainland. The larger island is home to Old Finkley. That's the last surviving lighthouse in the country. There are ruins of others, but Old Finkley is in good shape and well worth a visit. You can climb to the top and get a wonderful view of the whole northern tip. Now, in the centre of the northern tip – so pretty much between the two sites I've talked about – is Breedly Castle. There's not much left of it I'm afraid, but it was an important building in its day. It's a nice place to stop for a picnic. There are better preserved castles in other parts of the country. About a 20-minute drive south going back towards the west coast will take you down to the Kneads Estate. There's a lovely old manor house and some beautiful gardens. You can look around the manor house on Wednesdays and Saturdays. So, finally, heading back east and slightly to the south – and you might prefer to come here first as you drive up – is the Fowley Wildlife Park. It's more like a big farm than a wildlife park really, but the kids love it. There are all the usual farm animals and some llamas and deer too. They've got some go-karts too, if I remember rightly. So, I hope that's helped you and that …

C, D and E The aim now is to present students with three different types of listening task that are frequently applied to maps and plans – choosing one option from a number of options, matching and labelling.

It would be better during the presentation stage of the lesson to work on the exercises one at a time. Making an OHT or other visual medium of the maps will allow you to refer to them as you check answers.

C 🎧 Give students a moment to check the map again and read the instructions. Ask them if it matters that the hotel has a name they do not recognize – it should not, since all they have to do is choose a letter as an option. Play the recording and give students a moment to compare answers. Check the answer – if a significant number of students got it wrong, you may want to play the recording again, though they should get accustomed to listening once only. Use the copy of the map on the board to explain why options are wrong, if necessary.

Answer:
D

Tapescript 🎧 **58 (0 mins, 16 secs)**

C Listen to the first extract and circle *Las Gaviotas* (A, B, C, D or E) on the map.

[Play **Extract 1** of Track 57 again]

D 🎧 Give students a moment to read the instructions and check the map again. Ask them if they think they will need to write words they know or words that are new to them. Ask them if they think words will be spelt for them. Work through as C, but give students a minute to compare answers and write answers on the board for clarity.

Answers:
1. statue 2. museum 3. office 4. library

Tapescript 🎧 **59 (0 mins, 12 secs)**

D Listen to the second extract and label the plan with ONE WORD in each space.

[Play **Extract 2** of Track 57 again]

E 🎧 Give students a little longer to read the instructions and the list of landmarks that they have to listen for. Ask them if they think they will hear all the landmarks mentioned even though there are more landmarks than there are letters. Establish that they probably will – or they will hear a similar word as a distractor – and that this will make the task a little more challenging. Work through as with C and D, matching the letters to the numbers on the board for clarity as you check answers. Point out why any mistakes were made, matching *farm* with one of the numbers, for example.

Answers:
1. F 2. B 3. G 4. I 5. E

Tapescript 🎧 **60 (0 mins, 17 secs)**

E Listen to the third extract and label the map. Choose from the box below and write five letters from A–I next to the labels 1–5.

[Play **Extract 3** of Track 57 again]

Listening 2

Refer students to the Exam tip and give them time to read and absorb. Point out that repeating very specific information will often mean spelling it.

A 🎧 Play the whole recording once more and ask students to give you one or two examples of information that was repeated.

Tapescript 🎧 **61 (0 mins, 12 secs)**

A Listen again. Notice examples of a speaker repeating information.

[Play Track 57 again]

B Only work through this exercise if you feel it will be beneficial. If students have identified a number of examples of repeated information from listening, skip it and move on.

Listening 3

Students are now left to their own devices, though the context is set for them in the first line of instructions and they will have a couple of minutes to discuss predictions – remind them that this will not be the case in the exam.

A Read through the instructions with students, pointing out that *rep* is short for *representative*. Point out that here predicting does not mean guessing answers – it means predicting what you will hear.

Students should spend a minute looking at the plan and the task and making predictions individually, and then spend another minute comparing thoughts with a partner. Feedback is unnecessary.

B 🎧 Play the whole recording as students complete the task. Do not check answers as students will do so in Exercise C. Give students a moment to compare answers if you feel it would be beneficial.

Tapescript 🎧 62 (4 mins, 14 secs)

B **Listen and answer the questions.**

Voice: OK, are you all in now? Don't worry, the staff will bring your cases in from the coach. While they're doing that and while the reception get ready to check all your passports, I'll take you for a very quick mini-tour just so you get a feel for the hotel and know where everything is when you've unpacked and had a shower.

As you can see, this is the entrance area, or foyer, and the reception desk is here on your right. There's somebody at reception at all times – so if you have any problems, this is where to come. You can change travellers' cheques or exchange currency here at any time. Now, I'll show you outside in a moment. It's beautiful and sunny and I'm sure you all want to get out there, but let me just point out a couple of things in here first. The bigger room over to the left is the restaurant. There's the entrance you can see from the foyer and another entrance out on to the outside dining area. There are always tables outside when the weather's like it is now. The restaurant's mainly self-service, but there are chefs serving speciality dishes too. Next to the restaurant just here to the left is the main bar. You can buy drinks in the restaurant with your meals and from the bar that is set up outside in the evenings, but for an aperitif before you eat or a late drink after your meal, this is the best place to come. It's open from 11:30 right through to

1 a.m. Now, over to the right, next to the reception, is the shop. It's not huge, but you can buy guidebooks and maps and all sorts of gifts and souvenirs. There are newspapers and magazines from around the world too. OK, now if we walk through the foyer to the doors out to the back of the hotel, we'll see how lovely it is. When the weather's like this, you probably won't be in the hotel much at all.

So, immediately outside is this dining area. The outside bar is here on the left – it's not open now, but it'll be set up around 8 o'clock before dinner. On the right here, there's a little stage. We have performances two or three nights a week at this time of year and there'll be information about what's on in advance. Ahead of you is the beach and the sea – doesn't it look beautiful? You can see that the pool is close to the sea so you can hop back and forth from the pool to the beach, if you want to. As you might be able to see, there's a separate children's pool at one end. OK, the rooms are spread around the garden area. To the right, running up to the beach are rooms 8–14 and round the corner to the right are rooms 1–7. Rooms 15–21 are over to the left. Now, just round to the left at the end of the dining area is the towel collection and return. It's a sort of office I suppose – more like a hut really. You can collect a towel for the beach or pool and drop it off when you come back in the evening. I'm sure I don't need to say, but that means no towels from the rooms are to be taken down to the beach. Now, I said you can hop from the beach to the pool all day, but we do ask people to shower quickly as they come off the beach so that the pool area doesn't get too sandy. If you look across to the little pathway that takes you onto the beach, you'll see that just to the left are a couple of showers. They're warm, so there's no excuse for not quickly cleaning off before you jump back in the pool. OK, what haven't I mentioned? Ah, yes – the sauna. At the end of the row of rooms over there – that's rooms 15–21 – is the sauna and jacuzzi area. Some of you will have paid for that as part of your package and some of you will have to pay a small charge for using it. It's very popular so you do need to book. Go to reception the evening before you plan to use it.

OK, I think they're ready in reception to check all the passports now, but let me quickly mention horse riding. We have two horses in the stable, which is at the end of the path that runs along the beach from the back of the swimming pool. You need to book a ride at reception and then go to the stable about 15 minutes before your booking. Somebody will be there then to make sure you have the gear and run through a few things with you.

Anyway, I'm sure you all want to get to your rooms as quickly as possible – your cases will be in the rooms when you go in. There are plenty of other things to do and there's information about excursions and so on in reception. So, if you'd like to just come back into the foyer and have your passports ready, we'll …

C Checking and reflecting on answers is a constant feature of the skills modules. Give students sufficient time to check and think about why any answers were incorrect before moving onto D. You can decide if it would be beneficial to play the recording again, but avoid doing so simply to check individual students' wrong answers.

Answers:
1. E 2. G 3. J 4. C 5. H 6. I 7. A 8. B

D Students will be used to reflecting on tasks in this way by now. Note that, here, there are fewer points to consider and statements relate directly to the task type they have practised. Remind them that identifying what they are doing well and not doing so well is a very good way of focusing on what they can do better next time. Allow students time to reflect and complete the exercise and then ask them if they are happy with the number of correct answers.

Key vocabulary in context

Encourage students to attempt to complete the exercise without checking the tapescript first. They can work in pairs to pool resources. Tell them to check the tapescript if they really do not know an answer. As feedback, write the full phrases in the answers to consolidate and aid retention.

Answers:
1. off 2. to 3. on 4. at

Refer students to the Workbook exercises related to this module. Choose to work on them now, or set up for homework.

Reading

Objectives

- To further develop awareness of the purpose of topic sentences.
- To practise using topic sentences effectively to predict passage and paragraph content.
- To practise using topic sentences effectively to predict where specific information is likely to be found.
- To introduce an exam task that focuses on the writer's opinion.
- To practise understanding the writer's opinion.

The aim of this Reading Module is to develop what students learnt in the last unit about topic sentences. They are given further guidance on using topic sentences to predict both whole passage and paragraph content, and how to use topic sentences to locate information that answers specific questions.

The theme of *contrasting package holidays with independent travel* touched on in the first module is explored in greater depth. The first passage looks at *the impact that mass tourism is having generally*, while the second, more challenging text, focuses more specifically on *package tourism*. The second passage largely consists of the writer's opinion and students are introduced to the concept of recognizing and understanding opinion rather than fact.

Although students start by reading the heading of the first passage, the lead-in stage aims to prepare them for the content of both passages – they are closely linked. Note, however, that there is also a separate stage that prepares students for the second passage.

Reading 1

A Refer students to the heading and check the meaning of *weigh up*. Explain the connection with *balance* – use your hands to show how one thing can be weighed against another. Point out that we frequently talk about *weighing up advantages and disadvantages* or *weighing up pros and cons*. Ask students to define *tourism* as opposed to *travel*, and ask them when they think *tourism* first started. Refer students to the picture and use it to introduce the two questions.

Make sure students understand the two questions and then set a time limit of eight minutes for the discussion. Students can either work in pairs, as suggested in the instructions, or in groups of three or four. Monitor and assist with key vocabulary when necessary.

Use feedback to introduce concepts and vocabulary that will facilitate comprehension of the texts later, though avoid feeding too much information yourself. Get ideas in note form on the board in two columns. If students work in larger groups, they should appoint a spokesperson to give feedback on what the group discussed.

Possible answers:
Benefits: income / business expansion / employment opportunities / opportunity to meet people from places they will never visit
Damaging effects: destruction of global environment / damage to local environment / destruction of or change to traditional lifestyle / exploitation

Reading 2

A Tell students that they will develop the topic they have been discussing in a moment, but first they are going to focus on reading skills.

Students should read the questions and think individually before answering the questions in pairs. Check answers orally, but make sure they are clear. It would be worth writing supporting sentences on the board.

Answers:
1. the first sentence (It would be a good idea to point out now that the last sentence of a paragraph can sometimes serve as a sort of

topic sentence. It may summarize rather than introduce a paragraph and link one paragraph with the next.)
2. to introduce the main idea of the paragraph / to tell the reader what the paragraph will be about
3. support the topic sentence (give examples, develop, explain, etc.) / supporting sentences
4. when he or she wants to make a fresh point / change from one topic to another

B The first three steps in the exercise are very similar to the steps that students worked through in an exercise in the previous unit. The fourth step is a development, and students will need to know what they are doing. It would be best to work through steps 1–3 and then go on to step 4 separately.

Refer students to the topic sentences and make sure they appreciate that there are six and that there are six paragraphs in the passage they will read. Tell them not to read the sentences until they have checked the first three steps of the task.

Read through the three steps with them, pointing out that they did the same thing in the last Reading Module.

Students should spend five minutes reading the sentences and thinking individually and then discuss answers with a partner. Monitor and check that students have absorbed what they learnt in the last Reading Module. Guide and prompt when necessary. Check answers to steps 1 and 2 quickly, but not step 3. Step 4 develops the point and gives more direct guidance.

Possible answers:
1. The text will be about the benefits and negative effects of mass tourism.
2. It appears that the text will start by saying that tourism is having a huge impact and then go on to alternately present advantages and the related disadvantages.

Make sure students appreciate that in step 4, the six ideas are supporting ideas and not actually supporting sentences from the passage. The aim is for them to use the ideas to predict and then to identify the actual supporting sentences when they come to read the passage. Tell them that sometimes the link between the topic sentence and supporting sentence will be clear and sometimes not so obvious. Work through an example with them, if you think necessary.

They will probably need about ten minutes to work though this exercise and benefit fully from doing it.

Students should match the supporting ideas with the topic sentences individually. (You can suggest that they use a pencil so that answers can easily be changed when they read the passage.) They can then discuss answers with a partner. Check answers, but do not confirm or correct – students will read the passage to check in a moment.

C The aim here is simply to check answers to B. The matching task itself is easy since language is not paraphrased in the way it would be in this type of exam task.

Students should complete the task individually, changing any answers given previously. Then, they should compare answers with a partner. Check answers with students and ask them if they had to make any changes to answers in B. Show an OHT or other visual medium of the passage on the board. This will enable you to draw attention once more to the topic sentences and then to the supporting sentences in each paragraph.

Answers:
3. Students' own answers.
4. the conservation of an area of beauty = paragraph 3 (Point out that the supporting sentence here contrasts with the topic sentence – the topic sentence raises an issue – the supporting sentence suggests another viewpoint.)
   people becoming more tolerant = paragraph 6
   local people doing menial work = paragraph 5
   the cost of maintaining a tourist industry = paragraph 2
   the need for debate about tourism = paragraph 1
   unique customs and lifestyles changing = paragraph 4

Refer students to the Exam tip at the end of the text.

D The aim now is to reverse the process. Students remember what supporting information supported each of the topic sentences. Emphasize that they should use their own words and that they do not need to remember every piece of supporting information in every paragraph. Monitor closely to check what they have absorbed and whether or not they appear to have fully grasped the relationship between topic and supporting sentences. Feedback is unnecessary.

Reading 3

Although students should now be more independent when working on the practice part of the skills modules, the important thing here is to consolidate and practise using topic sentences and there is some preparation that focuses on that.

A Since this is the first time that students have worked with a passage that is largely the writer's opinion, it is a good idea to orientate them towards the theme and pre-teach a few key words and phrases to start with. Note that the concept of some people having a negative perception of other people's tastes and lifestyle may not be as familiar to some students as others, especially if they are young.

Since the aim of the lead-in stage is to prepare for the reading practice, you may prefer to conduct it as a whole-class discussion. Remember, though, that this will mean fewer students contributing and may mean stronger students dominating. If you conduct it as pairwork, set a time limit of five minutes. Go over answers quickly to check the concept has been grasped and that the highlighted phrases have been understood.

Possible answers:
1. They are convenient – everything is arranged in one go. / They are often cheaper. / People do not have to worry about practical issues while they are on holiday.
2. They are not adventurous. / People eat in the same place every day and evening. / People are sometimes forced to participate in activities. / People generally only meet other people from the same country or other tourists.

3. This depends on students – but generally speaking, yes. Some independent travellers are *snobbish* (they feel superior) and they *look down on* certain types of package holidays, especially packages that involve doing the same thing that can be done at home – eating familiar food and drinking a lot of alcohol.

B Students have worked through this process a couple of times now and know what to do and why it is a good idea. During the practice stage, simply give students five minutes to read the topic sentences and think about the questions. There is no need for them to discuss the process again or for you to check answers.

C This is the same task that students completed earlier, but it is now a part of real exam practice. Make sure students only read the lines of information and the topic sentences again – not the rest of the passage. Point out once more that the information is written as phrases or concepts – not as complete sentences.

Students should spend five minutes (one minute for each line of information) matching/predicting individually and then compare answers with a partner. Monitor and check whether the process is working and whether it appears to be helpful. Feedback is unnecessary since you will not be able to confirm answers.

D Before you leave students to their own devices to work through the practice tasks, tell them to look ahead to the second task (questions 6–12) and then to read the Question-type tip that follows. Give them time to read and absorb and then tell them to cover it. Select one student to tell you what advice it gave. Emphasize that they should apply the same strategies as for T/F/NG tasks.

Note that, although many IELTS materials suggest that students should practise distinguishing between fact and opinion, tasks very rarely require them to actually do that. Students need to recognize opinions, understand opinions and attribute opinions to different people mentioned in a passage, but not actually decide whether a statement is a fact or an opinion. A Y/N/NG task is the task most frequently applied when a passage is largely opinion.

Set a time limit of 12 minutes for the two tasks, pointing out that they have already done considerable work with the text. Remind them that answers to the Y/N/NG task will be found in order in the passage, and that that will also help them to know roughly in which part of the passage to look for information.

E Checking and reflecting on answers is a constant feature of the skills modules. Give students sufficient time to check and think about why they may have answered incorrectly. Students might want to know why some of their answers were not correct. Explaining some points may be necessary and beneficial, but going through all of them will be very time-consuming. It is best to tell students that they will learn more about how to do these tasks and that their scores will improve.

If you do want to identify the specific parts of the passage that provide answers to any questions, make an OHT or other visual medium of the passage and highlight those parts on the board.

Answers:
1. E 2. B 3. D 4. A 5. C
6. Y 7. NG 8. Y 9. N 10. NG 11. N 12. NG

F Students will now be familiar with this type of reflective process. Point out that, once again, points are related to exploiting topic sentences. Remind them that identifying what they are doing well and not doing so well is a very good way of focusing on what they can do better next time. Allow students time to reflect and complete the exercise and then ask them if they are happy with the number of correct answers.

Key vocabulary in context

Remind students that an effective way to learn and remember new vocabulary is to study it closely once it has been presented in context.

The aim is as much to increase students' awareness of positive and negative connotation and the use of predictable prefixes as to specifically learn these words. Seventeen words (though some will certainly be known) is a lot to absorb in one go and students should be selective about what they think will be usefully retained.

Students may claim to know some of the words and they can work out whether others are positive or negative from the prefix alone. However, they should use the context to understand the words properly and should check back to the text each time. They can either work individually and then compare answers or work in pairs so that they can communicate and compare knowledge as they go. If they work individually, suggest that they compare answers after working on each passage.

You may even prefer to set this exercise for homework and check it at the beginning of the next lesson when students are more familiar with the words.

A feedback stage could be fairly lengthy, but you will need to check the meaning of the words as well as simply the 50/50 answer. To make feedback more motivating, you could read definitions of words from each group as students shout out the words. Use the definitions with the answer key below.

Answers:

Text 1

1. burden (N) = unwanted responsibility
2. intrude (N) = become involved when not welcome
3. disrupt (N) = prevent something from operating smoothly / create a problem
4. impetus (P) = force that helps something to happen
5. unspoiled (unspoilt) (P) = natural / left alone
6. rewarding (P) = beneficial / giving satisfaction
7. menial (N) = unimportant / of a low status
8. distrust (N) = not trust / believe to be dishonest
9. conflict (N) = angry disagreement

Text 2

1. disapprove (N) = not be in favour of / not agree with
2. pittance (N) = tiny amount (usually payment)
3. luxury (P) = something very expensive / something you cannot usually afford
4. upmarket (P) = expensive / of a high standard
5. privileged (P) = only available to a small minority

6. uncertainty (N) = insecurity / not knowing what will happen
7. ruin (N) = destroy
8. inferior (N) = of low quality / of a lesser quality than something else

Refer students to the Workbook exercises related to this module. Choose to work on them now, or set up for homework.

Writing

Objectives

- **To introduce students to the concept of problem- and solution-type discursive compositions.**
- **To give further practice understanding Writing Task 2 instructions and appreciating what is required.**
- **To give further practice and increase confidence in terms of knowing what to say.**
- **To practise organizing ideas.**
- **To practise writing using topic sentences in written work.**

The Writing Module in this unit concentrates on Writing Task 2. The aim is to revise and develop the fundamental issues addressed in Units 2 and 4 and to improve the organization and natural flow of a discursive composition.

Writing 1

The first part of the module aims to orientate students to the theme and then revise the fundamental issues of discursive composition writing.

A The principal aim is to prepare for the writing focus rather than to provide extended speaking practice. Though students should be encouraged to develop a conversation, you may like to have a clear time limit in mind (five minutes, perhaps). Note that the conversation will develop with more focus as students discuss possible content of the Writing task. Point out that students should think back to some of the ideas they learnt about and discussed in the Reading Module.

Students should spend two minutes looking at the pictures, thinking and planning answers individually. Then spend three minutes answering the question in pairs. Monitor to check that students are discussing points that will help them tackle the exercises that follow, and guide them when necessary. Focus attention on the hotel in the first picture – ask them who they think owns the hotel and if they remember the word to describe the kind of work that local people might end up doing. Make a note of observations that will be useful during feedback. Keep feedback brief and concise and use it to make sure that students have the basic idea to take into B.

Possible answers:
Tourists can afford things that the people whose country they are visiting will never be able to. / Money from tourism does not find its way down to the local people in need. / Big hotels are not owned by local organizations – they are international chain establishments. / Local people do menial jobs. / Local people have a poor standard of living.

B Refer students to the Writing task instructions and read the line of rubric with them. Explain that *approach* for now means *plan* and *write*. Ask students if they would try to agree or disagree with a statement or write a balanced argument as they have done previously. What sort of points would they list before they started

to write? Do not help with anything in the instructions – that will be dealt with in a moment in Exercise C.

C Tell students that they will need to have their books open both on the current page and on the relevant page of Unit 2. Give them time to complete the exercise and then another minute or so to compare with a partner.

Make an OHT or other visual medium of the task instructions to show on the board. You can highlight parts and make notes as feedback and give students a model to work to (see suggestion below).

Refer students to the Exam tip and give them time to read and absorb. Tell them to cover the advice and go over what it said. Emphasize once more that the initial difficulty is knowing what to say – you will know how big an issue this still is to your students. Draw attention to the last part of the advice once more – point out that students may feel quite confident discussing the issue in their own language with friends, but far more worried about writing about it in English. Remind them that the starting point should often be to simply list ideas in their own language.

D You can answer the first question as a whole class, if you prefer. Get a general consensus as to who feels confident about tackling the task.

Put students into pairs to discuss the other two points. Set a time limit of four minutes. Get some quick feedback, but do not confirm or offer suggestions of your own – the task that follows develops the point and gives further guidance.

Write about the following topic:

I must list reasons (4/5 perhaps)

it makes a lot of money

In many of the world's poorest countries tourism is a huge industry. However, the profit made from tourism rarely benefits the poorest people living in the local community. What are some of the reasons for this situation and what are some possible solutions?

Give reasons for your answer and include any relevant examples from your own experience.

Write at least 250 words.

the poorest people don't get any of the money

I must suggest solutions (maybe NOT to all the problems)

I'm not sure (maybe I can mention friends that work as waiters)

E The aim is to present students with possible content for the composition and to prepare them to read the model. Completing the notes successfully is not in itself an aim, so accept suggestions that students make.

Students should spend five minutes completing the notes individually, before comparing answers in pairs. Write answers on the board for clarity.

Answers:
Reasons:
1. businesses / hotels   2. foreign
3. local   4. jobs / menial   5. globally

Solutions:
1. limit / restrict   2. assistance / subsidies
3. education   4. employ   5. tourists

F Give students three minutes to discuss the points in pairs. Monitor to check the ideas being suggested. Feedback is unnecessary as students will read a model composition in a moment.

Writing 2

A Start this part of the lesson with books closed – students should not be tempted to look ahead to the model. Either give the instructions orally or write them on the board. If you are planning to get some feedback before students read the model, write 1–5 down the side of the board in preparation.

Make sure students appreciate that they are making a very rough plan and set a time limit of three minutes. Monitor to check and assist where necessary.

Whether or not you work through a feedback stage should depend on how successfully students have organized ideas. If they have all made perfectly logical suggestions for each paragraph, it would be best to move on to the reading stage. Getting a rough plan on the board, however, will reinforce the way discursive compositions of this type should be organized.

Possible answers:
Paragraph 1 – introduce general idea / say that tourism is very profitable, but that it does not benefit everyone

Paragraph 2 – give some reasons / examples – businesses owned by foreign chains / locals do not get best jobs
Paragraph 3 – give more reasons / examples – tourists do not buy local products / use local facilities
Paragraph 4 – suggest possible solutions
Paragraph 5 – conclude / suggest (or repeat) most obvious solution

B Refer students to the model and ask them what they think is missing from the beginning of each paragraph. Tell them they will work on topic sentences in a moment. Emphasize that they should read and absorb the content and compare it with their own ideas and what is on the board.

C Ensure that the model topic sentences in D are covered. The aim now is to conclude the focus on topic sentences by getting students to write their own.

Note that, although the guidance they have been given should facilitate the task, students may find it more difficult to write topic sentences for an existing model than to write their own topic sentences that introduce an idea that they feel is theirs. Encourage them to work in pairs so that they can communicate and pool resources as they go.

Set a time limit of two minutes to write an opening sentence for the first paragraph and then check answers. Get ideas from three or four pairs and write the best on the board. Do not reveal the model topic sentence yet. Set a further time limit of eight minutes (two minutes per sentence) to complete the whole exercise.

Monitor to check progress and to make a note of good sentences that can help you to keep feedback brief. You may feel that a feedback stage is unnecessary and that students should go straight to D to see the model sentences.

D The task itself now should be easy. The aim is to start comparing.

Students should complete the task individually and then compare answers in pairs.

Answers:

Paragraph 1 = 3   Paragraph 2 = 5
Paragraph 3 = 1   Paragraph 4 = 4
Paragraph 5 = 2

E Students will have already started comparing. Give them another two minutes to read and absorb.

Writing task

The Writing tasks are found either in the Workbook or in the Exam Practice Module at the end of the unit. In this unit, the task is in the Exam Practice Module, and teacher's notes for it can be found in the notes for that module.

Consolidation

Instructions are given for Speaking exercises when the procedure is not clear from instructions in the Course Book. Set Vocabulary and Errors exercises either for individual completion and pairwork checking, or as pairwork when you feel immediate interaction is beneficial.

To correct errors in the final exercise, ask students to come and write the correct sentences on the board while other students offer help. You will need to write the corrections on the board to clarify.

Speaking

A The aim is to provide further practice in paraphrasing when a key word is not known. Students should use bilingual dictionaries here; otherwise they will simply read the definition given. Tell them that once they know what the word means, they should find a way of explaining it. Their partner should tell them if the meaning is clear from what they have said.

B The aim is simply to prepare students for the practice in C. Emphasize that they do not have to talk about the task card again – simply remember what they said previously.

C Students should answer the questions spontaneously, as they will have to when the examiner asks them follow-up questions. Do not

give them time to read and prepare answers. Monitor as students interact and give feedback as you go. A whole-class feedback stage is unnecessary.

Vocabulary

A **Answers:**

1. c 2. f 3. b 4. g 5. d 6. a 7. e

B **Answers:**

1. memorable 2. disapprove
3. unspoiled / unspoilt 4. sustainable
5. uncertainty 6. unwilling
7. escapism 8. managerial

Errors

Answers:

1. The journey from ...
2. ... arrived in Sydney...
3. ... reach the coast?
4. ... as big as I expected.
5. It's by far the ...
6. Venice was even more beautiful than ...

Exam Practice

Writing

This is the first time that a discursive Writing task (for which students need 40 minutes) has been the subject of the Exam Practice Module. This will be a good opportunity to set the Writing task itself in class time so that you can check timing and monitor to give assistance.

Even if you decide to set the Writing task itself for homework, work through the preparation stage (which involves pairwork) in class time and make sure that students agree to time themselves strictly.

A The aim is to revise and consolidate themes presented and discussed in the Writing Module and to prepare for and provide content for the Writing task. Students should be aware of this, and not simply talk about the pictures.

Students should talk in pairs. They can either identify each problem and suggest some solutions, or identify all the problems and then suggest solutions. Set a time limit of eight minutes (two minutes per picture).

Use feedback to get ideas on the board that will prepare for and facilitate the writing stage of the lesson. Note that suggesting solutions will not always be easy and you could remind students that they do not have to suggest a solution to each problem they identify.

B Work through as with Writing 1B in the Writing Module. Students should compare the notes they make on the task instructions with a partner.

C Encourage students to work in pairs so that they can pool resources and communicate. Of course, they will not work collaboratively on writing tasks in the exam, but preparing with a partner will boost confidence at this stage. Set a time limit of six minutes, pointing out that this should be an extension of the ideas suggested in A. Monitor and check that what students are doing really is preparing them to write their compositions. A feedback stage is unnecessary.

Refer students to the Exam tip and give them time to read and absorb.

D Once students start writing their compositions, take into account the time already spent preparing. They should need only 25 minutes. If they write at home, tell them to be strict with a time limit – they will not benefit from spending longer on the task than they will have when it comes to the exam.

When students have completed the task, they should compare it with the model composition on page 266. The model is reproduced opposite. Note that the model here is relatively long – point out to students that there is no maximum word limit, but that they must be realistic.

If you collect students' compositions to mark, concentrate on what has been the focus of the Writing Module – organizing points logically and using topic sentences effectively. You will want to start correcting more of the composition content, but remember that correcting every sentence will not be very motivating. You may still be correcting most of what they write.

Model composition:

As the tourist industry continues to develop, travellers are taken to ever more remote corners of the globe. Not long ago, holidaymakers were happy with a week in Spain, but now they want to experience exotic locations like Nepal and Madagascar. Unfortunately, as soon as even a modest number of tourists begin to visit a place, they have an impact which changes that place and makes it less appealing.

There are various ways in which the impact of tourism has a negative effect. Firstly, in order to support tourism, there needs to be construction and infrastructure. This might mean hotels, bars and shops built where they would never have been for local people. It might mean roads and railway links that spoil an area's natural beauty. Airports may not be built in remote places, instead they will be built somewhere nearby and planes will fly over areas that were previously peaceful.

Deserted beaches might become crowded and less clean. Hundreds of people start visiting sites that are not suitable as tourist attractions. In the worst cases, tourists damage countryside or coral reefs. Even a small amount of tourism probably means local people opening shops, bars and other businesses that are not typical of the culture. All this begins to make the destination less attractive.

It is difficult to suggest clear solutions since once development begins, it is impossible to reverse. However, some measures could be taken. The authorities could limit the number of large hotels and encourage small guest houses. They could limit the number of foreign-owned bars and restaurants and not allow fast-food chains to open.

The most important thing, in my opinion, is for the tourists to become more aware of the impact they have. They must be prepared to fly to an airport some way from their final destination and understand why they should support local businesses and buy local products.

Unit 6 Workbook answers

Vocabulary development

A

S	I	G	H	T	S	E	E	I	N	G
A	U	A	M	R	G	C	T	N	I	I
F	T	E	X	C	U	R	S	I	O	N
A	D	V	E	N	T	U	R	E	J	L
R	N	R	A	S	T	I	R	E	O	E
I	R	E	L	E	L	S	N	E	U	K
J	Y	S	O	U	V	E	N	I	R	A
P	E	O	M	C	A	M	P	I	N	G
Q	O	R	U	R	D	E	R	I	E	N
A	P	T	R	I	P	H	A	C	Y	R

B 1. e 2. d 3. f 4. c 5. h 6. a 7. b 8. g

C 1. away 2. down 3. out 4. up

D Text 1

1. the lion's share = the biggest part / the majority

2. fall victim to = be negatively affected by / suffer from

Text 2

1. it struck me = I realized / it occurred to me

2. on a shoe-string budget = planning to spend very little money

Listening

A 1. E 2. B 3. C 4. G

Tapescript 🎧 **63 (2 mins, 41 secs)**

A Listen to a conversation between a hotel receptionist and a guest and write the correct letter A–G next to the four places.

Guest: ... mm, that's right ... thank you. Can you tell me if the restaurant is still open? I know it's late, but I hardly had anything to eat on the plane – the meal was dreadful, actually.

Receptionist: I'm sorry, the restaurant's closed now, but there are two or three very nice places to eat within a few minutes of the hotel.

Guest: Oh, good. I'll have a quick shower and then get something. Which restaurant do you recommend?

Receptionist: Well, it depends what you fancy. Rosario's does pretty much everything, from steak to pizza, and it's very reasonable.

Guest: Where's that, then?

Receptionist: When you come out of the hotel, go left and then right. You'll come into a square and there are a few bars and restaurants around it. Rosario's is on the opposite side. You'll see it as you enter the square.

Guest: What are the other places in the square like?

Receptionist: They're all very nice, but a bit more expensive than Rosario's. Personally, I like the Chinese restaurant down by the harbour. That's only a few minutes' walk too.

Guest: What's it called?

Receptionist: The Lotus Flower. Again, you go left out of the hotel and then walk straight down. Turn left when you get down to the harbour and you'll see it there, close to the corner.

Guest: Thanks. Oh, is there a cashpoint nearby? I didn't have time to get any money at the airport.

Receptionist: Yes, there's a bank virtually next door. The cashpoint's inside the entrance area. You'll pass it on your way if you go down to the harbour.

Guest: Great. Oh, one more thing. I'll need to get a taxi quite early tomorrow to get to the conference. The taxi that brought me in dropped me right outside the hotel so I didn't see if there was a place to catch one. Shall I order a taxi from here or is there a rank nearby?

Receptionist: I can certainly order you a taxi from here but, frankly, it's better to just walk down to the rank. They charge a little more for picking you up here. You go right when you come out and walk straight down for three or four minutes. Then you take a right and the taxi rank is round the corner. I'll explain it again tomorrow morning, if you like. I'll be here when you leave.

Guest: Oh, that's good. I'm a bit tired to take it in now. Anyway, thanks again. I'll go and get changed now.

Receptionist: OK, I'll see you when you come back down. Enjoy your stay with us.

Reading

B going back to the classroom – C
wanting to be frightened – E
travellers not doing what everyone else is doing – A
enjoying extreme sports in the desert – B
staying in unusual surroundings – D

Writing

A 1. As   2. Not long ago   3. as soon as
4. in order to   5. In the worst cases
6. Even   7. since   8. However
9. The most important thing

7 Kill or cure

Speaking and Vocabulary

Objectives

- To practise talking about health and fitness.
- To practise interaction typical of all parts of the IELTS Speaking test.
- To practise using strategies that give you time to think in conversation.

The first module aims to bring the various parts of the Speaking test together. The first part presents and practises language related to *general health and fitness issues* and *minor ailments*, giving students an opportunity to exchange personal information. The last part of the lesson develops the theme and practises exchanges more typical of the third part of the Speaking test.

Start with books closed and write both the correct quotation and a wrong quotation on the board – *The greatest wealth is health* and *The greatest health is wealth*. Ask students which they think is the famous quotation for this unit. Once they have identified the famous quotation, ask them to explain what it means – they can talk in pairs for a minute, focusing on what it means and their reaction to it. Spend another two minutes discussing it as a class.

Virgil – Publius Vergilius Maro (October 15, 70 BC – September 21, 19 BC) was a classical Roman poet, best known for three major works – the Eclogues, *the* Georgics, *and the* Aeneid. *The quotation suggests that a rich man cannot be happy if he does not have his health and perhaps that it is unwise to aspire to wealth rather than ensure that good health is maintained.*

Speaking 1

A The aim is to orientate students towards the general theme of the whole unit and to provide them with the opportunity to exchange information about their own lives using language they already know. Since no new language is learnt here, set a time limit of six minutes.

Students should spend three minutes looking at the images, thinking and planning what to say individually. Then, they should discuss the questions with a partner. Monitor to assist with any necessary vocabulary and make a note of any contributions that could be shared during a feedback stage. As feedback, concentrate on the first question, taking the opportunity to introduce lexis that will be useful later – *lying around, working out, eating healthily / unhealthily, diet, alcohol consumption, drinking to excess, doing / taking exercise, yoga,* etc.

Two vocabulary exercises come together now and students are presented with a fairly large number of new words and phrases. The assumption is that some of these will already be known and will only need revising, and students should cope.

Vocabulary 1

The aim is to check core vocabulary and practise everyday spoken language that will widen students' range of options when discussing *lifestyle*. Note that some of the phrases mean more or less the same thing.

A Students should work in pairs, so that they can talk about the vocabulary items as they go. They should only use a dictionary if neither of them knows an item. Give them the time they need to work through the exercise. Monitor and assist when necessary. Keep feedback brief, concentrating on clarifying any remaining uncertainties. Note that you can use one of the highlighted words or phrases to help understand another. They are all very closely related.

Answers:
1. *Healthy* is more about being free from illness, diet and general well-being (and includes physical, emotional and psychological health). / *Fit* is more about staying in good shape physically.
2. *Be in good shape* and *stay in shape* are more about being fit.
3. *Out of condition* means not in good shape – not physically fit.
4. If you *look after yourself*, you keep fit / stay in shape. You probably take part in sports or go to the gym.
5. A *balanced diet* is a diet with the right amount of what is good for you – the right balance of meat, fish, vegetables, fruit and dairy products.
6. If you *feel under the weather*, you feel generally (temporarily) unwell. We do not use the phrase to mean generally unhealthy or unfit.

B Refer students to the example and then give them two minutes to plan questions. Monitor and check that questions are appropriate before they start asking them. Note that the appropriate question is *How are you feeling?* rather than *Are you feeling under the weather?*

Monitor again as students interact. Conclude by getting a show of hands for each question – *So, how many people think they have a balanced diet?*

Pronunciation check

Use the board to present the point. Write *healthy* and *weather* and ask a few students to pronounce the two words. Ask others if the sound of *th* is the same or different. Establish that the sounds are different and write them phonetically /θ/ and /ð/.

🎧 Refer students to the *Pronunciation check* and give them time to read and absorb. Make sure they then say the words aloud in their pair as they complete the exercise. Explain that *teething* applies to babies when they first grow teeth – it is a verb, but it is almost only used as an ~*ing* form. Play the whole recording as students check their answers and then again, pausing after each word to check the answers yourself. Point out the pattern that the noun is produced with an unvoiced /θ/, while the related verb is produced with a voiced /ð/.

Answers:
bath = /θ/   bathe = /ð/
breath = /θ/   breathe = /ð/
truth = /θ/   clothes = /ð/
teeth = /θ/   teething = /ð/

Tapescript 🎧 **64 (0 mins, 37 secs)**
Pronunciation check
Mark the words below /θ/ or /ð/ depending on how *th* is pronounced. Listen and check.

bath
bathe
breath
breathe
truth
clothes
teeth
teething

Vocabulary 2

The aim is to widen students' range of vocabulary when talking about *health issues* and *minor ailments*. Point out that they should be selective here. Some words and phrases will be more useful than others to each individual.

A Tell students that before they check the vocabulary they will engage in a mingling activity and talk to various classmates. Give them five minutes to read through the list and check items if necessary. Monitor and assist, but do not check anything at this stage. You can go over meaning more rigorously during a feedback stage after B.

B Make sure students understand that the aim is to find at least one *yes* answer for each question as they mingle and talk to classmates. Once somebody has answered *yes* to a question, they don't need to ask anyone that particular question again. The activity will end when three students have *yes* answers for all questions. Point out that most questions will be in the present perfect, *Have you ever ...?* but a few will be present simple. Tell students to ask follow-up questions if they are interested and write the example below on the board.

Have you ever had an electric shock?
Yes, twice, actually.
Really? When was the last time, and how did it happen?

When students are ready, make sure they walk around and talk to different classmates. Encourage them to talk to one other classmate at a time rather than in big groups where they can cross off three or four questions at a time. Tell them not to tell each other who has answered a question *yes* in order to find him or her.

As feedback, go through the questions yourself, checking vocabulary and consolidating by using it in context – *So, who has an allergy? Oh, really, what are you allergic to?* Clarify any remaining uncertainties and check pronunciation, drilling when appropriate.

Vocabulary suggestions

- You are *allergic* or have an *allergy to* something.
- We say *carsick*, but *seasick* rather than 'boatsick'!
- We can say *bad eyesight*, but the better collocation for written work is *poor*.
- A *wound* is a very deep cut or hole made by a bullet, for example. Contrast *wound* with *injury* – a wound is an injury, but an injury is not necessarily a wound. *Wound* is pronounced /wuːnd/, while the past form of *wind* (also spelt *wound*) is pronounced /waʊnd/.
- *Stung* is the past form and past participle form of *sting*. The noun is also *sting – a bee sting*.
- *Bitten* is the past participle form of *bite*. The past form is *bit*. The noun is *bite – a snake bite*.
- If you *burn yourself*, it is an accident, as it is if you *cut yourself* (See development in *Grammar check*).

Grammar check

Students have already studied the passive and should be fairly confident with it anyway. The aim here is to raise their awareness of a particularly frequent use when the agent of the action is typically expressed. Give them time to read and absorb the information. Clarify the fact that, in this case, what happens to somebody is more the focus than who or what performs the action, but who or what performs the action is also a very important part of the message. Emphasize that learning the passive is as much about being natural as about being right or wrong about how a structure is formed.

Refer students to the second part of the *Grammar check* and give them time to read and absorb the information. Refer back to the example in the communicative activity (*burnt himself*). Students should work individually to write the reflexive pronouns and then compare with a partner. Write answers on the board for clarity.

Answers:
1. myself 2. yourself 3. yourselves
4. himself 5. herself 6. itself 7. ourselves
8. themselves

Speaking 2

The aim now is to develop the theme and practise interaction more typical of the third part of the Speaking test. Remind students that the examiner will often stay with the general theme on the task card to start a conversation in the third part. The more specific aim is to present and practise ways of giving yourself time to think rather than blurting out an answer.

A Make sure students appreciate they should read and think and not start answering questions yet. Give them two minutes to do so. Check that they understand *acupuncture* and *aromatherapy* – more the fact that they are examples of alternative medicine than their specific individual meaning. Explain that an *ageing population* is one that, on average, is becoming older – more people between 65 and 80, for example. Revise the meaning of *burden* from the last unit, and clarify the whole phrase *health care burden on taxpayers* – people have to pay more tax to look after old people.

B 🎧 Tell students to cover C and read through the instructions and question with them. Tell them that they will hear four speakers, each of whom will use a strategy to give themselves time to think before answering the question. Tell them to focus on what the strategies have in common the first time they listen rather than trying to remember the specific expressions used. They will do that in a moment.

Play the whole recording and then give students a moment to answer the question in pairs. Establish together that they each make a comment about the question rather than try to answer it. Point out that one speaker repeats part of the question.

Tapescript 🎧 **65 (1 min, 17 secs)**

B Listen to some students answering the questions. How do they give themselves time to think?

1

Examiner: Do you think your generation has a healthier lifestyle than your parents' generation?

Student: Mm, I haven't really thought about it before. I guess there are certainly more fast-food restaurants …

2

Examiner: What do you think about alternative approaches to health care, like acupuncture or aromatherapy?

Student: Mm, alternative approaches. It's not a topic I've thought about very much, but I suppose …

3

Examiner: Does the government of a country have a responsibility to promote healthy lifestyle options?

Student: That's a very good question. I don't really think the government should interfere too much in …

4

Examiner: Is an ageing population placing too much of a health care burden on taxpayers?

Student: Goodness. I don't know if I can answer that in a few words. It's a very big question. Personally, I think …

C 🎧 Give students a moment to read the expressions and think about the gaps, though not to try and remember the answers. Play the recording, pausing after each exchange so that students can write answers. Play the recording again, pausing after each gapped expression to check answers. Making an OHT or other visual medium of the sentences to show on the board will enable quick, concise feedback and allow you to clarify any uncertainties efficiently. Playing the recording a final time as students read the tapescript will prepare them for D. You can decide whether or not drilling the expressions will be of benefit.

Answers:
See highlighting in tapescript for Track 65.

Tapescript 🎧 **66 (0 mins, 9 secs)**

C Listen again and fill in the gaps.

[Play Track 65 again]

Refer students to the Exam tip and give them a moment to read and absorb.

D Tell students they should give their own answers – not just repeat those from the recording – but emphasize that the real aim is to practise using the strategies that ensure thinking time. Tell them to spend two minutes preparing answers before they interact. Monitor and check performance. Feedback is unnecessary.

E Students continue working in the same pair. Give them three minutes to write three or four questions that they will ask their partner. Monitor to check the questions are suitable for the purpose – you may need to assist weaker students. Continue to monitor closely as they interact, making sure exchanges are natural. Make a note of particularly successful exchanges that can be read aloud to the class during a feedback stage.

Listening

Objectives

- **To introduce students to the concept of table completion as an exam task.**
- **To re-emphasize the importance of prediction and show students how looking at a table can aid prediction.**
- **To revise and give further practice listening for specific information and spelling answers correctly.**

Students are now familiar with tasks that involve completing sentences, notes and summaries. Completing notes organized in a table should be no more of a challenge. Note that, in the exam, it is unlikely that students will have to answer more than five or six questions working with a table. A table completion task will be one of three or four tasks that assess comprehension of a whole recording.

In this Listening Module, the one recording serves as the topic for all parts of the lesson.

Listening 1

The aim of the first part of the lesson is to orientate students towards a topic they have probably not thought much about and to motivate them for the listening tasks later.

A Conduct the lead-in as a whole-class discussion. Read the instructions with students and then give them two minutes in silence to look at the pictures and think. Students may suggest that the topic is *operations* or *medical surgery*, which is fine, but try to elicit *transplant*. Elicit the type of transplant that is shown in each image – a corneal transplant, a heart transplant, a hand transplant and a face transplant. Students will probably appreciate that an 'eye transplant' is not possible, but will not know the word *cornea*. Take the opportunity to present and revise vocabulary – *Which organ can you see in the second picture? How many stitches do you think are needed to sew a hand back on? What do you call the person who gives the organ or body part?*, etc. Avoid a lengthy discussion in which you reveal information that students should learn from listening to the recording.

B Developing the discussion in groups of three will give more individuals a chance to interact and express opinions. Make sure students appreciate that they are not expected to know the correct answers.

Students spend three minutes reading the questions and thinking individually, before comparing thoughts with a partner. Use a feedback stage to further consolidate vocabulary and motivate students. You do not need to worry about giving away answers to listening tasks, but you may prefer to tell students that you will not reveal the answer to question 2 as they will hear it in the lecture (it is unlikely they will correctly guess). For questions 1 and 3, elicit organs / body parts from students and write them on the board. Drill if and when necessary. You do not need to confirm that suggestions are correct.

Possible answers:
1. heart / liver / lung / kidney / pancreas / face / cornea, etc.
2. a corneal transplant
3. hand / face

C 🎧 The first stage of the listening is an extension of the lead-in – there are no exam-type tasks. The aim is to further orientate students so that they can properly benefit from making predictions about the tables later.

Give students a minute to read the questions before they listen, so they know what they are listening for. Play the whole recording and give students a moment to compare answers with a partner. Check answers yourself orally – you might think it best to write the definition that answers question 2 on the board. Students would benefit from hearing the introduction to the lecture again before engaging in the exam tasks, especially to understand the final part about the Chinese physician. Conclude by emphasizing that the lecturer says that transplant surgery has not been going on for very long.

Answers:

1. to find out more for themselves / to choose one of the transplants and do some detailed research
2. the moving of an organ from one body to another for the purpose of replacing a damaged or absent organ
3. it was conceptual / the physical operation never actually took place

Tapescript 🎧 **67 (2 mins, 51 secs)**

C **Listen to the introductory part of the talk. Answer the question below in pairs.**

Voice: Is everyone here? Could you come inside the room at the back there and close the door, please? You won't be able to hear me properly if you're standing out in the corridor. Thank you. I'm sorry there aren't enough seats for everyone. I'm afraid some of you will just have to make your notes leaning on a book or something. There are a few clipboards at the back of the room there if anyone wants one. Anyway, I'm not going to say a huge amount and you won't need to make copious notes. The idea is that the brief outline I give you now will help you decide what you want to find out more about for yourselves. I've got a few images to show you on PowerPoint too, so make sure you can see the screen.

Right, I'm going to talk about transplants. I'm going to give you an overview, hopefully whet your appetite, and motivate you to go away and find more information. I want you to choose one of the transplants I talk about and do some detailed research. That means that when we then go into each transplant type in

more depth over the next week or so, each of you feels that you're experts on at least one particular area of the topic. Clear?

OK, so – what is a transplant? No, I don't want you to shout out. I'll tell you. A transplant – at least in medical terms – is the moving of an organ from one body to another for the purpose of replacing a damaged or absent organ. So, how long have doctors been able to perform transplants? The answer is 'not very long', especially if we're talking about transplants of the major organs that we associate with this type of surgery. Of course, there are numerous accounts of transplants taking place long ago, but these were not successful and in many cases were simply notions. The Chinese physician Pien Chi'ao, for example, is reported to have exchanged the heart of a man of strong spirit but weak will, with the heart of a man of weak spirit but strong will in an attempt to achieve balance in each man! I think we can safely say that the physical operation never actually took place.

Listening 2

Refer students to the Question-type tip and tell them to look at the tables in Listening 2 and 3. Give them a moment to read and absorb.

A By now, students will be aware that discussion points like this are subsequently the focus of a Question-type tip. Discourage them from looking ahead if they appear to be doing so. Give them a minute to answer the question and then get some ideas from selected students. There is no need to confirm answers – tell them they will read the Exam tip after doing the first exercise.

B 🎧 Read through the instructions with students. Give them a little longer than usual to read the questions before they listen so they appreciate how the table helps organize ideas. Point out that tables usually consist of notes rather than full sentences. Ask them what they will write in the spaces for questions 1 and 2 – a date and an organ or body part.

Play the recording right through – do not pause for them to write answers. Check answers after C.

Tapescript 🎧 68 (2 mins, 9 secs)

B Listen to the first part of the talk and complete the table.

Voice: The first properly successful transplant was actually carried out in a small town in Czechoslovakia, now actually in the Czech Republic, in 1905. This was a corneal transplant, a surgical procedure where the damaged cornea is replaced by donated corneal tissue. Look at the screen here and you can see some images of eyes that have been operated on in this way. OK, let's move along. Now, it was a while – just over 50 years in fact – before the next major breakthrough occurred. In 1954, in Boston, in the United States, a successful kidney transplant was undertaken. The donor and recipient were identical twins and this minimized complications. Previously, a kidney transplant had been concluded in Illinois, but the recipient's body rejected the organ ten months later.

Now, we jump on another decade to the end of the 1960s, when there were some major advances in transplant surgery. The first pancreas transplantation was performed in 1966 in Minnesota in the United States. A pancreas, along with a kidney and a duodenum, was transplanted into a 28-year-old woman. The patient was, as is the case in most instances of pancreatic transplant, a sufferer of diabetes. Her blood sugar levels decreased immediately after transplantation. Anyway, I'll let you discover more there, if that's the area you opt for.

C Give students two minutes to compare answers and discuss the format. Play the recording again, pausing at appropriate points to check answers.

Making an OHT or other visual medium of the gapped table to show on the board will enable quick, efficient feedback. Ask students how they spelt words as you go. Clarify the meaning of *donate* and revise *donor* before going onto the next part of the lecture.

Answers:

1. 1905 2. kidney 3. identical twins
4. diabetes 5. blood sugar

Refer students to the Exam tip, give them a moment to read and absorb and then ask them if they agree with the advice given – *Did having a table make the Listening task easier in any way?*

Listening 3

A 🎧 Students are now left to their own devices, though having done so much preparation work should facilitate the process significantly. Give them two minutes to look at the questions and make predictions – this is four times what they will be allowed, but since the overall aim is to become familiar with table completion, they should spend time looking at tables. Once again, you might want to point out that in the exam, a number of different task types will be integrated to assess comprehension – students will not answer 15 questions in a table like this.

Play the whole recording as students complete the task. Do not check answers as students will do so in Exercise B. Give students a moment to compare answers if you feel it would be beneficial.

Tapescript 🎧 69 (5 mins, 13 secs)

A Listen to the rest of the talk and answer the questions.

Voice: Right, in 1967, the first liver and heart transplants were performed. The liver transplant was performed by a surgical team in Colorado. It should be stressed here that success is defined as one-year post-transplantation survival – a number of transplants that ultimately failed to sustain life had previously been attempted. The world's first human heart transplant was performed in Cape Town, South Africa, in the same year, on a man called Louis Washkansky – this is him on the screen. Less than 50 years later, 3,500 heart transplants are undertaken worldwide every year.

OK – lung transplants. This is complicated as, for so long, attempts failed due to bodily rejection of the donated organ. As early as the 1940s, doctors showed that the procedure was possible, but the first operation didn't take place until 1963 and then the patient lived for only 18 days. For the next 15 years, multiple attempts at lung transplantation failed because of rejection and problems with bronchial healing. It was only after the invention of the heart–lung machine, coupled with the development of immunosuppressive drugs, that a lung could be transplanted with a reasonable chance of patient recovery. The first properly successful operation involved a heart and lung transplant, performed at Stanford University in the United States in 1981.

Over the next 15 years or so, developments revolved around further successes with the organs we've already mentioned. It was in 1998 – not long ago at all – that we move into what some might think of as futuristic territory, when the first hand transplant was carried out. Again, there had previously been many failed attempts at the surgery over a long period – the first serious attempt was as long ago as 1944. Even this success in 1998 was only partial. The recipient failed to follow the prescribed post-operative drug and physiotherapy programme and in 2001 the transplanted hand was removed at his request. A year later, a fully successful operation was concluded – the recipient has almost normal use of his transplanted hand today. Look at the image here – I'm not sure if this illustrates either of the cases I've mentioned, but it shows you just how mammoth an operation this is.

In 2005, the first partial face transplant was a success in France. Previously, a patient's own face had been reattached and you can find out more about that if you want to. I warn you, the details are a bit grizzly! Two thousand and five saw the first case of a donor transplant. Isabelle Dinoire – this is her – underwent surgery to replace her original face that had been ravaged by her dog. A triangle of face tissue from a brain-dead human's nose and mouth was grafted onto the patient. In 2007, a report 18 months after the transplant stated that the patient was happy with the results, but that the journey had been difficult, especially with respect to the response of her immune system. In 2010, the surgery moved on to a new level. A team of 30 Spanish doctors carried out the first full face transplant on a man injured in a shooting accident.

So, there we have it. I'll finish there and you decide what you want to know more about. As I say, we'll be looking at each type of transplant in more detail, but if you have done some research yourself in preparation, you'll …

B Checking and reflecting on answers is a constant feature of the skills modules. Give students sufficient time to check and think about why any answers were incorrect before moving onto C. You can decide if it would be beneficial to play the recording again, but avoid doing so simply to check individual students' wrong answers.

Answers:
1. liver   2. heart   3. one year   4. 3,500
5. 1963   6. 18 days / eighteen days
7. patient recovery   8. hand   9. 1944
10. programme   11. partial   12. France
13. her dog / a dog   14. nose   15. mouth

C Students will be used to reflecting on tasks in this way by now. Remind them that identifying what they are doing well and not doing so well is a very good way of focusing on what they can do better next time. Ask whether anyone made silly mistakes, like not using a capital letter for *France*. Allow students time to reflect and complete the exercise and then ask them if they are happy with the number of correct answers.

No discussion stage is provided in the Listening Module of this unit, but you may feel there is plenty to talk about, ask *What have students learnt from the lecture? Are they surprised / shocked by anything? What will the future bring in terms of transplants – will brain transplants ever be possible?*

Key vocabulary in context

Students should work in pairs so they can communicate as they go. Encourage them to attempt to define the words without looking at the tapescript, and then to check the tapescript to fully understand the item in context. As feedback, tell students to cover the exercise and read the definitions in the answer key as they shout out the words and phrases.

Answers:
1. the donor = person who gives organ or body part
2. the recipient = person who receives organ or body part
3. a surgical procedure = operation
4. failed to sustain life = could not keep person alive
5. the prescribed programme = programme instructed by doctors
6. was grafted onto = cut from one body part and used to repair another
7. her immune system = system in body that protects against infection

Vocabulary suggestions

- Point out that *donate* means to give something to somebody who needs it more than you do – *you donate money to charity*. We use *donor* for somebody that gives money, or gives blood – *a blood donor.*
- *Recipient* is the opposite of *donor*, as *receive* is the opposite of *donate.*
- *Surgical* is from the noun *surgery*. The person who performs an operation is a *surgeon.*
- A doctor *prescribes* medicine or he gives a *prescription* – the patient takes the prescription to collect the medicine.
- *Graft* is the verb and noun – *a skin graft.*
- If somebody is *immune to* something, they cannot be affected by it. The noun is *immunity.*

Refer students to the Workbook exercises related to this module. Choose to work on them now or set up for homework.

Reading

Objectives

- **To practise dealing with unknown vocabulary in context.**
- **To help students use words they already know to understand related new words.**
- **To provide further practice with typical IELTS Reading tasks.**

- **To introduce students to a flow chart in preparation for the Writing Module.**

Students have practised understanding vocabulary in context in each of the Listening and Reading Modules, but the skill has not yet been the main focus of a Reading Module. It is important to appreciate from the outset that the aim of this unit is to practise understanding words and phrases in context and not to learn the numerous words and phrases that are highlighted in the passages.

In this Reading Module, students will complete both exercises that practise understanding vocabulary in context (non-exam exercises) and exam practice tasks that involve exploiting the skill practised.

As previously mentioned, the theme of *health* is combined with the theme of *global warming*. *The environment* generally is a frequent IELTS theme and students need to learn related language and practise talking about it. Language from this Reading Module is recycled in later units in the course.

Reading 1

The first part of the lesson aims to introduce the overall theme of the module – *global warming*, and to focus students' attention on the need to understand vocabulary in context. Students work with three short extracts related to the overall theme – in the practice stage of the lesson, they will work with a fresh passage.

A Since students are supposed to look only at the highlighted words, and the aim is really for them to say that they do not recognize most of them, start with those words written on the board. That way, you know students are not reading around the words and working out their meaning.

Focus attention on the words students might know and which they might be able to guess from parts of the word they do know – *widespread, hospitable* and *deadly*. Select students to explain or make guesses, but do not confirm or correct.

B The aim now is for students to get the general idea of the extracts in which the unknown words occur so that they can go on to work out what they mean from the context. Make sure they understand that the aim is to identify what all three extracts are about – not to summarize each extract.

Students should spend three minutes reading the extracts individually. Do not allow the use of dictionaries. Students should summarize the overall content with a partner. Check the answer orally, but make sure it is clear.

Answers:
The extracts are about how global warming might result in the spread of disease (especially diseases carried by small insects).

C Students should spend another four minutes reading the extracts and working out the meaning of the highlighted words individually. They can then compare thoughts with a partner. Monitor to check comprehension, but do not confirm or correct until students have worked through D.

Refer students to the Exam tip and give them a moment to read and absorb. Tell them to cover it and select a student to tell the class what advice was given.

D The aim now is to guide students towards better understanding words and phrases in context. If they successfully defined most of the words previously in C, they will be able to work through this fairly quickly. If they had difficulty understanding words, this process should be very helpful, and they should spend time thinking about what they are doing.

Students should spend four minutes answering questions individually. Then, they should compare answers with a partner, redefining any of the highlighted words if necessary. Monitor and check that the process is working. Assist if and when necessary. Show an OHT or other visual medium of the extracts on the board. This will enable you to draw attention to the highlighted words and the surrounding language as you go through a feedback stage.

Note that the answer key here provides answers for D and rough definitions that students should have suggested during the process. You can give clearer definitions if you feel it is necessary.

Answers:
1. thrived (was able to exist) / roaming (moving) / hasten (make quicker) = verbs
   midges / ticks (small creatures / insects) = nouns

widespread (over a large area) / hospitable (welcoming) / deadly (able to kill) = adjectives
You know because of the words that come after them.

2. midges and ticks – students will know *mosquitoes*
3. widespread – both parts should be known / deadly – though understanding *dead* does not necessarily mean understanding the adjective.
4. various possibilities – see example below.

Example:
Parts of Europe and North America are beginning to see cases of West Nile disease, which, as the name suggests, has previously only thrived in tropical and subtropical areas.

So, *thrived* must mean *was able to exist*.

E The aim is to focus specifically on understanding new words from parts already known and understanding new uses of words already known. Note that the idea is to work without a context to aid comprehension this time – you can provide contexts as you monitor to help when students have no idea of what an item means.

Students should spend two minutes thinking about the words and phrases individually, before discussing the meaning in pairs. Monitor and give guidance ~*less* as a suffix means *without*, so what does *bloodless* mean? Make a note of clear, concise definitions that can help you give feedback. As feedback, clarify the meaning of each item, but make sure students appreciate that the aim is not to learn these words and phrases specifically.

Answers:
1. heart-stopping = very exciting / very worrying (something makes your heart stop)
2. bloodless = without violence (a bloodless revolution)
3. jet lag = tiredness due to hours spent flying
4. fighting fit = very fit – ready for a fight (from boxing)
5. my feet are killing me = my feet hurt because I've been so busy / I need a rest

Reading 2

Although students should now be more independent when working on the practice part of the skills modules, an important aim here is to provide specific practice with new words and phrases. Students will need to have some idea of what the passage is about to do that successfully, and this part of the lessons aims to prepare and motivate them to read a challenging text about a complex issue.

A Read through the instructions with students and then point out once more that, occasionally, words that refer to a very specific area of interest are given in a glossary at the end of a passage. Pronounce each of the words.

Students should complete the matching task individually, before checking answers with a partner. As feedback, read the definition as students call out the newly learnt words.

Answers:
1. c 2. a 3. d 4. b

B The aim is for students to motivate themselves and set their own gist reading task. They should work in pairs so that they can communicate as they go. Monitor to assist and make a note of questions that could be shared with the class during a feedback stage. Note that some pairs will work more quickly than others and you should have a realistic time limit in mind.

Keep feedback brief. Choose three or four students to read their questions to the class. Writing them on the board is not necessary. If students feel that they can attempt to answer any of the questions, allow them to do so.

Reading 3

A The process is the same as with the extracts earlier, though students will need to look at words in the passage rather than on the board. Give them three minutes to look at the words, telling them that, in most cases, they will simply have to admit that they have no idea what they mean.

Get some quick feedback. This will largely be a case of establishing the fact that there are a lot of unknown words and phrases in the passage, but *hosts* and *season* should be known, *neighbouring* can be guessed at from knowing *neighbour*, and other items are likely to be very similar in the students' first language.

B Tell students to read all the instructions carefully and give them three minutes to do so in silence. Tell them to use the time to understand what they are to do – not to start reading the passage.

Give them eight minutes to read the passage, concentrating on answering questions 1 and 2.

A thorough feedback stage here could be very time-consuming and students will probably now want to get on with the exam practice tasks. Tell them to spend a minute with their partner checking which of their questions are answered, and then another two minutes discussing items highlighted in the passage. They should select four or five items rather than discuss all of them. There is no need to give feedback yourself, though you could conclude by checking with the whole class whether or not they understood the highlighted items in context once they had read the passage.

C There are a number of different tasks with this passage, as there will be in the exam. Note that students have not yet completed a flow chart, but the process should be no more challenging than other gap-filling tasks. The aim of introducing it here is partly to prepare students for the Writing Module. Spend a moment looking ahead to it before students start the tasks.

Set a time limit of 12 minutes, pointing out that they have already done considerable work with the text. Give them an extra three minutes if a number of students have not completed the exercise. Remind them that answers will be found in order in the passage and that that will help them to know roughly in which part of the passage to look for information.

D Checking and reflecting on answers is a constant feature of the skills modules. Give students sufficient time to check and think about why they may have answered incorrectly.

Students might want to know why some of their answers were not correct. Explaining some points may be necessary and beneficial, but going through all of them will be very time-consuming. It is best to tell students that they will learn more about how to do these tasks and that their scores will improve.

If you do want to identify the specific parts of the passage that provide answers to any questions, make an OHT or other visual medium of the passage and highlight those parts on the board.

Answers:

1. Outbreaks   2. active   3. prevention measures (*treatment* is uncountable, so not correct)
4. 15°C   5. 40°C   6. 10°C
7. parasites and viruses   8. geographic range
9. high-risk areas   10. malaria-free
11. food resources   12. fleas   13. contact
14. B   15. C (14 and 15 in either order)

E Students will now be familiar with this type of reflective process. Point out that, once again, points are related specifically to the reading skills practised. Remind them that identifying what they are doing well and not doing so well is a very good way of focusing on what they can do better next time. Allow students time to reflect and complete the exercise and then ask them if they are happy with the number of correct answers.

Key vocabulary in context

Remind students that an effective way to learn and remember new vocabulary is to study it closely once it has been presented in context. They will be familiar with this type of exercise from the Consolidation Modules. Tell them to attempt to answer questions without referring back to the passage first. They should then check answers in the passage. As you check answers, pronounce the words for students and drill when necessary.

Answers:

1. transmission   2. abundance
3. incubation   4. seasonal   5. immunity
6. favourable

Refer students to the Workbook exercises related to this module. Choose to work on them now, or set up for homework.

Writing

Objectives

- **To familiarize students with flow charts and the type of information that flow charts show.**
- **To revise the present simple passive and to practise its typical use when describing flow charts.**
- **To present and practise typical ways of linking together a description of a flow chart.**
- **To practise writing a report based on information shown in a flow chart.**

The Writing Module in this unit concentrates on Writing Task 1. The aim is to focus on the type of language typically used to describe flow charts and there is a fairly robust emphasis on grammatical form and linking devices. The theme of surgery explored in the Listening Module is revisited and there is some recycling of core vocabulary.

Students were introduced to a flow chart in the Reading Module, but have not yet practised writing a description of one. In many respects, describing a flow chart is the easiest of the Writing Task 1 questions. It is really a case of linking together the elements of the diagram given. They do not have to think so carefully about what to include or how to organize their ideas. Some students, however, may feel that understanding the process is difficult and that using passive structures is challenging.

Writing 1

The first part of the module aims to orientate students towards a concept and cultural phenomenon that is likely to be unfamiliar.

A If possible, start by showing an OHT or other visual medium of the advertisement on the board. Gradually reveal more of the advertisement as students work out what exactly is being sold. Start with only the main heading and picture – ask students to guess what *medical tourism* means. If anyone already knows, tell them to keep it to themselves for the moment. Reveal the next line – check the meaning of *save a fortune* and so on. Make sure that you either elicit or teach the terms *plastic surgery* and *cosmetic surgery* – point out the difference between these two terms. *Plastic surgery* is surgery that reconstructs or improves appearance after injury or illness. *Cosmetic surgery* is surgery carried out to improve appearance and is carried out at the patient's own request. By the end of the process, you will have answered question 1 together.

Put students into pairs to answer the remaining questions – questions 2–4. Point out that these are the links on the advertisement and that they can find answers to 2 on the page, but will have to guess answers to 3. Set a time limit of three minutes. Keep feedback brief, outlining answers and getting a few suggestions about what more would be interesting to know.

Answers:
1. private medical operations combined with a holiday
2. modern surgery techniques at low prices / travel to exotic locations
3. (Possible) less well-trained surgeons / fewer regulations about medical procedures / operations done hurriedly or cheaply
4. Students' own answers.

B Read through the instructions with students, pointing out the alterative phrase *health tourism*. You might prefer to conduct this as a quick whole-class debate, but remember that fewer students will be able to contribute. If you opt for pairwork, set a time limit of three minutes and tell students to give reasons.

C 🎧 The principal aim of having a listening stage is to further orientate and motivate – students will understand the flow chart better having listened to the interview. The additional listening practice will be beneficial, though, and there is some further practice with guessing unknown lexis in context.

Make sure students appreciate that the gist task is to compare what they discussed with what the doctor says. Tell them they will now listen a second time to take notes. Play the whole recording.

As very brief feedback, select one student and ask what new information they learnt from listening to the doctor.

Tapescript 🎧 **70 (2 mins, 50 secs)**

C **Listen to a doctor talking. Compare what she says with your ideas in Exercise B.**

Interviewer: Now, the terms *medical tourism, medical travel* and *health tourism* were initially coined by the media. Of course the concept existed, but the labelling made far more people aware, and those terms have become quite pejorative. So, would you say this development in tourism is all negative?

Doctor: Oh, no. I certainly wouldn't say it's all negative. I think there are concerns, but not all negative … no.

Interviewer: Before we go into that, can you tell me what medical care really means? Are we talking about cosmetic surgery, for example, that doctors in the patient's own country wouldn't perform?

Doctor: No, … well sometimes yes …, but generally no. People are travelling abroad to get operations done more quickly. There are long waiting lists in many countries and this is a way to queue-jump. Let's say that someone wants a hip replacement. They could be waiting up to a year in their own country. They look round and see that they can have the operation wherever they like. What makes it even more attractive is that it can be combined with a holiday. People choose places where the operation costs very little and then spend two or three weeks on the beach convalescing.

Interviewer: Can patients have any kind of surgery?

Doctor: Pretty much. Joint replacement – hips, knees and so on, is very common, but heart surgery is also popular and dental surgery is now taking off too.

Interviewer: So, why should all this be frowned on? Is it jealousy?

Doctor: No, I don't think it's just that. Perhaps people are sceptical about the idea of combining relaxation with something as serious as potentially life-saving surgery. Perhaps they do feel there's an element of wealthy people queue-jumping. But I think also, there's a concern about the standard of care. I mean concerns about the expertise of the people performing operations. In many of the countries in which medical tourism is popular, the people actually doing the operations may not be nearly as qualified as surgeons in the patient's own country. There are many stories of surgeons performing operations outside their immediate area of expertise and of trainee surgeons undertaking the most critical surgery.

Interviewer: So, are you saying that people are putting their lives at risk by seeking medical care – even serious operations – in places that they fancy going for a holiday?

Doctor: Mm … you put it in very stark terms. I'm not sure I'd put it quite like that, but then again I can't really say that it isn't the case.

D 🎧 As students have already listened, you should not need to pause the recording for them to take notes. Tell them to use single words and abbreviations rather than complete sentences. Play the whole recording and give students three minutes to compare notes.

As quick feedback, select two students to tell you what they found most interesting or worrying. Note that discussing the words and phrases in E will mean going into more depth with the meaning of specific parts of the interview.

Tapescript 🎧 **71 (0 mins, 9 secs)**

D Listen again and make notes

[Play Track 70 again]

E Give students a moment to read through the list of words and phrases individually. Ask them if they can remember them being used or if they would like to listen to the interview again to hear them in context – the process should not be a memory test. Give them the time they need to discuss the items in pairs.

To keep feedback brief, concentrate on defining the items for them. Tell them to read the tapescript later in their own time.

Answers:
joint replacement = replacing knees / hips, etc. (Point out that joints are where one bone joins another.)

convalescing = recovering / getting back to normal
waiting list = number of patients waiting for an operation
be frowned on = not be approved of / thought of negatively (show students what *frown* means)
queue-jumping = going before other people who have been waiting longer
expertise = in-depth knowledge in a specialist area

Writing 2

Since you do not want students looking ahead to the flow chart on the page, it would be best to present A and B on the board.

A Remind students that they saw a flow chart in the Reading Module – they will almost certainly have seen them previously in one capacity or another, anyway.

Students should spend two minutes reading and completing the task individually, before checking answers with a partner. Write answers on the board for clarity.

Answers:
1. process 2. effect 3. reason 4. direction

B As previously stressed, it is essential that students do not look ahead to the chart – showing the task instructions on the board will ensure the process works far more efficiently.

Students are now accustomed to looking at the task instructions with a figure and thinking about how to approach the task. Designing the figure themselves should make a welcome change. Give them a minute or so to read the task instructions and clarify any uncertainties. Set a time limit of five minutes for students to predict the stages of the flow chart in pairs – ideally pairs should draw their own flow chart.

Monitor and check progress. Tell pairs if you think an obvious key stage is missing. Students might like to compare their charts with other pairs, but it is not necessary.

C Refer them to the flow chart to compare with their own. Give them sufficient time to study and absorb. Clarify anything that is not clear. Check that they appreciate why the flow chart forks at the point where patients tour the hospital.

D Students can either answer the questions in pairs or you can answer them quickly as a class. You can provide the answer to question 3 or wait until they have completed E and the *Grammar check*.

Answers:
1. No   2. No   3. Passive forms – particularly the present simple passive

E Note that, in this Writing Module, students do not make an attempt at writing before seeing a model. Make sure they spend at least three minutes reading the model carefully, absorbing how each step on the flow chart has been expressed and linked before engaging in the exercise. Read the instructions and make sure they appreciate that there are two simultaneous tasks.

Students should complete both parts of the task individually and then check answers with a partner. Show an OHT or other visual medium of the model on the board to ensure efficient feedback. You can either write answers and delete options yourself or select students to come to the board. Each student should deal with three or four items. Point out that 1 is an example of a reduced relative clause – it is not necessary to say *which has been arranged* – and that in 10, when two participles relate to the same subject, it is not necessary to repeat the auxiliary verb. Note that this is also possible in 7, but there is rather a lot between the two subjects. You may need to clarify the difference between some of the linking options.

Answers:
The diagram shows the stages in the process of medical tourism <u>arranged</u> by a private company. It shows what happens from when an initial request for information <u>is received</u> to when the patient <u>enjoys</u> a post-care holiday.

***First of all**, when there is a request, information about specific services <u>is sent back</u>. **When** a specific request is received, it is sent to the hospital that the company <u>thinks (is)</u> appropriate. **At this point**, the patient's medical records <u>are checked</u> at the hospital and a recommendation of what treatment is appropriate <u>is provided</u>. This is sent to the patient, together with an estimate of the duration of their stay and what the treatment <u>costs</u>. A suitable package <u>is arranged</u> and the bill <u>(is) paid</u>.*

*The patient travels to Thailand, **where** he or she <u>is met</u> by a company representative. The patient can tour the hospital and meet the medical team that will provide the treatment or perform the operation.*

*If the patient <u>has chosen</u> a pre-care holiday, he or she can **now** enjoy that before the treatment. If not, the patient <u>undergoes</u> the medical treatment directly. **Finally**, the patient can enjoy a post-care holiday before <u>returning</u> home.*

> **Grammar check**
>
> Students have already been advised about the various uses of the passive. Here it is brought up again specifically to reinforce its frequency in this type of writing task. Note that the final point about a reduced relative clause has not previously been made. Give students time to read and absorb the information.

Refer students to the Exam tip and give them time to read and absorb. You will know whether your students need practice with irregular verbs. If they do, you could write some verbs on the board as they check the participle forms in pairs.

F The aim is to focus students' attention back onto the model now that they can see a final version with all the correct options. Give them two minutes to compare ideas in pairs and then get some quick feedback.

G The aim is to conclude the lesson rather than develop an extended debate. You will know whether your students will enjoy and benefit from a small group discussion or whether a quick whole-class discussion will suffice. Whatever approach you take, encourage students to use core language learnt in the module.

Writing task

The Writing tasks are found either in the Workbook or in the Exam Practice Module at the end of the unit. In this unit, the task is in the Workbook.

Even if you decide to set the task for homework, students will benefit from a short preparation stage during which they can compare ideas and start planning.

The topic of the flow chart is closely related to the topic of the Listening Module, so they should not need too much fresh orientation. They will, however, need to make sure that what is shown is clear and check the vocabulary.

A Remind students of the importance of making sure they understand what the figure shows before they do anything else – this is as true of flow charts as any other figure.

Refer them to the task instructions and flow chart and give them three minutes to read and absorb in silence.

Make an OHT or other visual medium of the flow chart to show on the board and refer to key parts to check core vocabulary. Point out that *exploratory* is from *explore* – surgery that identifies a problem – and that *consultation* is from *consult* – a formal meeting in which a condition is discussed.

Tell students to close their books and try to remember the steps shown in the chart.

B Once they start writing their reports, take into account the time already spent preparing. They should need only 15 minutes. If they write the report at home, tell them to be strict with a time limit – they will not benefit from spending longer on the task than they will have when it comes to the exam.

When students have completed the task, they should compare it with the model composition on page 266. The model is reproduced below.

If you collect students' reports to mark, concentrate on whether the basic description of the process is clear. Look at how they have used appropriate structures and linked parts of the description together.

Model report:

The flow chart shows the stages in the process of a liver transplant. It shows what happens from the moment a patient is first referred to a hospital to the point where the operation is performed in the liver transplant unit.

First of all, when a patient is referred to the hospital, he or she attends an initial interview and then undergoes exploratory surgery at the specialist unit. Each patient's case is then submitted for discussion at a weekly meeting, where it will either be accepted or rejected. If the case is accepted, it is placed on the waiting list and the next part of the process begins. If the case is rejected, further evaluation might be agreed or alternative treatment could be suggested.

When a case is accepted, a suitable donor organ is selected. At this point, all medical checks are undertaken before there is a final consultation with the patient. Finally, the transplant is performed.

Consolidation

Instructions are given for Speaking exercises when the procedure is not clear from instructions in the Course Book. Set Vocabulary and Errors exercises either for individual completion and pairwork checking, or as pairwork when you feel immediate interaction is beneficial.

To correct errors in the final exercise, ask students to come and write the correct sentences on the board while other students offer help. You will need to write the corrections on the board to clarify.

Speaking

A Give students a minute to look at the points on the card. They should not start talking yet. Ask them if they think it is an easy topic to talk about. Establish that the speaker needs to use a range of past tenses appropriately.

B 🎧 Give students a minute to read the questions before they listen so they know what they are listening for. Note that the speaker makes a number of grammatical mistakes, but do not focus on that at all the first time students listen. Play the whole recording and give students time to answer the questions. Check answers orally, but make sure they are clear. Students might want you to write *snorkel* on the board.

Answers:
1. on holiday in Egypt / snorkelling
2. A jellyfish stung her.
3. He (a lifeguard) put fresh water on her arm.

Tapescript 🎧 **72 (1 min, 34 secs)**

B **Listen to a student talking and answer the questions.**

Examiner: OK, so are you ready?

Student: Yes, I think so. OK, … I was on holiday … on holiday in Egypt. I was swimming or more … um … you know, with a snorkel. There were lots of very coloured fishes and it was so beautiful. Suddenly … um … I felt a pain. Not a big big pain, but quite … err … well, it hurt. Then I couldn't feel one arm. I was afraid and I swam back to beach. It wasn't easy to swim when I couldn't feel one arm. I lay on the beach and I couldn't feel at all one arm and all the side of my body. I went to the lifeguard and told him. I was surprised because he laughed. He said it was a … err … a medusa … no … I mean … err … a jellyfish. He said it happened every day for someone. He put some fresh water on my arm and said I must lie and wait for it go away. It was about 20 minutes and then it went away. I didn't go back in the sea that day.

C You may prefer to conduct this as a quick whole-class discussion, but pairwork will allow more students to be involved. Give them a minute or so to discuss the point and then get some feedback. If very few students noticed inaccuracies or other elements of poor performance, play the recording again. Monitor and check points being made. Keep feedback brief, establishing that the speaker was not fluent – there was a lot of hesitancy, her pronunciation was not clear, she made a number of grammatical errors and she used some words wrongly – *coloured* instead of *colourful*, and *medusa* when she did not know the word *jellyfish*.

D 🎧 Read the instructions with students and play the whole recording. Give them a minute or so to discuss the point and then get some feedback. The aim is not to identify the correction of every error previously made. Establish that she is fluent, her pronunciation is clear, there is almost no hesitancy, she uses grammatical structures accurately and she finds the right word to express what she means.

Tapescript 🎧 **73 (1 min, 28 secs)**

D **Listen to the same student speaking again. What does she do better the second time?**

Examiner: OK, so are you ready?

Student: Yes. Well, this was about six months ago. I was on holiday in Egypt and I was snorkelling. There were hundreds of colourful fish that were swimming right round me. It was absolutely beautiful. Suddenly, I felt a pain, a sharp pain and I didn't know what it was. Then one of my arms went completely numb. I couldn't feel it at all. I was scared and I swam back to the beach, which wasn't easy not being able to feel one arm. By the time I got to the beach, I was numb all down one side of my body. There were lifeguards all along the beach and I told one of them what had happened. I couldn't believe it when he started laughing. He said it was a jellyfish and that this happened every day, at least once.

> He poured some fresh water from a bottle on my arm and told me I had to lie down and wait for the numbness to go away. It was about 20 minutes before my side started to feel normal. I didn't go back in the sea that day, I can tell you.

E Students take it in turns to talk about the points on the task card in pairs. Make sure they follow the usual procedure.

Vocabulary

A Answers:
1. in 2. out 3. after 4. under 5. in 6. to
7. at 8. to 9. to 10. on / upon

B Answers:
endangered species / balanced diet / immune system / food poisoning / joint replacement / climate change / liver transplant / queue-jumping

Errors

Answers:
1. … ever been chased …
2. … think of themselves as …
3. … do it ourselves.
4. … is received, it is sent …
5. At this point …
6. … in China, where …

Exam Practice

Listening

The Exam Practice Module aims to practise the skills practised in the Listening Module – completing a table.

A Note once more that students will not have an introductory exercise like this when it comes to the actual exam, nor will they be told what each listening section is about. The aim here is to facilitate the listening process and to motivate students to do as well as possible in the tasks.

You may feel the best approach here is to conduct a quick whole-class discussion, but remember that discussing the questions in pairs will give more opportunity for more students to contribute. Keep to a time a limit of five minutes, whether you opt for pairwork or a whole-class discussion.

B Remind students that they will only have 30 seconds to read the questions in the exam, but that here you want them to focus especially on how the table helps them to predict and that they have longer. Tell them to read points 1–3 – you might like to read through with them systematically – and then give them three or four minutes to look through the tasks. There is no need for feedback – go straight into the exam practice now.

C Play the whole recording. Check answers. You can decide if students should hear the recording again to check why any answers were incorrect.

Answers:
1. I 2. M 3. K 4. D 5. B
6. tap 7. meat 8. ice 9. bottled water
10. peel 11. (mosquito) nets 12. shutters
13. shorts 14. ankles 15. stray dogs
16. sunstroke 17. exposure

Tapescript 🎧 **74 (5 mins, 46 secs)**

C Listen and complete the tasks.

Female student:	So, the summer break's coming up soon. I take it you're both off somewhere exciting.
Male student:	Mm, well, it'd be nice, but I'm going to have to work for the first few weeks to save enough to go anywhere worthwhile.
Female student:	What about you, Tim?
Tim:	Oh, I've already saved enough. There's no way I'm studying all year and then sitting around here all summer. I'm off to Asia – India, Nepal and then on to Thailand and Vietnam.
Male student:	Wow, that sounds amazing.
Tim:	Yeah, except one thing.

Male student:	What's that?
Tim:	I've got to have my jabs this afternoon – malaria, tetanus, typhoid and hep B.
Female student:	Ouch! I hate jabs. So, is it supposed to be dangerous where you're going?
Tim:	I'm not sure *dangerous* is the right word, but it's best to be safe.
Male student:	Here look – I'm checking on my laptop. There's a site with loads of advice for students travelling to far-off places. Actually, it looks like you might be safer staying here.
Tim:	What does it say?
Male student:	Well, apart from the jabs you're having, there are several other diseases you might go down with – yellow fever, rabies and dengue fever are apparently quite common as well as those you've mentioned.
Tim:	Well, I'll just have to deal with those when I get them.
Female student:	Are you sure you need jabs for all of those? I thought most people took malaria tablets these days.
Male student:	Yes, they say here that that's an option. Mm, I didn't know you had to pay for precautionary treatment before travelling. None of this is on the NHS, then?
Tim:	No, I'm going to have to cough up a small fortune on top of all the physical pain.
Male student:	Well, speaking of small fortunes, they also insist on extensive travel insurance.
Female student:	Oh yes – that's good advice … especially if you've got an existing medical condition of any kind. You have to tell them about anything like that, or you're not covered.
Male student:	I trust that's all in order.
Tim:	Erm … I wouldn't say it was extensive. I've got insurance, though.
Female student:	So, come on then … what else should we be careful of if we go travelling?
Male student:	Well, they divide it up into a number of categories. The first category is all related to what you eat and drink. The most common complaint among travellers – students or otherwise – is a simple stomach bug.
Female student:	You mean sickness and diarrhoea?
Male student:	Yes – and there's nothing you can do about it.
Tim:	Well, nothing once you've got it, but plenty to stop you getting it in the first place. Most people just take silly risks like drinking water straight from the tap, or eating meat that hasn't been cooked properly.
Female student:	Yes, bottled water is the only sensible choice. I think everyone knows that.
Male student:	Yes, that's more or less the advice they give, but it's easier said than done when you run out of money. Something they say here, that you might not have thought about, is to stay away from ice.
Female student:	Oh yes, they'll put ice in your juice in cafes and so on, won't they?
Male student:	They also say – well in some countries anyway – that you should stay away from fruit and salad – certainly unpeeled fruit anyway.
Female student:	Oh dear, you like eating fruit with the skin on, don't you?

Tim: I'm sure I can peel it for a few weeks. I'll just have to eat lots of bananas.

Male student: The second category is about insect bites – oh, and bites from other animals.

Tim: Other animals? What like tigers?

Male student: No, like dogs, but I'll tell you about that in minute.

Female student: What do they say about insects, then?

Male student: Well, you can probably guess that mosquitoes are the biggest concern.

Female student: Will they have mosquito nets in the countries you're going to?

Tim: I think they have nets in the nicer hotels. I'm not so sure about hostels. They only protect you at night though. I'll take plenty of insect repellent – cream and sprays. I think you can get little devices that you plug into the wall too.

Female student: And don't let insects come into rooms during the day. They'll probably have shutters everywhere you stay, so you can open the windows. Even if you haven't got air con, don't leave doors open, and don't be tempted to open up the shutters. They let enough cool air in, but keep the mosquitoes out.

Male student: The most important thing really is covering up. I know it's hot in the places you're visiting, but baggy trousers instead of shorts is advisable, and socks are a really good idea, especially in the evening, apparently. However much cream you put on, your ankles are exposed under tables and so on.

Female student: So, what was it they said about dogs, then?

Male student: Oh, yes – there might be lots of stray dogs around. Don't approach or try to pet stray dogs. They're not friendly, and a bite will mean ending up in hospital … even if you've had all the right jabs.

Female student: They probably say something about staying out of the sun too, don't they?

Tim: Well, that's something I'm usually careful about – ever since I got burnt in Mexico.

Male student: Apparently, there's no such thing as a safe suntan. The bottom line is that exposure to sunshine increases the risk of skin cancer – even if you think you're tanning gradually. Young travellers spend more time at the beach and are more at risk, especially in places where they're not used to the temperatures.

Tim: Like Mexico. I've learnt my lesson.

Male student: It's not just about sunbathing, though. Very high temperatures that you're not used to can cause sunstroke. They say, gradually increase exposure to daytime sunlight. Don't go out and spend your first day walking round temples in extreme heat.

Tim: So, is that it? Can I start thinking about enjoying my trip yet?

Male student: Erm, no, we haven't mentioned accidents yet. Accidents are especially common …

D Set for homework or as a five-minute in-class exercise. If you opt for the latter, monitor to check what students have identified.

E The aim is to focus attention onto some expressions used in the Listening task. Note that students may have already highlighted these in Exercise D. Either refer them to the tapescript to check how the expression are used in context or play the parts of the recording in which they occur again. Check answers orally using the definitions below.

Answers:
1. go down with = contract / catch / get (used almost exclusively with illnesses)
2. cough up = pay for / spend (very informal)
3. the bottom line = the fundamental message

Unit 7 Workbook answers

Vocabulary development

A 1. condition = illness or ailment that constantly or regularly affects a patient
allergy = negative reaction to something you eat, breathe in or touch.
2. out of condition = not fit
under the weather = not well
3. injury = physical damage to the body (could be a wound)
wound = deep cut or hole made in flesh – involves bleeding
4. bitten = with teeth (by dog, for example)
stung = by poisonous creature (insect / jellyfish, for example)
5. transplant = operation that replaces organ or body part
graft = operation that involves using a piece of skin, bone, etc., from one part of the body to repair another
6. virus = tiny living thing that enters the body and causes disease
parasite = creature that lives in or on another creature and feeds on it
7. outbreak = sudden start of a disease affecting a large number of people
epidemic = disease that spreads very quickly and affects a huge number of people
8. moisture = small amount of water in the air or on a surface

precipitation = scientific word for water in the atmosphere (*rain*, *snow*, *hail*, etc.)
9. cure = medicine or treatment that makes a patient better
treatment = care/medicine that aims to make a patient better or improve his/her condition.
10. operation = one case of a surgical procedure (countable)
surgery = medical process during which the body is cut open (uncountable)

B 1. shape 2. weather 3. killing 4. fit 5. slope

C 1. becoming unwell 2. quick return to health
3. fresh enthusiasm 4. died 5. died

D 1. recipient 2. surgical 3. deadly 4. incidence
5. expertise 6. representative 7. consumption
8. fertility 9. irresponsibly 10. tolerance

Listening

A 1. Martin Thompson 2. 63 3. Place 4. 5RQ
5. 07789 4356496 6. Thursday, 11:15 a.m.
7. February 2011

Tapescript 🎧 **75 (2 mins, 47 secs)**

A Listen to a receptionist at a dental surgery talking to a patient and complete the form below.

Receptionist: Good morning, Albion Hill Dental Practice.
Man: Oh, good morning. I'd like to make an appointment. I haven't been in for some time now.
Receptionist: But you are a patient at the practice?
Man: Yes.
Receptionist: And the name is?
Man: Martin Thompson.
Receptionist: Hm … ah, yes … Is that Thompson with a P or without?
Man: With a P … T-H-O-M-P-S-O-N.
Receptionist: Yes, I've got you here. You're at 63 Montreal Place, aren't you?
Man: Yes, that's right.
Receptionist: Now, since you haven't been in for a while, can you just update the postcode. Some of them have changed recently. Is it still MD2 4RQ?

Man: No, it's now 5RQ. They've decided we live further out of town.

Receptionist: Yes, mine changed too. Now, I've got a phone number, but not a mobile number – have you got a mobile?

Man: Yes, but I don't know the number from memory. Hang on … it's just on the side here. … It's 0 double 7 89 4356496.

Receptionist: 07789 4356496.

Man: Uh huh.

Receptionist: Right, so do you want an appointment for this week?

Man: If possible.

Receptionist: Well, Thursday's not too full up. How about 11:15 on Thursday morning?

Man: Yes, that's fine. After I've seen the dentist, I usually see the hygienist. Can I book that now too?

Receptionist: Actually, you can't. See your last appointment was such a long time ago, the dentist will want to check and then refer you.

Man: Was it really so long ago?

Receptionist: It was February 2011.

Man: Was it really? OK, I'll sort out the hygienist when I'm in.

Receptionist: Yes, that's best. Is that all, then? We'll see you on Thursday.

Man: Oh, actually, there's something else … I nearly forgot. I want to book an appointment for my daughter.

B   8. Naomi Thompson   9. 7 / seven
10. Monday, 3:45 p.m.

Tapescript 🎧 76 (1 min, 2 secs)

B   **Listen to the patient making an appointment for his daughter and complete the form below.**

Man: I nearly forgot. I want to book an appointment for my daughter.

Receptionist: Is she on our books too?

Man: Yes, her name's Naomi.

Man: Naomi Thompson. Ah, yes, I've got her here. She's seven now,

then. That's a lovely age. My daughter's eight.

Man: Well, she's lovely some of the time. Can I make the appointment for her straight after mine?

Receptionist: Let me see. No, sorry, I can't. It'd have to be a couple of hours later.

Man: No, that's not very convenient. What about another day?

Receptionist: Erm … next Monday. What time?

Man: Well, after school's best. I don't want her to miss class time if she doesn't have to.

Receptionist: OK, I can slot her in at 3:45. Can you make it here by then?

Man: Yes, that should be ok. Thanks.

Receptionist: OK, We'll see you on Thursday and then again next Monday.

Man: OK, bye bye.

Reading

A   1. T   2. F   3. T   4. NG   5. T   6. NG
7. F   8. NG

B   swept across = moved very quickly over a large area
parish = a district with its own church (Christian)
pits = holes in the ground
ghastly = horrible
inflamed glands = glands are in your body and produce essential chemicals – *inflamed* is swollen
compulsive vomiting = *vomiting* is being sick – *compulsive* is uncontrollable
splitting = very painful / extreme (used especially with *headache*)
agonizing = extremely painful
wiped out = killed in large numbers
corpses = dead bodies
at its peak = when it had most impact
perished = did not survive / died
sealed = closed to stop exit or entry
condemning = forcing into a situation / offering no chance of reprieve
mercy = sympathy / forgiveness
cart = simple wooden vehicle
fled = escaped
vivid = colourful and dramatic
pestilence = disease carried by pests (rats, fleas, etc.)

Writing

A Model report:

The diagram shows the stages in the process of medical tourism is arranged by a private company. It shows what happens from when an initial request for information is received to when the patient enjoys a post-care holiday.

First of all, when there is a request, information about specific services is sent back. When a specific request is received, it is sent to the hospital that the company thinks appropriate. At this point, the patient's medical records are checked at the hospital and a recommendation of what treatment is appropriate is provided. This is sent to the patient, together with an estimate of the duration of their stay and what the treatment will cost. A suitable package is arranged and the bill paid.

The patient travels to Thailand, where he or she is met by a company representative. The patient can tour the hospital and meet the medical team that will provide the treatment or perform the operation.

If the patient chooses a pre-care holiday, he or she can now enjoy that before the treatment. If not, the patient undergoes the medical treatment directly. Finally, the patient can enjoy a post-care holiday before returning home.

Writing task

See notes in the Course Book Writing Module.

8 Bricks and mortar

Unit overview

The eighth unit presents language related to an overall theme of *construction* – the physical presence of buildings. The title of the unit, *Bricks and mortar*, is an expression used to express just that – *bricks*, the blocks which a building is made of, and *mortar*, the substance (cement) between, which holds the bricks in place. The topics within the general theme are varied, developing from architecture to buying property to standards of accommodation.

(Note that the phrase *bricks and mortar* is currently also used to refer to a physical, rather than an online, business – the *bricks and mortar* part of the business is the shop or other outlet where customers can go to buy things in person.)

There is clear recycling of language from one module to another within the unit. Students are presented with, and practise, specific tasks from the Speaking, Listening, Reading and Writing tests that make up the IELTS exam.

Speaking and Vocabulary

Objectives

- To practise talking about construction and architecture.
- To present and practise vocabulary that describes the aesthetic quality of buildings.
- To practise interaction typical of all parts of the IELTS Speaking test.
- To revise and practise language of obligation.

The first module aims to bring the various parts of the Speaking test together. The first part gives students an opportunity to express personal taste and exchange information about their own situation. The last part of the lesson develops the theme and practises exchanges more typical of the third part of the Speaking test.

Since the quotation at the beginning of this unit is so specific to one area of life, it would be best to orientate students to the theme before they read and discuss it. Work through Speaking 1 and then discuss the quotation once students know who Frank Gehry is.

Speaking 1

A and B The aim is to orientate students towards the general theme of the module and to prepare them to learn the vocabulary in the second part of the lesson (see Vocabulary 1C). Since students will discuss the same buildings in that part of the lesson using newly acquired lexis, keep this first stage relatively brief. Note that a range of buildings likely to provoke both positive and negative reactions has been selected – you can choose to show students different buildings.

Read the instructions with the class and give students three minutes to look at the buildings and think individually. Point out that the picture of Shanghai shows the city skyline rather than one specific building. Give them a further five minutes to talk in their group. As feedback, get a one-line impression of each image.

As an alternative, show an OHT or other visual medium of the page on the board. Start with books closed and reveal each building one by one. Discuss each as a whole class, establishing the name of the building, where it is, roughly when it was built and what the impression is. You do not need to feed vocabulary, as a whole range of descriptive language is presented in the next part of the lesson, but you should encourage students at this level to go beyond *nice, beautiful, ugly*, if possible. Show different or additional buildings as desired.

The buildings are:

a. The Bullring Shopping Centre (Birmingham, UK) – note that this is frequently cited as one of the world's ugliest buildings!
b. The Walt Disney Concert Hall (Los Angeles, USA) – designed by Frank Gehry
c. Dancing House (Prague, Czech Republic) – designed by Frank Gehry
d. the National Capitol Building (Havana, Cuba)
e. the Shanghai skyline (various buildings, China)
f. The Alhambra Place (Granada, Spain)
g. Rheinauhafen Harbour (Cologne, Germany)
h. The Grand Palace (Bangkok, Thailand)

Draw attention to the Walt Disney Concert Hall and Dancing House again and refer students to the quotation. You could show further examples of Gehry's work if easily accessible. Students should discuss the quote in pairs for a minute or two, focusing on what it means and their reaction to it. Spend another two minutes discussing it as a class.

> *Frank Gehry is a Canadian American architect based in Los Angeles, California. His buildings, including the Walt Disney Concert Hall in Los Angeles, the Guggenheim Museum in Bilbao and the Dancing House in Prague, have become tourist attractions. His works are considered to be among the most important and original works of contemporary architecture. The quotation can best be explained by breaking it into its three parts – architecture must be modern and exciting, it must be appropriate to the place where it exists, but most importantly, it must have the potential to transcend time – people should appreciate and admire it as much in 500 years time as they do at the time of construction.*

Vocabulary 1

The aim is for students to learn the new descriptive vocabulary and to then talk about the buildings again, appreciating the wider range they have

acquired. The challenge of the exercise will depend, to an extent, on their first language – you will know how many of these words are cognates.

A Read the instructions with students and make sure they appreciate that they have to decide what the three categories are themselves as they check the words and phrases. Tell them not to worry about the part of speech an item is – there are adjectives and nouns, but that should not influence the division. They should work individually and wait until the next exercise to compare ideas. Give them around ten minutes to complete the task. Monitor and assist, but do not do the exercise for them.

B Give students five minutes to discuss the exercise and to clarify the meaning of items they are unsure of. As feedback, divide the board into three columns, but do not give them headings. Get students to tell you which column each item goes in, and then decide on headings. Deal with any remaining uncertainties, pronounce and drill items when appropriate.

There are no specific vocabulary suggestions here – they are too numerous – but point out that the positive adjectives all have a general meaning of *impressive* rather than *beautiful*. Emphasize that the negative items are very negative and that though some can be used to describe other things, care should be taken – saying that a person is *hideous*, for example, is inappropriate. The adjectives in the third column can be used to describe a whole range of things.

Answers:

very positive	very negative/ugly	unusual (neutral)
magnificent	hideous	peculiar
spectacular	ghastly	weird
splendid	a monstrosity	eccentric
imposing	unsightly	quirky
grand	an eyesore	
	a blot on the landscape	

C Students can talk in pairs. Set a time limit of five minutes. Monitor to check use of newly acquired language. Feedback is unnecessary.

D Conduct as pairwork or as a whole-class discussion. If you opt for pairwork, monitor and make a note of suggestions that could be shared with the class during a feedback stage.

Speaking 2

The aim now is to develop the theme, practise interaction more typical of the third part of the Speaking test and at the same time to revise and check structures of obligation.

A By now, students will appreciate that the aim is to use questions as an opportunity to express ideas, and that they should expand and give reasons and examples.

Students should spend two minutes reading the questions and thinking individually. Then answer the questions and develop a conversation with a partner. Your feedback will depend on whether students are all from the same city or various different countries. If it is the former, briefly get a general consensus on each question. If it is the latter, select one student to give some class feedback on each question.

B Give students a minute to think about the question individually. Make sure they do not start answering it yet. Clarify the meaning of *restriction* and *level of construction* – the amount of building that goes on.

C 🎧 Students may expect to hear good and poor answers as they have done previously. Tell them that that is not the aim here – they will hear good answers, which should encourage them to give an answer of their own in a moment. They will also learn some key vocabulary related to the issue and start thinking about the topic of the Listening Module – understanding unknown vocabulary in context.

Play the whole recording, with pens down, so that students can simply listen and absorb. When they are ready to take notes, play it again, pausing briefly after each speaker to give them a moment to write. Tell them not to try to take down everything the speakers say. Give them three minutes to compare notes. Monitor and check what has been understood.

As feedback, check comprehension by asking *Which two speakers talked about construction spoiling the countryside? Which speaker talked about construction spoiling the coast?* Do not attempt to build up notes on the board.

Tapescript 🎧 **77 (1 min, 44 secs)**

C Listen to three students answering the question and make notes for each exchange.

Speaker 1
Examiner: Do you think there should be restrictions on the level of construction in certain places?
Student: Definitely. Some of the biggest cities in the world are enormous – ridiculously big in my opinion. I think the authorities must have some kind of green belt around the city where construction is not permitted.

Speaker 2
Examiner: Do you think there should be restrictions on the level of construction in certain places?
Student: Yes, I do. In many parts of my country, the coastline is ruined by overbuilding. Now, everyone knows it was a mistake to allow such levels of construction and some of it has stopped. In some places, buildings are not allowed to be over a certain height – two or three storeys, for example.

Speaker 3
Examiner: Do you think there should be restrictions on the level of construction in certain places?
Student: Well, I think authorities and town planners have a duty to make use of brownfield sites rather than

greenfield sites. I mean, they must build in the city centre where there's empty land or where buildings are derelict. In some towns in my country, building on greenfield sites is forbidden. There's a kind of green belt around the town to protect it from expanding any more.

D   🎧 Give students a moment to look at the items and then pronounce them for them. Point out the spelling of *storeys* – not *stories*. Ask students if they recognize the items from the recording, but do not deal with meaning yet. Make sure they understand that the third time they hear the recording, they are to focus on understanding these key items. Point out that they will practise this skill as the focus of the Listening Module.

Play the recording and then give students two minutes to discuss the items. Give feedback after E.

Tapescript 🎧 **78 (0 mins, 13 secs)**

D   Listen again, and then, in pairs, discuss the meaning of the words and phrases below.

[Play Track 77 again]

E   🎧 Students can choose whether or not to listen again as they read the tapescript. Check comprehension by reading the definitions below as students shout out the newly acquired items.

green belt = area around a town or city that nobody can build on
two or three storeys = levels / floors of a large building
brownfield site = parts of a town or city that have already been built on. Buildings there have either fallen down or are ready to be replaced by new ones.
derelict = no longer fit for human habitation / falling down

Tapescript 🎧 **79 (0 mins, 13 secs)**

E   Listen one more time as you read the tapescript and check your answers in Exercise D.

[Play Track 77 again]

Grammar check

There is a crossover of vocabulary and grammar with this language point. Students might not know the words *forbidden* or *banned*, but be able to use them easily once they do. On the other hand, they might know the words, but not use them accurately (see the *Watch out!* box). Give students time to read and absorb the information, making sure they look at the *Watch out!* box.

F   Students will need a little time to prepare if they are to apply the grammatical structures, as well as newly acquired vocabulary, to the questions they answer. Tell them they should answer the first question with their own ideas, but that they can use ideas from the model answers if they want to.

Students should spend four minutes thinking individually and planning answers, and then answer the questions and develop a conversation with a partner. Conclude the lesson with a quick whole-class discussion on the first question.

Listening

Objectives

- **To help students deal with words and phrases they do not know when they are listening.**
- **To help students guess the spelling of words they do not know but need to use as answers to exam questions.**
- **To give further practice listening for specific information to complete notes.**

In the Reading Module of the last unit, the focus was on understanding unknown vocabulary in context. To an extent, this module is a development of that, but it is important to understand that the strategies advised when reading do not all apply when listening. Students cannot see the word or phrase and have far less time to understand the surrounding language.

Listening 1

The first part of the lesson introduces the concept of understanding vocabulary in context. The first extract orientates students towards the theme of the practice stage – looking at a property with a view to buying it.

A The aim is to prepare and motivate students for the listening tasks that follow and to re-emphasize the need to make predictions before listening, especially if any visual support is provided. Give students three minutes to talk in pairs. Get very brief summaries as feedback – *They're on a building site – perhaps she's a surveyor; a salesman is selling something; an estate agent is showing some people a house that's for sale.* Do not feed information that students will listen for in the next exercise.

B 🎧 Read through the instructions with students and make sure they know what to do. Play the whole recording, and check answers. Do not play the recording a second time as students will listen again in a moment with a more guided task.

Answers:
1. c   2. a   3. b

Tapescript 🎧 80 (3 mins, 11 secs)

B Listen to three extracts. Match each with a picture from Exercise A. Write the letter in the space.

Extract 1

Estate Agent:	Well, this is it – The Cedars.
Client 1:	Oh, it does look nice, doesn't it?
Estate Agent:	People's first impressions of this property are always really good, and I have shown it to a few people already, I warn you. We'll go inside in a moment, but just take a closer look at some of these shrubs and bushes. Mm, I can smell that jasmine from here.

Client 2:	Those shrubs growing around by the gate, they're magnolia, aren't they?
Estate Agent:	Yes, they certainly are. The lawn is absolutely beautiful, look. Frankly, it wouldn't look out of place as the green on a top golf course. Can you see the fish pond over in the corner, there, too? I certainly wish I could get my lawn looking like this! When we've seen the house, I'll show you the back garden – believe me, it's …

Extract 2

Inspector:	Oh, hello … hello.
Workman:	Hi. Can I help?
Inspector:	Yes, I'm here from health and safety. I'm a little bit later than I planned, I'm afraid.
Workman:	Oh, right.
Inspector:	Can I just ask straightaway about that scaffolding there? I mean, has it been up long?
Workman:	Mm, I'm not sure – about a week I think.
Inspector:	Really? Well, it doesn't look as stable as it could. I noticed it as soon as I arrived. Anyway, I guess I'd better tell the right person.
Workman:	Yes, the state of the scaffolding's not really my business – you'll need to speak to the foreman.
Inspector:	Yes, of course. Where I can find the foreman?
Workman:	He's probably in his office now. That's over there, look. See the portable cabin with the blue car by it? He'll be in there. I'd take you over, but I've got to get on with …

Extract 3

Salesman:	There are a number of advantages.
Customer:	Yes, but I think I've heard them all before.
Salesman:	In a house like this, having double glazing saves you money in the long term. It may cost you money now, but I can guarantee you won't be sorry you've had it put in.

Customer:	But we've recently had the roof insulated and that was supposed to save us money. It won't save us money if we then have to have double glazing as well.
Salesman:	Well, it will. Having insulation is always a good idea. It stops heat escaping through the roof, which is the main source of heat loss. However, draughts come in through doors and windows too, and if that's still happening, you don't get the full benefit of the insulation. Good insulation and double glazing complement each other.
Customer:	Mm.
Salesman:	What's more, you're pretty near the road here. I bet you can hear the traffic most of the time you're in the house. You'd be amazed at the reduction in noise levels once you've had …

Refer students to the Exam tip and give them a moment to read and absorb.

C 🎧 Tell students that the aim of the exercise is to practise the point referred to in the Exam tip. Give them time to read through the multiple-choice options so they know what they are listening for. You may need to explain that *virtues* means *good points*. Tell them to concentrate on choosing the correct option, but to think about the key word that provides the answer. Play the recording again, pausing briefly between each extract. Check answers, but do not discuss the key word yet.

Answers:
1. a 2. c 3. b

> **Tapescript** 🎧 **81 (0 mins, 11 secs)**
>
> **C** **Listen again and choose the correct letter a, b or c.**
>
> [Play Track 80 again]

D Students should do this quietly in pairs so that they do not reveal the answer if they already

know the word. Give them a couple of minutes. Monitor and check, but do not check answers – they will be given further guidance in E.

Refer students to the second Exam tip and give them a moment to read and absorb. Tell them to cover it and then ask one student to summarize the advice.

E 🎧 Read the instructions with students and then give them time to read the gapped sentences. Tell them not to write in the words (even if they know them) until they have listened again. Play the recording again, pausing after each extract. Do not pause directly after each key word as that will negate the objective. Give students a minute or so to compare answers. Write answers on the board for clarity or show an OHT or other visual medium of the exercise and ask students to come up and write answers in the spaces on the board.

Answers:
1. shrubs 2. lawn 3. scaffolding
4. foreman 5. double glazing 6. insulation

> **Tapescript** 🎧 **82 (0 mins, 14 secs)**
>
> **E** **Listen again and write key words and phrases in the spaces. You may need to guess the spelling.**
>
> [Play Track 80 again]

Listening 2

The aim now is to provide listening practice which necessitates understanding unknown words and phrases and spelling them. Because the nature of the focus is quite challenging, students are provided with some preparation and a gist task so that they are familiar with the recording before attempting the exam practice.

A The aim is more to prepare the students for the listening content and to motivate than to provide extended speaking practice. However, during this first phase, students create their own gist task, so they will need to spend long enough on it to accomplish that. Read through the instructions with them and clarify the meaning of *renovate* – to make something old seem new again. Set a time limit of five minutes. Provide brief feedback, but be careful not to pre-teach words and phrases that are answers in the listening tasks.

Possible answers:

1. The price is usually lower. / You can renovate and decorate it to your own taste.

2. You might need to repair roof / floors / walls / ceilings, put in new electric / water systems, replace doors / windows, paint walls / doors / window frames, lay paths / patio, plant trees / shrubs / flowers.

B 🎧 Make sure students appreciate that they are listening simply to check their own ideas. They will listen again with exam tasks in a moment. Play the whole recording. Feedback is unnecessary.

Tapescript 🎧 **83 (4 mins, 1 sec)**

B **Listen to a couple talking about buying an old house and check your ideas in Exercise A.**

Jenny: Hello.

Dan: Hi, Jenny.

Jenny: Oh, hi, Dan.

Dan: So, did you go and see the house?

Jenny: Uh huh.

Dan: And?

Jenny: Pretty good. Well, as good as most of what we've seen so far. It'd certainly be worth you checking out. I've put it on the 'to see again' list.

Dan: So, where is it exactly? I wasn't really sure where Abbey Road was.

Jenny: It's where we went to that party a few months ago. You know, that friend of Steve's.

Dan: Mm, I vaguely remember the party, not the place though.

Jenny: You know when you come out of London Road station … onto London Road? Abbey Road's kind of opposite, but just to the right. You walk up about 30 yards and then it's opposite.

Dan: Oh yeah … I remember … it runs directly off London Road. So, where's the house?

Jenny: It's a little way up on the left … not far from the house with the party.

Dan: So, what's good about it then?

Jenny: Well, there's quite a lot really. It needs work, but work we could definitely do … or that wouldn't cost too much to get done. The price reflects the condition.

Dan: So, are they all semis around there?

Jenny: No, no … it's detached. There's quite a decent-sized garden. It isn't huge, but it's definitely a possibility.

Dan: Four bedrooms?

Jenny: Yeah, but the loft could easily be converted into a fifth. I looked up there. It's big enough for a bedroom with a shower room. One of the two bigger bedrooms has a nice balcony overlooking the garden too, big enough to walk out onto and maybe put a couple of chairs.

Dan: That sounds nice.

Jenny: It's got a good-size cellar too. It's been left unloved and it's a bit dark and damp, but I reckon we could dry it out and make a really useful space out of it.

Dan: That's good too. What about the state of the plumbing and the heating and so on?

Jenny: Not good. That would need a complete overhaul. The central heating system's had its day. The radiators are old and I'd say the water tank needs replacing too.

Dan: That'd be quite a big expense then.

Jenny: It would … but we'll talk about it. The whole place needs rewiring too. The electrics look quite dodgy, frankly. Plumbing and electrics would be the biggest jobs.

Dan: OK, I guess anywhere we buy will need rewiring. What about the walls and so on … you know, general upkeep?

Jenny: Not too bad. There's plaster coming away from the walls in places. It's worst in the hall. I'd say some rooms need replastering, but not necessarily from scratch.

Dan: Mm ... you know what's it's like. It's often easier to just take it all off and start again.

Jenny: Yeah, I guess so. Some floorboards need replacing too. There are a few gaps. The floors will all need to be stripped and treated, but a few boards will definitely need replacing.

Dan: OK, what about ...?

Jenny: Oh ... sorry, I interrupted ... but the roof'll need a bit of work too.

Dan: Tiles coming off?

Jenny: No, not that so much ..., though I didn't really check. It's more the chimney and guttering. The estate agent warned me that the chimney had been a bit damaged and since there's an open fire in the living room, we'd have to look at it carefully. The guttering's coming away from the roof all along the front elevation ... the drainpipe down is pretty rickety too. I think that'll all need to go.

Dan: Well, that's not a huge job. Anything we go for will probably need that sort of thing doing. I'm guessing the kitchen's pretty old too.

Jenny: Oh yeah ... well, that goes without saying. We'll need to fit a new kitchen and probably replaster it first. There are some really gross grey tiles all over the kitchen. They'll have to come off and I doubt what's underneath's very pleasant!

Dan: OK ... well, you can fill me in on anything else when I get back this evening. I guess I'd better get back and do some work now. Remind me of the price again.

Jenny: It's on for 420,000, but I'm pretty sure they'd come down. The estate agent wouldn't say it directly, but I think he knows they won't get the asking price.

Dan: Yeah, 420's a bit steep. Anyway, thanks for going and seeing it. Would it be a good idea for you to get back onto the agent again to arrange for both of us to go ...

C 🎧 Give students a little longer than usual to read the questions as they will be listening for some words that are likely to be new to them. Do not check unknown words in the notes already made – they will not need to know exactly what all of these mean to complete the task. Encourage them to make predictions, but not assumptions, as they read.

Once again, you might want to point out that in the exam, a number of different task types will be integrated to assess comprehension – students will not write answers to 14 questions on a page of notes like this.

Play the whole recording – do not pause for them to write answers. Check answers after D.

Tapescript 🎧 84 (0 mins, 9 secs)

C   Listen again and answer the questions.

[Play Track 83 again]

D Checking and reflecting on answers is a constant feature of the skills modules. Give students sufficient time to check and think about why any answers were incorrect before moving onto E. You can decide if it would be beneficial to play the recording again, but avoid doing so simply to check individual students' wrong answers. It will probably be more beneficial to listen again later as they read the tapescript. As they check, monitor and make a note of words that were misspelt.

Answers:
1. D
2. Detached   3. balcony   4. loft   5. cellar
6. central heating   7. rewiring   8. Plaster
9. floorboards   10. chimney   11. guttering
12. kitchen   13. 420   14. asking price

E Students will be used to reflecting on tasks in this way by now. Remind them that identifying what they are doing well and not doing so well is a very good way of focusing on what they can do better next time. Allow students time to reflect and complete the exercise. Ask whether anyone heard words but misspelt them or, more positively, managed to spell answers correctly without really understanding them. Conclude by asking them if they are happy with the number of correct answers.

As a brief discussion point, you might like to ask students whether they like the idea of buying an old house to renovate or whether they would prefer to buy a modern house that is ready to live in.

Grammar check

Write on the board, *We'll need to replace the water tank.* and *The water tank needs to be replaced.* and elicit the difference – active and passive. Then point out that the woman in the recording did not actually use either of these structures and elicit what she did say. Refer students to the information given and then tell them to read and absorb. Tell them to look out for more examples when they read the tapescript later to work on vocabulary.

Key vocabulary in context

Students have previously worked through a less guided *Key vocabulary in context* exercise like this so will know how to approach it. It is beneficial for them to check and learn vocabulary independently, choosing what they personally feel they need to retain. Students might ask about some of the informal expressions rather than only about language that relates directly to the topic. Tell them that there is a Workbook exercise (Vocabulary development D) that focuses on these informal expressions, amongst others, from the Listening Module.

Students should spend five minutes reading the tapescript individually and then compare noted vocabulary with a partner. Monitor to check how useful the exercise appears to be. A feedback stage is unnecessary.

Refer students to the Workbook exercises related to this module. Choose to work on them now or set up for homework.

Reading

Objectives

- **To introduce students to two types of summary completion task.**
- **To show students strategies for completing both types of summary task.**
- **To provide further practice dealing with unknown vocabulary in context.**

In this Reading Module, students are introduced to and practise two types of summary completion task – using words from the passage to complete a summary, and choosing words from a list of options to complete a summary. While the first task type demands a similar approach to tasks which require completion of sentences and notes, the second task type is different from anything they have yet practised.

The module is divided into three parts. The first part serves to orientate students towards the overall theme and provide a passage through which the summary tasks are introduced in the second part of the lesson. The second part of the lesson introduces the two task types and gives rigorous advice on approach strategies – there are more exam tips giving concrete advice on how to go about a task than has so far been the case. The third part of the lesson, as usual, practises what has been learnt through authentic exam practice tasks.

Though the two passages are quite separate, the theme of *slum accommodation* is common and ideas and language from the first passage are recycled in the second.

Reading 1

A The aim is to introduce the overall theme of the unit – *slum accommodation* – but more specifically to prepare for the first passage rather than to provide extended speaking practice. However, pairwork would be a better option than a whole-class discussion as everyone will be able to make a contribution and so be better motivated.

Start by referring students to the two pictures and ask them where they think the areas might be. Listen to suggestions and then tell students that, in fact, the first image is Haiti and the second Mumbai in India. Read through the questions with students so that you can guide and help with vocabulary as you go. Read question 1 and tell them to find the key word in a dictionary. Read question 2 and clarify *settlement* – a place where people *settle*, i.e., build homes and live. Check the pronunciation of *characterize* and explain the meaning if necessary.

Students should spend four minutes thinking and planning answers individually. Then, they should answer the questions and develop a conversation with a partner. Students will read the passage to check their ideas, but you might like to get some quick feedback before they read. Avoid a lengthy discussion that simply repeats what has already been said. Do not confirm or correct any suggested answers.

B Make sure students appreciate that they are reading the passage with the aim of checking and possibly correcting their own ideas. Tell them not to use dictionaries as they will work on vocabulary in a moment. For now, they should highlight words and phrases and longer parts of the text that relate directly to the questions and anything they suggested, even if that means guessing the meaning of some items to start with.

Students should read carefully and will need sufficient time to benefit from the process – set a time limit of ten minutes. Monitor and check what students are highlighting. Ask some individuals what they are highlighting, and why. Pairwork checking is not necessary, nor is class feedback. Students will discuss the passage in the exercises that follow. It would, however, be useful to clarify that these settlements are referred to as *slums*.

C The aim is twofold. Students will need to understand the passage in more depth to fully benefit from the summary completion practice later (some of these words are either gapped or paraphrased in the summary) and they revise the skill that was the focus of the previous Reading Module. Once again, make sure students are given sufficient time to complete the exercise properly. By now, they will know that the idea is to give definitions that show they have a rough understanding of what the items mean.

Students should spend eight minutes (one minute per item) checking the words and phrases in the passage individually. Then compare ideas with a partner. As feedback, tell students to close their books. Read the definitions below as students shout out the newly acquired words. Deal with any remaining uncertainties, though bear in mind the principal aim.

affluent = wealthy
slum dwellers = people who live in slums
shacks = simple homes (usually made from wood or corrugated iron)
alleys = narrow pathways between buildings
prone to = susceptible to / likely to be a victim of
trash = rubbish
displacement = becoming homeless / losing your home
squatter = person who lives in a residence illegally (They do not own it, nor do they pay rent.)

D Make sure students appreciate that the aim is to assess what they have absorbed – not to remember the passage word for word. They should use largely their own words, incorporating the key words and phrases they have just learnt when appropriate. Each student in a pair should answer two questions – do not allow the stronger individual in a pair to dominate. Monitor and check performance. Another feedback stage is unnecessary.

Reading 2

Refer students to the first Question-type tip and read through it with them.

A By now, students will be accustomed to discussing task types and then reading an Exam tip to check ideas. Tell them to cover the Exam tip below the summary so they are not tempted to read ahead. Read the instructions with them, but tell them not to start comparing thoughts yet. They should spend sufficient time looking at the summary in silence first. Give them three minutes to read and think.

Read the exercise instructions again together and make sure that, in pairs, they discuss strategies and not the answers. You could tell them that they are ultimately guessing what the Exam tip will say if you think that will direct them. Set a time limit of three minutes. Monitor to check ideas and make a note of anything that could be shared during feedback. As feedback, get a few ideas, but do not confirm – they will read another tip after they have done the task.

B Make sure students continue to cover the Exam tip as they complete the summary task. Students should complete the task individually, and then compare answers with a partner and reflect on any mistakes made. Show an OHT or other visual medium of the summary on the board. You can write in answers as students call them out and refer to the passage to explain or clarify anything, if necessary.

Answers:
1. characteristics   2. shacks   3. natural disasters
4. social problems   5. disease   6. trash

Refer students to the Exam tip and give them time to read and absorb. Show an OHT or other visual medium of the summary on the board and go through it one line at a time together.

- Ask which section of the passage the summary summarizes – establish that it covers the third and fourth paragraphs.
- Point out that when students first read the summary, they should have notes that all the gaps are to be filled by nouns or noun phrases.
- Highlight some examples of paraphrasing – *their characteristics vary between geographic regions / different parts of the world have different characteristics*, for example.

C and D Work through as you did with A and B – so students read the Question-type tip, discuss strategies and complete the task before reading the Exam tip that advises them on the best approach.

Answers:
1. C   2. D   3. I   4. F   5. H

Note that, once more, the Exam tip is robust and you should go through it with them, referring to the passage and task in question. Give examples of correct options being similar in meaning to incorrect options – *buildings, construction, structure* and *shelter* are all related nouns, but are not all appropriate as answers. Clearly, a task of this nature will be designed to 'trick' students – providing a list of totally unrelated options would make it all far too easy!

Reading 3

Students should now be more independent when working on the practice part of the skills modules, and only a brief orientation/facilitation stage is provided with this fresh passage.

A Tell students to look at the picture and read the heading first – ideally show an OHT or other visual medium of these on the board so that students can focus only on them to start with. Give them a moment to think and then ask where they think this is. Read the exercise instructions to confirm.

Make sure students understand that they are to use the listed features to predict passage content. Point out that if they were making general predictions without any guidance, they should organize their thoughts in this way. Run through the list of features with them, checking the meaning of *ventilation* if necessary – fresh air that passes through a building. Students should talk in pairs. Set a time limit of four minutes.

Use a feedback stage to facilitate the reading process, but do not feel that you must pre-teach a large amount of vocabulary. Make some brief notes on the board.

Possible answers:
space = There's very little space/room. / Rooms are tiny. / Inhabitants share a small space. / They are living in cages like animals.
furniture and facilities = Furniture is basic / broken. / They have only a bed. / Facilities don't work. / Perhaps there's no electricity.
heat / ventilation = It's very hot / stuffy / airless. / It might be cold at night.
cleanliness = It's dirty. / Perhaps there's no running water. / There might be rats and cockroaches.

B Set a strict time limit of four minutes to skim/scan the passage, checking ideas. As feedback, tell students to close their books and ask two students to tell the class one thing each that stood out for them.

C Set a time limit of 12 minutes, pointing out that they have already prepared and skimmed the text. Give them an extra three minutes if a number of students have not completed the task. You can decide if students will benefit from comparing answers with a partner before checking the answer key.

D Checking and reflecting on answers is a constant feature of the skills modules. Give students sufficient time to check and think about why they may have answered incorrectly.

Students might want to know why some of their answers were not correct. While going over each answer individually will be fairly time-consuming, it will probably be beneficial with this first attempt at summary completion. Show an OHT or other visual medium of the passage on the board and refer to it as you check answers in the summary. To start with, you can blow up the relevant parts of the passage – the fifth, sixth and final paragraphs for the first summary, and the first, second and fourth paragraphs for the second summary. Point out how language is paraphrased around each answer and how in the second task, options could easily be confused.

Answers:

1. Chinese rule   2. economic boom
3. refugees   4. units   5. more affluent (just *affluent* is acceptable)   6. new tenants
7. J   8. E   9. N   10. L   11. B   12. F

E Students will now be familiar with this type of reflective process. Point out that once again, points are related specifically to the reading skills and task strategies practised. Remind them that identifying what they are doing well and not doing so well is a very good way of focusing on what they can do better next time. Allow students time to reflect and complete the exercise and then ask them if they are happy with the number of correct answers.

Key vocabulary in context

Remind students that an effective way to learn and remember new vocabulary is to study it closely once it has been presented in context.

Here, students learn independently but are directed to the type of language they should focus on. Point out that while the passage is factual, it is written in a colourful, rather dramatic style to have maximum impact. Refer students to the list of items and run through them. Ideally, refer to them on an OHT or other visual medium of the passage

that is on the board. Pronounce each item and clarify meaning if necessary (see below).

damp = a little wet
meagre = small in quantity / not generous
stuffed under his pillow = the implication is that there is nowhere else to put them – *stuffed* implies that they are not cared for like most people's clothes
cramped = too small

Set a time limit of five minutes for students to read again and make notes individually. Then allow them three minutes to check lists in pairs. Monitor to check whether lists have been made logically and usefully. As feedback, write a selection of the words and phrases on the board, checking meaning and pronunciation as you do so.

Possible answers:

roughly constructed / rusty / crawl / the draught from holes / filthy / wet / broken / abandoned / below the poverty line / worsening deprivation / downtrodden / vulnerable / unacceptable hardship / paltry / bleak / at the very thinnest end of the wedge

Refer students to the Workbook exercises related to this module. Choose to work on them now or set up for homework.

Writing

Objectives

- **To improve students' awareness of appropriate style and register in discursive compositions.**
- **To present and practise fixed expressions that introduce opinion.**
- **To revise various features that contribute to a well-written discursive composition.**

The Writing Module in this unit concentrates on Writing Task 2. The principal aim is to focus on issues of style and register and on introducing opinions appropriately, but various aspects of good composition writing are also revised. The overall theme allows recycling of language introduced in the first module.

Writing 1

The first part of the module aims to orientate students towards the theme and to present the Writing task they will subsequently work with.

A The principal aim is to prepare for the writing focus, rather than to provide extended speaking practice. Though students should be encouraged to develop a conversation, you may like to have a clear time limit in mind (six minutes, perhaps).

Students should spend three minutes looking at the pictures, thinking and planning answers individually. Then spend another three minutes answering the questions in pairs. Monitor to check that students are discussing points that will help them tackle the exercises that follow and guide them when necessary.

Keep feedback brief and concise, ideally just getting *yes/no* answers to the questions. Students might like to know more about the pictures. On the left is the Swiss RE building (known informally as 'the Gherkin') in London and on the right is the Old State House in Boston.

B Refer students to the Writing task instructions and read the question in the rubric with them. Give them a minute to read through the task instructions and check they understand everything. Revise *historic* – old and important culturally. Point out that the statement is worded strongly and that the question then asks whether the reader approves or disapproves – students might feel that the question invites them to disapprove, though they certainly do not have to. Get a general consensus as to whether it is a writing task students feel confident about.

Note that, in this Writing Module, there is no stage where students discuss possible composition content. They may be pleased about that, but you may feel it is something they need more practice with. If so, spend five minutes together brainstorming possibilities – *Why are old buildings pulled down? What is built instead? Why should it be beneficial? Who is negatively affected? Aren't new buildings today, historic buildings of the future? Whose responsibility is the protection of old buildings?*

Writing 2

In the second part of the lesson, students will compare two model compositions. Make sure they do not look ahead and read the second improved composition before they have worked with the first.

A Tell students to cover B (the teacher's comments) before they read the model composition. They have previously assessed compositions written by students but have, until now, been given more guidance and direction as to what to look for. Here they work more independently, deciding for themselves what the strengths and, more importantly, the weaknesses are. Be aware that some students might find this challenging.

Give students just two minutes to read the composition, and then ask whether they think it is good, quite good or not so good. Do not confirm or give your own opinion. Tell students that later they will see what a teacher said about the composition, but now they are going to say more about what they think.

Students should spend five minutes reading and making notes individually and then another three minutes comparing their assessment with a partner. Monitor to check what they are saying, but do not give any feedback before they see the teacher's comments.

B Read through the rubric with students. Note that some students may not feel comfortable putting themselves in the teacher's shoes, but it is fairly easy to see which of the comments are totally unfair. Keep in mind that the aim is to draw attention to aspects of composition writing – not to get all the answers correct in this exercise. You could point out that it is unrealistic that this student would make no spelling or grammatical mistakes – however, the aim here is to focus on other aspects of good writing.

Students should spend ten minutes (a minute per comment) completing the exercise individually. Then, they should spend another three minutes comparing their assessment with a partner. As initial feedback, simply tell students which comments are certainly fair – write the numbers of the comment on the board. This will prepare them to work through C.

Answers:

1. U – The composition is easy to follow. Points are made too strongly and rather randomly, but the message is clear.
2. F (*... and I find this really shocking,* early in the first paragraph)
3. U – Every point made is relevant.
4. U / F – This is probably unfair. Points are expressed rather too randomly, which suggests a lack of planning, but ideas are organized fairly well – the train of thought is easy to follow.
5. F (See point 6 + whole of final paragraph.)
6. F (*... the biggest of these constructions are complete eyesores!*)
7. U – Topic sentences are used to organize thoughts.
8. F – See Writing 3.
9. U – See comment in notes above.
10. F – (*It's terrible that ...*)

C Give students three minutes to work individually. They should have already identified examples if they worked properly through B. Give them another two minutes to compare with the same partner.

To ensure that feedback is efficient, show an OHT or other visual medium of the comments on the board. Go through them, clarifying and giving examples. Emphasize that points 5 and 6 are especially relevant in terms of what this writer does well and not so well.

Answers:

See answers above for 2 / 5 / 6 / 8 / 10

D Students should be keen to read the improved composition. They should not worry about the highlighted expressions for now. Give them time to read and then start comparing thoughts with a partner. Monitor and make a note of salient points that could be shared during a feedback stage.

As feedback, show an OHT or other visual medium of the composition on the board. Draw attention to the most obvious improvements – a balanced introduction that shows the writer fully understands the issue and appreciates that there are two opinions / better use of topic sentences to organize thoughts / points and opinions expressed in a more sophisticated way / opinions introduced with suitable expressions / opinions expressed more appropriately / a concluding paragraph that both summarizes and concludes.

Writing 3

A Use the OHT or other visual medium of the composition that is on the board. Tell students to cover all of B or they will be tempted to look ahead. Look at the first introductory word *unfortunately* together. Ask a student to explain its use. If that explanation is not clear, ask another student. Establish that *unfortunately* is used to introduce a negative point and that it means something like *sadly* or *it's a shame that*.

Students should spend two and a half minutes reading and thinking individually and another five minutes discussing with a partner. Monitor and check ideas, but do not confirm or correct. The exercise that follows develops and gives further guidance. Check to see if students are using any of the alternatives in B as they talk.

B Refer students to the list of alternative words and phrases and give them a moment to read and absorb. Read through the instructions with them and make sure they know what to do. Since you have already suggested *sadly* as an alternative to *unfortunately*, don't use it as an example here. Use *Personally* as another example, pointing out that the whole introductory line would change to, *In my opinion, it is sad when ...* Students should work in pairs so that they can communicate and compare knowledge as they go.

Refer to the composition as you check answers. Clarify any remaining uncertainties and point out changes that need to be made to accommodate an alternative in the existing model (see additional guidance below).

Answers:

1. In my opinion = Personally (See change suggested in example above.)
2. Of course = I admit (Of course, new buildings are ...)
3. Sadly = unfortunately
4. Significantly = importantly
5. To sum up = In conclusion
6. Possibly = Perhaps (When we pull down a magnificent old building, we possibly show ...)

7. To my mind = Personally (To my mind, it is sad when ...)
8. Regrettably = unfortunately
9. All in all = In conclusion
10. Crucially = Importantly
11. It goes without saying = I admit

Refer students to the Exam tip and give them a moment to read and absorb.

C Students should spend six minutes writing individually and then three minutes comparing sentences with a partner. Note that if you want students to think more carefully and fully benefit from this practice exercise, it may be better set for homework. Students can then compare at the start of the next lesson.

Grammar check

The passive has been the focus of a number of *Grammar checks* already. The aim here is to practise recognizing and labelling complex passives, which will be essential when reading authentic academic texts. Students should start thinking about whether they would feel confident using them in compositions of their own. Give students time to read and absorb the information and to think about the forms used in the examples. Give them three minutes to discuss and label in pairs. Monitor to make a note of who can best provide feedback. Write answers on the board for clarity.

Answers:
A passive *~ing* form or passive gerund / a passive infinitive after a modal verb / a passive infinitive expressing a future intention

Watch out!

On this occasion, in the same pairs, students should correct the sentences in the *Watch out!* box.

Answers:
A new school is to be built.
It means more houses being built.

Writing task

The Writing tasks are found either in the Workbook or in the Exam Practice Module at the end of the unit. For this unit, the task is in the Workbook.

Even if you decide to set the Writing task for homework, students will benefit from a short preparation stage during which they can compare ideas and start planning.

The topic of the discursive composition is very similar to that in the Course Book, so students should not need fresh orientation. They will, however, almost certainly need some guidance with what to say. You may feel that students should now be more independent in terms of deciding what points to make, but remember they are still finding it difficult to express sophisticated ideas in English, let alone expressing them if they have nothing to say! You will know whether or not your students are likely to have opinions on the topic and you can decide how much assistance to give with possible content.

A Give students time to read and absorb the Writing task instructions. Point out that, again, the statement is quite forceful and students might feel that they are invited to disagree. Check the meaning of *appealing* – pleasant to look at – and *ruined*. Point out also that while it is perfectly acceptable to agree with a rather contentious statement, it is probably more difficult to find supporting arguments, and a more balanced approach is usually a better option. Give students five minutes to read through the points and think. They should make notes if they want to.

B Students spend another five minutes comparing ideas with a partner or in small groups. Encourage them to make notes now – they should use shared ideas to plan their composition.

If you feel your students are struggling for ideas, conduct a feedback stage, during which as a class you brainstorm ideas that answer questions 2 and 3 in Exercise A. Look ahead to the model for arguments that you could suggest. If you feel that your students have enough to say, skip a feedback stage and let them start writing.

C Once students start writing their compositions, take into account the time already spent preparing. They should need between 25 and 30 minutes. If they write at home, tell them to be strict with a time limit – they will not benefit from spending longer on the task than they will have when it comes to the exam.

When students have completed the task, they should compare it with the model composition on pages 266 and 267. The model is reproduced below.

If you collect students' compositions to mark, concentrate on what has been the focus of the Writing Module – organizing points logically and introducing and expressing opinions appropriately. You will want to start correcting more of the composition content, but remember that correcting every sentence will not be very motivating.

Model composition:

These days, it is common to hear people, especially older people perhaps, complaining that modern buildings are ruining the appeal of town and city centres. They claim that modern architecture is ugly and that buildings are out of place in historical centres close to magnificent old buildings and beautiful squares. Though I understand this view and appreciate that there is some truth in it, I tend to disagree.

First of all, it is important to remember that when many of these magnificent old buildings were built, they were probably seen as modern and unsuitable for the existing city landscape. People flock to Barcelona to see La Sagrada Familia, *but many people would say that it is an ugly building. When the Eiffel Tower was built, there was uproar that such a hideous construction would ruin the beauty of Paris.*

It is probably true that less time and money is spent on the construction of buildings nowadays. Centuries ago, it took years to build and furnish a cathedral and that is simply not possible now. However, that does not mean that modern buildings are ugly. In cities from London to Shanghai, there are wonderful examples of architecture that generations of people will grow to love. Modern buildings like airports will be viewed as works of art in the same way that medieval town halls and churches are today.

Certainly, I agree that some modern constructions like tower blocks and leisure centres do little to add to the appeal of the urban landscape, but generally speaking, I feel that it is unfair to claim that modern architecture is ruining cities.

Consolidation

Instructions are given for Speaking exercises when the procedure is not clear from instructions in the Course Book. Set Vocabulary and Errors exercises either for individual completion and pairwork checking, or as pairwork when you feel immediate interaction is beneficial.

To correct errors in the final exercise, ask students to come and write the correct sentences on the board while other students offer help. You will need to write the corrections on the board to clarify.

Speaking

The aim is to provide more focus on and practice with sounding natural and interested rather than abrupt and disinterested. The point develops the one made in the Writing Module about expressing opinions too forcefully.

A 🎧 Give students a moment to read through the exchanges and then play the whole recording. Ask the class what they think. Try to elicit responses like *abrupt, rude, not friendly* and so on.

> **Tapescript** 🎧 **85 (0 mins, 55 secs)**
>
> **A** Look at the exchanges between an examiner and some students. Listen to the students answering the questions. What do you think about the students' answers?
>
> 1
>
> **Examiner:** So, tell me about a part of your city that you like.
>
> **Student:** I don't like any part of my city. It's a horrible city.

2

> **Examiner:** So, Paris must be a lovely to place to study. You're very lucky.
>
> **Student:** No, it's overrated. Everything's too expensive for a student like me.

3

> **Examiner:** What do you think of that amazing new museum they've just built?
>
> **Student:** I hate it. It's a blot on the landscape.

B 🎧 Make sure students understand what they are listening for. Play the second recording right through, simply allowing students to listen and absorb. Play it again, pausing after each exchange to get and give feedback. Establish that the students still express a negative idea and challenge the examiner's view, but do so in a far more appropriate manner. Answers are fuller and the speakers adopt a far more friendly tone. There is no need to identify the introductory expressions that speakers use as students will do that independently when they check the tapescript in Exercise C.

Tapescript 🎧 **86 (1 min, 03 secs)**

B **Listen to these students answering the questions again. How are their answers better?**

1

> **Examiner:** So, tell me about a part of your city that you like.
>
> **Student:** Actually, there are not many parts of my city that I really like. To tell you the truth, I'm getting bored of it and I'll be glad to move away next year.

2

> **Examiner:** So, Paris must be a lovely to place to study. You're very lucky.
>
> **Student:** Mm, yes and no. Of course, there are some amazing buildings and the tourists love it. For a poor student like me, though, everything's a bit too expensive.

3

> **Examiner:** What do you think of that amazing new museum they've just built?

> **Student:** Mm, if I'm honest with you, I'm not very keen on it. Some people say it's a blot on the landscape.

Refer students to the Exam tip and give them time to read and absorb. Ask them if they can remember any words or expressions used to introduce a disagreement during the exchanges. Do not confirm or write suggestions on the board – they can check the tapescript.

C 🎧 Refer students to the tapescript and give them time to read and highlight. Listen to the recording once more. Monitor to check that they highlight useful language. Show an OHT or other visual medium of the exchanges on the board and highlight the items that students should have noticed.

Tapescript 🎧 **87 (0 mins, 11 secs)**

C Look at the tapescript and listen again.

[Play Track 86 again]

D Students should practise the exchanges once with books open and then again with books closed to assess what they have absorbed and retained.

Vocabulary

A **Answers:**
1. unsightly   2. imposing   3. permitted
4. plush   5. boom   6. rusty

B **Answers:**
1. to   2. into   3. to   4. on / upon   5. into   6. for

C **Answers:**
1. Illiteracy   2. powerless   3. reportedly
4. spectacular   5. unacceptable

Errors

Answers:
1. Smoking is not allowed in … / You are not allowed to smoke …
2. Speaking during the exam is forbidden. / You are forbidden to speak …
3. … need replacing.
4. … divided into cages.

5. ... to be collected at ...

6. ... changes being made.

Exam Practice

Reading

The Exam Practice Module aims to practise both types of summary completion introduced in the Reading Module. It also aims to practise working on a passage that is more about a very specific area of interest than most of the reading passages have been up to now (see Exam tip at the top of the first page in the Course Book). With this in mind, there is a more robust preparation stage.

Note that students must not look ahead and read the passage until they have completed C, which focuses on topic sentences.

Start by referring students to the Exam tip. Read just the first line and then refer them to the pictures. Ask them to guess what the passage will be about and if they think it will be interesting. Do not worry if they say *no*. Allow them to read the rest of the tip. Point out once more that technical words and phrases are occasionally defined in a glossary at the end of the passage – not, however, when their meaning can easily be deduced or when they are used as answers.

Note that the advice given here does not apply only to summary completion. Generally speaking, passages in this Course Book have been chosen because the subject matter is likely to be of general interest to a range of students. The passages are likely to motivate and provoke a degree of discussion. Some of the passages in the exam itself are likely to be of a more specific nature and hence less likely to be of real interest to the majority of students. When asked what they find especially challenging about the IELTS Reading test, a high percentage of students identify unfamiliarity of topic as a major issue. They feel daunted by the fact that passages are about subjects they know nothing about. While it is hoped that the subject of this Exam Practice will be of some interest to your students, the aim is to provide authentic practice and not to inspire them.

A Refer students to the pictures again and then to the title of the passage (make sure they do not start reading the passage). Reassure them that they are not expected to understand the title. Refer them to the three questions and again emphasize that they are not expected to know answers – the idea is to guess and deduce.

Students should spend three minutes reading the questions and thinking individually. Then, they should spend three minutes answering the questions with a partner. Use feedback to facilitate the reading process. Get suggestions from the class and develop ideas, making notes on the board.

Possible answers

1. covering pieces of wood with some kind of plaster
2. It looked attractive. / It was strong. / It was flexible.
3. It is visually appealing. / It preserves traditional building techniques. / It is part of our heritage.

B The aim is to further facilitate reading a challenging passage, but also to revise the use of topic sentences and reinforce their importance. Make sure students understand that the seven sentences are the topic sentences from the paragraphs of the passage they will read. Point out that at least half of the boxed words are very specific to the area of interest and they will have to use dictionaries. Note that some students will have dictionaries that do not include all the words – *infills*, in particular. As you monitor, tell them you will explain during feedback.

Students should spend seven minutes completing the task individually and another three minutes comparing answers with a partner. Students will be able to check their answers as they read the passage, but it would probably benefit them to see the completed topic sentences before they read. Go through answers orally, clarifying the meaning of any gapped words if necessary, but not the meaning of the complete sentences.

Answers

1. timber (wood / wooden)
2. infills (material used for filling)
3. movement

4. panels (areas of a material – glass, wood, plaster, etc. – that make up a surface in a building)
5. limewash (wash with a special substance)
6. gables (parts of a roof)
7. damage

C Give students just a minute to discuss in pairs what they can predict about the passage. Feedback is unnecessary.

D Although students have been prepared for the passage, they will need at least another 20 minutes to complete the tasks. They will not have to answer 20 questions on one passage in the actual exam. Note also that, in the exam, multiple-choice questions will usually apply to one part of the passage and will not involve reading the whole passage again, as is necessary here. You may decide to go over answers to the summary completion tasks and then set questions 17–20 as a follow-up task.

You can decide whether students should compare answers before you give feedback. Write answers on the board for clarity or provide them with a copy of the answers.

Students might want to know why some of their answers were not correct. Explaining some points may be necessary and beneficial, but going through all of them will be very time-consuming. It is best to tell students that they will learn more about how to do these tasks and that their scores will improve.

If you do want to identify the specific parts of the passage that provide answers to any questions, make an OHT or other visual medium of the passage and highlight those parts on the board.

Answers:
1. character 2. materials 3. matrix 4. staves
5. withies 6. lime plaster 7. concealed
8. structural movement 9. insulation
10. blotting paper 11. I 12. F 13. L 14. B
15. O 16. M
17. b 18. d 19. c 20. a

E The aim is to conclude the lesson rather than develop an extended debate. You will know whether your students will enjoy and benefit from an extended pair or group discussion, or whether a quick whole-class discussion will suffice. Whatever approach you take, encourage students to use core language learnt in the module.

Unit 8 Workbook answers

Vocabulary development

A 1. rusty 2. affluent 3. derelict 4. meagre
5. macabre 6. plush 7. damp 8. hideous
9. cramped 10. flimsy

B 1. f 2. d 3. h 4. b 5. g 6. c 7. a 8. e

C 1. f 2. c 3. a 4. d 5. h 6. e 7. b 8. g

D 1. place 2. out 3. day 4. in 5. down
6. steep

E 1. it wouldn't look out of place = it is good enough to be …
2. checking it out = taking a good look at it
3. has had its day = is past its best
4. fill me in on = give me the details
5. come down = lower their asking price
6. a bit steep = too expensive / more than it's worth

Listening

A Exchange A = 3   Exchange B = 1
Exchange C = 4   Exchange D = 2

Tapescript 🎧 **88 (6 mins, 12 secs)**

A **Listen and match each social exchange with a situation. Write the number of the situation as your answer.**

Exchange A
Woman: Hello.
Student: Hello, I'm phoning about the place advertised in *The Gazette*. Is it still available?
Woman: Yes … well, I think so, anyway. Some people saw it yesterday, but they haven't got back to me.
Student: Oh that's good. I expected it to be gone. Places are going so quickly now term's started. I know there are four bedrooms, but there are actually five of us looking. Are any of the bedrooms big enough to share or could the dining room be another bedroom?

Woman: Mm, there isn't really a separate dining room – it's part of the living room. The biggest bedroom is quite big, but there's only one bed. You'd have to get another bed yourselves and it'd be a bit of a squash with five in the house. I think we'd have to talk about that.

Student: OK, well we can decide on that if we come over and take a look. It might depend on the number of bathrooms – five of us trying to share one – especially when we're all getting ready in the morning – might be impractical.

Woman: There's only one bathroom, but there's a cloakroom downstairs. I'm afraid you would all be fighting over the bathroom.

Student: And is there any outside space – I mean some kind of garden?

Woman: There's a small yard. It's been paved over and there are a few shrubs in pots. It's not really a garden, though.

Student: That's fine – as long as there's somewhere to sit out when it's nice. Anyway, I think the best thing is to come over and see it. Would this evening be OK?

Woman: Mm, let me think. I'm busy till six, but I could get over there by about half past. Does that suit you?

Student: That'd be fine. Lorna Road's near the church on West Hill, isn't it?

Woman: Yes, that's right. It's number 35. If you wait outside, I'll see you there. Will you all be coming?

Student: I'm not sure. Probably not – but three or four of us perhaps.

Woman: OK. I look forward to meeting you all. Bye.

Exchange B

Male: So, this is the Court of the Lions. I've heard about this part.

Female: Yes, I've been reading a bit about it – it's one of the most important parts of the whole palace.

Male: So, tell me about these lions then.

Female: This is the Fountain of the Lions. There are 12 of them and, apparently, they represent strength and courage.

Male: They're not very big, though, are they? I mean, you'd expect them to be a bit more imposing.

Female: I don't know about that.

Male: So, what are they made of … marble?

Female: Yes, they're made of marble. The basin of the fountain's alabaster, but the lions are marble.

Male: Well, you certainly did do a bit of reading up. I wouldn't have expected you to know what the basin of a fountain was made of. Perhaps I should've made a bit more effort …

Exchange C

Interviewer: So, how did you decide to go into this particular line?

Architect: It was all very natural. Teachers and family friends recognized from an early age that I had talents that seemed to combine both science and art. I was drawing plans of buildings and town layouts as a hobby – rather a strange one, I guess – from the age of ten.

Interviewer: So, tell us what you really do. I mean, it's not just about drawing a plan is it?

Architect: No, there's far more responsibility than that and the role changes as the project develops. To start with, it's all about making sure that the plan allows the client to envisage the finished building. They want to know exactly what it's going to be like – not wait until it's finished and then be horribly disappointed. It's the architect's job to organize and manage the engineers and the various designers involved in the project right through the process.

Interviewer: What is it you enjoy most about what you do?

Architect: There's huge satisfaction as a project comes to fruition and you realize that what you've achieved will have an impact on people's lives. I wouldn't enjoy doing this nearly so much if it were just an art form – I mean, if people simply looked at and admired my work. For me, the joy is creating something that'll be used by people.

Interviewer: Tell us about some of your favourite buildings.

Architect: Mm, that's difficult. There are so many …

Exchange D

Interviewer: What exactly is the difference between green building and conventional building?

Owner: I think it's all about using common sense. Too much construction focuses on the finish – I mean the aesthetic appeal – what the building looks like both inside and out. For us, the central issue is always the structure and systems – how the building is built. Green building means optimizing the infrastructure – the power, the heat and the water systems – and making the most of natural daylight to ensure efficient use of resources.

Interviewer: What are a couple of concrete examples?

Owner: Well, take water. Hot and cold water should be provided from a single trunk line. Branch lines should be minimized. Hot water pipes should be insulated to the point of use. That's not usually the case with most construction.

Interviewer: And is recycling and reusing an important aspect of this?

Owner: Absolutely. We reuse materials whenever we can. Timber off-cuts are used for smaller jobs – many builders throw so much away. If we can't make use of materials on a current site, we'll store it for …

B Exchange A:
1. 4   2. dining room   3. cloakroom   4. yard
5. 6.30 p.m.   6. 35

Exchange B:
1. 12   2. strength   3. courage   4. basin
5. marble

Exchange C:
1. science   2. hobby   3. client   4. engineers
5. designers   6. impact

Exchange D:
1. structure   2. systems   3. natural daylight
4. trunk line   5. hot water pipes   6. timber

Tapescript 🎧 89 (0 mins, 11 secs)

B Listen again and in each case, complete the notes.

[Play Track 88 again]

Reading

A 1. B   2. B   3. A   4. C   5. E   6. B   7. A   8. D

B 1. office blocks   2. economic boom
3. colonial era   4. vast   5. fleeing   6. partitioned
into   7. affluent

D 1. thatcher   2. the lifespan   3. stack   4. aerial
5. fixings   6. vermin   7. moss   8. the eaves
9. rot

Writing

A 1. a) ✗
    b) ✓
    c) ✗✗
2. a) ✗✗
    b) ✗
    c) ✓
3. a) ✓
    b) ✗
    c) ✗✗

B Possible answers:
1. Personally, I think the new museum in my city could be more visually appealing.
2. It is regrettable when modern buildings with little aesthetic appeal are built in pretty town centres.
3. In my opinion, there are modern sculptures in many cities that are far more interesting than historic statues.

C (as in the Course Book Writing Module)

Personally, I find it sad when an interesting old building is destroyed and I think it should always be the last option. Preserving historical buildings and monuments is one way of passing our history on to the next generation. Children learn from visiting these buildings and develop an interest in and respect for the past. Perhaps when we pull down a magnificent old building, we show a lack of respect for the architect and his work.

Writing task

See notes in the Course Book Writing Module.

Review 2

Overview

The review units are very much reviews rather than revision units. The aim is for students to consolidate what they have learnt about the IELTS exam and how to go about getting the grade they require. There are exercises which are purely designed to encourage students to reflect and discuss, and there are exercises which consolidate and have correct answers. Teacher instructions for the review sections are brief as the aims and procedure for each exercise are largely self-explanatory.

Speaking and Vocabulary

A Give students three or four minutes to discuss the questions in pairs and then go over answers as a class.

B The aim is to practise typical exam questions and assess whether or not students have gained in confidence. Students should not allow their partner to see the questions they ask. Encourage them to practise asking for repetition if they do not catch something in the question. Monitor carefully and check students' performance. Do not go through each question as feedback as it will be repetitive and not beneficial.

C Give students a moment to look at the web and then read through the headings with them. Start by telling them not to look back at the Course Book units to see what they have retained. After five minutes, allow them to look back, adding words and phrases from the unit. Encourage them to do this in order to store new language rather than simply fulfil a task.

Listening and Reading

A Students should complete the exercise in pairs and share knowledge as they go. Answers can be checked orally, but make sure they are clear.

Answers:
1. third / two
2. summary
3. answers / paraphrased
4. grammatically
5. repeat

6. organized / topic
7. context / spelling

B Work through as with A.

Answers:
1. topic / supporting
2. headings / heading
3. opinion / knowledge
4. meaning
5. text or passage / list / relevant
6. speech

C Suggest that students read all questions, think and answer individually and then compare ideas with a partner. Give them around eight minutes to read and make choices and another six or seven to discuss them.

Note that pairwork gives everyone the opportunity to talk about their strengths and weaknesses – a quick whole-class feedback stage will not allow that. The benefit here is in identifying strengths and weaknesses and discussing them. No solutions can be offered to each student individually right now.

Writing

A 🎧 Make sure students understand that they will listen to an examiner and that she will talk about the Writing test. Read through the interviewer's question with them and give them a moment to read the statements that follow. Play the whole recording as students answer and then again, pausing appropriately to check answers.

Answers:
1. F   2. NG   3. T

Tapescript 🎧 90 (2 mins, 24 secs)

A Look at the interviewer's first question and then listen to the first part of the interview. Mark the statements below (T) true, (F) false or (NG) not given.

Interviewer: Do students tend to do better in Writing Task 1 or 2?

Examiner: Mm, that's difficult to say because, of course, the second task carries more marks and students have more time to write it. There are students who practise writing reports and know how to do them very well. Their reports are well-organized and easy to read. In contrast, they find the composition more of a challenge. Perhaps they don't know quite what to say and they don't organize ideas well. However, they actually score slightly better for the second task because the whole idea is that it's more challenging.

Interviewer: So, it's a question of balance?

Examiner: Yes, it is. Students must time themselves and not write too much for the first task even if they feel this is where their strength lies. They have to leave enough time to do the second task properly as they gain more from that.

Interviewer: So would you say the first task is easier?

Examiner: Well, it depends. I wouldn't say it's easier – even though it carries fewer marks. It's a much shorter piece of writing and students don't need to use complex grammatical forms like conditionals and so on, but for some students it's actually more difficult. They clearly find it quite hard to read the information properly and decide what's relevant. It's a very stylized piece of writing and that suits some people more than others. Some students clearly feel more comfortable debating an issue and expressing an opinion.

B 🎧 Give students three minutes to read through the notes and make predictions – the aim is to make predictions both as a listening skill and to revise Exam tip advice. Play the whole recording as students answer and then again, pausing appropriately to check answers. Ideally, you should write answers onto an OHT or other visual medium of the notes on the board.

Answers:
1. relevant   2. creative   3. practice
4. looking at   5. complex   6. explain

Tapescript 🎧 91 (3 mins, 5 secs)

B Listen to the second part of the interview about Writing Task 1 and complete the notes.

Interviewer: So, what are some things you notice about the first task in particular?

Examiner: Well, certainly the students who do best are the ones that keep things fairly simple. By that, I don't mean they use very basic English – that depends on their level – but that they say what needs to be said and no more. They pick out what's relevant and what will interest the reader and then they express that using the most appropriate language. I think they understand that report writing is formulaic. They don't try to be creative or explain why they think something is a trend, for example.

Interviewer: Is practice important?

Examiner: Oh, very much so – for both writing tasks, in fact – but I think I notice it more for the first task. An advanced learner – perhaps even a native speaker – would find writing a report, based on two pie charts say, challenging if they'd never practised it. It's like somebody who's been driving for years might not pass a driving test if they suddenly had to take one again.

Interviewer: What are the most typical problems with the first task?

Examiner: The most typical problem is trying to report too much of the information. Students who can probably write very well make the mistake of trying to comment on almost everything shown by the figure. They write far too much or try to cram too much information into a sentence. It's very important to spend some time looking at the figure before starting to write. In theory, it's the language used that's important and not what information the student has chosen to report. However, if a very obvious piece of stand-out information has been ignored while something fairly irrelevant is the focus of a paragraph, it suggests that the student hasn't really understood the figure. Another common mistake is for students – usually lower-level students – to try to use complex language they don't really know how to use well. Of course, there are marks for well-expressed sentences that express comparison and contrast, but students must stick to language they can use confidently.

Interviewer: Do many students make the mistake of trying to explain the reason for information?

Examiner: It's not a common mistake, but it does happen. Some students seem to think that all writing is creative and they just can't resist suggesting why a trend might have occurred at a certain time, for example.

c 🎧 Read through the interviewer's question with students and give them time to read through the list so they know what they are listening for. Play the recording right through as students answer and then again, pausing appropriately to check answers.

Answers:

5 organizing points
9 using the appropriate style and register
4 using the right number of words
3 planning what to say
1 answering the question
7 using reference words and linking devices
8 using vocabulary and grammar
2 getting plenty of practice
6 using paragraphs and topic sentences

Tapescript 🎧 **92 (4 mins, 55 secs)**

C **Put the points into the order in which you hear them.**

Interviewer: What about Writing Task 2 – the discursive composition? What do you look for?

Examiner: Well, there are various things to look for and it depends on the level of the student. I can see straightaway if the composition is written by a lower-level student or by a more advanced learner. There are certain aspects of a composition that are essential – and that's the same for any student taking the exam. Firstly, what the student writes must be relevant to the question – it doesn't matter how well-written the composition is, it's no good if it doesn't answer the question. It's quite common that a student can clearly write English well, but he or she just didn't really know what to say about a particular issue. I think they panic and then start inventing things that are off the point. Again, practice is vital. Many of the composition topics come up quite frequently. If students practise writing discursive compositions, there's a reasonable chance that an issue they've written about before will come up in the exam and then it's much easier to have plenty to say.

Interviewer: So, is it important to plan and make notes?

Examiner: It's absolutely essential! IELTS Writing tasks are quite sophisticated, but they're not designed to trip students up. I mean the issues are always issues that an educated person would have something to say about. The idea is not to resolve the issue or even to say anything especially intelligent, but what is said must be relevant, and a bit of time spent thinking and jotting down some ideas is invaluable. Trying to think of what to say as you write is almost impossible.

Interviewer: How important is the word count?

Examiner: It's also vital. The second composition must be at least 250 words and a very short composition will lose marks. Again, planning is so important. Students can easily ensure a composition is the right length by giving an example from their own experience or an extra reason to support an opinion they've expressed.

Interviewer: And does planning mean better organization?

Examiner: Definitely. In a discursive composition, points must be made in a logical order and ideas should be introduced and concluded. You can't do that if you make it all up as you go. Apart from a general logical flow of ideas, students should understand the purpose of paragraphs and introduce each with a topic sentence that helps the reader follow the train of thought. Students with a higher level of English should be able to use a range of reference words – that is, words that refer back to an earlier idea or forward to something that has not yet been introduced – and suitable linking devices.

Interviewer: What about vocabulary, spelling and accurate grammar?

Examiner: It's all about a sensible balance. Lower-level students should stick to saying what they know how to say, but more capable students need to show they can use a range of language. I'm not saying they should try to use really complex structures for the sake of it or show off with advanced vocabulary that isn't totally appropriate, but they do need to show the examiner what

they can do. I get the impression that some very capable students don't really stretch themselves by using vocabulary they probably know. They should make a list of suitable words and phrases that relate to the issue while they're planning. Stronger students should be able to use the appropriate grammatical structures without having to try too hard – I mean they should come naturally. Finally, the student needs to use language that is appropriate in style and register. I see too many compositions that contain inappropriately informal expressions and are full of contractions. Even though I'm impressed that the student knows an expression, I can't give extra marks if it's used inappropriately.

D 🎧 Students should read the tapescript as this gives invaluable information about the Writing test as you play the recording again.

Tapescript 🎧 **93 (0 mins, 9 secs)**

D **Listen again as you read the tapescript.**

[Play Track 92 again]

E Tell students not to be too critical or modest. Once they have given themselves a score, have a quick class discussion and get a general consensus as to whether writing skills are improving.

What next?

You might like to tell students to read this at home. You can check by asking questions or by having a brief feedback session at the beginning of the next lesson. If there is time to read it in class, it would be better to read through one section at a time and get some feedback rather than reading it right through in one go.

9 Words and pictures

Unit overview

The ninth unit presents language related to an overall theme of *art and literature*. While some of the vocabulary presented relates specifically to the theme, most is flexible and can be applied to other areas of life. Language learnt to talk about *aesthetic quality* in the last module is recycled. Students are presented with, and practise, specific tasks from the Speaking, Listening, Reading and Writing tests that make up the IELTS exam.

Speaking and Vocabulary

Objectives

- **To present and practise vocabulary related to art and literature.**
- **To present and practise new ways of expressing taste.**

The first module aims to orientate students towards the overall theme of the unit and to provide an opportunity for students to learn and practise ways of expressing taste and opinion.

Ask students if they know anything about Alexander Solzhenitsyn. Give them two minutes to read the quotation and think. Give them a minute to discuss it in pairs, focusing on what it means and their reaction to it. Spend another two minutes discussing it as a class.

Aleksandr Isayevich Solzhenitsyn (1918–2008) was a Russian novelist, dramatist and historian. Much of his work was suppressed by the Soviet state and he was expelled from the Soviet Union in 1974. He returned to Russia in 1994 after the collapse of the Soviet system. The quotation is best explained as an expression of the importance of art and literature – without it, a person would understand only his or her own small world and what he or she has personally experienced.

Speaking 1

The aim is to orientate students towards the general theme of the module and to prepare them to learn the vocabulary in the second part of the lesson, rather than to provide lengthy speaking practice. Though students should be encouraged to talk about the books and paintings here, have a time limit in mind and discourage individuals from going into too much detail about one particular piece.

A The items are among the best-known works in history and students should know something about most of them. They should talk in pairs. Encourage them to identify the title and the artist or writer in each case and say a little more if possible. Monitor to give guidance and help with pronunciation if necessary.

Use feedback to confirm or correct suggestions and to provide essential information (see below).

Romeo and Juliet – William Shakespeare (16th century)
The Persistence of Memory – Salvador Dali – (1931)
One Hundred Years of Solitude – Gabriel Garcia Marquez (1967)
Weeping Woman – Picasso (1937)
Mona Lisa – Leonardo da Vinci (circa 1503–1519)
Wheatfield with Crows – Vincent Van Gogh (1890)
The Da Vinci Code – Dan Brown (2003)

B Students should spend four minutes thinking and planning individually and then another six minutes exchanging thoughts with a partner. Monitor to assist as appropriate. As feedback, select one or two students to tell the class about a favourite work. Avoid a lengthy repetitive feedback phase with too many exchanges of opinions.

Vocabulary 1

The aim is for students to learn the new vocabulary and to then apply it to the same books and paintings, appreciating the wider range they have acquired.

A Students should work individually. They will discuss the items in a moment. Make sure they know what to do and set a time limit of five minutes. Tell them to use dictionaries when they are unsure. Monitor to assist, especially with pronunciation, but do not explain each word to any one individual.

Provide the answers without going into the meaning. That can be done after B.

Answers:

novel = L	landscape = A	character = L
abstract = A	surreal = A	plot = L
best-seller = L	portrait = A	exhibition = A
fiction = L	poetry = L	chapter = L
watercolour = A	play = L	classic = L
sketch = A	biography = L	paperback = L
masterpiece = A / L		

B Encourage students to talk again about the books and paintings in the pictures as a means of clarifying any of the new vocabulary they are not sure of. They should concentrate on items that are not clear – not discuss each item one at a time. Monitor to assist and then provide some feedback, dealing with any remaining uncertainties (see suggestions below).

Vocabulary suggestions

- Refer to the Van Gogh painting as an example of a *landscape*.
- An *abstract* painting is made up of colours and shapes that don't seek to represent reality.
- Refer to the Dali painting as an example of *surreal art* or *surrealism*.
- *Plot* and *story* are easily confused. The plot is a series of events that make up a story. *Cinderella* is a story – not a plot.
- A *best-seller* is a very popular book (usually a novel) that is bought by many people.

- Refer to the Picasso painting as an example of a *portrait*. A *self-portrait* is an artist's painting of himself or herself.
- An *exhibition* is *displayed* in a *gallery*. Each item in an exhibition is an *exhibit*.
- Contrast *fiction* with *non-fiction* – a biography, for example.
- *Poetry* is uncountable, as is *literature* – *poem* is countable, as is *novel* or *story*.
- Contrast *watercolour* with *oil painting*.
- Refer to *Romeo and Juliet* as an example of a *play*. A play is written to be performed in a *theatre*.
- A *classic* is (usually) a novel that has been popular and had much influence over a long period of time.
- A *sketch* is a quick drawing or an outline that has not been painted.
- Contrast *biography* and *autobiography*. A *biography* is a story of someone's life written by someone other than the subject. An *autobiography* is the story of a person's life written by them.
- Contrast *paperback* with *hardback*. Most books have a limited number of hardback copies when they are first published. A *paperback* is often used to refer to a popular novel that you can read in a day or two – *I usually take three or four paperbacks on holiday*.
- Conventionally, a *masterpiece* is a great painting – *Mona Lisa* is a masterpiece. However, it is also used to describe any piece of work that is considered to be the creator's best – *the band's first album is still their masterpiece, to my mind*.

C Students should spend three minutes thinking and planning individually, before exchanging thoughts with a partner. Feedback is unnecessary.

Speaking 2

The aim is to expand lexical range. At this level, students should be able to express the same idea in a variety of ways. In the interview, it is likely that they will express an opinion at some point and they will impress the examiner if they can use natural expressions that a native speaker might use.

A Start with books closed. Write on the board, *I like* and *I don't like*. Brainstorm various other ways – more extreme ways – in which each could be expressed. Do not feed expressions yourself. Refer students to the exercise and tell them to work in pairs. Emphasize that they are not expected to know all the expressions – the idea is to see what they do know. Set a time limit of three minutes. Check ideas, but do not confirm or correct answers yet.

B 🎧 The aim is to present the expressions in natural spoken exchanges. Students are answering an examiner's question in each case. Point out that students should absorb these exchanges as examples of good interaction, but not necessarily feel they should be able to achieve this level of fluency and sophistication.

Play the whole recording with pens down, so that students can simply listen and absorb. Play it again as students write answers, and then a third time, pausing after each exchange to check answers. Though students should read the tapescript at some point, writing the full expressions on the board will aid retention. Before clarifying meaning, put students back into their pair to complete the task. Go over the final part of the task, dealing with any remaining uncertainties. See suggestions below.

> **Vocabulary suggestions**
>
> • *It's not really my thing* is typically used as a negative comment. *Now, this is more my thing* is positive.
> • *I'm not very keen on* is as frequently used as the affirmative form.
> • *It doesn't do much for me* and *I don't know what … see in …* are used as negative comments.
> • If you *go off* something, you stop liking something that you previously liked.
> • *I can't / couldn't put it down* is used only to talk about a gripping novel.

Answers:
1. I absolutely adore … L (Note that *love* is a perfectly acceptable alternative.)
2. It's not really my thing. D
3. I'm very keen on … L
4. It doesn't do much for me. D

5. I don't know what they see in him. D
6. I've gone off him. D
7. I couldn't put it down. L
8. I'm a huge fan of … L

Tapescript 🎧 **94 (3 mins, 21 secs)**

B Listen and check your answers. Then make each expression (L) like or (D) dislike.

1
Examiner: So, since you're studying art, tell me which artists you like and why.
Student: Well, I absolutely adore Picasso. I know he's not to everyone's taste, but I think he was brilliant. His work is so powerful. Some people would call some paintings weird, but they're actually very accessible. I saw …

2
Examiner: And what about poetry? Do you ever read poetry?
Student: Mm, it's not really my thing. Of course, I've read some poetry as part of the course and there are poems I like, but really I prefer a good story.

3
Examiner: Which period are you especially interested in?
Student: I like modern art and I'm very keen on pop art, especially from America. I like Andy Warhol and Jasper Johns … I really like that they exploit mass media and the fact that there was music at the time that complemented their work.

4
Examiner: And do you like contemporary art as well?
Student: I'm afraid most of it doesn't do much for me. I guess it depends what you call contemporary, but there's nothing much from the last 50 years that I'm very impressed by. Like I said before, I really like …

5

Examiner: And what about a novelist from your own country? I mean, Kafka is one of the greats, isn't he?

Student: Mm, not for me I'm afraid. I just don't know what people see in him. I mean, of course, I appreciate the quality of the writing, but I find the content very dull and the plots are so complicated.

6

Examiner: Well, having studied so much Shakespeare, I guess he's one of your favourites?

Student: Actually, I've gone off him. Maybe I studied him too much. Now I prefer something a bit more up to date.

7

Examiner: So, what's the best book you've read recently?

Student: That's interesting. Normally I'm not so keen on biographies – you know, I prefer fiction. But I've just read a biography of Elizabeth Taylor – I liked her very much as an actress. Really, I couldn't put it down. It was really fascinating.

8

Examiner: What kind of books do you like reading yourself?

Student: I'd like to say the classics, but I really read paperbacks – you know, stories I can read quickly and are not too heavy. I'm a huge fan of Stephen King. I think I've read nearly all his …

Pronunciation check

Give students time to read and absorb the information about stress and intonation. Make sure they understand what they are listening for in each exchange.

🎧 Play the whole recording. Refer students to the tapescript to practise. Make sure they appreciate that trying to reproduce the complete exchanges will be difficult and not very beneficial. Monitor as they practise, check performance and give positive feedback when appropriate.

Tapescript 🎧 95 (0 mins, 13 secs)
Pronunciation check

Listen again to the exchanges and focus on the speakers' pronunciation.

[Play Track 94 again]

C The aim is to provide exam-type speaking practice, but also to specifically practise the newly acquired expressions. Note that *worship* is added to the range of options – you might need to check its meaning.

Students should spend two and a half minutes thinking and planning answers individually, and then answer the questions with a partner. To vary feedback, get students to ask you each of the questions. They will be interested to hear your answers and you can use the opportunity to provide some authentic on-the-spot listening practice.

D Read the instructions with students. Refer to the artists mentioned to see if they recognize the artists' names. Provide examples of a selection of works by these artists on an OHT or other visual medium (see list below for suggestions). Once students have looked at the paintings, tell them to read the two questions and then give them another three minutes to plan which new language from the module they want to use. Once interaction begins, monitor and make a note of comments and opinions that could be shared during a feedback stage. Information about the paintings is provided below.

Alternatively, this could be set for a homework task and then discussed in a future lesson.

1. René Magritte – *Time Transfixed* (*La Durée poignardée*) 1938
2. Frida Kahlo – *The Love Embrace* (1949)
3. Andy Warhol – from a series of Marilyn Monroe prints (circa 1962)
4. John Constable – *The Haywain* (1821)
5. Damien Hirst – *Deadly Roses* (2005)
6. Leonardo da Vinci – *The Last Supper* (1495–98)

Grammar check

Refer students specifically to Exchange 6 in the tapescript. Ideally, refer to an OHT or other visual medium that you can show on the board. Underline or highlight *having studied* and see if students can label the form. If they cannot, do not worry – just move on. They can read the information in the *Grammar check* in a moment. See if they can rephrase the sentence. Suggest that they start with *since* or *because* or use *so* and switch the clauses round. There is a lot of information in the *Grammar check* and the more students work out for themselves before they read, the more they are likely to take in.

Refer students to the *Grammar check* and give them time to read and absorb. Bear in mind that there is a lot to take in and they will probably grasp the point better from working through the practice phase in a moment. Do not try to explain more.

Refer them to the three sentences for completion. Students should work in pairs, so that they can communicate as they go. Give them a minute for each sentence and monitor to make a note of suggestions that can be shared during feedback. Choose three sentence endings to write up on the board.

Possible answers:
1. Having worked hard on her novel for a year, Tina finally found a publisher.
2. Having sold a painting for £100,000, James decided to take a year off to go travelling.
3. Having met so many famous artists, I suppose you think of them as ordinary people.

Note that reading the *Grammar check* and completing the sentences can alternatively be set as a homework task. It is a fairly complex point and students might benefit from studying it alone without time constraints. You can check their sentences at the beginning of the next lesson.

Listening

Objectives
- **To introduce students to the concept of matching features of a recording to items in a list.**
- **To practise coping with more complicated task instructions.**

The principal aim of the Listening Module is to introduce and practise a matching task that students have not yet seen – certainly not on this course anyway. As with all modules that focus on one particular exam task type, the underlying aim is to practise the listening skill applied to the task – in this case, listening for clues and key words and phrases that apply to categories into which the content has been divided. The task is referred to as *matching features* since students match one feature of a recording with another. Note that the task type is also applied to reading passages (students will practise that in the next unit). The task is potentially more challenging than some other tasks since students have to listen and, at the same time, refer to a list, which can include five or six options.

In this Listening Module, the one recording serves as the topic of all parts of the lesson. Note that, since Part 4 of the Listening test is the focus here, the degree of challenge is higher. You may need to remind students that even when their understanding of a whole lecture is limited, they can complete tasks successfully.

Listening 1

The aim of the first part of the lesson is to orientate students towards the specific theme of the module and facilitate the presentation and practice of the tasks that come later.

A Before students open their books, tell them they are going to see a picture. Tell them they should not shout out anything they know about it. Refer them to the picture and read the rubric through with them. Revise the meaning of *masterpiece*. Put them into pairs or groups of three to answer the questions – tell them to talk quietly.

Monitor to see which pair or group seems to know most. Students will listen to check answers in a moment, but a feedback stage is a good idea, especially if some pairs or groups have very few answers. Get some suggestions from various pairs or groups, but do not confirm or correct (see answers after B).

B 🎧 Make sure students appreciate they are listening to check their own (or other students') suggested answers. Play the whole recording with pens down so that they can simply listen and absorb. Tell them to make notes the second time you play it. Give them a minute or two to compare answers and then play the recording a third time, pausing to check answers. Dealing with this introductory part of the lecture so rigorously will give students a solid platform that will facilitate the challenging tasks that follow. Write answers to questions 1–3 from Exercise A on the board for clarity. Refer students to C as a check to question 4.

Answers:
1. Brontë
2. Charlotte / Emily / Anne
3. *Jane Eyre* / *Wuthering Heights* / *The Tenant of Wildfell Hall*

Tapescript 🎧 96 (1 min, 43 secs)

B **Listen to the introduction of a talk and check your answers.**

Voice: Over the next term, we're going to be looking especially at great female writers and where better to start – certainly for me anyway – than with the Brontës? I'm quite sure you all know something – perhaps quite a lot – about the Brontës, so forgive me if I tell you things you already know. I hope my introduction will help you to enjoy the four novels that we'll be working on. So, the Brontë family lived in Hawarth, a village in West Yorkshire, in the 19th century. The environment was hugely instrumental as you'll come to appreciate. The literary sisters were Charlotte, born in 1816 – the best-known of her stories is, of course, *Jane Eyre*, but *Shirley* and *Villette* are also major works. Emily, born in 1818, – known for her one astonishing novel *Wuthering Heights,* and Anne, born in 1820, perhaps less known than her two sisters, but known for perhaps the most controversial of all the Brontë sisters' novels, *The Tenant of Wildfell Hall*. The sisters

and their brother, Branwell, were very close and they developed vivid childhood imaginations through the collaborative writing of poems and stories. There were also two older sisters, but they died in childhood and this, together with the early death of their mother in 1821, had a huge impact on Charlotte, Emily and Anne's future work.

C Conduct as a whole-class round-up. Students can put up their hands to offer suggestions. Write answers on the board in note form in order to check spelling and to ensure that more background information is provided to facilitate the next phase of listening.

Possible answers:
lived in West Yorkshire in the 19th century / two older sisters died in childhood / early death of mother

Listening 2

The idea is that students will attempt a matching features type task and then reflect on it. They will learn strategies that will help them to attempt it again in the practice part of the lesson.

A 🎧 Show an OHT or other visual medium of the whole task on the board and talk through it. However, do not explain so much that the reflection exercise (B) is negated.

Tell students that they will hear the next part of the lecture about the Brontë sisters. Draw attention to the box and emphasize that these are the sisters' names. Explain that their names – the letters A, B or C, will be the answers to the questions. Now draw attention to the statements 1–8. Point out that these will often be shorter, unpunctuated phrases (as with other matching tasks) rather than statements. Ask students which order they think the sisters will be mentioned in, but do not confirm or correct. Then ask them if they think the statements will also be mentioned in the order they appear on the page, i.e., 1–8. Again, do not confirm or correct.

Give students two minutes to read through the statements. They should check any words they are unsure of. Play the whole recording and then give students time to compare answers with a partner. Play the recording, pausing at the appropriate point to check answers. In this way, you can emphasize how students must keep looking at the statements as they listen. Draw attention to paraphrasing as you go (see guidance with answers below).

Answers:

1. B (Emily attended the girls' school where Charlotte was a teacher, ...)

2. A (Charlotte claimed that the dreadful conditions at the school were a major contribution to ... the early death of her two elder sisters.)

3. B (Surviving diary pages show ... the extraordinary imagination and originality responsible for *Wuthering Heights* ...)

4. C (... while the older siblings found it difficult to establish a relationship with the ... aunt ..., Anne was shown real affection and was said to be her favourite.)

5. C (She had great difficulty controlling them and ... little education was achieved. Anne was soon dismissed ...)

6. B (Emily was at first furious that her privacy had been invaded ...)

7. A (Charlotte completed *The Professor*. Though this was rejected for publication, ...)

8. C (This first novel, though successful, was overshadowed by the epic *Jane Eyre* and dramatic *Wuthering Heights*. Anne's second novel, ...)

Tapescript 🎧 **97 (5 mins, 33 secs)**

A **Look at the statements 1–8. Listen and match each statement with the correct sister A, B or C.**

Voice: So ... Charlotte was the eldest of the surviving sisters and probably the most successful in terms of the amount of writing actually published. Like her two sisters, she used a male pseudonym rather than her real name. At the time, it was not considered appropriate for women to be writers, and it was assumed that success was far more likely if readers thought that the story had been written by a man. Charlotte wrote mainly under the pseudonym of Currer Bell. After the death of their mother - as I've said that was in 1821 -

Charlotte was sent with three of her sisters, Emily, Maria and Elizabeth, to the Clergy Daughters' School in Lancashire. This was later the model for the school in *Jane Eyre*. Charlotte claimed that the dreadful conditions at the school were a major contribution to her own poor health and physical development, and the early death of her two elder sisters, Maria and Elizabeth. Back at home – their father took them out of the school when the girls died – Charlotte became the guardian and mother figure to her two younger sisters despite their aunt, their mother's sister, living almost permanently at the house as a carer. This is when the children began narrating the lives and struggles of characters from their imaginary worlds. Charlotte wrote tales of imperfect heroes, while Emily and Anne wrote articles and poems. At the end of her education, Charlotte worked briefly as a teacher and then as a governess to the children of wealthy Yorkshire families. This latter experience greatly influenced her writing. Around this time, together with Emily and Anne, Charlotte published a collection of poetry under the assumed names of Currer, Ellis and Acton Bell. Although only a handful of copies were sold, the inspiration to write for publication was born and just a little while later, Charlotte completed *The Professor*. Though this was rejected for publication, it was only a year later that the masterpiece *Jane Eyre* became an instantly popular phenomenon. Emily, the second sister, known really for her one novel *Wuthering Heights*, but what a novel! Emily, as I've said, was removed from school when her older sisters died and was educated at home. During this period, she and her younger sister Anne spent hours creating stories and poems about an imaginary island, Gondal. The girls even enacted scenes from their stories. Surviving diary pages show clearly that the extraordinary imagination and originality responsible for *Wuthering Heights* blossomed at this time. When she was 17, Emily attended the girls school where Charlotte was a teacher, but managed to stay only three months before being overcome by extreme homesickness. She tried working as a teacher herself for a while, but the 17-hour day was too much and she returned home, becoming the housekeeper of the family. It was in 1845 that Charlotte discovered how much poetry Emily and Anne had written and she insisted that the work be published. Emily was at first furious that her privacy had been invaded and refused to allow her work to be shared. She relented when she realized that Anne too had been so prolific. As previously suggested, it was this, despite the commercial failure of the collection, that drove the sisters to keep writing, and Emily was compelled to write her masterpiece.

The youngest sister, Anne, certainly isn't a household name like Charlotte and Emily, but nonetheless, her contribution to literature is notable, as I previously suggested, *The Tenant of Wildfell Hall* is possibly the bravest … certainly for its time … of all the Brontë novels. Anne spent most of her life with her family in Hawarth. She was only a year old when her mother died, and while the older siblings found it difficult to establish a relationship with the rather stern aunt who now cared for them, Anne was shown real affection and was said to be her favourite. For a couple of years, Anne went to a boarding school, but when her older sisters were brought home, she was too and, as we've heard, the great period of creativity began. Anne and Emily were especially inseparable and started writing their tales and poems about Gondal. Anne worked, like her eldest sister, as a governess, but the children in Anne's charge were wild and spoilt, and persistently disobeyed her. She had great difficulty controlling them and very little education was achieved. Anne was soon dismissed and returned home to join Charlotte and Emily. This episode was so traumatic for Anne that she reproduced it in almost perfect detail in her first novel, *Agnes Grey*. This first novel, though successful, was overshadowed by the epic *Jane Eyre* and dramatic *Wuthering Heights*. Anne's second novel, *The Tenant of Wildfell Hall*, was published in 1848 and was an instant phenomenal success, selling out within six weeks.

B By now, students will be accustomed to reflecting on new types of task, having attempted them. They should answer the questions in pairs. Check answers before referring them to the Question-type tip as consolidation.

Answers:
1. the sisters – features A–C
2. the statements 1–8
3. You must read the statements clearly and then continue to look at them all as you are listening.

Refer students to the Question-type tip and give them time to read and absorb. Emphasize that in order to make the task a task, either the names OR the statements have to be mentioned in a random order. Point out that there can be more features in the box (see practice task later) and that they might then be in a random order and the statements mentioned in order.

Listening 3

Since the lecture continues for the practice part of the lesson, there is no need to refocus students and they should be left to work independently. Note, however, that B is an additional task that means playing only part of the recording again, and it should be dealt with separately.

A 🎧 Give students a little longer than usual to read through the various features and understand what they have to do. Encourage them to use the statements to make general predictions about the content of the next part of the lecture, but point out that predicting the answers is not possible. Play the whole recording. Do not check answers as students will do so in Exercise C. Give students a moment to compare answers in pairs if you feel it would be beneficial.

Tapescript 🎧 **98 (5 mins, 17 secs)**

A **Look at the statements 1–8 about four of the Brontë sisters' novels. Then listen to a continuation of the talk and match each statement with the correct title A, B, C or D.**

Voice: Now, onto a quick overview of the Brontë novels we'll be focusing on this term. I'm sure from what I've already said that you can guess which novels those will be – well, at least three of them. *Jane Eyre* is Charlotte's gift to literature – one of the most important pieces of Victorian writing, perhaps most important of any time. It was described at the time as an influential feminist text because of its in-depth exploration of a strong female character. Apart from the intricate plot, there is a great deal of social criticism. The story has a strong sense of morality at its core and the actions of characters are so expertly depicted. It is in many respects a rites of passage novel, following Jane's development from abused child through to mature woman. The story of Jane's transformation from a poor, plain girl into a charming, confident, self-reliant lady was certainly ahead of its time. During Jane's childhood, she's emotionally and physically abused by her aunt and cousins. During her education at Lowood School, she makes friends and learns from role models, but also suffers oppression. During her time as a governess at Thornfield Hall, she falls in love with her charismatic employer, Mr Rochester. All this is clearly influenced by Charlotte's background, which I described earlier. Charlotte's third novel, *Villette*, published in 1853, reworked ideas from her unsuccessful first novel, *The Professor*. The protagonist, Lucy Snowe, travels to the fictional city of Villette to teach at an all-girls school, where she is pulled into adventure and romance. The novel is celebrated more for its study of Lucy's character than for its plot. Earlier themes are revisited. Once again, there is a fiery male schoolmaster and once again there is no smooth passage to love. The final pages are ambiguous. Lucy – the story is told in the first person – says that she wants to allow the reader to imagine a happy ending, but she strongly implies that, in fact, the story ends in tragedy.

Emily's *Wuthering Heights* – and once more I should stress that this was her only major work – is one of the best-loved and frequently studied stories of all. The novel met with mixed reviews when it first appeared, mainly because of its dark description of mental and physical cruelty. Though Charlotte's *Jane Eyre* was generally considered the best of the sisters' works for most of the 19th century, more recent critics of *Wuthering Heights* have claimed that it was a superior achievement. Interestingly, the second edition of *Wuthering Heights* was edited by Charlotte after Emily's death. The narrative tells the tale of the passionate, but tragically thwarted love between the protagonist Catherine Earnshaw and Heathcliff, an abandoned boy who is adopted into her family. The unresolved passion eventually destroys them and people around them. For many people, it seems incredible that Emily Brontë, a young sheltered girl, who spent her time looking after the family home, could write a story of such intense emotion.

And finally, Anne's second novel, *The Tenant of Wildfell Hall*, published in 1848 under the pseudonym Acton Bell. As I've said, perhaps the bravest, even the most shocking of the Brontës' novels. It had an instant phenomenal success and sold out. After Anne's death, however, Charlotte prevented its republication. The novel, like Anne's first, is written in a sharper, more realistic style than the romantic style of her two sisters. It tells the story of a mysterious widow, Helen, who arrives with her young son at Wildfell Hall, a country mansion that has been empty for many years. She lives there under an assumed name and soon finds herself the victim of cruel gossip. In her diary, Helen writes about her husband's physical and moral decline through alcohol, and the world of cruelty and shame from which she has escaped. The novel is considered to be one of the first sustained feminist novels. Aspects of the story caused great controversy in Victorian Britain, where, by fleeing from her husband, Helen violates not only social conventions, but also English law at the time.

B Since the features matching task exploits the entire recording, students would not be expected to complete a second task at the same time, nor try to remember the answers. For this reason, it is necessary to treat the task as additional practice and play part of the recording again. Work through as previously with gap-filling tasks.

Note that students have the advantage of having listened once already, but that they will almost certainly spell *rites* incorrectly as 'rights'. During a feedback stage, point them to the question in Exercise F and remind them that they will rarely need to spell words with which they are totally unfamiliar. Here, the item is included partly to lead onto the discussion point in F.

Tapescript 🎧 99 (1 min, 31 secs)

B Listen to the part of the talk about *Jane Eyre* again. Complete the sentences below.

Voice: *Jane Eyre* is Charlotte's gift to literature – one of the most important pieces of Victorian writing, perhaps most important of any time. It was described at the time as an influential feminist text because of its in-depth exploration of a strong female character. Apart from the intricate plot, there is a great deal of social criticism. The story has a strong sense of morality at its core and the actions of characters are so expertly depicted. It is in many respects a rites of passage novel, following Jane's development from abused child through to mature woman. The story of Jane's transformation from a poor, plain girl into a charming, confident, self-reliant lady was certainly ahead of its time. During Jane's childhood, she's emotionally and physically abused by her aunt and cousins. During her education at Lowood School, she makes friends and learns from role models, but also suffers oppression. During her time as a governess at Thornfield Hall, she falls in love with her charismatic employer, Mr Rochester. All this is clearly influenced by Charlotte's background, which I described earlier.

C Checking and reflecting on answers is a constant feature of the skills modules. Give students sufficient time to check and think about why any answers were incorrect before moving onto D. You can decide if it would be beneficial to play the recording again, but avoid doing so simply to check individual students' wrong answers. It will probably be more beneficial to listen again later as they read the tapescript. If you do want to draw attention to parts of the recording that provide answers, show an OHT or other visual medium of the tapescript on the board and highlight key parts as you pause the recording.

Answers:
Exercise A:
1. C   2. D   3. B   4. A   5. C   6. A
7. C   8. D

Exercise B:
1. strong female character
2. rites of passage
3. background

D Students will be used to reflecting on tasks in this way now. Remind them that identifying what they are doing well and not doing so well is a very good way of focusing on what they can do better next time. Allow students time to reflect and complete the exercise. Conclude by asking them if they are happy with the number of correct answers.

E and F The aim is to conclude the lesson rather than develop an extended debate. You will know whether your students will enjoy and benefit from an extended pair or group discussion, or whether a quick whole-class discussion will suffice. Whatever approach you take, encourage students to use core language learnt in the module.

Key vocabulary in context

Students have previously worked through *Key vocabulary in context* exercises like this, so will know how to approach this one. They should work in pairs, so they can communicate as they go. Encourage them to attempt to define the words without looking at the tapescript, and then to check the tapescript to fully understand the item in context. Remind them that the aim is to practise understanding unknown lexis in context rather than to retain all of these items specifically – they should be selective.

As feedback, tell students to cover the exercise and read the definitions in the answers below as students shout out the words and phrases.

Answers:
1. pseudonym = name that a person (usually an author) uses instead of their real name
2. blossomed = developed and became successful (literal meaning applies to flowers on a tree opening)
3. prolific = producing many works or ideas / productive – *the team's most prolific goal-scorer*

4. a household name = a name that everyone recognizes

5. stern = serious and strict

6. inseparable = very close / not able to be apart

7. traumatic = extremely upsetting – note that the noun is *trauma*

8. ahead of its time = very modern at the time of production – perhaps too new for some people to understand

9. charismatic = having strong qualities that attract other people – note that the noun is *charisma*

10. ambiguous = not clear / possible to interpret in different ways

11. thwarted = stopped from developing

12. sheltered = protected from experiences that others have had

Refer students to the Workbook exercises related to this module. Choose to work on them now or set up for homework.

Reading

Objectives

- **To practise recognizing facts and opinions.**
- **To practise distinguishing between fact and opinion.**
- **To practise exam tasks that require recognizing and understanding opinion.**

Students looked at fact and opinion in Unit 6, when the main focus was topic sentences. In this Reading Module, recognizing and understanding fact and opinion is the main focus.

The module is divided into three parts. The first part orientates students towards the overall theme of modern art and the concept of expressing strong opinions about popular culture. The second part focuses on task types that require recognition and comprehension of opinion. The third part, as usual, practises what has been learnt through authentic exam practice tasks.

Though the two passages are quite separate and very different in style and genre, the theme of *reaction to modern art* is common, and ideas and language from the first passage are recycled in the second. Language related to *art* from the first module is recycled.

Reading 1

A The aim is to provide students with examples of modern art that are likely to divide opinion. Your students might recognize or have heard about one or more of the pieces, but it does not matter if they have not. You will need to give them a little information in order for them to answer the questions.

Draw attention to the pictures, either in the book or copied onto an OHT or other visual medium on the board. If the images can be blown up but still be clear on the board, it will be an advantage. Remind students of the meaning of *exhibit* and ask them what they think these exhibits have in common. Depending on the age of your students and the knowledge they have, you will get a range of answers. Tell them that these are all examples of *conceptual art* – the idea is that the creativity is in the concept of the work, not necessarily the aesthetic value of the finished piece. Give them the background information below.

Tracey Emin – *My Bed* (1998) – The exhibit consists of the artist's bed with bedroom objects littered around it. It gained huge media attention when it was put forward for the Turner Prize (the UK's most prestigious annual prize for artists). It did not win the prize, but it has become a symbol of controversial conceptual art.

Damien Hirst – *The Physical Impossibility of Death in the Mind of Someone Living* (1991) – The exhibit is a shark in formaldehyde in a large tank. It sold for £50,000. The shark had been caught by a commissioned fisherman in Australia and had cost £6,000. Since then, the work has gained almost iconic status.

Ai Weiwei – *Sunflower Seeds* (2010) – The exhibit was installed at a London gallery, where it was scattered over a large area of the exhibition hall floor. It consisted of 100 million porcelain 'seeds', each individually hand-painted in the town of Jingdezhen by 1,600 Chinese artisans. The artist intended visitors to walk across and roll in the work to experience and contemplate the essence of his comment on mass consumption in China. In 2011, a 100 kg pile from *Sunflower Seeds* sold for $559,394.

Refer students to the three questions and give them time to think and plan answers. Monitor as they talk in pairs to make a note of salient comments that can be shared during a feedback stage.

As feedback, choose three different students to briefly answer each of the questions for the class. Avoid starting another lengthy debate as the next part of the lesson develops the theme.

B Make sure students appreciate what the genre of the passage is – ask them if they ever read or make comments on online forums. Read the instructions with them and tell them to read with the principal of aim of deciding who they agree with. Point out that they will not need to understand every word, but that they can use a dictionary for up to three words or phrases which they feel are essential to comprehension. Tell them to highlight lines which they particularly like. Set a time limit of ten minutes and make sure they work individually for now. Monitor to check what students are highlighting or looking up and assist students who are having difficulties.

As feedback, get a very quick idea of how many students agree with each forum contributor. Tell them that they will discuss who they agree and disagree with in more depth later when they better understand the comments.

Reading 2

A As previously stated, students will almost certainly not have to distinguish between fact and opinion as part of an exam task, but they will have to complete tasks that require them to recognize and understand opinion. The aim here is to prepare them for the more direct exam practice tasks that follow and to develop a general reading skill that is essential for students at this level. Note that whether some of the

sentences express fact or opinion is debatable – at this level, it would be pointless to present students with sentences that are clearly one thing or the other. You will need to clarify during a feedback stage.

Students should spend four minutes completing the task individually and then compare answers with a partner. Show an OHT or other visual medium of the sentences on the board so that you can refer efficiently to parts of each to provide feedback and clarify.

Answers:
1. F – a specific date is given, 15,000BC, which shows it is a fact.
2. O – The writer uses a dramatic, exaggerated image to make his point.
3. F – The main clause, *It saddens me* ..., is certainly fact. It could be argued that, ... *so many people hate conceptual art* is opinion, but it is probably true that most people hate it.
4. O – The statement might be true, but the writer does not know this. She claims that this is the case.
5. O – It is a true statement for the writer, but it is very personal. It is more an opinion of a situation than a factual statement.
6. O – As with question 4.

Refer students to the Exam tip and give them time to read and absorb. Tell them to cover it and ask one student to go over the advice given.

B The aim now is to practise the two exam task types that require understanding of opinions expressed in a passage. Though the tasks are presented as exam practice tasks, remember that this is still the presentation part of the lesson and students should be guided and assisted and should compare ideas with other students.

Tell students to work individually on questions 1–4, to compare answers with a partner and then to do the same with questions 5–8. Remind them to look for paraphrased language (which should by now be a matter of course). End the exercise when the majority of pairs have finished it.

To ensure that feedback is efficient, show a copy of the forum on the board. Identify the lines and phrases that provide answers as you check them (see additional guidance in answer key).

Make a point of explaining the expression *stuck in the past* as this is deliberately introduced here to link in with the main reading passage.

Answers:

1. Debbie (… artists felt that there was nothing left to say by drawing or painting …)
2. Jill (… a group of pretentious wannabes … a tiny elite of even more pretentious art critics, who wield far too much power.)
3. Toby (Those who criticize conceptualism are just stuck in the past!)
4. Dom (… so-called artists …)
5. N (… trying to persuade people that … + general message of whole comment)
6. NG (She cannot paint like Michelangelo, but that does not mean she says she paints badly.)
7. Y (… a tiny elite … wield far too much power.)
8. Y (… are just stuck in the past!)

Note that, in the exam, students' comprehension of a single expression will not be tested more than once as is the case here.

C The discussion will both provide an opportunity for students to express their own opinions, and help you assess how much they have really grasped so far. Give them a moment to remind themselves of what they did in Exercise A and then put them into groups. Set a time limit of five minutes. Monitor and, as feedback, simply tell the class what the general consensus of opinion seems to be. The main reading passage will develop the theme.

Reading 3

Students should now be more independent when working on the practice part of the skills modules. Since the passage continues the theme of the first part of the lesson, students should feel fairly well-prepared anyway. The passage, however, is quite challenging and it contains a number of cultural references. A brief orientation/facilitation stage is provided to ensure that students have a platform from which to tackle the practice tasks.

A The aim is to make sure that students understand the basic message of the passage before they engage in the tasks. Read through the instructions with students and tell them to read carefully through the options a–d before they skim the passage. When they are all ready to read, set a strict time limit of three minutes.

Check the answer by getting a show of hands or asking a number of students what their answer is. Establish that the correct option is c. Point out now that *Stuckism* is not an established art movement like *Surrealism*, which they would find in their dictionaries, but a modern underground movement that not many people know about.

B Set a time limit of 12 minutes, pointing out that students have already prepared and skimmed the text. Give them an extra three minutes if a number of students have not completed the task. You can decide if students will benefit from comparing answers with a partner before checking the answers.

C Checking and reflecting on answers is a constant feature of the skills modules. Give students sufficient time to check and think about why they may have answered incorrectly.

Students might want to know why some of their answers were not correct. Explaining some points may be necessary and beneficial, but going through all of them will be very time-consuming. It is probably best to reassure them that with more practice their scores will improve.

If you do want to identify the specific parts of the passage that provide answers to any questions, make an OHT or other visual medium of the passage and highlight those parts on the board.

Answers:

1. D 2. F 3. C 4. B 5. E
6. Y 7. N 8. N 9. NG 10. NG 11. Y
12. Y 13. N

D Students will now be familiar with this type of reflective process. Point out that, once again, points are related specifically to the reading skills and task strategies practised. Remind them that identifying what they are doing well and not doing so well is a very good way of focusing on what they can do better next time. Allow students time to reflect and complete the exercise and then ask them if they are happy with the number of correct answers.

E The aim is to conclude the lesson rather than develop an extended debate. You will know whether your students will enjoy and benefit from an extended pair or group discussion or whether a quick whole-class discussion will suffice. Whatever approach you take, encourage students to use core language learnt in the module.

Key vocabulary in context

The aim of the first two exercises is more to practise understanding new lexis in context as it is to learn the specific words and phrases. Most of the words in the third exercise are flexible, high-frequency items that students should try to retain.

A Students can discuss the idioms, which are italicized in the first paragraph of the passage in the Course Book, in pairs. They will have already had time to think about them. You can point out that they all mean something very similar, but students should work this out themselves from the context. Give them three minutes and then check answers. If students are all from the same country, agree on whether there is a similar idiom in the first language. If students are from various countries, choose one student to tell the class about each idiom.

Answers:
each to his own = each person has his or her own taste
beauty is in the eye of the beholder = the person looking at something or somebody decides whether or not it or he/she is beautiful
one man's meat is another man's poison = what one person likes, another person hates

B Students will need some time to individually check the items in context before comparing with a partner. As feedback, read the definitions below as students shout out the compounds as answers.

Answers:
self-appointed = not put in a position by other people / not elected
one-time = previously / no longer
age-old = historic / traditional
so-called = labelled as this but not really so

C Work as Exercise A.

Answers:
worthy = of value
eminent = in a high position / respected
humble = ordinary / not special
censor = say what is not allowed and stop people having access to it
suppress = stop something happening freely
pontificate = make judgements in a superior way

Refer students to the Workbook exercises related to this module. Choose to work on them now or set up for homework.

Writing

Objectives

- **To present and practise reports which describe physical change.**
- **To practise using tenses appropriate to describing change.**

The Writing Module in this unit concentrates on Writing Task 1. It presents and practises a type of task that students are perhaps less likely to have previously seen. Though reports describing graphs, charts and tables are more frequently set as Writing 1 tasks, students need to be familiar with this task type and practise it. Note that the task type is designed so that students at different levels will be capable of writing reports of lesser or greater sophistication. At this level, students will generally be expected to use more complex perfect tenses.

Writing 1

The first part of the module aims to orientate students towards the theme and motivate them to write the report later in the lesson.

A Read through the instructions with students and make sure they talk about change and not just about libraries – the aim is that they start using structures like *used to, are more / less than …,* *have become more* … and so on, though for now they should not be directed to do so.

Students should spend three minutes thinking and planning what to say individually and then compare ideas with a partner. Get and give some brief feedback. Avoid getting into a discussion that answers questions in B.

B Read through the questions with the class, telling them to think and plan answers as you go. Pause briefly between questions. Point out that *public* here means *open to everybody – not private*, and explain that *be in tune with* means *be more aware of / understand better*. Give them five minutes to answer the questions with a partner. Monitor to make a note of salient contributions that could be shared during a feedback stage. As feedback, choose one student to give their thoughts on each question briefly. Do not attempt to confirm or correct.

C Make sure students appreciate that they are reading to check the ideas they discussed – they should highlight points that relate to what they or their partner mentioned. They should not worry about understanding every word, but they can use a dictionary selectively when an item is essential to comprehension. Monitor to check what students are highlighting and looking up. Assist if and when necessary. Feedback on this stage is unnecessary.

D The idea is not to try to remember chunks of each extract. Students use their own words to summarize and compare points of interest. Set a time limit of three minutes. Monitor to check comprehension of the extracts and fluency of interaction.

Use feedback to check selected vocabulary and conclude. Select individuals and ask questions like, *So, why are students using libraries less? What is the disadvantage of getting information online? Why is the future of UK libraries described as gloomy? Have adaptations to libraries had any effect?*

E If students are all from the same town or city, they can compare a library they both know. If they are from various parts of the world, they can exchange information. Your feedback should reflect this.

Writing 2

A It is important to appreciate that the aim here is for students to understand and talk about the plans that will be the subject of the Writing task, but not yet use the language they will have to use to actually write the task. Here they will use various forms – present perfect especially – while in the written task, they will use future forms.

Read through the instructions with students and refer them to the plans. Emphasize that the first plan is labelled *2005* and the second *today*. Ask them about the local history room and write suggestions on the board. Students may say, *It is now a coffee shop*. That is fine, but the stage will not be very beneficial if students describe only the second plan in these simple terms. Elicit or suggest alternative ways of saying the same thing. Emphasize the need to talk about change and write a few suggestions on the board – *It has become a coffee shop, They've made it into a coffee shop* and *It has been turned into a coffee shop.* You may need to explain that the male and female symbols are the cloakrooms. You will probably need to explain *cloakrooms*.

Set a time limit of five minutes. Tell students they do not have to use each of the forms for each change, but they should vary the structures they use. Monitor to check the logic and accuracy of points made and to make a note of what could be used to provide feedback. Aim to get five or six sentences on the board during a feedback stage. Concentrate on forms that are more appropriate to report writing now – point out that using a neutral *they – They've moved the …*, for example, is used more in spoken language.

Possible answers:
A new computer centre has been added.
The children's library has been expanded.
The information desk is now in the centre of the floor.
The newspapers and journals section is now in the area where the old computer stations were.
There are fewer reading tables, but access to Wi-Fi (wireless Internet) has been made available.

B Since this is the first time students have seen this task type, make an OHT or other visual medium of the task instructions and refer to parts of them as you talk go through the task together. Point out which plan each line of instructions refers to and draw particular attention to the phrase *will be completed by the end of next year*. Do not actually mention future forms yet – students can work that out when they answer the questions in a moment. Note that, in an actual exam task, years will be given, rather than time references like *now* and *next year*.

Students should read the questions and think individually, before answering the questions with a partner. Monitor to check what students are saying and get brief feedback to the first question before students look at the Exam tip. Simply establish that future forms will be required instead of present and present perfect forms.

Refer students to the Exam tip and give them time to read and absorb. Tell them to cover the tip and ask one student to summarize the advice for the class.

C   Tell students to read and absorb the content of the model report before they attempt to focus specifically on the tenses used. Ask them if the changes identified and described are the same as those discussed. Emphasize that the instructions say that more than one form is sometimes possible and then suggest they work individually on the task. They can compare answers with a partner before checking the completed model on page 267. Monitor and assist as they work. Point out any errors so that students can try to correct themselves before seeing the answers.

If students find the exercise challenging, you could show an OHT or other visual medium on the board and write in the answers one at a time as you elicit them. This will help you to focus on each form and to explain why it is used. The model is reproduced below for your convenience.

Answers (alternative forms in brackets):

The diagrams show that by the end of next year, some radical changes will have been made to Poolsville library.

There are plans to add a whole new computer centre, part of which will be a coffee shop. This will mean dispensing with the local history room and music and video library. A DVD library will be available in the computer room.

The children's library will be expanded (will expand), meaning that the cloakrooms will have to be moved to the other side of the floor. There will be fewer reading tables, but Wi-Fi access will be available in that area.

To make room for the new computer centre and the expansion of the non-fiction reading area, the information centre will be moved (will move) to the centre of the floor. The newspapers and journals section is going to be (will be) in the area where the old computer stations were.

D   Refer students to the model and give them time to study it carefully. Clarify any remaining uncertainties, but bear in mind they will read the *Grammar check* in a moment.

Grammar check

If the various forms were revised and dealt with during the feedback stage to D, this should really be a matter of consolidation. It may help students to compare the future perfect with the present perfect and past perfect – it is simply a matter of transferring the concept to another point in time. Use timelines if you know they help your students. Point out that the future perfect is relatively rare – it is not frequently necessary to look back at a point in time from a more advanced point in the future like this. Emphasize that although the future perfect is strictly speaking formed with *will*, other modal verbs are just as likely.

Give students the time they need to read and absorb and suggest they correct the errors in the *Watch out!* box in pairs. Tell them to check the information again in their own time.

Answers:

By the end of the week, I'll have finished my ...
By 2020, a cure will have been found.
To create space for ...

Writing task

The Writing tasks are found either in the Workbook or in the Exam Practice Module at the end of the unit. In this unit, the task is in the Exam Practice Module, and teacher's notes for it can be found in the notes for that module.

Consolidation

Instructions are given for Speaking exercises when the procedure is not clear from instructions in the Course Book. Set Vocabulary and Errors exercises either for individual completion and pairwork checking, or as pairwork when you feel immediate interaction is beneficial.

To correct errors in the final exercise, ask students to come and write the correct sentences on the board while other students offer help. You will need to write the corrections on the board to clarify.

Speaking

A Answers:
   1. I absolutely adore it.
   2. I don't know what they see in it.
   3. It's not really my thing.
   4. I've gone off it.
   5. I'm very keen on it.
   6. I couldn't put it down.
   7. It doesn't do much for me.
   8. I'm a huge fan of his.

B and C Work through as with previous task card tasks.

Vocabulary

A Answers:
   vivid imagination / traumatic experience / household name / social conventions / self-appointed judge / humble beginnings

B Answers:
   1. notable   2. cruelty   3. influential   4. imaginary
   5. privacy   6. validity

C Answers:
   1. exhibition   2. charismatic   3. pseudonym
   4. inseparable   5. eminent   6. bureaucracy
   7. suppress   8. criticism

Errors

Answers:
   1. Having taken …
   2. Having worked a ten-hour …
   3. … books will have become …
   4. … should have found …
   5. To improve my English, …
   6. … will mean moving away …

Exam Practice

Writing

Since the shorter writing task is in the Exam Practice Module for this unit, it would be a good opportunity to set it in class time and make it part of the lesson. By the time students have prepared and planned with a partner, they should need only about 15 minutes for the actual writing stage.

A This exercise and the one that follows are not essential to the writing process. The aim is to orientate and provide an engaging lead-in stage. Adding a competitive element to the exercise should motivate students. Put them either into pairs or small groups to complete the task.

Answers:
1. d   2. g   3. h   4. f   5. b   6. a   7. c   8. e

B Conduct either as pairwork or as a quick whole-class discussion. If anyone has visited any of the galleries, they should tell the class about the experience.

C The aim is to orientate students more specifically to the content of the writing task and to link it with the Writing task in the Writing Module. Set either as pairwork or as quick whole-class discussion.

D Remind students of the importance of making sure they understand the information shown before they do anything else – this is as true of this task type as of any other.

Refer them to the task instructions and plans and give them three minutes to read and absorb in silence. Ask them if the changes have been made already or if they are planned for the future. Clarify that a *temporary exhibition or visiting exhibition* is one that is shown at a gallery for a limited period of time.

Students should spend three minutes looking at the plans carefully and making notes individually. They can then compare ideas with a partner. As an alternative, tell students to look at the plans for two minutes and then to close their books. In pairs, they should talk about the planned changes in their own words. The changes they have remembered are likely to be those they want to mention in the report.

Refer students to the Exam tip and give them time to read and absorb.

E   Point out how similar to the Writing Module task this Exam Practice task is. Students should refer to the model and use it as framework for this report. Once they start writing their reports, take into account the time already spent preparing. They should 15 minutes.

If they write the report at home, tell them to be strict with a time limit – they will not benefit from spending longer on the task than they will have when it comes to the exam.

When students have completed the task, they should compare it with the model composition on page 267. The model is reproduced below.

If you collect students' compositions to mark, concentrate on how they have used appropriate structures and linked parts of the description together.

Note that the Exam tip here should be read after checking the model report. Give them a moment to read and absorb. The Workbook writing exercises specifically focus on these verbs.

Model composition:

The diagrams show that within three years, some fairly major changes will have been made to the Crowley Gallery.

There are plans to provide a new interactive education centre, which means the existing temporary exhibition gallery will have to be moved. That will be located within the area that was the portrait gallery, meaning that the portrait gallery be will be smaller. A photography gallery will be a brand new feature.

The cafeteria will be transformed into a bar and restaurant and a separate coffee shop will open

next door. To make that possible, the book and gift shop will move to the other side of the floor next to the information desk.

The stairs to the second floor will remain in place, but a lift will be installed too. To accommodate this, the toilets will be relocated.

Unit 9 Workbook answers

Vocabulary development

A   1. paperback   2. chapter   3. classic
4. thwarted   5. affection   6. controversial
7. stern   8. reactionary   9. humble
10. opposition

B   1. to   2. in   3. of   4. under   5. to   6. to
7. with   8. in / to   9. of   10. from / to
11. in   12. to

C   admire L   loathe D   detest D   adore L
idolize L   worship L   abhor D   despise D
revere L

Listening

B   Picture a = sound art
Picture b = Internet art
Picture c = street art

Tapescript 🎧 **100 (7 mins, 15 secs)**

B   **Listen and label each picture with the name of the movement it is an example of.**

Interviewer: So, do you feel that there have been any significant developments in art over the last 20 or so years, or is it a case of simply redefining and dressing something up as new?

Speaker: Well, that's a good question because, of course, so many so-called art movements really are all about rehashing – I mean rather pretentiously claiming that something is fresh and innovative when actually it's very little different to what's come before. For that reason, I want to concentrate on three movements that I really do believe are innovative. They may not be totally new in terms of the images created, but they are certainly fresh in the way that the work is available – I mean how and where people access the work.

Interviewer: And you're going to concentrate on developments or movements, if you like, that have emerged since the domination of conceptual art that defined the art world during the 70s and 80s.

Speaker: Yes, I am. Let me start in the 1980s, in fact, with sound art. Now, sound art was really a direct step on from conceptualism – I mean the idea that anything could be art. Personally, I'm not a huge fan of sound art, but I do think it's challenging and interesting. Many people might argue that it's actually more about music than art, but I think that's short-sighted. The aim of the artist isn't to make music. It's to make a statement through the medium of sound, often combined with visual imagery – paintings or sculpture – and very frequently with an environment or installation of some kind. The relationship between the sound and the other features of the art is the essential element. It's also different from music in that acoustics are more important than notes or melodies – I mean the way the sound travels and interacts with physical objects.

Interviewer: Isn't that what experimental music is supposed to be about?

Speaker: Yes, I admit there's still debate about whether sound art can really be categorized as art or whether it would be better labelled as experimental music. In 2010 – it took a long time to catch on! – the Turner Prize was won by an artist who sang various overlapping versions of an ancient Scottish song played back through loudspeakers. There was no visual element at all and the honour was seen as an important boost for this relatively new genre.

Interviewer: Mm, interesting. I know you want to talk about the Internet now and how that's changed art, or at least where people look at it.

Speaker: Yes, now I'm a bit sceptical about all the different labels and movements that are supposed to exist. In the 90s, we had new media art and Internet art. Now, we have video game art and virtual art. Frankly, they're all a slight twist on what's ultimately the same basic concept. Internet art, or net art, as it's often called, is digital artwork distributed over the Internet. For me, the interesting thing is that this form of art has bypassed the traditional dominance of the gallery system, delivering aesthetic experiences directly to the viewer – that may be at home or while they're at work. The viewer is often drawn into some kind of interaction and messages – just like many forms of art over the centuries – are frequently social and political in nature.

Interviewer: So, I assume that a Van Gogh painting downloaded and sent as an attachment is not net art.

Speaker: No, certainly not. Simply digitalizing existing images is not the point. Lots of traditional artists now exhibit their work in online galleries. That doesn't mean they're net artists. Net art relies intrinsically on the Internet to exist, taking advantage of interactive interface and connectivity to multiple social and economic cultures. Net art can be created through websites, e-mail collaborations, original software projects and the creation of games. It may also include video and audio elements.

Interviewer: It sounds to me as though you're saying that the Internet itself is art – I mean, that almost any feature on the net can be seen as an art form. Couldn't this have been said about all sorts of previous aspects of design, like packaging?

Speaker: I think it was.

Interviewer: Mm. You're going to tell us about street art now. I don't know a great deal about it, but I'd like to. I sense that there's something a bit more substantial here – something really a bit different.

Speaker: Well, perhaps, though, as I said, it's where the art exists that is different – not necessarily the imagery itself. Street art is any art created in public spaces – that is, usually in the streets. Street art typically refers to unsanctioned art rather than government or local authority-sponsored art. Very much as with graffiti, once it is allowed and people accept it, it loses some of its purpose and appeal.

Interviewer: So, is street art really graffiti, then?

Speaker: No, definitely not. While traditional graffiti artists used free-hand aerosol paints, street art encompasses a range of media and techniques, including mosaic and tiling, murals and stencils. Street installations are popular, as is video projection. A new angle is sticker art, where art is produced and then stuck onto walls or other surfaces in public places.

Interviewer: So, in many respects, it's traditional art that's been taken out of the studio and gallery, and onto the street?

Speaker: Absolutely. Street artists claim that they don't aspire to change the definition of art, but rather to question the environment in which it exists.

Interviewer: So, what are the legal implications? I mean, graffiti was and still is often just vandalism. Is street art more acceptable?

Speaker: Some street artists have become very popular very quickly, and have sold work to well-known collectors or have been commissioned to create work for advertisers. Street art has a veneer of respectability that graffiti didn't. However, most street artists create their work in order to spread a social or political message and some of it is still quite simple and very subversive. For this reason, street art is sometimes referred to as post-graffiti. I'd say that most street artists don't wish to become part of the establishment.

Interviewer: Yes, I'd be interested to know how exactly a collector goes about buying a painting on the wall of a city centre building or a video projected onto a bridge in the middle of the night. It does seem that once …

C 1. C 2. A 3. C 4. B 5. A 6. B 7. A 8. C

Tapescript 🎧 **101 (0 mins, 17 secs)**

C Look at the statements 1–8. Listen and match each statement with the correct movement A, B or C.

[Play Track 100 again]

Tapescript 🎧 **102 (0 mins, 15 secs)**

D Read the tapescript as you listen again. Make a note of any new words and phrases that you think are useful.

[Play Track 100 again]

Reading

A 1. I 2. I 3. P 4. P 5. P 6. P 7. N 8. N
9. N 10. I 11. I 12. P

B of course / Now / I ask myself / In short

C 1. N 2. Y 3. NG 4. Y 5. NG 6. Y

Writing

A dispensing with = sacrificing
expanded = enlarged
moved = relocated
provide = install
located = situated
installed = fitted
accommodate = make room for

B 1. introduced   2. reduce   3. adapt
4. enhanced   5. divided   6. restored

10 Rain or shine

Speaking and Vocabulary

Objectives

- To practise talking about weather conditions.
- To revise, present and practise vocabulary related to weather conditions.
- To practise interaction typical of the first and third parts of the IELTS Speaking test.
- To introduce the concept of the weather as a metaphor for human emotions.

The first module aims to bring the various parts of the Speaking test together. The first part gives students an opportunity to exchange information about their own situation. The last part of the lesson develops the theme and practises exchanges more typical of the third part of the Speaking test.

Start with books closed. Show an OHT or other visual medium of the quotation on the board and gradually reveal it. Start with just *Weather is a great metaphor for life* and clarify the meaning of *metaphor*. Give an example previously learnt – *I'm snowed under with work*, in which being very busy is compared to being stuck in snow. Reveal the next part – *sometimes it's good, sometimes it's bad, and there's nothing much you can do about it but ...* and see if students can guess the ending. Finally, reveal *carry* and see if students can work out the last two words. Give students two minutes to think about the quotation and then a minute to discuss it in pairs, focusing on what it means and their reaction to it.

> *Terri Guillemets is a quotation anthologist from Phoenix, Arizona, who has collected quotes since the age of 13. Her passion is sharing inspirational, thought-provoking and humorous quotations with a worldwide audience via her website The Quote Garden at www.quotegarden.com. Her own quotation here is itself a metaphor. She is saying that life is full of unexpected events and all you can do is try to protect yourself.*

Vocabulary 1

Students at this level will have learnt weather vocabulary numerous times. It is assumed that they will already know basic nouns, adjectives and verbs to talk about frequent conditions. Some common lexis is revised here – *rainbow, thunder and lightning*, etc. – but most is likely to be new or at least not perfectly clear. Students should be selective if they feel they are overloaded with new items.

A Students should work individually in silence. There is an opportunity to interact and clarify the meaning of new lexis in B. Encourage them to use dictionaries only for items they really do not know – they can discuss those they are simply unclear on later. Point out that the context in each sentence will help them understand new items. Set a time limit of ten minutes. Monitor and check what students are looking up. Give assistance if and when necessary.

Pronunciation check

The aim is to check this pronunciation feature before students use the language in B. Write *lightning* on the board and get several students to say it. It is unlikely that anyone will produce it correctly, and each time you should just say *no*, or *not quite*. If anyone produces it with three syllables, point out that that is totally wrong! If anyone does produce it with the appropriate nasal sound, get them to repeat and make sure other students listen. Refer students to the information and give them time to read and absorb. Make sure they look at the list of examples before you play the recording.

🎧 Play the whole recording and then again, pausing to drill. Note that the sound is very difficult for many students to produce and the real aim is to make them aware of it. Say the words yourself, showing students physically what you are doing, if possible. Give them time to practise saying the words in pairs and monitor to see if there is improvement.

Tapescript 🎧 103 (0 mins, 34 secs)
Pronunciation check

Listen to these words that contain the sound. Then practise saying them.
1 lightning
2 frightening
3 frightened
4 certainly
5 important

B How this exercise works will depend largely on whether students are all from the same town or city, or from various parts of the world. If students are in a pair with a partner from another part of the world, they should both exchange information and clarify the meaning of any new vocabulary. If students are from the same place, they will have to focus on checking that they have the same sentences ticked and discussing vocabulary they are uncertain of.

Rather than conduct a repetitive feedback stage, give students a short test. Tell them to cover the exercise and then give them definitions as they shout out the newly acquired words and phrases – *What does snow turn to when it starts to melt? What do we call something between rain and*

snow? Tell students to ask you about any remaining uncertainties.

Refer students to the Exam tip and give them time to read and absorb.

C The aim is as much to increase students' awareness as it is to learn these items specifically. Read through the instructions one part at a time with the class. Read the first part and write *salt – salty* and *speed – speedy* to show that these adjectives can come from any topic area. Emphasize that these adjectives are often informal – native speakers sometimes make them up! Read the last part and write *sun – sunny* and *rain – rainy* on the board, pointing out how often these adjectives are related to the weather.

Students should work in pairs so that they can communicate as they go. Encourage them to focus on the meaning of the whole phrase – not just the adjective. Native speakers expect to see these words together.

As feedback, give examples of where these expressions might be seen or heard rather than simply explain them. Point out the suffix *~less* on *cloudless* and explain that *~less* often creates the adjective which is the opposite of one with a *~y* ending.

Answers:
wintry showers = sleet / hail (on a weather forecast)
a stormy night = a night with rain and thunder and lightning (to set the scene in a scary story)
icy conditions = roads with snow and ice (a TV or radio warning for drivers)
patchy cloud = some blue sky, but with some cloud (on a weather forecast)
a summery dress = a light, comfortable dress

Speaking 1

The aim is fourfold – to present students with further examples of good Part 1 interview practice, to provide some authentic listening practice, to introduce some additional useful vocabulary and to set a context for the grammar point.

A 🎧 Tell students they will hear three extracts from interviews. Tell them that they have no clues this time – they will not see the examiner's questions first, for example. They should listen carefully to the question as though they were asked it themselves in an interview and then make notes when the student answers. Play the recording, pausing briefly between extracts to give students time to write.

Tapescript 🎧 **104 (1 min, 49 secs)**

A   Listen to some interview exchanges. Make notes about what each student says.

1

Examiner: Do you have four seasons, like in European countries?

Student: No, we don't. We have a rainy season and a dry season. It's the rainy season now so we expect some rain most days. Sometimes it's just overcast or there are a few showers, but on other days there are severe storms and very heavy rain. It can be very humid – muggy, I think you say.

2

Examiner: Would you say the weather influences the Spanish lifestyle?

Student: Definitely – probably like in all countries where there is a lot of sunshine. We can depend on the weather to be good for several months of the year and this allows us to enjoy an outdoor lifestyle. People drive to the coast at the weekend or arrange parties in their gardens. You see people sitting outside restaurants to have dinner – not like in the north of Europe, where everyone eats inside.

3

Examiner: So, what do you think of our English weather?

Student: Um, I don't want to sound too negative, but I get a bit fed up of it. I have to carry an umbrella all the time, but I still get soaked on the way to college most mornings. I think the frequent bad weather stops people doing a lot of outdoor activities and it discourages them from arranging to meet friends for a picnic or barbecue. In Brazil, we have social events like that very often.

B   Give students three or four minutes to compare and then get some feedback. Write the questions on the board as students remember them (see tapescript) and a brief summary of each answer. Write *severe* and *get soaked* on the board and see if students managed to catch the meaning.

C   🎧 Give students a minute to read the questions before they listen so they know what they are listening for. Play the whole recording. There is no need to pause directly after each gapped item. Show an OHT or other visual medium of the exercise on the board and write the answers in as feedback. Make a point of eliciting the correct grammatical form of the missing verbs.

Answers:
1. to enjoy   2. doing   3. from arranging

Tapescript 🎧 **105 (0 mins, 10 secs)**

C   Listen again and complete the sentences.

[Play Track 104 again]

Grammar check

The information should simply serve as consolidation. There is quite a lot to take in, however, and rather than simply allowing students to read through it, you could show an OHT or other visual medium on the board and reveal the information in more absorbable chunks. Students should work individually on the exercise and then compare answers with a partner. Write answers on the board for clarity.

Answers:
1. to enjoy   2. from taking
3. (from) having to   4. to cancel

Speaking 2

The aim now is to develop the theme and practise interaction more typical of the third part of the Speaking test. At the same time, vocabulary related to *extreme weather conditions* is revised/presented.

Refer students to the Exam tip and give them time to read and absorb. Remind them that *environmental issues* and *climate change* are themes that commonly arise in all parts of the IELTS exam.

A You will know whether or not there has been a recent extreme weather event which students will be able to talk about. There is usually at least one event at any given time. Tell them to think about the event or events they want to talk about and then to check the specific vocabulary. They can learn the other words in the box later.

As feedback, choose two or three students to give brief feedback. Avoid getting into a long discussion to which very few students will contribute. Then go over the words in the box, checking pronunciation and dealing with any uncertainties. Relate each to a part or parts of the world where they are likely to occur. You could point out that tornadoes are often called *twisters* in parts of the United States where they are frequent.

B Previously, students have listened to answers and then answered the questions themselves. This time, they answer the questions first and then listen to compare their performance with the models. Set a time limit of 30 seconds for each student to answer each question.

Students should spend three minutes reading the questions and thinking individually. Then, they should answer the questions and develop a short conversation with a partner. Monitor to check performance and assist where necessary. Make a note of good answers that could be shared with the class as feedback. You may prefer to skip a feedback stage and go straight onto hearing the model answers.

C Tell students that they will hear model answers. Emphasize that these answers have been designed as good answers and that they should not feel that their answers are inferior. Refer them to the task instructions and play the recording right through as they match.

Answers:
Student A = 2 / Student B = 1 / Student C = 3

Tapescript 106 (2 mins, 8 secs)

C Listen and match each student with a question in Exercise B.

Student A
Student: That's a very difficult question. I think it's possibly a bit of both. Of course, we know that glaciers and ice caps are melting and there have been extreme heatwaves in some countries, but the winters are still very cold – maybe even colder than before. It seems more a case of the weather becoming more extreme, rather than it just getting hotter. I think there are some reports that spread panic.

Student B
Student: Well, many people say it is and sometimes I think it is. It seems that summer days are hotter each year and winters go on for longer. Now, it seems there's no spring at all – one day it's cold and then it's summer! However, when I think back to when I was little, it was just the same. I remember at least two winters when there was lots of snow and summers when it was too hot to go out.

Student C
Student: It's a good question. I think some events like hurricanes probably have always happened and will always happen, but there are other events like floods and mudslides that people cause. I don't understand completely, but I heard that we cut down too many trees and then they don't hold the rainwater. This results in floods that we say are 'acts of God' even though we made them happen. Also, we build towns and villages in places where we know there are extreme conditions. I think we must say then that we are partly to blame if there's a catastrophe.

D As has previously been stated, one of students' biggest concerns is that they do not know about some of the topics which are typical in the IELTS exam. The principal aim here is to reassure students that they can give a perfectly good answer without being an expert on a topic. Refer students to the tapescript and play the recording again. Pronounce and drill the difficult word *catastrophe* /kəˈtæstrəfiː/.

Vocabulary 2

A Read through the instructions with students and remind them of the quotation at the beginning of the module. They can talk in pairs. Note that they learnt the first expression earlier in the course.

As feedback, tell students to cover the exercise and read the definitions below as students shout out the expressions.

1. I'm feeling a bit under the weather. = I'm not very well at the moment.
2. They've had a stormy relationship. = Their relationship has not been smooth.
3. I was given a very warm welcome. = People treated me very kindly when I arrived.
4. He was given a frosty reception. = People were unfriendly when he arrived.

B Conduct in small groups or as a quick whole-class discussion. Explain that by *area of metaphor*, we mean that we compare one whole area with another, *sport and war* or *time and money*, for example. Ascertain whether in students' own first language or languages, there are similar whole areas like this and whether the expressions in A exist.

Listening

Objectives

- To practise listening in order to understand cause and effect.
- To practise listening to complete a flow chart.
- To provide further practice spelling answers correctly.

Students have practised with flow charts in both reading and writing lessons and so will understand their purpose and how they are organized. They have seen that having information organized into a table facilitates listening and should appreciate the benefit of being able to follow a flow chart in the same way.

Apart from the various elements of listening practice, the aim of this module is to teach students about an important feature of environmental change. It will benefit students to understand the process of deforestation and its consequences.

In this Listening Module, the one recording serves as the topic of both parts of the lesson.

Listening 1

The aim of the first part of the lesson is to orientate students towards the overall theme, to present core vocabulary and to provide basic background knowledge that will facilitate the exam practice listening later.

A Read through the instructions with the class and refer them to the pictures. Tell them to think about the connection for a moment before they start looking at the words and phrases in the box.

Students should spend three minutes checking the words and phrases individually, before discussing the connection between the pictures with a partner. Monitor and give individual assistance, but do not give class feedback or rigorously check the vocabulary until they have listened to the first part of the lecture (see *Vocabulary suggestions* after the notes for C). It will be difficult to clarify the meaning of individual items without going into the process.

B 🎧 Make sure students appreciate they are listening only to the introduction to a lecture and that they are listening to check what they have just discussed. Play the recording through and then give them a moment to discuss what they heard in pairs. Do not give feedback yet.

Tapescript 🎧 108 (1 min, 35 secs)

B Listen to the first part of a lecture about how deforestation can cause mudslides. Check your ideas in Exercise A.

Voice: So, we've been looking at global warming and this week we've been focusing on deforestation and thinking about some of the consequences of that. If you remember, I told you that an area something like the size of Panama is cut down in various parts of the globe each year – a huge rate of destruction. We've seen how deforestation deprives wildlife – not to mention the very few indigenous tribes that still reside in the rainforest – of natural habitat and how the loss of unique plants may mean losing opportunities to find the natural remedies for disease – we may be wiping out future cures of cancer in our haste to build roads and infrastructure. Today, we're going to concentrate on the so-called natural disasters that can be a direct cause of deforestation – how mudslides occur on steep slopes stripped of vegetation when torrential rain or earthquakes destabilize them. Mud can flow down the slopes, sometimes at high speeds, gathering rocks and debris, and can completely destroy buildings and bury villages.

C 🎧 Read through the question with students and play the recording again. Give them another couple of minutes to discuss what they heard the second time they listened.

The feedback stage should be fairly rigorous, ensuring that students understand the basic process before they go on to hear more of the lecture. Go through the process with them, checking and expanding on the vocabulary. Ask why certain key points – wildlife, indigenous tribes, diseases, etc. – were mentioned. You can decide whether or not to play the recording again as students read the tapescript.

Tapescript 🎧 109 (0 mins, 13 secs)

C Listen again and write down some of the other effects of deforestation that were mentioned.

[Play Track 108 again]

Vocabulary suggestions

- Use the picture to check *log* – explain that *logging* means cutting down large numbers of trees for timber.
- *Rainforest* is countable or uncountable, as is *forest*. A rainforest is a large area of forest in a region, where it rains a lot. Contrast with *jungle*.
- Show how *deforestation* is formed with a prefix and suffix added to *forest*. There is a verb *deforest*, but the noun is more frequently used.
- Explain the difference between *soil* and *mud*. *Soil* refers to what plants grow in and has a positive connotation. *Mud* is wet soil and has a more negative connotation – *covered in mud*.
- The verb from *erosion* is *erode*. If soil is eroded, it is carried or blown away.
- A *mudslide* is also referred to as a *landslide*. *Slide* is both a noun and verb – if mud or land slides, it loses its support and moves downwards.

Listening 2

A 🎧 Read through the instructions with students and give them a minute to study the flow chart. Ask what sort of information is required – they should be able to predict that there will be a list of causes. Play the recording through and give students a minute to compare answers with a partner before you check them. Play the recording again, pausing to write answers. Ideally, write answers on an OHT or other visual medium of the chart shown on the board. Point out how *ranching*, a word that students will probably not know but can understand in context, is repeated.

Answers:
1. ranching   2. logging   3. construction
4. mining

Tapescript 🎧 110 (1 min, 14 secs)

A Listen to the next part of the lecture and complete the first part of a flow chart.

Voice: So, what are the reasons for deforestation in the first place? Let's go back over the causes before we move on. First of all, *ranching* – that is, clearing land so that cattle can feed. Of course, this is not the cattle of local farmers, but ranching on a huge scale that provides produce for international markets. Secondly, *logging* – that's cutting down the trees for timber – not simply burning the rainforest to clear it, but to use the wood the trees provide. Thirdly, *construction* – this is more often than not road building as parts of countries are linked. It may also be the construction of new residential areas as populations increase. Finally, forests are cleared for *mining* – gold and silver mining are common in areas where rainforest exists and new sources of precious metals are exploited wherever they may be.

B Students will be aware that discussion points like this are subsequently the focus of an Exam tip. Discourage them from looking ahead if they appear to be doing so. Give them a minute to answer the question and then get some quick feedback. Encourage students to tell you that a flow chart facilitates the listening process in the same way that a table or a summary does – it helps you predict how the lecture will be organized.

Refer students to the Question-type tip and give them a moment to read and absorb.

Listening 3

A 🎧 Since there is no need to refocus, students can be left to their own devices for the practice part of the lesson. Give them a little longer than usual to read the questions as they should appreciate how the flow chart format helps them to make predictions.

Once again, you might want to point out that in the exam, a number of different task types will be integrated to assess comprehension – students will probably not write as many as seven answers on a flow chart like this.

Play the whole recording – do not pause for them to write answers. Check answers after B.

Tapescript 🎧 111 (3 mins, 42 secs)

A **Listen to the rest of the lecture and complete the flow chart.**

Voice: Onto the specific theme of today's lecture then – mudslides. You've probably heard the term *landslide* before – that's pretty much the same thing, but we use *mudslide* when the soil and debris that slides consists of a lot of water – it's wet – it's mud! To illustrate how serious an event a mudslide can be, let me say that in 1999, a mudslide in Venezuela was responsible for taking 20,000 human lives when torrential rain pounded down onto deforested hillsides. The trees in the rainforest stop soil eroding in various ways. Most importantly, underground, their tight-knit root systems keep soil in place and hold it to the bedrock below. Tree litter – that's fallen leaves, branches and twigs – slows water runoff which occurs when it rains. Obviously, when the rain is torrential, this water runoff is far more evident and causes far more damage. It carries away topsoil, weakening the foundation that lies below. When land, especially land on slopes and hillsides, is stripped of vegetation, this whole layer of protection disappears. When there are storms, and rain is especially heavy, often during the rainy season, in many areas where mudslides occur the chances of a catastrophe are far higher. Large areas of hillside or chunks of rock give way and start sliding downwards. In some cases, a single relatively small chunk of hillside can cause untold damage if close to an area of residence – perhaps just an isolated farmhouse or a tiny mountain village. Generally speaking, however, the area of land that slides is high up on the hillside and the potential for catastrophe is even greater. By the time the original breakaway chunk arrives at the foot of the slope, it may be far, far bigger. As the land slides – and let's remember that we're talking about thick wet mud, so perhaps we should say *flows* rather than *slides* – it picks up more soil as well as rocks and any other debris in its path. If the slide has already destroyed one or two hillside homes, it will have picked up and be carrying substantial amounts of solid matter – perhaps even cars and other large pieces of machinery. When the mudslide arrives at the bottom of the slope, it can completely destroy whatever is in its path and bury whole villages. In 2006, a mudslide completely covered a village in the Philippines, killing 57 people in just two minutes. As deforestation accelerates – and remember we've said that an area of rainforest the size of Panama is cleared annually – catastrophic mudslides increase in frequency. The most pessimistic estimates conclude that our rainforests could vanish within 100 years. Fortunately, there's now awareness and a realization that destruction cannot continue and governments in many of the countries which …

B Checking and reflecting on answers is a constant feature of the skills modules. Give students sufficient time to check and think about why any answers were incorrect before moving onto C. You can decide if it would be beneficial to play the recording again, but avoid doing so simply to check individual students' wrong answers. It will probably be more beneficial to listen again later as they read the tapescript. As they check, monitor and make a note of words that were misspelt.

Answers:
1. root systems   2. bedrock   3. tree litter
4. topsoil   5. isolated   6. (other) debris / solid matter   7. whole villages

C Students will be used to reflecting on tasks in this way by now. Remind them that identifying what they are doing well and not doing so well is a very good way of focusing on what they can do better next time. Allow students time to reflect and complete the exercise. Ask whether anyone heard words but misspelt them or, more positively, managed to spell answers correctly without really understanding them. Conclude by asking them if they are happy with the number of correct answers.

D The aim is to provide an additional comprehension and discussion task rather than additional exam practice. It will give them a further opportunity to absorb features of the topic for future reference. Students should work in pairs so that they can communicate as they go. Monitor and check for comprehension and fluency of answers. Assist if and when necessary. Class feedback is unnecessary. See the highlighted words in the tapescript for answers.

Key vocabulary in context

Work through the exercises one at a time as they are very different in type.

A Students should work individually and then check answers in pairs. Encourage them to match without checking the tapescript and then to check for confirmation. As feedback, tell students to cover the exercise and elicit the four compounds to write on the board. Check pronunciation as you go.

Answers:
1. indigenous tribes   2. natural habitat
3. precious metals   4. solid matter

B Work through as A. As feedback, tell students to cover the exercise and read out the definitions as students shout out the newly acquired vocabulary.

Answers:
1. f   2. e   3. c   4. a   5. b   6. d

C 🎧 Give students a moment to look at the list before you play the recording. If necessary, do one as an example showing them how to underline the stressed syllable or draw a little box above it. Play the recording through and then again, pausing after each item to check answers. As you write the answers on the board, show where weak forms occur as well as marking the stress. Emphasize the shifting stress on 4 and 5. Drill the words and then give students a couple of minutes to practise saying them aloud in pairs.

Answers:
1. in'digenous   2. 'precious   3. ac'celerate
4. ca'tastrophe   5. cata'strophic

Tapescript 🎧 112 (0 mins, 32 secs)
Key vocabulary in context

C   **Listen and mark the main stress on the words from the lecture.**

1 indigenous
2 precious
3 accelerate
4 catastrophe
5 catastrophic

Refer students to the Workbook exercises related to this module. Choose to work on them now or set up for homework.

Reading

Objectives

- **To emphasize the importance of understanding referencing in a text.**
- **To practise understanding what is being referred to in a text more quickly.**
- **To provide further practice with a range of typical IELTS Reading tasks.**

The principal aim in this Reading Module is to practise a general reading skill rather than exam strategy – students will not have to identify referencing features as a task in the exam. Students will complete exercises that focus on referencing directly (non-exam tasks) and exam practice tasks that aim to indirectly practise the skill acquired.

Apart from the various elements of reading practice, the aim of this module is to teach students about an important feature of environmental change. It will benefit students to understand more about global warming and its possible consequences. Note that ideas and language from the Reading Module in Unit 7 are recycled.

In this Reading Module, the one passage serves as the topic of both parts of the lesson.

Reading 1

The first part of the lesson introduces the overall theme of the module and the reading skill.

A To best focus students' attention, start with books closed and show an OHT or other visual medium of only the heading and the figure on the board. If students do refer to the figure in the book, make sure they do not start reading the supporting information with it – the aim at the moment is to get a very rough idea of the concept. Check vocabulary in both the heading and figure to aid comprehension (see *Vocabulary suggestions*).

Set a time limit of two minutes for this initial discussion. Get some quick feedback, but do not confirm or correct – B develops the theme and provides further guidance.

Vocabulary suggestions

- *Urban* means *of the city*. Point out that it is an adjective, but is almost always used immediately before a noun and usually forms fixed expressions as here. Contrast it with *rural* – *of the country*.
- Point out the prefix on *suburban* and explain that it means *close to* or *around the city* – if houses are *in the suburbs*, they are in areas around the city.
- *Downtown* is used more in American English and means *the city centre*. It is both a noun and adjective – *a downtown restaurant.*
- A *pond* here is American English. In British English, a large expanse of water as here is a *lake*. In British English, a *pond* is a much smaller body of water – in a garden, for example.
- A *warehouse* is a large building where products are stored.

B Students should complete the matching task individually and then compare answers with a partner. Provide answers, dealing with any uncertainties, and then give students another minute or so in their pair to decide whether or not the vocabulary has helped them understand the concept. Get some further brief feedback. Do not worry if students say that the vocabulary has not helped them. Do not be tempted to explain ideas yourself – students will read the passage to check in a moment.

Answers:

1. e 2. a 3. d 4. b 5. c

C Make sure students appreciate they are reading the passage with the aim of checking their own ideas. Emphasize that they should not consider the highlighted items yet – they are part of another exercise entirely. Give them the time they need to read within reason – it is important that they fully grasp the basic concept now before they focus on the referencing and go on to read the next part of the passage. Make sure they read the information that supports the figure as well as the main text. As feedback, simply ascertain whether the passage confirmed ideas and if it was interesting. Tell students they will discuss it in more depth later (see E).

D Students will probably have studied simple referencing devices, like using pronouns and possessive adjectives, but perhaps not the more sophisticated devices presented here. At this level, students should appreciate how a whole range of referencing features help to organize and create cohesion in a text. They should now be using some of these features in their own written English.

Read through the instructions with students. Show an OHT or other visual medium of the passage on the board and show how *their* refers back to *urban areas*.

As urban areas develop, changes occur within their landscape.

Emphasize that the references can point both back and ahead in a text, but do not give another example. Any uncertainties can be clarified during a feedback stage and students will have an opportunity to practise later.

Students should work in pairs so that they can communicate and compare knowledge as they go.

Feedback should be rigorous, ensuring that all is clear and that students are prepared for the practice part of the lesson. Show an OHT or other visual medium of the passage and mark it as below. Use the answer key that follows to clarify how each reference works.

Answers:

their = possessive adjective (reference shown as example)
features = general noun referring back to given examples
These changes = general noun phrase summarizing previously given explanation (avoidance of repetition)
exposed urban surfaces = general noun referencing ahead to given examples
its = possessive adjective referencing back to given noun
The graphic = alternative noun replacing previously used noun phrase (avoidance of repetition)
bodies of water = general noun referencing ahead to given examples

Urban Heat Islands

As urban areas develop, changes occur within their landscape. Buildings, roads, and other features of infrastructure replace open land and vegetation. Surfaces that were once permeable and moist become impermeable and dry. These changes cause urban regions to become warmer than their rural surroundings, forming an 'island' of higher temperatures within the landscape.

Heat islands occur on the surface and in the atmosphere. On a hot, sunny summer day, the sun can heat dry, exposed urban surfaces, such as roofs and pavement, to temperatures up to 50°C hotter than the air, while shaded or moist surfaces, often within more rural surroundings, remain close to air temperatures. Surface urban heat islands are present day and night, but tend to be strongest during the day when the sun is shining.

In contrast, atmospheric urban heat islands are often weak during the late morning and throughout the day and become more pronounced after sunset due to the slow release of heat from urban infrastructure. The annual average air temperature of a city with a population of 1 million or more can be 1–3°C warmer than its surroundings. On a clear, calm night, however, the temperature difference can be as much as 12°C.

The heat island sketch below shows how urban temperatures are typically lower at the urban–rural border than in dense downtown areas. The graphic also illustrates how parks, open land, and bodies of water, such as lakes, ponds and reservoirs, can create cooler areas within a city.

Refer students to the Exam tip and give them time to read and absorb. Tell them to cover it and select one student to summarize for the class.

E   Make sure students appreciate that the aim is to assess what they have absorbed – not to remember the passage word for word. They should use largely their own words, incorporating the key words and phrases they have learnt when appropriate. Monitor and check performance. Another feedback stage is unnecessary.

Reading 2

The aim of the second part of the lesson is as much to consolidate and practise referencing as it is to provide exam practice. The more rigorous preparation stage reflects that.

A   The aim is to link the two parts of the passage and give students an opportunity to predict content. They will need to skim the passage for gist before engaging in the challenging gap-filling exercise that follows, and here they set their own gist task. Read through the questions, clarifying *measures* and pointing out the phrase *take measures*. Students should answer the questions in pairs. Monitor to check the validity of ideas and to make a note of points that could be shared during a feedback stage.

Keep feedback brief, getting a couple of suggested answers for each question. Do not confirm or correct and do not try to feed answers yourself – there are far too many possibilities. Students should read the passage to check their ideas.

B   Before students read, tell them to look at the passage and its layout and ask them what is going to help them skim read. Establish that the subheadings, particularly in the *Effects* section of the passage, answer the questions. Tell them that they should concentrate on the subheadings and skim the rest of each paragraph for key information.

Make sure they understand that they are reading to check what they discussed and not to worry about the gaps and the box of words and phrases for now. It is a fairly long, challenging passage and they will need sufficient time to

read with any real purpose. Set a time limit of five minutes.

A feedback stage could be very time-consuming. A shortcut will be to tell students to close their books and then in pairs, remember one effect and one measure that stood out for them. Do not allow students to compare all their thoughts with the content of the passage.

C   Read through the instructions with students and make sure they know what to do – the task is challenging, but fairly straightforward.

It is an exercise that will take around 15 minutes to complete – students will need to read carefully and then choose from the options. Some students will prefer to work individually and have time to think, while others will prefer to share ideas and communicate right away – they should decide for themselves. One option would be to work on each section individually and then compare ideas before moving on. They should certainly compare answers with a partner at the end of the task since they will probably have changed a number of them retrospectively.

As feedback, show an OHT or other visual medium of the passage on the board and write answers in as you check them. Checking answers orally will suffice, but make sure they are all clear.

Answers:
1. most   2. health issues   3. it   4. them
5. Vegetation   6. approach   7. they   8. their
9. these finance-related considerations
10. They   11. those   12. its   13. properties
14. this drawback   15. their   16. term
17. materials   18. ones

D   The exam tasks may seem secondary having done so much work on referencing, but students should approach them as they have done so previously. Note that here there are two tasks with a similar number of questions in each, as will be the case in the exam. Set a time limit of ten minutes, pointing out that they have already read the text in depth and should know where to locate answers. Give them an extra two minutes if a number of students have not completed the exercise. You can decide if students will benefit from comparing answers with a partner before checking the answers.

E Checking and reflecting on answers is a constant feature of the skills modules. Give students sufficient time to check and think about why they may have answered incorrectly.

Students might want to know why some of their answers were not correct. Explaining some points may be necessary and beneficial, but going through all of them will be very time-consuming. It is probably best to reassure them that with more practice their scores will improve.

If you do want to identify the specific parts of the passage that provide answers to any questions, make an OHT or other visual medium of the passage and highlight those parts on the board.

Answers:
1. plant-growing season   2. cooling
3. power plants   4. discomfort   5. storm water
6. D   7. C   8. B   9. D   10. A   11. B   12. A

F Students will be familiar with this type of reflective process. Point out that again, points are related specifically to the reading skills and task strategies practised. Remind them that identifying what they are doing well and not doing so well is a very good way of focusing on what they can do better next time. Allow students time to reflect and complete the exercise and then ask them if they are happy with the number of correct answers.

Key vocabulary in context

Remind students that an effective way to learn and remember new vocabulary is to study it closely once it has been presented in context. One aim is to practise understanding new lexis in context, but the words here have been selected as flexible, high-frequency items and students should try to learn and retain them. Work through the exercises one at a time to emphasize the different parts of speech that are the focus.

A Students have worked through exercises like this a number of times now and will know how to approach this one. They will need some time to individually check the items in context before comparing with a partner. As feedback, read the definitions opposite as students shout out the newly acquired items as answers.

Answers:
1. lengthen = make longer
2. utilize = use for a specific purpose
3. maintain = care for
4. outweigh = be more important than
5. absorb = take in
6. filter = take out harmful elements
7. deflect = change the direction of
8. soak in = absorb

B Work through as with Exercise A.

Answers:
1. dense = thick
2. strategic = proceed with thought and care to achieve a specific purpose
3. aesthetic = relating to what is pleasing to look at (usually before a noun in a fixed expression)
4. emerging = newly invented

Refer students to the Workbook exercises related to this module. Choose to work on them now or set up for homework.

Writing

Objectives

- **To give further practice and increase confidence in terms of knowing what to say in a discursive composition.**
- **To give specific guidance as to where content can be expanded to ensure the word count is met.**

The Writing Module in this unit concentrates on Writing Task 2. The issue of students not knowing what to say is revisited and, more specifically, the issue of not having enough material to meet the word count. Advice and guidance is given as to how points made in a discursive composition can be expanded.

In this Writing Module, there is more reading than has been the case. The aim is to provide students with ideas that they can use in the written composition.

Writing 1

The first part of the module aims to orientate students towards the specific theme of the Writing task and to start introducing ideas that might be used in the composition later.

A The discussion relates directly to the issue that is the subject of the Writing task. You will know whether or not your students are likely to have considered the question before and just how much guidance they will need. Remind them that the question was answered briefly by one of the students they listened to in the first module. Read through the instructions/question with students. Ask why *natural* is in inverted commas and establish that disasters are blamed on nature when in fact some are clearly caused by human behaviour. Do not give specific examples as that is to be discussed. Do not go through the words for each disaster beforehand – most were presented in the first module and students can check any they do not know as they go. Advise students to spend a minute or two thinking individually before engaging in pairwork.

Use feedback to check the words for each disaster and find out what students already know. They will read to check ideas in a moment, so do not feed ideas or allow an extended debate to develop.

Disasters are:
a. earthquake   b. volcanic eruption   c. flood
d. tidal wave   e. drought   f. wildfire

B Set a time limit of two minutes for students to skim the extract. Make sure they understand that the principal aim is to decide whether the text says that disasters really are natural or whether they are caused by human behaviour – not to decide whether each disaster pictured is natural. Get some quick feedback and establish that the text claims that most disasters are not totally natural.

Give students another three minutes to read the text more carefully. Allow them to use dictionaries to look up a maximum of two words, which they feel are essential for comprehension. Tell them to close their books and summarize the text quickly in pairs, using their own words. As feedback, select individuals and ask, *What is the*

anthropocene? What are the effects of global warming? What do scientists and insurance companies have in common?

Writing 2

The second part of the lesson presents the task and then concentrates on identifying points that could be made and planning the actual content of the composition.

A Students will now be accustomed to studying Writing task instructions and then discussing them. Refer them to the instructions and give them a minute to read through and check they understand everything. Encourage them to highlight key words or phrases and make notes as they learnt to earlier in the course. Do not allow them to use dictionaries now.

Show an OHT or other visual medium of the instructions and highlight *so-called*. Select a student to remind the class of its meaning. Highlight *attributed to* and do the same. When students are ready, they should answer the questions in pairs. Note that the first question is posed again as having enough to say is the focus of the module.

Get some brief feedback. Establish that students must write at least 250 words. Point out that writing an excessively long introduction or conclusion without much in the middle is not a good idea, but that making sure both the introduction and conclusion are solid is a good way of achieving the word count.

B This stage should serve as an interim between what has been suggested so far and what will be suggested in the reading stage that follows. Students should spend some time suggesting their own ideas before they are fed any more. Read through the instructions with students and make sure they look at the examples and appreciate that they support each side of the debate. Students can work in pairs or groups if you think that will increase the likelihood of productivity. Set a time limit of five minutes. Monitor to check and assist and to make a note of contributions that can be shared during feedback.

As students will go on to read and gather more ideas in a moment, keep feedback fairly brief. Get one point from each pair or group. You can decide whether making notes on the board will be beneficial.

C The principal aim is to provide further arguments that can be used in the composition, but students will benefit from the additional reading practice, the opportunity to exchange information orally and the additional knowledge they gain about this common topic.

For the process to be beneficial, it must be organized and managed properly. Make sure the class can be divided into the required groups. You may have to have one or two groups with only four students, in which case you should give the strongest student in the group two reports to read. If you have one or two students too many, form one or two groups of six, and tell two of the weaker students to read the same report.

Read through the instructions with students and then time each step. Give them three minutes to read without using a dictionary and then a further two minutes to check vocabulary. They can use dictionaries or ask you – if the same word or phrase is a difficulty for a number of students, check it with the whole class more rigorously. Note that vocabulary typical of disaster reporting occurs in more than one of the extracts – *destroy*, *be buried*, etc. – and that the first extract recycles vocabulary learnt earlier in the unit.

When students are ready, emphasize that they should exchange the core information using their own words – they should not try to remember long chunks of the text and should certainly not read parts aloud. If students are confident, tell them to close their books.

Once students are interacting, monitor closely to check that the right information is being exchanged and for accuracy and fluency. A feedback stage is unnecessary as it will only be repetitive.

D Students can either discuss this in the group they are in or go back into pairs. Give them sufficient time to think and answer the question properly. If you think it's necessary, give them an

example – *Logging seems to be widespread, and so should be mentioned. / Toboggan riders causing an avalanche isn't a very important concern.* Further feedback is unnecessary.

Writing 3

A Students should be keen to see how the ideas they have been discussing have been expressed in the composition. They will probably quickly see what the problem is, but should read carefully enough to appreciate that, in other respects, the composition is very good. Give them three minutes to read in silence and then together establish that the composition is too short. Ask them how the composition could be lengthened – does the writer need to introduce another complete argument?

B Tell students that they will now look at ways that the composition could be lengthened. Make sure they cover the second version of the composition so they are not tempted to look ahead. Read through the questions systematically with the class, giving them a moment to think between each. Make sure they understand that, for now, they are not to actually start rewriting or adding to the composition.

Students should spend three minutes individually reading the composition again carefully and planning answers. They can then spend three minutes comparing thoughts with a partner. As feedback, show an OHT or other visual·medium of the composition on the board. Select students to come up and show you where they have expanded, added or given examples. There is no need to confirm or correct suggestions as the exercise that follows develops and gives further guidance.

C Students are now engaged in more or less the same task, but with additional guidance. They should first compare their own ideas with what has been suggested in the model and then think about what to actually write. Note that this is ultimately the writing stage of the lesson – you will probably set the Writing task for homework – and students will need around 20 minutes to work through it properly.

Students should spend five minutes reading and thinking individually. They should then spend at least 15 minutes comparing ideas and writing collaboratively with a partner. Note that some students, whilst happy to discuss ideas with a partner, are reluctant to actually write collaboratively. Ideally, this process should be communicative and an opportunity to share resources, but if some students want to work individually it may be counterproductive to force them to work in pairs. Monitor closely and assist and advise where necessary.

As feedback, refer students to the model on pages 267 and 268. Give them time to read and absorb. Clarify any remaining uncertainties. The model is reproduced below.

Model report:

Not long ago, when people talked about natural disasters, they assumed that they really were all natural – 'acts of God' some might say. As the human race has developed and as we understand more about the consequences of our actions, we realize that some of these events are in fact caused by what we do to the planet.

The huge floods that we have seen recently in many parts of the world are often caused by deforestation. When whole forests of trees are cut down, there is nothing to hold the rainwater and it washes down into rivers, which then overflow. Mudslides are another result of destroying the rainforests. Areas of deforested land break away from a hillside and can cause tremendous damage. Droughts are increasing and becoming common in places where once they were unknown. We produce far higher levels of greenhouse gases, which we release into the atmosphere, causing temperatures to rise. In my country, sandstorms have become more frequent because so many people now drive large vehicles in the desert. People drive too fast and disturb the top layer of sand.

Even disasters that are not actually caused by our interference with nature can have more serious consequences because of the way we live. Earthquakes hit hardest in areas where land has been destabilized by overuse and can easily come away from a hillside. Hurricanes and

tornadoes seem to affect the poorest people since they live in the least stable housing.

Of course, not all disasters can be blamed directly on man. There have always been earthquakes, volcanoes and hurricanes and there always will be. However, I agree that we are moving into an age when man is at least partly to blame for more of these events.

Refer students to the Exam tip and give them time to read and absorb. Tell them to cover it and select one student to summarize for the class.

Writing task

The Writing tasks are found either in the Workbook or in the Exam Practice Module at the end of the unit. For this unit, the task is in the Workbook.

Even if you decide to set the Writing task for homework, students will benefit from a short preparation stage during which they can compare ideas and start planning.

The topic of the discursive composition is very similar to that in the Course Book so students should not need fresh orientation. They will, however, almost certainly need some guidance with what to say. You may feel now that students should be more independent in terms of deciding what points to make, but remember they are still finding it difficult to think of sophisticated ideas in English, let alone express them, if they feel they have nothing to say!

You will know whether or not your students are likely to have opinions on the topic and you can decide how much assistance to give with possible content.

A Give students time to read and absorb the Writing task instructions. Get them to highlight and make notes. Point out that the statement is quite forceful, but that here they are unlikely to simply disagree. Give students five minutes to read through the points and think. They should make notes if they want to.

B Students spend another five minutes comparing ideas with a partner or in small groups. Encourage them to make notes now – they should use shared ideas to plan their composition.

If you feel your students are struggling for ideas, conduct a feedback stage, during which as a class you brainstorm ideas that answer questions 2, 3 and 5. Look ahead to the model for arguments that you could suggest. If you feel that your students have enough to say, skip a feedback stage and let them start writing.

C Once students start writing their compositions, take into account the time already spent preparing. They should need 25–30 minutes. If they write at home, tell them to be strict with a time limit – they will not benefit from spending longer on the task than they will have when it comes to the exam.

When students have completed the task, they should compare it with the model composition on page 268. The model is reproduced below.

If you collect students' compositions to mark, concentrate on what is positive, as well as weaknesses and errors. You will need to start correcting more of all aspects of students' written work now, but remember that correcting every sentence will not be motivating.

Model composition:

When people think about climate change or global warming, as it is now frequently called, they tend to think of it as an issue that we are all affected by equally, whether we are man, woman or child, and regardless of whether we are wealthy or poor. Perhaps we should remember too that it is not only humans who own this planet – climate change is having a terrible impact on animals too!

If people stop to think more deeply, however, they will soon realize that climate change is bound to affect the world's poorest people more than anyone else. They rely more directly on natural resources, are more vulnerable to disaster and are less protected.

We have seen for many years how droughts in parts of Africa result in crop failure and lead to famine. Now, with temperatures rising, those parts of the world are becoming even hotter and drier and the desert is spreading. There is little hope for the world's poorest farmers. In many parts of Asia and South America, floods and

landslides are caused by deforestation. You can be sure that it is the poor who live in rural areas at the foot of the hillside who are hit hardest by any catastrophe. It seems that some countries, usually very poor countries, are especially unlucky – Haiti and Honduras seem to just be recovering from one disaster when they are hit by another.

Of course, there are natural disasters that hit large cities in the first world and climate change is having an effect on all of us. We must look at this situation as one that we are all in together if we have any hope of addressing the problem. However, we must also remember that educated people with skills can escape from areas that become unbearably hot, dry or cold and that it is the poorest who are left behind to suffer.

Consolidation

Instructions are given for Speaking exercises when the procedure is not clear from instructions in the Course Book. Set Vocabulary and Errors exercises either for individual completion and pairwork checking, or as pairwork when you feel immediate interaction is beneficial.

To correct errors in the final exercise, ask students to come and write the correct sentences on the board while other students offer help. You will need to write the corrections on the board to clarify.

Speaking

A Students should answer the questions spontaneously as they would in the interview. Remind them to think for a moment to organize their thoughts. Both students in each pair should answer all the questions. They should aim to each talk for 30–45 seconds for each answer. Monitor to check for fluency and accuracy. Feedback is unnecessary.

B Encourage students to interact and develop a conversation rather than treat each point as a question. Have a time limit in mind.

Vocabulary

A **Answers:**

1. drizzle 2. a rainbow 3. slush
4. breeze / gale / hurricane 5. frost
6. sleet / hail 7. chilly 8. a heatwave
9. muggy 10. Students' own answers.

B **Answers:**

greenhouse gases / solar energy / precious metals / global warming / indigenous tribes / power plant / soil erosion / natural habitat / solid matter

Errors

Answers:

1. … stopped people enjoying …
2. … discouraged people from leaving …
3. … forced us to change …
4. … allows us to spend …
5. … made me wear …
6. … outweigh its drawbacks

Exam Practice

Listening

The Exam Practice Module practises completing a flow chart as one of a number of integrated tasks. By now, students should not need excessive practice specifically with flow charts – the strategies they adopt are similar to those adopted with other note completion tasks. The Listening task in the Workbook provides further practice.

Note once more that students will not have introductory exercises like these when it comes to the actual exam, nor will they be told what each listening section is about. The aim here is to facilitate the listening process and to motivate students to do as well as possible in the tasks.

A Refer students to the pictures and establish that they show *water pipes*. Read through the questions with them and clarify *avert* – prevent something harmful from happening before it happens. Students should answer the questions in pairs.

Use feedback as an opportunity to pre-teach core vocabulary. Select students to answer the questions for the class and either highlight key words they use or teach alternatives (see guidance below).

Possible answers:

1. Temperatures are very low. / The pipes are covered in ice / frozen. / The water in the pipes could freeze. / The pipes could burst. (irregular verb – *burst, burst, burst*)
2. The pipes have been covered / insulated.

B Read through the rubric with students and make sure they understand the prediction task. Give them a moment to think individually and then give them four minutes to talk in pairs. Tell them to check unknown words in a dictionary as they go. Make sure they appreciate that if they have no idea why an item will be mentioned, they should simply move on – they are not expected to know. Monitor to assist and make a note of suggestions that can be used during a feedback stage.

Keep feedback brief, simply asking individuals if they can makes guesses. Do not confirm or correct, and certainly do not feed answers yourself. You may feel that feedback is unnecessary, but note there is no skim reading phase during which they would check ideas this time.

C 🎧 You can decide whether to give students only 30 seconds to read the questions. You may feel that they still need a little longer. There is probably more to read than there will be in an actual exam section.

Play the whole recording. You can decide whether or not students should check answers in pairs before you provide them and whether or not they should hear the recording again to check why any answers were not correct.

Answers:

1. building insulation 2. cold spells
3. homeowners 4. walls
5. temperatures 6. left empty 7. in the freezer
8. expands 9. Water pressure 10. pipe bursts
11. Water escapes
12. B 13. B 14. C 15. A

C Listen to the talk and answer the questions.

Voice: Now, I'm sure you're all here to find out what to do to stop your water pipes freezing and bursting, but first let me say something about why pipes burst and why here in the south, where it's warmer than in many parts of the country, you're actually more at risk. Most people assume that in cold northern climates there's more risk of pipes freezing up, but in fact, houses in northern climates are generally built with the water pipes located on the inside of the building insulation and that, of course, protects them from sub-zero temperatures.

Houses in slightly warmer climates are more vulnerable to winter cold spells. Water pipes are more likely to be located in unprotected areas outside of the building insulation, and homeowners are very often not as aware of freezing problems, which probably only occur once or twice a year. Pipes in lofts and attics, pipes in basements and crawl spaces and pipes in outside walls are all vulnerable to freezing, especially if there are cracks or openings that allow cold, outside air to flow across them. Holes in an outside wall where a television cable or telephone lines enter can also provide access for cold air that can affect water pipes.

So, water pipes freeze and burst because cold air gets to them – remember that when you're warm inside, temperatures outside might be far lower and water pipes that are exposed might be getting much colder than you realize. I don't want to alarm you though – the majority of burst pipes occur when homes are left empty for a while or when the heating inside is simply not sufficient to keep the whole house warm enough. Now, water expands when it freezes – have you ever put a can of soda or a bottle of wine in the freezer to chill it quickly, but then forgotten about it? What happened? It exploded and you spent an hour clearing up the mess! Well, when water freezes in a pipe, it expands in the same way. If it expands sufficiently, the pipe bursts, water escapes and there's some serious damage to contend with. Now, what surprises people is that it isn't ice forming in a pipe that directly causes a break – the split doesn't occur where the ice blockage is. The expansion of the ice against the wall of the pipe isn't the issue. What actually happens is that when a pipe is completely blocked by ice, the water pressure increases downstream – that is, between the blockage and a closed tap at the end. Upstream from the ice blockage there's no danger as water can always retreat back towards its source – there's no build-up of pressure. A water pipe usually bursts where little or no ice has actually formed. This doesn't really matter much to the homeowner, though, as he or she is faced with a clean-up and repair bill when water escapes.

So, what can homeowners do to stop water pipes freezing? Well, quite a lot in fact - pipes that are protected along their entire length by placement within the building's insulation, insulation on the pipe itself or by a sufficient level of heating within the building, are safe. The ideal solution is to place water pipes only in heated parts of the house and to keep them out of the vulnerable areas we've mentioned – lofts, attics, basements and so on. Of course, in modern buildings this is taken for granted and there's really not an issue. In existing houses, it's sometimes possible, though not always practical, to re-route pipes to protected areas. A more realistic and common solution is proper insulation. Vulnerable pipes that are accessible should be fitted with insulation sleeves or wrapped with insulation – the more the better. It's important not to leave gaps that expose the pipe to cold air. Hardware stores and DIY centres will have the necessary materials – sleeves are usually made of foam rubber or fibreglass. Specialist plumbing supply stores will have pipe sleeves with extra-thick insulation and you may feel that the added protection's worth the extra cost. Even if your pipes are well-insulated, it's important to seal cracks and holes on outside walls as these allow cold air in. Another simple solution is to allow taps to drip – this won't guarantee that pipes don't freeze, but it makes it less likely. If there's a spell of extremely cold weather, allow taps to drip. It's not that a small flow of water prevents freezing – this helps, but water can freeze even with a slow flow. It works because opening a tap slightly prevents the build-up of pressure that we've said actually causes the burst in the pipe. If there's no excessive pressure, a pipe won't burst, even if the water inside the pipe freezes.

So, this brings me to what to do if a pipe does freeze or if you suspect that you have a frozen pipe somewhere in the house. If you open a tap and no water comes out …

Unit 10 Workbook answers

Vocabulary development

A 1. b   2. c   3. a

B 1. They are formed by adding an ~en suffix.
2. It is formed by adding ~en to a noun rather than an adjective.

C 1. harden   2. threatening   3. soften   4. sharpen
5. strengthen   6. lighten

D 1. harden = A
2. threatening = N
3. soften = A
4. sharpen = A
5. strengthen = N
6. lighten = A

E 1. *outweigh* – means to *weigh more than*, or in this instance to be *more significant*; to have *greater value* or *importance* than something else.
2. more than

F 1. was far superior to   2. live longer than
3. last longer   4. travel faster than
5. being cleverer than
6. performs better than

G *Slight* is the opposite of all the other adjectives.

Listening

A 1. the United Kingdom and North Africa (the Sahara Desert)
2. It doesn't usually rain sand.

Tapescript 🎧 114 (2 mins, 55 secs)

A Listen to a news report about an unusual weather event and answer the questions.

Newsreader: People in parts of the UK woke up this morning to find their houses and cars coated in a layer of yellowy-brown dust. The cause was sand, which had been carried on the wind all the way from the Sahara Desert. Meteorologists quickly allayed any fears, saying that the settled dust was harmless and posed no health risk. The sand, which was blown at high altitude from North Africa, fell overnight during showers of light rain while most people were in bed, so any possible disruption was limited.

The event is very rare – the last time something similar was reported was nearly 15 years ago. Airstreams that affect the UK usually arrive from the Atlantic, but recently winds have been blowing in from the desert region of Africa. Areas of Spain and France were also affected. In France, drivers reported reduced visibility, though the majority of journeys were completed. Spain was harder hit, and a number of flights from airports in the south were delayed due to conditions deemed to be unsafe. I'm joined now by Tim Atkins from our weather team, who's going to explain what probably happened. Tim.

Weather forecaster: Yes, well, as wind blows across the Sahara every day, it lifts off particles of sand – huge amounts of it in fact. When there are sandstorms – and that's quite common in the Sahara – greater quantities of sand are picked up and carried over long distances. A light wind starts a sandstorm by lifting the top layer of very fine particles. These particles start vibrating and then saltate – that means jump around. As the particles swirl around, they loosen more sand, which also saltates. Before long, the sand is travelling in suspension and a sandstorm is underway. Large sandstorms can cover a huge area and it's little wonder that some of this sand is then carried over long distances. As you said, the unusual wind direction meant that on this occasion sand was carried all the way to Europe.

Newsreader: Thanks Tim. I'll finish by saying that though people here may have been inconvenienced, what they experienced is nothing compared to one of the most notorious cases of Sahara sand over Europe. In 1947, many parts of the Swiss Alps were turned pink and remained pink for several days after red dust was carried on winds from Algeria after a severe sandstorm.

B 1. The Sahara Desert / North Africa
   2. harmless   3. in bed   4. 15 years ago
   5. The Atlantic   6. reduced visibility   7. Spain
   8. top layer   9. loosen   10. in suspension
   11. long distances
   12. 1947   13. Swiss Alps   14. red dust

Tapescript 🎧 115 (0 mins, 9 secs)

B **Listen again and answer the questions.**

[Play Track 114 again]

Reading

A 1. one   2. This   3. That   4. they   5. these

B 2. global warming is melting Antarctic ice more rapidly than had previously been believed
   3. floods and mudslides
   4. wealthy nations to reduce their own emissions while providing assistance to developing countries
   5. all that comes before the reference phrase

C 1. aspect   2. features   3. practice   4. policy
   5. approach

Writing

A See model composition in the Course Book.

Writing task

See notes in the Course Book Writing Module.

11 Sink or swim

Unit overview

The eleventh unit presents language related to an overall theme of *success and failure*. The specific themes within the modules are more varied in this unit than in most, ranging from *qualities that determine achievement* to *survival in the animal kingdom*. The topic of literature from the last unit is revisited and the common theme *the environment* is once again the focus in the Exam Practice Module. Language from previous units is recycled, as is language from one module to another. Students are presented with, and practise, specific tasks from the Speaking, Listening, Reading and Writing tests that make up the IELTS exam.

Speaking and Vocabulary

Objectives

- **To present and practise vocabulary related to success and failure.**
- **To practise answering the examiner's questions properly.**

The first module aims to orientate students towards a very general overall unit theme and to present and practise core vocabulary that will facilitate the tasks in the skills modules.

Start with books closed and write the unit title *sink or swim* on the board. You may know whether or not there is a similar phrase in the students' first language. Establish what the phrase means literally first, pointing out that a person *drowns* if he sinks under water and that if he does not want to sink, he must swim. Ask students what they think the phrase really means, reminding them of metaphors. Establish that it a synonym for *accept failure or do everything to succeed*.

Ask students if they know anything about Gore Vidal – they will probably not. Give them two minutes to read the quotation and think. Give them a minute to discuss it in pairs, focusing on what it means and their reaction to it. Spend another two minutes discussing it as a class. Tell students that later they will listen to a short extract in which the concept is exemplified.

Gore Vidal (1925–2012) was an American author, playwright, screenwriter and political activist. He ran for political office twice and was a long-term political critic. The quotation is cynical, claiming that success means nothing unless it proves that you are better than other people. Doing better than other people rather than simply doing your best is what matters.

Speaking 1

The first part of the lesson aims to develop the concept of the quotation and provide students with an opportunity to think about and discuss their own definition of success.

You can either tell students to refer to the pictures as they look through the list of definitions or use them to begin a discussion. As a class, you can discuss what concept of success each picture shows.

A Read through the list of definitions with students – there are a few words that may need clarifying and you should draw attention to some common collocations – *fulfil potential, overcome difficulties*, etc. Explain that *contentment* means long-term happiness – having from life what you want.

Students should spend four minutes reading steps 1–4, thinking and planning answers individually. They should then spend ten minutes exchanging thoughts with a partner. Monitor to assist and make a note of salient comments that can be used during a feedback stage. Allow students to discuss their own definition (B) before getting and giving feedback.

B Extend the discussion in A for a minute. Students may feel that one of the definitions listed is their own ideal definition.

Keep feedback brief and concise – avoid an extended class debate. Perhaps get a show of hands for each definition or ask one or two students to sum up their thoughts for the class.

C Drill *failure* and point out that *~ure* is not a common suffix for forming nouns. Tell them to think of something more imaginative than simply *not succeeding* and set a time limit of two minutes. Listen to each pair's definition and decide as a class which one you like best.

D 🎧 Read through the instructions with students and explain that they should answer the questions themselves as they listen. Play the whole recording and give them a moment to think. Ask them if they are ready to compare the situation in pairs or if they want to listen again – they will probably have understood everything, but want to check. There is no point in them discussing the situation if students have not properly understood it. Play the recording again if necessary. Give them time to discuss the situation.

A whole-class conclusion is a necessary stage here, but have a time limit in mind. There is no point in going round in circles. Concentrate on one or two students who freely admit that the important thing is to do better than others, and one or two who say they would be happy simply to get a high score.

Tapescript 🎧 **116 (1 min, 6 secs)**

D **Listen to somebody describing a situation and answer each of the questions she poses. Then discuss the situation in your pair.**

Voice: Imagine you are waiting for the results of a test or exam that you've just done at school or university. You go into class and your teacher or tutor tells you that you scored 95% in the test. How do you feel – proud, delighted? Are you looking forward to comparing your result with other students

when they arrive? The other students start to arrive and the teacher tells them their scores. All of the other students have scored between 97% and 100% – half of the class, in fact, have scored full marks. Your score is actually the lowest in the class! Does this change the way you feel? Can you explain why? What's important to you – doing well and fulfilling your potential or doing better than other people?

Grammar check

Tell students to close their books and write on the board: *Success is doing what you said you would do*. Ask students which one word can be deleted and why that is possible. Write on the board: *My sister always said she would be famous and she …*, and elicit the missing word *is*. Write, *My great grandfather said he would be famous and he …*, and again elicit the missing word. Ask students to explain why in this case it is *was* and not *is*. Establish that the speaker knows which auxiliary to use from the context. Point out than in conversation, it is not always easy to decide which verb to use.

Refer students to the *Grammar check* and give them time to read and absorb. Make sure they read the examples carefully and clarify any remaining uncertainties. Ask them to correct the sentence in the *Watch out!* box.

Answer:
She said she would win and she did.

Vocabulary 1

In the three exercises A–C, there is a lot of new vocabulary to take in. There is an assumption that some of the words will be known and only need revision, but students should be selective if they feel overloaded. Note that students whose first language is of Latin origin will understand many of the items even if they are new, and that students will know words like *drive* and *hunger* with different meanings.

A Emphasize that the words are all qualities, so they are all nouns. Point out that they are in alphabetical order. Read through the list, pronouncing the words carefully as students listen and think.

Students should complete the exercise individually, using a dictionary when necessary. They can then compare answers with a partner. Use a feedback stage to check answers. Clarify and develop vocabulary as appropriate. However, do not go into the form of related adjectives yet (see B).

Answers:

ambition = S / belief = S / courage = S / cowardice = F / defeatism = F / desire = S / determination = S / drive = S / faith = S / hesitation = F / hunger = S / indecision = F / insecurity = F / optimism = S / persistence = S / pessimism = F / purpose = S / resignation = F / resilience = S / self-confidence = S / self-doubt = F / self-pity = F / strength of mind = S / weakness = F / willpower = S

Vocabulary suggestions

Emphasize that these words, as qualities, are all uncountable. Most of them also have a countable form. Some of them are virtually synonymous with others.

- Contrast *belief* as a quality with *a belief*, which is more related to religion. You have *belief in yourself* or *self-belief*.
- *Cowardice* is the opposite of *courage*. A person who displays *cowardice* is a *coward*.
- *Defeatism* is similar to *pessimism* and *resignation*. The person is a *defeatist*.
- *Desire* as a quality is very similar to *ambition*. The phrases *burning desire* and *burning ambition* are both common.
- *Drive* is only uncountable. *Drive* is very similar to *determination*.
- *Faith* as a quality has the same meaning as *belief*. You have *faith in* your ability.
- The verb is *hesitate*. The noun *hesitancy* also exists.
- *Hunger* is only uncountable. As a quality, it is very similar to *desire*. You can be *hungry for success*.
- *Optimism* is the opposite of *pessimism*. A person is an *optimist* or a *pessimist*.
- The verb is *persist*. If you persist, you refuse to *give up* or to *admit defeat*.
- Contrast *purpose* as a quality with *a purpose*. Purpose is similar to ambition and

determination. The phrase *a sense of purpose* is very common.
- If you *resign* or *resign yourself to* something, you *give up*.
- *Self-doubt* is very similar to *insecurity*.
- If you have *self-pity*, you *feel sorry for yourself*.
- *Strength of mind* and *willpower* are very similar and are both similar to determination. *Will* is similar to desire, while *willpower* is the ability to persist or refuse to give up.

B Since students have spent some time working individually, they should work in pairs now to share knowledge and pool resources. They will probably need to check some words in a dictionary as they go. Check answers when the majority of pairs have completed the exercise. As feedback, tell students to close books, and read out the nouns as they shout out the adjectives they have learnt. Check pronunciation and drill when necessary as you check answers.

Answers:

1. ambitious 2. courageous 3. cowardly
4. determined 5. driven 6. hesitant
7. indecisive 8. insecure 9. optimistic
10. persistent 11. purposeful 12. resilient

C Students should work in pairs, communicating and sharing knowledge as they go – saying the phrases aloud should help them decide if they are possible or not.

Establish which phrases are not possible and then tell students to close their books. See how many of the possible expressions from each list they remember.

Answers:

set an ambition / overcome a plan / fulfil your optimism – are NOT possible.

D Read through the instructions and the example with students and make sure they know what to do. Give them three minutes to plan what they want to say before they interact. Monitor to check what they have absorbed and are now confident with. A class feedback stage is unnecessary.

Pronunciation check

Tell students to close their books and write *setback* on the board. Ask a few students to say it and then model it yourself. See if students can explain what happens to the *t* and the *b* that follows. They should be able to say that the *t* is not pronounced clearly and, perhaps, that the *b* sounds more like a *p*. Write *good care* on the board and proceed in the same way. Do not worry if students cannot give a clear or accurate description of what happens – the aim is more to make them aware. Refer students to the *Pronunciation check* and give them time to read and absorb the list of phrases they will hear.

🎧 Play the whole recording. You may prefer to allow them to say the phrases in pairs before they listen, so they predict what they will hear. Students will probably want to hear the phrases three or four times before they practise. Model the phrases yourself, if you are confident. Monitor as they practise, check performance and give positive feedback when appropriate.

Tapescript 🎧 117 (0 mins, 35 secs)
Pronunciation check

Listen to the words and phrases carefully and then practise saying them in pairs.

1 my big break
2 set goals
3 last chance
4 make plans
5 don't hold back
6 take good care

Speaking 2

The aim is to develop the theme and practise interaction more typical of the third part of the Speaking test and specifically to practise making sure the examiner's questions are answered. At the same time, students will practise using vocabulary acquired in the lesson.

A By now, students will be accustomed to looking at questions like these but not actually answering them. Give them two minutes to read and think. Make sure that there is no interaction yet.

B 🎧 Read through the instructions and the two questions with students, making sure they know what to listen for. Make clear that they will hear four students and that only one gives a good answer to the examiner's question. Play the whole recording and give students two minutes to discuss with a partner. Play the recording again, pausing after each exchange to get and give feedback, using the answers provided below. Note that students will read the tapescript in a moment so you do not have to clarify every line.

Answers:

1. Speaker 3 gives a good answer – she has understood the question and gives a good balanced answer.

2. Speaker 1 does not understand the question and does not ask for clarification. Speaker 2 gives a confident, fluent answer, but does not answer the question. He defines *success*. Speaker 4 appears to understand the question, but tries to use words that he does not really know how to. His answer is grammatically inaccurate in a number of places – *and It depends on the person / somebody that / who is very contented with his life / It works both ways.*

Tapescript 🎧 118 (1 min, 43 secs)

B **Listen to some students answering the questions.**

1
Examiner: Does succeeding mean doing better than other people?
Student: No, I don't think so.
Examiner: … So, what do you think success really means …

2
Examiner: Why do you think some people succeed while others fail?
Student: Mm, that's a good question. For me, succeeding is all about achieving what you set out to achieve and perhaps even becoming well-known for doing that – somebody who writes a novel or an athlete who wins a gold medal in the Olympics, for example.

3

Examiner: Is it easier for people from certain backgrounds to succeed?

Student: Yes, I think you have to say that it is. Of course, there are many examples of people from poor backgrounds who do great things – they succeed against all the odds, if you like – but in reality, people who have a good education and are surrounded by successful people are much more likely to do well in life.

4

Examiner: Do you think success brings happiness or that happiness equals success?

Student: I think both of these can be true and depends on the person. If somebody achieves his … erm … his …, you know, it will make him happy. But also, somebody what is very … err …. contented with his life can say he is successful. It goes both ways, I think.

Refer students to the Exam tip and give them a moment to read and absorb. Alternatively, show an OHT or visual medium of the tip on the board and reveal one point at a time, helping students to focus and absorb.

C 🎧 Refer students to the appropriate tapescript and play the recording again as they read. Students will probably ask you to explain the expressions *set out to* and *against all the odds*. Note that informal expressions from the unit are practised in the Workbook (see Vocabulary development D).

Tapescript 🎧 **119 (0 mins, 9 secs)**

C **Look at the tapescript and listen again.**

[Play Track 118 again]

D Both students in each pair should answer all the questions. They can either take it in turns to answer each question, or play student/examiner roles and answer all the questions before changing roles. They should spend two minutes thinking and planning answers before they interact. Monitor to check performance, especially to see whether they answer the question and how well they use language acquired in the lesson.

Feedback is unnecessary, but you could conclude the lesson by debating the final question as a class for a few minutes.

Listening

Objectives

- **To practise recognizing the four sections of the IELTS Listening test.**
- **To familiarize students with the different register adopted in the four sections of the Listening test.**
- **To practise various exam listening tasks with a focus on the register adopted.**

The overall aim of this Listening Module is to consolidate and conclude rather than to present a new concept – by now, students will be familiar with the four sections of Listening test. However, they will not necessarily have recognized the different register – formality or informality of language – that is likely to be adopted in each.

Listening 1

The first part of the lesson largely involves listening for gist and identifying sections of the Listening test.

A Students will know that answers to questions in this type of exercise will be given in the Exam tip that follows. Make sure they cover the tip before they begin. Students should answer the questions in pairs. Check their answers, but do not confirm or correct – they will read the Exam tip later.

Tapescript 🎧 120 (4 mins, 32 secs)

B Listen to extracts from each section of the Listening test. Identify which section you think each extract comes from.

Extract A

Father: Look, what we're saying is that we moved heaven and earth to get you onto this course and now you're just not making the most of the opportunity.

Lucas: What do you mean, moved heaven and earth?

Father: You know exactly what I mean. Your exam results weren't that good and we had to persuade the college to accept you. We talked about the fact that there would be other students on the course who'd find it less challenging and you promised to make an effort.

Mother: Yes – that's all we ask – make an effort – do your best. We don't expect miracles and we're not asking for super high marks or anything.

Lucas: So, why do you assume I'm not making an effort?

Father: Oh, come on Lucas. We've read the report – you've read the report. It's just like all those school reports we fell out about, isn't it? The bottom line is there's always something you'd rather be doing than working towards a future.

Extract B

Voice: It's interesting that the Russian anarchist philosopher, Peter Kropotkin, viewed the concept of survival of the fittest not as competition or in any way the modern perception of people climbing over one another to succeed, but as supporting co-operation. He coined the phrase 'mutual aid', having concluded that the fittest was not necessarily the best at competing individually, but often the community consisting of those best at operating together. In the animal kingdom, the vast majority of species live in societies – association is the best strategy in the struggle for survival. Struggle for survival understood, of course, in its wide Darwinian sense – not as a struggle for the sheer means of existence, but as a struggle against all natural conditions unfavourable to the species. The animal species, in which individual struggle has been reduced to a minimum, and the practice of mutual aid has attained the greatest development, are invariably the most numerous, the most prosperous and the most likely to make further progress.

Extract C

Voice: Secondly, those who run successful businesses develop a business blueprint. It's what we often refer to as a strategic business plan. This describes clearly their business concept, their mission and their overall philosophy of business. It sets out personal and corporate goals and draws up specific timelines and a set of strategies that will ensure these goals are achieved.

Owners of a successful business develop a structure that functions as a well-oiled machine. This structure – including all its policies and procedures – will encourage staff and associates to perform to their maximum capabilities. It'll aim to reward people who shine in proportion to the contribution they make. It'll probably also describe how to discipline anyone who deviates from acceptable behaviour – what the organization expects of them. Positions, duties and responsibilities are defined and communicated and performance is assessed on a regular basis.

Extract D

Interviewer: And what do you consider to be your greatest strength?

Speaker: I think I have a number of strengths. I especially pride myself on my customer service skills. I think I'm good at resolving problems and making sure that difficult situations are not allowed to develop. That applies both when dealing with customers and other members of staff, I think.

Interviewer: And do you have any weaknesses?

Speaker: Mm, I suppose I have to admit that I can be too much of a perfectionist – I mean, perhaps unrealistic in terms of how well something needs to be done. I sometimes spend too long on a project or task, or accept a job that could easily be delegated to somebody else. I never miss deadlines, but I do need to improve in terms of knowing when to say a job is complete and to move on to the next. I guess I need to be more trusting about handing tasks over to other people. I tend to feel that if a job needs doing, I should do it myself.

C Give students time to answer the questions in pairs and then check as a class before looking at the Exam tip.

Answers:

Exercise B:
Extract A: Section 3 / Extract B: Section 4 / Extract C: Section 2 / Extract D: Section 1

Exercise C:
1. the number of speakers / the situation / the register
2. Extract A – A mother and father are talking to a teenage son about his school report.
Extract B – A lecturer is discussing the expression survival of the fittest.
Extract C – A speaker is talking about what makes a business successful.
Extract D – An interviewee is talking about her strengths.

There is a lot to absorb in this Exam tip and it would be best presented on an OHT or other visual medium so that you can read through with the class. Reveal one point at a time, eliciting key information as you go.

D 🎧 Play each extract separately as students note specific examples. They should briefly compare ideas with a partner before you check with them. The most efficient way to provide feedback is to show an OHT or visual medium of the tapescript on which you can highlight examples students suggest or that you want to identify.

Tapescript 🎧 **121 (0 mins, 12 secs)**

D Listen again and note examples of formal and informal use of language.

[Play Track 120 again]

Listening 2

Since the four sections are unrelated, it would be best to treat each as a separate practice stage. In one section of the Listening test in the exam, students will not have to listen to a number of extracts like this, nor will they have as many questions to read through and answer. Note that each extract is similar in length to a complete Listening test section.

A 🎧 Since students have already heard the first part of each section, there is no need to refocus and they can be left to their own devices. Make sure they understand that they will now hear the sections in order and that each extract is now extended.

Allow students 30 seconds to read the questions for each section (perhaps longer to read the summary) and then play the recording for that section only. You can decide if they should compare answers in pairs before moving on to the next section. They should check the answers when they have completed all four sections (see B).

Tapescript 🎧 **122 (8 mins, 57 secs)**

A Listen to longer versions of each extract and answer the questions.

Section 1 extract

Interviewer: And what do you consider to be your greatest strength?

Speaker: I think I have a number of strengths. I especially pride myself on my customer service skills. I think I'm good at resolving problems and making sure that

Interviewer: And do you have any weaknesses?

Speaker: Mm, I suppose I have to admit that I can be too much of a perfectionist – I mean, perhaps unrealistic in terms of how well something needs to be done. I sometimes spend too long on a project or task, or accept a job that could easily be delegated to somebody else. I never miss deadlines, but I do need to improve in terms of knowing when to say a job is complete and to move on to the next. I guess I need to be more trusting about handing tasks over to other people. I tend to feel that if a job needs doing, I should do it myself.

Interviewer: So, can you describe one particular challenge and how you dealt with it?

Speaker: Well, last year we were having a few issues with one particular client. They were threatening to take their business elsewhere. I felt that some people on our side were not being … how shall I put it? – as diplomatic as they could be. I met personally with representatives of the client and managed to persuade them that we could handle their account in a way that suited them better. It all ended up very amicably.

Interviewer: Good. Now, if I asked somebody who knows you well why you should be offered this position, what would he or she say?

Speaker: I think they'd say I possess the skills outlined in the job description and I bring seven years of expertise with me. I've heard people describe me as hard-working, professional and trustworthy, and everyone knows me as a team player.

Interviewer: OK – that's good to hear. And, what about your expectations of salary? Is that something …

Section 2 extract

Voice: Businesses that succeed must have something that sets them apart from businesses that fail. First of all, successful businesses – or the people who run them – generally have a very positive attitude towards their business and a positive outlook on life in general. Successful business owners will see opportunities rather than obstacles, for example. They'll take risks and accept failure – I've heard so many people say that they regret not having tried something far more than they regret trying something that didn't work out. Again, it's that sense of a chance not seized – a fish that got away!

Secondly, those who run successful businesses develop a business blueprint. It's what we often refer to as a strategic business plan. This describes clearly their business concept, their mission and their overall philosophy of business. It sets out personal and corporate goals and draws up specific timelines and a set of strategies that will ensure these goals are achieved.

Owners of a successful business develop a structure that functions as a well-oiled machine. This structure – including all its policies and procedures – will encourage staff and associates to perform to their maximum capabilities. It'll aim to reward people who shine in proportion to the contribution they make. It'll probably also describe how to discipline anyone who deviates from acceptable behaviour – what the organization expects of them. Positions, duties and responsibilities are defined and communicated and performance is assessed on a regular basis.

Finally, the owners of successful businesses develop support systems. The objective is to support and make efficient all the activities carried out by the organization, relieving management of irksome routine tasks and giving owners more time to think and plan ahead. These tracking systems provide critical information about sales, cash flow and various financial performance data so that senior management can take action as soon as change occurs. Problems are flagged before they have a chance to become unmanageable.

So in summary, before I move on, the four areas I've outlined are …

Section 3 extract

Mother: Lucas, can we have a chat about college? You know we've been looking at the report, don't you?

Lucas: Oh, all right, I guess so.

Father: Don't you want to talk about it, then?

Lucas: Well, no, not really. I know what you're going to say.

Mother: Which is?

Lucas: That you're disappointed and I should've done better.

Father: Yes, you're right that we're disappointed, but it's not really that you should've done better – though that would be nice – it's the lack of commitment.

Lucas: Look, how is it that everyone seems to know that I've got no commitment? Maybe I just think …

Mother: Because we can all see that you're not making an effort. The report isn't just about the grades. Every one of the tutors has commented that you're not trying.

Father: Look, what we're saying is that we moved heaven and earth to get you onto this course and now you're just not making the most of the opportunity.

Lucas: What do you mean, moved heaven and earth?

Father: You know exactly what I mean. Your exam results weren't that good and we had to persuade the college to accept you. We talked about the fact that there would be other students on the course who'd find it less challenging and you promised to make an effort.

Mother: Yes – that's all we ask – make an effort – do your best. We don't expect miracles and we're not asking for super high marks or anything.

Lucas: So, why do you assume I'm not making an effort?

Father: Oh, come on, Lucas. We've read the report – you've read the report. It's just like all those school reports we fell out about, isn't it? The bottom line is there's always something you'd rather be doing than working towards a future.

Lucas: Look, maybe I just don't see my future sitting at a keyboard in some stuffy office.

Mother: So, what exactly does inspire you, then? Could you share it with us? Times are getting harder for everyone and if you have no qualifications, it'll be almost impossible.

Father: I suppose you think you think you're going to make a fortune playing those dreadful drums, don't you? Well, let me tell you, it doesn't work like that – not for the vast majority of …

Section 4 extract

Voice: So, we have seen that the term *survival of the fittest* has been rather misused over the years and in fact, has probably been misunderstood by the vast majority of people who have used it. I think we can certainly say that it isn't a direct synonym for *natural selection*, which, as I've said, was what Darwin first used the term in relation to.

It's interesting that the Russian anarchist philosopher, Peter Kropotkin, viewed the concept of survival of the fittest not as competition or in any way the modern perception of people climbing over one another to succeed, but as supporting co-operation. He coined the phrase 'mutual aid', having concluded that the fittest was not necessarily the best at competing individually, but often the community consisting of those best at operating together. In the animal kingdom, the vast majority of species live in societies – association is the best strategy in the struggle for survival. Struggle for survival understood, of course, in its wide Darwinian sense – not as a struggle for the sheer means of existence, but as a struggle against all natural conditions unfavourable to the species. The animal species, in which individual struggle has been reduced to a minimum, and the practice of mutual aid has attained the greatest development, are invariably the most numerous, the most prosperous and the most likely to make further progress.

Applying this concept to human society, Kropotkin presented mutual aid as one of the dominant factors of evolution. He claimed that we can retrace co-operation to the earliest stages of our development and in it find the origin of our ethical values. In the progress of man, mutual support rather than mutual struggle has had the upper hand. He also believed that despite the obvious conflict between people in modern society, mutual aid is the only way we can hope to continue to evolve.

B Checking and reflecting on answers is a constant feature of the skills modules. Give students sufficient time to check and think about why any answers were incorrect before moving onto C. You can decide if it would be beneficial to play the recording again, but avoid doing so simply to check individual students' wrong answers. It will probably be more beneficial to listen again later as they read the tapescript. If you do want to draw attention to parts of the recording that provide answers, show an OHT or other visual medium of the tapescript on the board and highlight key parts as you pause the recording.

Answers:
Section 1: 1. difficult situations 2. perfectionist
3. delegated 4. client 5. expertise
6. team player
Section 2: C / E / F
Section 3: 10. report 11. commitment
12. exam results 13. future 14. office
15. no qualifications
Section 4: 16. natural selection
17. community 18. animal 19. evolution
20. ethical values

C Students will be used to reflecting on tasks in this way. Remind them that identifying what they are doing well and not doing so well is a very good way of focusing on what they can do better next time. Allow students time to reflect and complete the exercise. Conclude by asking them if they are happy with the number of correct answers.

Key vocabulary in context

The aim is to further develop awareness of formal and informal style rather than learn specific words, phrases and expressions that occur in the exercise. However, some of the items will be useful and students will almost certainly ask for clarification. Guidance is given with the key below.

A Students should work individually and then compare answers with a partner before you check. Show an OHT or visual medium of the exercise on the board so that you can highlight and draw attention to key items.

Answers:
1. F – *pride myself on* = I am particularly proud of
2. F – *possess* = have
3. I – *a fish that got away* = a chance not seized / an opportunity not taken
4. I – *functions as a well-oiled machine* = runs very smoothly
5. I – *moved heaven and earth* = did everything possible
6. I – *the bottom line* = the fundamental truth / the basic fact (not necessarily informal)
7. F – *has had the upper hand* = has been dominant

B Set either as a class-time consolidation exercise or as a homework exercise. Once again, note that D in the *Vocabulary development* section of the Workbook practises a range of informal expressions.

Refer students to the Workbook exercises related to this module. Choose to work on them now or set up for homework.

Reading

Objectives

- **To introduce students to a sentence completion task and to focus on the skills required.**
- **To further develop skimming and scanning skills.**
- **To practise a sentence completion task.**

The module is divided into three parts. The first part orientates students towards the overall theme of *turning failure into success*, and specifically to the theme of the first passage – *successful people who were once deemed failures!* The second part introduces the new task type and suggests strategies for approaching it. The third part, as usual, practises what has been learnt through authentic exam practice tasks.

Though the two passages are quite separate, the theme of *an initial failure becoming a success* is common, and ideas and language from the first passage are recycled in the second. Vocabulary from earlier modules in the unit is recycled in both passages.

Note that a sentence completion task probably occurs less frequently in the exam than some other task types, but students will need to know how to approach it. It involves scanning to identify the relevant part of the text and then reading very carefully to check the text says the same as the two parts of the sentence in the task.

Reading 1

A Start with books closed and write the proverb on the board. If all your students are from the same country, discuss question 1 together. Then put students into pairs to discuss questions 2 and 3. If your students are from various countries, they should discuss all three questions in pairs. As feedback, get a general consensus as to whether the advice is good and then get one student to tell the class about a personal experience.

Ask students which of the qualities learnt in the first module the proverb relates to and revise those words – *determination, persistence, resilience, willpower,* etc.

B Tell students to cover the passage on the page so that they are not tempted to look ahead. If possible, isolate the exercise by showing it on an OHT or other visual medium on the board.

Refer students to the pictures and give them a moment to simply look at them and think. Point out that they may not know some of the people, but that that does not matter.

Students should read the questions and think about answers individually. They should then answer the questions and develop a conversation with a partner. Students will read the passage to check answers, but some class feedback will help to further orientate and motivate. Spend two or three minutes checking which of the people and their achievements are known and how the proverb applies in each case. Students will probably be able to apply it to the Wright Brothers, who failed many times before succeeding. An answer key is not provided as the passage answers all questions.

C Make sure students appreciate that they are reading the passage the first time with the aim of checking their own ideas. Note, however, that they will go on to answer questions about the passage and should spend enough time reading to be able to take in the information. Set a time limit of four minutes. There is no need for further feedback at this point.

D The aim is to assess global comprehension before students engage in the exam task and to provide some further interaction with students using their own words and words acquired in the unit. It should not be a memory test and students should simply move on if they do not know an answer. Make sure they cover the passage again and answer the questions in pairs. Monitor to assess comprehension and make a note of salient points that can be shared during a feedback stage. Keep feedback brief, getting concise answers to each question. Clarify any remaining uncertainties and take the opportunity to consolidate key vocabulary.

Possible answers:
1. The Wright Brothers (a) – proved people wrong. Albert Einstein (b) – overcame early difficulties. Walt Disney (c) – persisted despite many rejections.
   Thomas Edison (d) – overcame early difficulties. / He proved people wrong.
   Oprah Winfrey (e) – overcame early setbacks. / She confronted self-doubt.
2. The person got lucky or benefited from being in the right place at the right time. / The person was very intelligent or talented. / The person had the right connections (knew people who could help).

3. A refusal to allow setbacks and failures to get in the way.

Reading 2

The second part of the lesson exploits the passage that students have read to introduce the new task type and encourages students to reflect on the strategies they need to adopt.

Refer students to the Question-type tip. Note that the tip students read before attempting the task simply tells them how the task works. They will read another tip that focuses on the strategies they need to adopt after they have attempted the task. Tell them to read the tip and look at the task below it as they read.

A Do not give students any advice about how to approach the task yet. They will reflect on it and read the second Exam tip having attempted it. Note that having already read and discussed the content of the passage will make the task far easier. Give students the time they need to complete the task – perhaps check answers when the majority of students have completed the exercise. They should check answers in pairs before you provide them.

Feedback should be thorough – the aim is to become familiar with the task type and students will need to know why any answers are incorrect for that to happen. Show an OHT or other visual medium of the passage on the board and highlight the parts that provide answers, demonstrating once again how language is paraphrased (see guidance in answers below).

Answers:
1. D (all of first paragraph – the quote implies a degree of annoyance)
2. H (… had a slower start than many of his childhood peers)
3. A (… a local church minister took pity … and hired him to draw cartoons)
4. J (… a partially deaf …)
5. G (… was fired from one of her first positions …)

B Make sure students cover the Exam tip before answering the questions. Give them two minutes to talk and then refer them to the Exam tip. Tell students to cover the tip and then check the various pieces of advice given. Conclude by asking students if they found the task easy or

difficult and find out how many students answered all the questions correctly.

Reading 3

Students should now be more independent when working on the practice part of the skills modules, but the passage is quite challenging and contains a number of cultural references. A brief orientation/facilitation stage is provided to ensure that students have a platform from which to tackle the practice tasks.

A If students recognize some of the titles, it should motivate and boost confidence. Read through the instructions with them and allow them to communicate in pairs. Set a time limit of five minutes – students should briefly describe any titles they know, but not give an in-depth account. Make sure they do not start reading about any of the titles in the passage. A feedback stage is unnecessary, but you could simply get a show of hands for each title.

B Answer the question as a class. Establish that all of the books were initially rejected by publishers.

C You can decide whether to allow students to skim the passage as suggested or go straight into the practice task. It will depend on how deeply you discussed the answer to B. If students do skim the passage, make sure they appreciate that they are reading to confirm their own predictions or what you discussed as a class. You might like to remind students how important it is to accept that they will not understand every word – the passage is challenging, but identifying language that paraphrases the sentences' endings in Exercise D should be manageable.

D There is only one task with this passage and students have already prepared and skimmed. Set a time limit of ten minutes, but allow an extra two minutes if a number of students have not completed it. You can decide if students will benefit from comparing answers with a partner before checking the answer key.

E Checking and reflecting on answers is a constant feature of the skills modules. Give students sufficient time to check and think about why they may have answered incorrectly. Students might want to know why some of their answers were not correct. Since this task type is new to them, you might think it wise to establish why answers are correct or not. To identify the specific parts of the passage that provide answers to questions, show an OHT or other visual medium of the passage and highlight those parts on the board. Additional guidance is provided in the answer key below.

Answers:

1. F (… publisher who read the original manuscript … must have spent much of his career … regretting his words.)
2. B (… publishers would only accept the work if they personally had sympathy for a Trotskyite viewpoint.)
3. G (… 38 publishers … told author … that they didn't give a damn – *ironic because that is a line from the story*).
4. I (… the Chief Executive's eight-year-old daughter read the book and declared it a winner.)
5. D (*All of relevant paragraph, especially …* expressed the exact opposite opinion.)
6. H (… create a story to go along with his illustrations in the hope that the story might spark more interest.)

F Students will be familiar with this reflective process. Point out that, once again, points are related specifically to the reading skills and task strategies practised. Remind them that identifying what they are doing well and not doing so well is a very good way of focusing on what they can do better next time. Allow students time to reflect and complete the exercise, and then ask them if they are happy with the number of correct answers.

Key vocabulary in context

A Students have worked through this type of exercise previously and will know what to do. Note once more that the aim is to practise the skill of understanding new words and phrases in context, as well as actually learning the selected words and phrases. Discourage dictionary use.

Students should complete the exercise individually, before comparing answers with a partner. Answers can be given orally, but must be clear. Alternatively, delete the wrong option on a copy made on the board. Clarify any

---

remaining uncertainties and check pronunciation. When answers have been checked, tell students to cover the exercise. Read out the correct definitions as they shout out the newly acquired key word.

Answers:

1. challenge it 2. overcome difficulties
3. sympathy 4. protected
5. gives up easily 6. rejected or thrown away
7. positive 8. shame and embarrassment

Refer students to the Workbook exercises related to this module. Choose to work on them now or set up for homework.

Writing

Objectives

- **To give further practice and increase confidence in terms of knowing what to say.**
- **To revise the various features which contribute to a well-written report.**

The Writing Modules in the final two units of the course – Units 11 and 12 – aim to revise various elements of good writing practice. Unit 11 focuses on Writing Task 1. Note that, in this unit, students collaboratively write a report before they work with a model report, meaning that ultimately there are two Writing tasks.

Writing 1

The first part of the module aims to orientate students towards the theme and motivate them to write the report later in the lesson.

A You may prefer to conduct this as a whole-class discussion, clarifying language in the questions as you go, especially if your students are all from the same country. Note, however, that pairwork will allow more individuals to contribute.

Read through the questions with the class, giving each student time to think and plan an answer as you do so. This will also allow you to check the pronunciation of key words as you go – contrast the difference between *graduate* as a noun and as a verb. Emphasize that students are not expected to know answers – if they do not, they should simply say so and move on. Students can talk in pairs.

Get and give brief feedback, but avoid discussing examples of compromises when you answer question 4 – students discuss this point specifically in D.

B Tell students they will read the extract twice. Make sure they appreciate that the first time they read, the purpose is to check what was discussed in A. Set a time limit of two minutes. Tell them that they will summarize the extract in their own words. Give them another two minutes to read more carefully.

C Make sure students cover the extract and use their own words – the aim is not to memorize chunks of the text. Monitor as they interact to check comprehension and how well they summarize. Choose one pair's summary to share with the class as feedback.

D The aim now is to prepare for the Writing task – students predict information shown in the figure. Look ahead yourself to the figure, so that you know what sort of compromises students should suggest. Make sure students do not look ahead. Clarify the meaning of *compromise* if necessary – point out that it is a verb, but that it is also frequently used as a noun in the phrase *make compromises*. Students should discuss the point in pairs, though you may decide to suggest one example as a class to get the ball rolling. Set a time limit of three minutes. Monitor to assist and guide if necessary.

Get some brief feedback, but do not feed ideas that students fail to suggest themselves. They can check the figure in a moment.

E Refer students to the bar graph and give them time to read and absorb. Clarify where necessary. Point out that *unfavourable hours* does not necessarily mean long hours. It means working when you would rather not be working – in the evening or at weekends, for example. Explain that *no health benefits* means no health care provided by the company – large, private companies frequently offer this as a benefit.

Writing 2

In this part of the lesson, students are presented with task instructions and then write the report collaboratively in class time. By now, they should be ready to attempt the report themselves and then compare their work with a model. Note that managing students as they write collaboratively can be problematic and advice is given. Note also that there will not be time to write two reports in the one lesson and the Writing task in the Workbook will certainly need to be set for homework this time.

A Students will now be accustomed to studying Writing task instructions and then discussing them. Refer them to the instructions and give them a minute to read through and check they understand everything. Encourage them to highlight key words or phrases and make notes as they learnt to earlier in the course. Do not allow them to use dictionaries.

B Students are accustomed to discussing data shown in a figure in this way, but not necessarily as direct preparation for an immediate writing stage. Tell them they are going to write the report in the lesson and give them five minutes to talk in their pair. Monitor to check that they are identifying the right information and to assist and guide if necessary. A class feedback stage now is unnecessary unless you feel that stronger pairs can help weaker pairs to identify relevant data. Look ahead yourself to the model report if you want to suggest information that should be highlighted.

C As previously suggested, some students, whilst happy to discuss ideas with a partner, are reluctant to actually write collaboratively. It could be argued that it is not a very natural process, but students generally benefit from the communication and the pooling of resources. Emphasize that they will write the actual Writing task for the unit individually at home, and that this stage should be seen as preparation and practice. Tell students that only one report per pair should be produced – if you see them both writing, you will take one of the reports away.

Make sure pairs are compatible – stronger and weaker students can work together, but make sure the stronger student does not dominate and make all the suggestions. In each pair, one student should write while the other makes suggestions and checks. Suggest that the weaker student writes – in this way, the stronger student does not take over and write the report while the weaker student sits passively. You might like to suggest that some pairs swap roles halfway through the process.

Read through the steps with them and insist they stick strictly to the time limits. At the end of the 20 minutes, they will exchange reports. Monitor to check progress and give limited assistance.

D Encourage each pair to read two or three reports written by other pairs and to give feedback. Take the opportunity to read some of the reports yourself and give your own feedback. You can decide if you wish to collect all the reports and to mark them more formally. Tell students that they will see a model report, but that they will have to piece it together. Make sure they do not look ahead to the complete report yet.

Writing 3

The aim is to focus attention onto various aspects of good report writing.

A and B Show the exercise instructions on an OHT or other visual medium on the board so that you can focus attention on one step at a time and ensure that students know what they are doing and why. Show the first line, *Below and on the next page are possible sentences that make up a model report.* – and refer students to the jumbled report. Give them a moment to look at it and establish that there are more sentences than there will be in the report and that the sentences are not in the correct order. Make sure they can see that each paragraph is dealt with separately so the task is less daunting than it may first appear.

Now show the next line, *Before you read them, look at the points below.* and then reveal the bullet points one by one, checking that students are absorbing the information. Students can either work in pairs to communicate and share resources as they go, or work individually and then compare answers. Give them the time they need to complete the task.

Although students will look at the model report, you might feel that going over answers methodically will ensure better focus and retention. Show an OHT or other visual medium of the jumbled passages and fill in answers on the board as students explain choices and why alternative lines are inappropriate.

Answers:
1. e   2. c
3. k   4. h   5. i
6. q   7. n   8. p

C Allow students time to read and absorb the model report at the back of the Course Book on page 268. The model is reproduced below.

Model report:

The bar chart shows the various compromises that graduates in the United States might make in order to find their first job. It shows the percentage of graduates that made each of those compromises in the years 2006–2007 and 2009–2010.

The most noticeable increases were in the percentage of graduates earning less than they expected, the percentage working with no health benefits and the percentage accepting a temporary position. Those earning less than expected rose from 28% in 2006–2007 to 39% in 2009–2010, while the percentage working with no health benefits increased by over a third to 23%. The percentage accepting a temporary position was still quite low in 2009–2010, but had climbed by a third.

Apart from 'working outside area of interest', all the compromises increased in frequency over the period. The percentage of graduates who moved to another part of the country rose by 2%, as did the percentage working unfavourable hours. The percentage working below their education level rose only slightly, but was high anyway at around 33%.

Writing task

The Writing tasks are found either in the Workbook or in the Exam Practice Module at the end of the unit. In this unit, the task is in the Workbook.

Since students have already written a report in the lesson, you will almost certainly elect to set the Writing task for homework. However, the topic of the task is completely fresh and students will benefit from the orientation provided by the short preparation stage if conducted in class time. The first lead-in exercise is designed to be communicative and should motivate.

A   As in the Course Book Module, students predict information that is revealed by looking at the figure. Make sure they cover the figure before answering the questions. You might like to isolate the picture and questions by showing them on an OHT or other visual medium on the board.

Introduce an element of competition by telling students that you want to see which pair can get the most correct answers. Give them time to read and answer.

Refer students to the figure to check answers. Do not check them in advance as identifying them in the data provided should be part of the practice process.

B   Refer them to the task instructions.

Students should spend two minutes reading and absorbing the information in silence. Then, they should spend another four minutes discussing the task with a partner.

C   Tell students that they must take into account the time already spent preparing. They should spend about 15 minutes writing. Tell them to be strict with a time limit – they will not benefit from spending longer on the task than they will have when it comes to the exam.

When students have completed the task, they should compare it with the model report on pages 268 and 269. The model is reproduced below.

If you collect students' reports to mark, concentrate on what is positive, as well as weaknesses and errors. You will need to start correcting more of all aspects of their written work now, but remember that correcting every sentence will not be motivating.

Model report:

The bar chart shows the number of gold medals that the United States and China won at each of the Olympics Games between 1984

and 2008. It reveals that over that period, China gradually caught up with the United States and finally overtook them.

In 1984, the United States won over 80 gold medals, by far their biggest tally over the period shown, and at least double what they won at any other Games. By contrast, China won around only 15 medals that year.

At the next Games in 1988, The United States' tally was halved to fewer than 40, while China's tally dropped to only three or four. This was the lowest number of gold medals they won within the period shown.

Over the next 20 years, the number of gold medals won by the United States remained fairly constant at around 40, while the number won by China rose steadily. In 2004, China won almost as many gold medals as the United States. Four years later, in the 2008 Games, China won more gold medals than the United States for the first time.

Consolidation

Instructions are given for Speaking exercises when the procedure is not clear from instructions in the Course Book. Set Vocabulary and Errors exercises either for individual completion and pairwork checking, or as pairwork when you feel immediate interaction is beneficial.

To correct errors in the final exercise, ask students to come and write the correct sentences on the board while other students offer help. You will need to write the corrections on the board to clarify.

Speaking

A   By now, students will be accustomed to looking at questions like these, but not actually answering them. Give them two minutes to read and think. Make sure that there is no interaction yet.

B   🎧 Students will also be accustomed to listening to and assessing students' answers to interview questions – they are probably making predictions about what a good and poor answer might be before they listen. In this case, emphasize that they will not necessarily hear a poor answer. The aim is to discuss the merits of various answers and to use those they like as models. Tell them that they are not necessarily correct answers – they should tick the speaker whose answer they like for whatever reason. Play the whole recording, pausing briefly after each answer to give students a moment to think and write their answer. They should not comment at this point.

Tapescript 🎧 123 (4 mins, 8 secs)

B   Listen to some students answering the questions. For each question, tick the student that you think gives the better answer.

Question 1 – Student A

Examiner: Give me an example of somebody who you think has been very successful.

Student: Mm, there are so many people I could choose. I prefer to say someone who has triumphed over adversity as it means more to succeed when you started with nothing. For me, Barack Obama is the perfect example. I know he didn't start exactly with nothing, but he was born into a normal family. To become the first black president of the USA was an incredible achievement.

Question 1 – Student B

Examiner: Give me an example of somebody who you think has been very successful.

Student: I think my father has been very successful and I have a lot of respect for him. He worked hard to start his own business and it grew into a very big business. I work for him and I want to be so successful as he.

Question 2 – Student A

Examiner: What has been your biggest achievement so far?

Student: Oh, that's difficult – I'm still young. Maybe, to be the captain of my football team in school was it. I was very proud and my father was very proud too.

Question 2 – Student B

Examiner: What has been your biggest achievement so far?

Student: Mm, I am not sure – I have to think. Last year, I ran in the marathon. It was not a full marathon but a shorter one – 10 km. I felt it was an achievement not just because I finished, but because I did it for the right reason – for a good cause. I raised about 500 euros for orphan children in my country.

Question 3 – Student A

Examiner: Is it important to persevere or is it best to give up if you know that something is bound to fail?

Student: Yes, it's very important not to give up. I think you say if you don't succeed first time, you must try again or something like that. To give up is the failure in my mind.

Question 3 – Student B

Examiner: Is it important to persevere or is it best to give up if you know that something is bound to fail?

Student: It's a good question. People say you should never give up or that you must keep on trying, but I'm not sure that's true. You can't be good at everything. I knew, for example, that I would never be a singer even though I had some singing lessons. I was happier when I gave up.

Question 4 – Student A

Examiner: What have you failed to achieve recently and how did that make you feel?

Student: That's easy – my driving test. It made me feel really bad because I thought I would pass easily – maybe I was too confident. Now I must take it again next month.

Question 4 – Student B

Examiner: What have you failed to achieve recently and how did that make you feel?

Student: Mm, recently, I'm not sure. I think everyday there's something that is a little success and something that's a little failure. Maybe a specific example is not getting a job I applied for last year. I thought I did OK in the interview, but they gave the job to someone else. I wasn't too disappointed because I know there were many people who wanted this job. I had to pick up myself and try again.

C 🎧 Give students two or three minutes to discuss in pairs and then play the recording again. This time, pause after each pair of speakers, give students another minute to compare the two speakers in their pair and then get and give feedback.

Note there are eight different students speaking.

Possible answers:

Question 1:

Student A gives a very full answer, which she introduces naturally. She uses a range of impressive vocabulary, including idiomatic expressions.

Student B gives a good answer, but it is more simplistic. He makes a grammatical mistake (*I want to be as successful as he is.*).

Question 2:

Student A gives a good answer, but it is quite simplistic. *Maybe, to be the captain of my football team in school was it.* is not very natural.

Student B gives a very full answer, which she introduces naturally, giving herself a moment to think. She uses grammatically complex structures confidently.

Question 3:

Student A gives a good, but possibly predictable, answer. He uses the proverb to illustrate his point well, but makes a mistake in the final line (*To give up is the failure in my mind.*)

Student B gives a more interesting, less conventional answer, which he introduces

naturally. He gives an example from his own experience to support his opinion.

Question 4:

Student A gives a good answer, though it is rather simplistic.

Student B gives a very full, interesting answer, which he introduces naturally, giving himself a moment to think. He uses a range of grammatical structures accurately and a fairly good range of vocabulary, including informal expressions, but makes a mistake in the final line (*I had to pick up myself and try again.*)

Tapescript 🎧 **124 (0 mins, 16 secs)**

C **Listen again to the students' answers. In pairs, discuss why you feel that one student's answer was better in Exercise B.**

[Play Track 123 again]

D Both students in each pair should answer all the questions. They can either take it in turns to answer each question, or play student/examiner roles and answer all the questions before changing roles. Monitor to check performance and give individual feedback.

Vocabulary

A **Answers:**
1. failure   2. setback   3. cowardice   4. self-pity
5. optimism   6. resilience

B **Answers:**
1. adversity   2. defeatism   3. courageous
4. hesitation   5. pessimism   6. quitter
7. unfavourable   8. countless   9. unmanageable

Errors

Answers:
1. … but he didn't.   2. … but she won't.
3. … but he didn't.   4. … succeeded in making …
5. … prides herself on her …
6. If you've set your heart …

Exam Practice

Reading

The Exam Practice Module practises a sentence completion task integrated into a whole practice stage that includes three tasks with 18 questions in total. It is a long, challenging passage and students will not be expected to answer so many questions on a single passage in the exam. With this in mind, there is a more robust preparation stage, which includes revision with topic sentences. By now, students will know that this will not be the case in the exam.

As previously suggested the topic – *environment and ecology* – is a common IELTS topic and students will benefit from knowing about it and learning more related vocabulary.

The first part of the lesson aims to orientate students towards the fresh theme and to motivate. Note that, although the specific topic is fresh, the overall theme of *fail or succeed* is developed and language from earlier modules is recycled.

A Start with books closed and write the phrase *survival of the fittest* on the board. You can either discuss as a class or in pairs as suggested in the instructions. You will know whether or not students really understood the phrase from the Listening Module and whether they will be able to define it easily.

Establish that the phrase has been interpreted in different ways. Literally, it might simply mean the strong live, while weaker members of the species or community die. In modern times, it has been used cynically to define the concept of people climbing over one another in order to succeed. On the recording in the Listening Module, students learnt that the phrase might refer to a whole community consisting of individuals who best operate together.

B The aim now is to orientate students to the specific theme of the passage. Refer them to the pictures and ask how they think they relate to the phrase *survival of the fittest*. Establish what it says in the rubric – some animals have had to adapt to new environments in order to survive. Read through the rubric with the class, revising the exact meaning of *urban*. Run through the words for the animals shown as a couple of them are difficult to pronounce (bear/pigeons/sparrow/grey squirrel). Set a time limit of five minutes.

Note that not all the animals are mentioned specifically in the passage so students will not be reading their ideas, as has often been the case. Get and give some feedback and encourage students to talk about their own experience or about documentaries they have seen.

C The aim is to demonstrate once more how reading the topic sentences can provide a good overall understanding of the message. Students need to work through the steps systematically to properly benefit. If you can show an OHT or other visual medium of the page on the board, it will ensure that setting up is efficient.

Focus attention onto the first line of instruction, *Read only the title of the article below* …, and give students a moment to read the title. Check the meaning of *biological diversity* – the degree of variation of life forms within an ecosystem. Point out the phrase is often abbreviated to *biodiversity*.

Focus attention onto the rest of the first line of instruction, … *and the topic sentence at the beginning of each paragraph*, but do not allow students to start reading the topic sentences yet. Focus attention onto the final line of the instruction, … *tick what you think is the correct summary of the article below*, and then onto the three options. Give students a minute to read the options so that they know what they are looking for as they read the topic sentences. Note that they will probably think the second option is correct from only the title and the lead-in discussion. Tell them that they should read the options again carefully once they have read all the topic sentences. Set a time limit of three minutes to read the topic sentences and select the correct option – students should read the sentences carefully, but not worry if there is one they do not understand or words within the sentences they do not understand – the sentences are supposed to serve as a framework, not ensure total comprehension of the passage. Students can compare their choice quickly with a partner before you check the answer.

Answer:

1 is the correct summary

D Checking these key items before reading the passage will facilitate comprehension and ensure that students enjoy reading and learning about the topic more. Students will certainly not know words like *teeming* and *culling* – the idea is to check them in a dictionary and then, once understood, discuss why they will occur in the text.

Students should check the items and think about why they will occur individually. They can then discuss each item with a partner. Monitor and assist when necessary. Discuss some of the items with selected pairs. A class feedback stage that checks why each item is mentioned is unnecessary, but you might like to consolidate the vocabulary, some of which will be useful to retain.

E Although students have prepared for the passage, they will need another 20 minutes or slightly more to complete the tasks. For the summary, tell them that the focus is on birds and that they will need to read more than one specific part of the passage to find information. You can decide whether they should compare answers before you give feedback. Write answers on the board for clarity or provide students with a copy of the answer key.

Students might want to know why some of their answers were not correct. Explaining some points may be necessary and beneficial, but going through all of them will be very time-consuming.

If you do want to identify the specific parts of the passage that provide answers to any questions, show an OHT or other visual medium of the passage and highlight those parts on the board.

Answers:

1. I 2. E 3. L 4. C 5. H 6. A 7. N
8. F 9. B 10. K
11. b 12. b 13. a
14. favourable 15. shelter 16. noise
17. genetic 18. migrate

Unit 11 Workbook answers

Vocabulary development

A 1. making 2. missed 3. make 4. seize
5. took 6. made

B 1. insecurity 2. cowardice 3. indecision
4. resilience 5. hesitation 6. optimism
7. persistence 8. adversity

C self-doubt = insecurity
self-confidence = faith in your own ability
self-pity = feeling sorry for yourself
1. c 2. a 3. d 4. e 5. b

D a. makes them different / makes them stand out
b. overcomes huge difficulties
c. decided they must have something
d. do everything possible
e. The fundamental truth
f. when things become difficult
g. an opportunity that was not taken

E 1. pull 2. stop 3. set 4. made 5. going
6. fell

Listening

A Small businesses being affected by recession.

> **Tapescript** 🎧 125 (3 mins, 53 secs)
>
> **A** Listen to two extracts from a Listening test, one from Section 2 and the other from Section 3. What is the common theme of both extracts?
>
> **Section 2 extract**
> **Voice:** During any recession, small businesses are more dramatically affected than larger, more established businesses. Of course, we read about the giant high-street stores going to the wall, but we rarely hear about the small concerns that are folding every day. So, what can a small business do? The simple answer is that they must adapt and diversify, but what does that really mean? Well, the most common tactics are pretty obvious – launch new product ranges and trade at weekends – if, of course, you weren't doing that previously. More than

half of all small business owners admit that they've adapted in order to survive the downturn. Everywhere, we see businesses diversifying and offering new products or services that target new customer groups.

Now, this might mean that some businesses are no longer operating within their specific area of expertise – in their comfort zone, so to speak. Diversification is potentially risky, as I'm sure you can appreciate. Of course, it's essential that managers and thinkers remain entrepreneurial and that they can anticipate market change. They have to be versatile and ready to respond to any opportunity that presents itself. However, it's also vital that they remain focused on their original business plan and retain a very clear image of what their original objectives were when they set up in the first place.

Now, there are other options that businesses are taking – perhaps more drastic options – and they involve paring down the workforce. Many companies have been forced to make staff redundant, even though it's the last step they want to take. An alternative is cutting …

Section 3 extract

Student 1: Well, as business students, we ought to be able to suggest some solutions quite easily, don't you think?

Student 2: Yeah, I don't think it's too difficult. What was the exact brief again?

Student 1: Let's see. Here we are. To make a list of some of the measures that small businesses are taking in order to survive the recession. It's just a brainstorming task really – we're going to go into it more deeply in tomorrow's lecture.

Student 3: OK, well to start with, let's establish why we're focusing on small businesses. Have they been hit harder than bigger businesses?

Student 1: Yeah, I think so. Businesses that have been around for a while can weather the storm – you know, they already have loyal customers and probably more to fall back on. Smaller, newer businesses are more vulnerable and find it harder to stay afloat.

Student 2: OK, so they need to branch out.

Student 3: What does that mean exactly?

Student 2: Well, they need to find new products to offer.

Student 3: Or services.

Student 2: OK – and they need to aim them at new customers.

Student 1: True – but doesn't that mean that businesses lose sight of their original business plan? I mean they become a sort of Jack-of-all-trades. Every business ends up selling the same thing as everyone else.

Student 2: Mm, a bit of an exaggeration, but I take your point. There are certainly pros and cons to diversification.

Student 3: I think in the current climate, one of the ways that business people need to adapt is to become more of an all-rounder. I mean, no, they shouldn't start trying to operate within markets they know nothing about, but they need to be adaptable.

Student 2: OK, I think we've said that now. What else is there?

Student 1: Well, I'm not sure if it's really an adaptation, but I guess quite a few businesses have had to lay people off.

Student 3: Or cut their pay. I think it's always a last resort, but …

B See answers given in Exercise E.

Tapescript 🎧 **126 (0 mins, 16 secs)**

B Listen again. Can you identify any examples where the same idea is expressed formally in one extract and informally in the other?

[Play Track 125 again]

C   1. c   2. a   3. b

Tapescript 🎧 **127 (0 mins, 15 secs)**

C   Listen to the Section 2 extract and for each
    question choose a, b or c as your answer.

[Play **Section 2 extract** of Track 125]

D   1. hit harder   2. loyal   3. branch out
    4. new customers   5. original business plan
    6. lay off

Tapescript 🎧 **128 (0 mins, 12 secs)**

D   Listen to the Section 3 extract and
    complete the notes.

[Play **Section 3 extract** of Track 125]

E   1. d   2. a   3. e   4. c   5. f   6. b   7. e

Reading

A   2 is the correct definition.

D   1. equated with / celebrities   2. G

E   1. G   2. E   3. B   4. H   5. C   6. A

Writing

A   1. made   2. working   3. accepting   4. taking
    5. to work   6. accepted   7. rose   8. became
    9. found   10. remained

Writing task

See notes in the Course Book Writing Module.

Unit overview

The final unit presents language related to an overall theme of *crime, punishment* and *anti-social behaviour*. There is less noticeable recycling of language from previous units here, but there is clear recycling of language from one module to another within the unit. Students are presented with, and practise, specific tasks from the Speaking, Listening, Reading and Writing tests that make up the IELTS exam.

Speaking and Vocabulary

Objectives

- **To present and practise vocabulary related to crime and punishment.**
- **To practise interaction typical of the IELTS Speaking test, Parts 2 and 3.**

The first module aims to orientate students towards the overall theme of the unit and to present vocabulary that will facilitate working through the skills modules. There are two vocabulary parts to the lesson – the first focuses on basic crime terminology and types of offence, while the second focuses on words and phrases related to the criminal justice system and punishment. There is a lot of vocabulary to take in and though the assumption is that some of it will already be known, some students may need to be selective in terms of what they expect to retain. The speaking focus is on the kind of serious debate that is typical of the second and third parts of the Speaking test and there is practice with complex conditional structures.

Start with books closed and write the eight words from the quotation in a random order on the board. You could write the words onto pieces of paper that you hand out, meaning that students physically move them around to form the sentence. Tell students that there is a comma in the middle. Put them into pairs to form the quotation. Refer them to the quotation in the book when three or four pairs have succeeded.

Give them another moment to think about the quotation and then a minute to discuss it in pairs, focusing on what it means and their reaction to it. Spend another two minutes discussing it as a class.

Henry Thomas Buckle (1821–1862) was an English historian and the author of an unfinished history of civilization in England. The quotation can be seen as a liberal or left-wing view of crime – society creates problems like poverty and homelessness and so, of course, some individuals will commit crime in order to survive. The implication is that the criminal is not to blame for his or her actions, which students may want to disagree with.

Vocabulary 1

A Students should answer the questions in pairs. They can take a moment to look words up and think about differences between questions if they need to. Monitor to assist and make a note of observations that can be shared during a feedback stage.

Feedback will need to be clear. Concentrate on making sure words are defined and differences between items are clear. Expand as necessary using the suggestions below with the answer key.

Answers:
1. *Crime* and *offence* are often used synonymously, but there is a difference in usage. In simple terms, a crime is considered

more serious than an offence – note the term *criminal offence*. Parking a car on double yellow lines is an offence, but it is not a criminal offence. *Criminal* and *offender* can be used synonymously, but also have a different usage. A criminal is certainly an offender – an offender is not necessarily a criminal. A person defined as *a criminal* has probably committed a number of crimes or offences – *the offender* is the person who committed a particular single crime.

2. commit
3. more or less – but see the difference between *crime* and *offence* in 1. *Breaking the law* means *committing any offence* rather than necessarily committing a crime.
4. There is very little difference. If an act is *illegal*, it contravenes criminal law. If an act is *unlawful*, it is simply not allowed – that could apply in sport. *Against the law* is used more in spoken language to mean illegal.
5. *Offensive crime* is not possible. The others are common phrases. *Petty crime* is non-serious crime – the committing of *minor offences*.
6. a serious crime

B At this level, students should have already learnt a long list of different crimes. Rather than list them all again in an exercise here, students are encouraged to revise and share what they know. Suggest that they categorize the crimes as they list them, putting all kinds of stealing, for example, together. Keep to a strict time limit and then build up a list together on the board. Do not go into detail about the exact meaning of each crime suggested as you may negate C. A list of common crimes that students should know is provided below.

murder / terrorism / hijacking (a plane) / kidnapping / rape / assault / (armed) robbery / burglary / shoplifting / mugging / smuggling / drug dealing / blackmail / fraud

C Work through as A.

Answers:
1. attempted murder = intending to murder but failing
   manslaughter = unintentionally murdering
2. theft = stealing without the use of force
   robbery = stealing with the use of force
3. shoplifting = stealing from shops
   burglary = breaking into and stealing from houses

4. fraud = the crime of cheating somebody in order to get money or goods illegally
   forgery = the crime of copying money, documents, etc., in order to cheat people
5. blackmail = demanding money (or other favour) in return for not revealing information
   bribery = offering money (or other favour) in return for illegal favour
6. vandalism = deliberately damaging property
   arson = setting fire to property

Vocabulary suggestions
- The person who murders is a *murderer*.
- *Theft* is a general noun that means stealing – burglary and shoplifting are more specific examples of theft.
- A *thief* is a person who steals – a burglar or shoplifter are more specific examples of a thief.
- *Thieve* is a verb that means *steal*, but it is not very commonly used.
- The verbs *rob* and *steal* are easily confused. You *rob a bank* – you *steal the money*. The person who robs a bank or shop is a robber. *Armed robbery* is using a weapon, especially a gun, to commit robbery.
- The verb is *burgle*. The phrasal verb *break in* is commonly used. A *break-in* is a burglary.
- *Shoplift* used as a verb refers to the crime of stealing items from a shop/store.
- *Blackmail* is both a noun and verb. The person who blackmails is a *blackmailer*.
- *Bribe* is the verb and *a bribe* is the favour offered. There is not a word for a person who bribes.
- *Vandalize* is the verb. A person who vandalizes is a *vandal*.

D Read through the instructions with students and tell them to look carefully at the example. See if anyone knows the correct word. Tell them you will reveal the word when they have defined some similar crimes themselves. Give them three minutes to practise in pairs. Monitor to make a note of good examples that can be shared during a feedback stage. Finally reveal the crime for the example – *embezzlement*.

Speaking 1

A By now, students will know how to go about reading the points on the card and thinking about answers. Make sure they understand that, this time, they are not to start communicating immediately – they will listen to some model answers first. Give them a minute to look at the points on the card. You can ask if they think it is an easy or challenging topic to talk about.

B 🎧 Explain that the aim here is not to assess the answers they hear. They will hear two very good answers and they should concentrate on comprehension and then on using the answers as models.

Treat each card as a separate task. Make sure students are ready to take notes and give them another minute to check the points on task card A again. Play the first part of the recording and give them a moment to compare notes with a partner. Go over answers orally, writing key words on the board. Play the recording again as students read the tapescript.

Answers:
1. carjacking   2. young men – often just boys
3. victims are very frightened and feel violated

Work through card B in the same way.

Answers:
1. online crime / identity theft
2. some are still very young / some are better organized – groups working together
3. really bad / like somebody had burgled my house / also it was my fault

---

Tapescript 🎧 **129 (3 mins, 27 secs)**

B Listen to two students talking with an examiner.

Speaker 1

Examiner: So, are you ready?

Student: Yes, I think so. Well, I want to talk about a crime that is very typical nowadays. Of course, in many big cities, it's not always safe to walk around, especially after dark. Street robbery – I think you call it mugging – is common, and for women there are specific dangers too. However, people think they're safe if they drive – at least they used to. Now, that's maybe not so true. Carjacking is happening more and more. It's like hijacking, but it's not a plane – it's a car waiting at traffic lights or at a busy junction. The people who do – no, commit – this crime are usually young men – often just boys. They are poor and probably quite desperate, but that doesn't make it OK. The victims are very frightened and feel violated – sometimes there's violence if the car driver tries to hold on to a bag or a jacket, for example.

Examiner: So, do you mind if I ask if you've personally ever been the victim of this kind …

Speaker 2

Examiner: So, are you ready?

Student: Yes, I think so. I think the most obvious crime of the modern age is online crime – I mean theft of bank details and so on, and even identity theft, though I'm not sure exactly how that works. Online crime is becoming more and more common and it seems that the criminals are always one step ahead of the programmers who make the online safety software. Um, oh yes, the people who commit this crime I guess are getting more clever though I heard many are still very young. I read that now they are better organized – you know, not just one person vandalizing a site, but groups working together to steal money from accounts. They are cracking even secure sites.

Examiner: … And how do the victims of online crime feel?

Student: Oh yes. Well, I can say from experience. When I was shopping online, I suddenly had a message about a big offer to save money. Stupidly, I clicked it and the next thing I had a virus. It was a fake –

you know, it said that my credit card details had been stolen and I must download this program to protect myself – they try to make you panic. If I'd run the program, then they would have asked for my details to pay for the protection and then I would have really been in trouble. As it was, I had to pay a lot for my computer to be cleaned – you know, put back to normal. It made me feel really bad, like somebody had burgled my house – they were in my computer. Also, I felt it was my fault – if I hadn't clicked the window with the offer, it wouldn't have happened.

C   Monitor as students interact and give individual feedback. Ask students if they would like to practise a second time with a new partner to gain confidence.

Vocabulary 2

A   Read through the instructions with students and make sure they appreciate that a number of the words relate to more than one area. They should, however, choose the area they think is most specific. Students work individually, using a dictionary. They will discuss the lexis in B. End the exercise when the majority of students have completed it. Those who have not can check any remaining words with a partner in a moment.

B   Set a time limit of ten minutes – there are a lot of words to discuss and if you do not give them enough time, you will only spend longer giving feedback.

As feedback, show an OHT or other visual medium of the exercise on the board and mark the words appropriately as students make suggestions. Clarify any remaining uncertainties and check pronunciation when necessary. Expand on vocabulary as appropriate, using the suggestions in the answer key. Note that C deals with verb–noun collocations, so do not go into that yet.

Answers:
suspect – P   trial – C   inmates – PR
verdict – C   life sentence – C/PR   arrest – P
jury – C   investigation – P   judge – C
search – P   cell – PR   an oath – C
witness – PR   rehabilitation – PR
evidence – P/C   the accused – P/C
crime scene – P   parole – P   statement – P
barrister – C   plead guilty – C   defence – C
wardens – PR   enquiries – P   prosecution – C

Vocabulary suggestions

- *Suspect* is a noun and a verb – the *suspect* is the person *suspected of* committing the crime. The noun is pronounced with the stress on the first syllable – the verb with the stress on the second syllable. The adjective *suspicious* and noun *suspicion* are formed from *suspect*.
- Contrast *suspect* with *accuse* – if the police *suspect* a person, they believe he may have committed a crime. If they *accuse* the person – they tell him they believe he committed the crime. In court, once a suspect has been *charged*, he is referred to formally as *the accused*. The noun is *accusation* – you *make an accusation*. The accused is also the *defendant* – his barrister defends him in court.
- Suspects and witnesses *make a statement*. They write their version of events as evidence.
- *Witness* is a noun and a verb.
- The defendant can *plead guilty* or *not guilty*. He cannot 'plead innocent'.
- *Search* is a noun and a verb. The police can search a building or a person or they can *conduct a search*.
- *Parole* is permission to leave prison before the sentence has been completed if behaviour is good. A released prisoner is *on parole* for a period of time.
- Contrast *trial* with *case*. The trial is the process that takes place in court. The police investigate a case and there might be three or four cases heard during a day in court.

C   Students should work individually, using a dictionary when necessary and then check answers in pairs. As feedback, ask the class questions which mean using the complete phrases – *What must a witness do in court before he or she gives evidence? What does the judge do at the end of the trial?* and so on. Clarify any remaining uncertainties and check pronunciation when necessary.

Answers:

1. h   2. f   3. d   4. c   5. b   6. a   7. e   8. g

Speaking 2

The aim is to develop the theme and focus on interaction more typical of the third part of the Speaking test. At the same time, conditional structures common to the topic area are presented and practised.

A By now, students will be accustomed to looking at questions like these, but not actually answering them. Give them two minutes to read and think. Make sure that there is no interaction yet.

B 🎧 Make sure students appreciate that they are listening for comprehension, not to assess performance. They should make brief notes as they listen. Play the whole recording and give them two minutes to discuss with a partner. If they have not understood enough to decide whether or not they agree with the points made, play the recording again, pausing after each speaker for them to discuss again or to discuss together as a class. Play the recording one more time as students read the tapescript and go over key vocabulary – *behind bars, an eye for an eye* and *deterrent*, for example.

Tapescript 🎧 130 (2 mins, 35 secs)

B **Listen to some students answering the questions. Do you agree with any of the points they make?**

1

Examiner: Should prisoners be released early if they show remorse or seem to be rehabilitated?

Student: Mm, I'm not sure. I guess you could say that there must be some incentive to behave well in prison. I mean, if you feel there's no hope of getting out before 20 years, say, is up, there's no reason to improve yourself. On the other hand, criminals that commit terrible

---

crimes really shouldn't be released until they've served their whole sentence.

2

Examiner: Would there be so much crime if people were more equal?

Student: I think there'd still be crime – I mean, certain crimes are committed by people from any background. But, perhaps there would be less crime and certainly less crimes that are driven by need – you know, like theft, robbery and so on. I'm quite sure there are prisoners everywhere who are thinking that if they'd had a few more opportunities when they were younger, they wouldn't be behind bars now.

3

Examiner: Is crime ever acceptable if driven by extreme poverty?

Student: I don't think you can say a crime is acceptable or that you condone it, but you might say it becomes more understandable or forgivable. You know, if your children were hungry, you might decide to steal some food from a shop for them.

4

Examiner: Is the main role of prison to punish or to rehabilitate offenders?

Student: I don't think prison should be just a punishment – that's like an eye for an eye philosophy. I'm against the death penalty because it's so clearly just a punishment. Prison should also be a deterrent – I mean it should discourage people from committing crime. That's why prisons must be places that people are afraid of – not too soft. As for rehabilitation, I don't know. Yes – a period in prison should rehabilitate the offender, but I'm not convinced that really happens very often. I read that most people released from prison commit more crime.

Grammar check

Students find conditionals challenging, both conceptually and structurally. At this level, they often know what they want to say, but cannot remember all the various parts of the structure as they communicate. They should spend two or three minutes studying the sentences individually. Tell them to read the advice given after the sentences carefully first. Give them another two minutes to discuss with a partner.

Show an OHT or other visual medium of the sentences on the board so that you can refer to parts of each sentence as you discuss them together as a class during a feedback stage.

Answers:

1. This is sometimes referred to as *zero conditional* – both clauses are in the present tense and relate to the present. *If* could be replaced with *when*.
2. This is usually referred to as *second conditional*. The *if* clause contains a past simple verb, but relates to a hypothetical present. The *would* or result clause relates to a hypothetical present or future concept.
3. This is usually referred to as *third conditional*. The *if* clause contains a past perfect verb, but relates to hypothetical past time. The *would* or result clause contains a perfect infinitive and relates to a hypothetical past concept.
4. This is sometimes referred to as *mixed conditional*. The *if* clause relates to hypothetical past time, but the *would* or result clause relates to a hypothetical present concept.

To help students understand the more complex structures, ask concept questions:

1. Are people equal?
2. Is there a lot of crime? Why is there a lot of crime?
3. Did he click the window? How does he feel about that? What would he do differently?
4. Did they have opportunities? What is the result of that now?

Watch out!

Refer students to the tapescript to identify further examples of conditionals. Then give them two or three minutes to correct the sentences in the *Watch out!* box in pairs. Write the correct sentences on the board for clarity.

Answers:

If society were fairer, there …
If hadn't stolen that money, I wouldn't have ended up in prison.
If he hadn't robbed that bank …
If I'd studied harder at school …

Pronunciation check

Give students time to read and absorb the information about word stress and weak forms and intonation. Make sure they understand what they are listening for in each sentence.

🎧 Play the whole recording for students to simply listen and absorb. Play the recording again, pausing after each sentence to drill. Drill the sentences in parts and then as whole sentences. Give them the time they need to practise.

Tapescript 🎧 131 (0 mins, 41 secs)
Pronunciation check

Listen to some native speakers saying the sentences from the *Grammar check*.

1 If you feel there's no hope of getting out before 20 years, say, is up, there's no reason to improve yourself.
2 Would there be so much crime if people were more equal?
3 If I hadn't clicked the window with the offer, it wouldn't have happened.
4 There are prisoners everywhere who are thinking that if they'd had a few more opportunities when they were younger, they wouldn't be behind bars now.

C Both students in each pair should answer all the questions. They can either take it in turns to answer each question, or play student/examiner roles and answer all the questions before changing roles. They should spend two minutes thinking and planning answers before they interact. Monitor to check performance, especially to see whether they answer the question and how well they use language acquired in the lesson.

Class feedback is unnecessary, but you might like to conclude the lesson by briefly summarizing each of the points as a whole class. Have a time limit in mind and keep it brief. A lengthy whole-class debate could be unfocused and stronger students will dominate.

Listening

Objectives

- **To practise transferring answers to an IELTS Listening test answer sheet.**
- **To practise a range of Listening test task types.**

The overall aim of this Listening Module is to consolidate and conclude. Students complete a range of task types and specifically practise writing their final answers on the provided answer sheet. The one recording serves as the topic of all parts of the lesson, but the recording is divided into parts that practise the various sections of the Listening test.

Listening 1

The aim of the first part of the lesson is to orientate students towards the overall theme and facilitate the presentation and practice of the tasks that come later.

Start the lesson with books closed and write *theft* and *thief* on the board. Elicit and revise various types of theft – noun and verb – and the person who commits each crime.

A Refer students to the pictures. Tell students in advance that if they do not want to answer question 4, they do not have to.

Students should spend three minutes reading the questions and planning answers individually, before answering the questions with a partner. Keep feedback brief, selecting one student to answer each question. If students are all from

the same town or city, they can agree on an answer to 2. Concentrate on consolidating specific vocabulary.

Answers:
1. a – A thief is stealing from a motor vehicle. This is theft (perhaps a robbery, as force has been used), not a burglary.
   b – A thief is picking a man's pocket (the perpetrator is a *pickpocket* – there is no word for the crime).
   c – A burglar is breaking into a house.

B 🎧 The aim is to listen once for gist so that they can better benefit from the specific practice later. Play the recording right through and check answers. Do not give any explanations.

Answers:
1. b   2. c   3. a

Tapescript 🎧 **132 (6 mins, 7 secs)**

B Listen and match the Extracts 1–3 with the pictures a–c.

Extract 1

Police officer: Hello, what can I do for you?

Student: I've just had my purse stolen.

Police officer: Oh dear – I'm sorry. Where was this?

Student: In the High Street. I didn't phone from there as somebody told me the police station was so close.

Police officer: OK, well, how long ago did this happen?

Student: Just now – I came straight here.

Police officer: I'll put 2.20, then, shall I? That's ten minutes ago.

Student: Yes, OK – I don't really mind. Is there anything you can do? I mean, is there any chance of finding whoever stole it?

Police officer: Well, tell me what happened first and then we'll see. Did somebody grab the purse from you? Did you see the person?

Student: No, it was a pickpocket. The purse was in a loose bag that I was carrying over my shoulder. I didn't realize it was missing until I was in a shop buying something.

Police officer: Ah, so it could've been stolen longer than ten minutes ago.

Student: No – well certainly not much longer than ten minutes – I had it just before that when I bought something in another shop.

Police officer: I'll be honest. If you didn't see anybody and you're not sure exactly when this happened, there's not much chance of catching anybody – we don't know who we're looking for. The best thing now is if you give me some details and describe the purse. Very often, thieves take what they want and then throw a bag or purse away. You might get it back and some of whatever was in it. Now, what's your name?

Student: Joanna – Joanna Moore.

Police officer: Is that double *o* and an *e* on the end?

Student: Yes.

Police officer: Is that name on anything in the purse?

Student: Erm, I don't know – yes, it'll be on debit cards – if they're still in the purse. It'll be on my student ID card too.

Police officer: OK, I'll take an address and so on in a moment. Tell me what the purse looked like first.

Student: It's silver with a golden clasp.

Police officer: Gold clasp?

Student: No, just coloured gold I mean. It's not an especially expensive purse. It has a sort of checked design. I mean checks sort of in the leather – not different coloured checks.

Police officer: OK, and what was in it?

Student: There was about £70 cash, two debit cards and a credit card. As I say, my student ID was in there and probably my student bus pass too.

Police officer: And nothing else was taken from the bag on your shoulder?

Student: No, thankfully no – I think they just reached in and …

Extract 2

Voice: Now, this may seem really obvious, but always lock before you leave. In an average year, over 5,000 houses are burgled because the occupier fails to lock their front door. It's easy to forget to lock the front door, especially when you're in a hurry or distracted, and you'd be amazed how many people just don't bother if they're popping out to the local shop or on a school pick-up. It only takes five minutes to get in and make off with a DVD player, laptop or iPod when the occupier makes it so easy. Leaving the front door unlocked on just one occasion is enough. The vast majority of burglars are opportunists – they look for an easy way to get in that won't take long and won't arouse suspicion. The front door is often the first thing they try.

Burglars choose a target that presents them with the fewest obstacles. Again, this may seem obvious, but a building that appears to be unoccupied and insecure is far more likely to be targeted than one which is properly secured. Access to open windows, even at the top of the building, are an invitation, as are unlocked gates to the rear of a property and high fences or trees that obscure a natural view. Needless to say, leaving ladders out where they can be used to assist a break-in is asking for trouble. People who live in multi-occupancy blocks should be mindful not to grant entry to people they don't know via an intercom system, and to be suspicious of anyone who appears to be trying to follow them into the building.

Extract 3

Police officer: Police.

Man: Oh, hello. I want to report a car theft.

Police officer: Your car's been stolen?

Man: No, no – my car's been broken into. Some little … somebody's smashed the back windscreen and stolen quite a few bits and pieces. Can you send somebody here?

Police officer: Well, probably yes, but tell me what's been stolen first.

Man:	A briefcase and a jacket – there were quite a few valuable items in the case too.
Police officer:	Such as?
Man:	My mobile and iPod – oh, and two flight tickets as well – I'd forgotten about them. Urgh, it makes me so …
Police officer:	Yes, I understand. Can I ask why you left the items in the car? I mean, presumably they were in easy reach if they deliberately targeted the back windscreen.
Man:	I only stopped for a few minutes to nip into a restaurant to give somebody a message. I was double parked for goodness sake. I can't believe that nobody saw, or heard, it happen. It's a busy enough street.
Police officer:	OK, so where are you exactly?
Man:	In Upper Street about 30 m down the road from La Fourchette.
Police officer:	How do you spell that?
Man:	La – L-A and then F-O-U-R-C-H-E double T-E.
Police officer:	Thirty metres north or south?
Man:	Towards the tube station – that's north, isn't it?
Police officer:	Yes. And what's the name?
Man:	Brian. Brian Rafferty. That's R-A double F-E-R-T-Y.
Police officer:	OK, I'll get a patrol car to you as soon as possible and they'll take further details. I can't promise it'll be immediate, but it'll be in the next 15 minutes or so.
Man:	OK, thanks.

Listening 2

The first extract is now exploited to present the concept of transferring answers to the answer sheet.

A 🎧 Read through the instructions with students and give them a minute to read through the police report making predictions. Ask them what sort of information is required in each space and what mistakes are possible. Play the whole

recording once only. Students can compare answers in pairs, but do not check them yourself until they have completed B. The answer key is provided then.

> **Tapescript** 🎧 **133 (0 mins, 11 secs)**
>
> **A** **Listen to the first extract again and complete the police report.**
>
> [Play **Extract 1** of Track 132 again]

B Students can work in pairs. They should recognize mistakes and appreciate why some answers will be marked as wrong. They should also compare their own answers with these.

Show an OHT or other visual medium of the exercise on the board. Either you or students can make corrections and establish what the correct answers should be.

Answers:
1. correct   2. answer spelt wrongly
3. answer spelt wrongly   4. correct
5. misheard number   6. too many words used

Corrected answers:
2. Moore   3. purse   5. 70 / seventy
6. bus pass

Refer students to the Exam tip and give them time to read and absorb. Tell them to cover it and summarize the advice given together.

Listening 3

A 🎧 The fact that students have prepared for the topic and already listened to the recording should make the tasks more manageable and ensure that they have a sufficient number of answers to transfer and practise the target skill.

Make sure students understand that they should not try to write answers into spaces in the exercises on the page – they should write on a piece of paper or in their notebooks. Tell them to look ahead to the answer sheet provided further down the page. Tell them they will have ten minutes to transfer answers onto it when the recording has finished. Allow them 30 seconds to read the questions – the time they will have in the exam – and then play the recording.

A Listen to the second and third extracts again and answer the questions.

[Play **Extracts 2** and **3** of Track 132 again]

B Students must work individually in silence to transfer answers to the answer sheet. Give them exactly ten minutes.

C Checking and reflecting on answers is a constant feature of the skills modules. Give students sufficient time to check and think about why any answers were incorrect before moving onto D. You can decide if it would be beneficial to play the recording again, but avoid doing so simply to check individual students' wrong answers. If you do want to draw attention to parts of the recording that provide answers, show an OHT or other visual medium of the tapescript on the board and highlight key parts as you pause the recording.

For this particular Listening Module, instead of students checking the answer key at the back of the Course Book, you may prefer to show an OHT or other visual medium of the answer sheet on the board and write answers in, so that students fully appreciate the correct process.

Answers:
1. front door   2. local   3. 5 minutes / five minutes   4. suspicion   5. unoccupied
6. natural view   7. intercom system
8. (back) windscreen   9. briefcase
10. flight tickets   11. a message
12. Upper Street   13. La Fourchette
14. Brian Rafferty

D Students will be used to reflecting on tasks in this way now. Here, the three questions refer directly to transferring answers. Remind them that identifying what they are doing well and not doing so well is a very good way of focusing on what they can do better next time. Allow students time to reflect and complete the exercise. Conclude by asking them if they are happy with the number of correct answers.

Key vocabulary in context

The aim is as much to practise understanding vocabulary in context as it is to learn these specific words and phrases. Students should work individually to check each item in context in the tapescript and then compare answers with a partner before you check. Do not allow dictionaries.

As feedback, tell students to cover the exercise. Read out the definitions below as students shout out the newly acquired items.

Answers:
1. make off with = steal (and escape with)
2. arouse suspicion = make people suspicious
3. asking for trouble = taking an unwise risk
4. be mindful = be aware
5. grant entry = allow in

Refer students to the Workbook exercises related to this module. Choose to work on them now or set up for homework.

Reading

Objectives

- To emphasize the importance of timing when reading under exam conditions.
- To practise reading more quickly and to improve reading speed.
- To practise a range of typical IELTS Reading tasks.
- To practise writing answers directly onto the answer sheet.

The overall aim is to consolidate and revise rather than introduce a new concept. By now, students will have started thinking about how to time themselves and how long to spend on each of the three passages. There is a longer practice stage with two passages, which students can work through as exam practice. They have practised transferring answers onto the answer sheet in the Listening test – here they practise writing answers directly onto the answer sheet.

Reading 1

The aim of the first stage is to revise what students know about the Reading test and to emphasize the need to think about timing systematically.

A   Tell students to cover the Exam tip. By now, they will know that the answers to the questions will be answered in the tip.

Students should read the questions and think about answers individually, before answering the questions with a partner. There is no need to provide feedback. Refer students to the Exam tip to check answers. Give them time to read and absorb. Alternatively, show a copy of the whole Exam tip on an OHT or other visual medium on the board, revealing one part at a time to focus attention.

B   Read through the instructions with students and make sure they understand that they are planning how they are going to approach each of the three passages in the Reading test – how they are going to divide 20 minutes into smaller periods of time. Students should work individually and then compare with a partner. It is important that students appreciate that there are no hard and fast correct answers here, but you should provide a rough guide as feedback.

Answers:
1. one minute   2. three minutes
3. two minutes   4. 12 minutes
5. two minutes

Reading 2

The practice part of the module is divided into A and B for convenience, but the two passages are intended to make up 40 minutes of the 60-minute Reading test. Note that question numbers continue through from 1–27 and students write their answers directly onto the answer sheet at the back of the Course Book on page 262. You can decide if you want to work through a complete 40-minute test in class time or if you would prefer to work through one passage and then the other. Note that, if you choose the second option, students will not be as independent in terms of timing themselves on the two passages.

The two passages are completely separate, but are related to the overall unit theme of crime. Point out to

students that passages will not be related in this way in the exam.

There is no orientation/preparation stage here – students must use the headings and visual support to tune in to the theme of each passage.

A and B   Either set a time limit of 20 minutes for the first exercise or 40 minutes for both exercises. If you choose the latter option, tell students to decide for themselves if they need a little longer for the second, slightly more challenging passage. Refer them to the page where they are to write their answers.

If students check the answer key for the first passage at the end of 20 minutes, make sure they do not see the answers for the second passage. You can decide if students will benefit from comparing answers with a partner before checking the key.

C   Checking and reflecting on answers is a constant feature of the skills modules. Give students sufficient time to check and think about why they may have answered incorrectly. Students might want to know why some of their answers were not correct. To identify the specific parts of each passage that provide answers, show an OHT or other visual medium of the passage and highlight those parts on the board.

Answers:
Exercise A:
1. viii   2. v   3. iii   4. i   5. vii   6. vi   7. F
8. NG   9. T   10. T   11. F   12. NG

Exercise B:
13. B   14. G   15. A   16. E   17. C   18. F
19. a journalist   20. lengthy and dull
21. vehicle number plates   22. Big Brother
23. police patrols   24. Luton (railway station)
25. E   26. G   27. C

D   Students will be familiar with this reflective process. Points are related specifically to the skills and strategies practised. Note that the answer to the first question will depend to a degree on whether or not they worked through the two passages as one practice test. Remind them that identifying what they are doing well and not doing so well is a very good way of focusing on what they can do better next time. Allow students time to reflect and complete the exercise and then ask them if they are happy with the number of correct answers.

Note that the Consolidation Module also provides an opportunity for students to discuss the content of the two passages.

Key vocabulary in context

Note once more that the aim is to practise the skill of understanding new words and phrases in context, as well as actually learning the selected words and phrases. Students should work in pairs so that they can communicate and share knowledge as they go. They should look back at how any words they are unsure of are used in context. Discourage dictionary use. Monitor to assist and make a note of salient points that can be used during a feedback stage.

Feedback can be given orally, but all must be clear. Involve students, but concentrate on clarifying any remaining uncertainties yourself.

Answers:

1. harass = constantly annoy / upset somebody
   intimidate = deliberately frighten somebody
   victimize = single one person out to intimidate and harass
   terrorize = (more extreme) repeatedly frighten and harass
2. sympathy = feeling of sadness for what somebody else has experienced
   remorse = feeling of regret / shame / guilt for your own actions
3. rumours = (countable) pieces of (often untrue) information about a person's private life
   gossip = (uncountable) conversation about people's private lives
4. disturbing = upsetting
   sinister = potentially damaging / evil
5. supervise = be in charge of / manage
   monitor = check behaviour / performance/ progress
   patrol = move regularly around in order to monitor
6. install = put in place (usually piece of equipment)
   deploy = use for a specific purpose (often people)

Refer students to the Workbook exercises related to this module. Choose to work on them now or set up for homework.

Writing

Objectives

- **To give further practice and increase confidence in terms of knowing what to say.**
- **To revise the various features which contribute to a well-written discursive composition.**

The focus of the last unit was to revise various elements of good report writing. The aim now is to revise and practise various elements of good discursive composition writing.

Writing 1

The first part of the module aims to orientate students towards the theme, present key vocabulary and motivate them to read and write the compositions later in the lesson.

A Conduct as pairwork or put students into groups of three or four if you think it will encourage more debate. Read through the first line of instruction with them and check *imprisonment* – being put in prison. Read through the discussion steps with them, giving them a moment to absorb and think between each. As you read the second point, emphasize that in most cultures, a first offence, depending on what it is, is usually dealt with less severely. You might like to also say that a punishment can depend on whether or not somebody is hurt. Give students two minutes to look through the list of crimes and think individually.

Remember that the principal aim is to prepare for the writing stage, so have a time limit in mind for the discussion. Monitor to assist and make a note of salient comments that can be used during a feedback stage. As feedback, try to summarize – avoid allowing a whole-class debate to develop.

B Tell students to close their books and ask them the question that begins the rubric, *What is the purpose of prison?* Write suggestions on the board, helping out with key words that they want to explain, but do not know.

Refer students to the book again and give them time to read through the reasons. Tell them to look at the pictures as they read. Note that words that might be new are explained. Check pronunciation and drill if necessary. Tell students to cover the exercise and check the key words by asking questions – *Which verb is similar to* discourage? *Which process means prisoners reflecting on their crime and learning new skills?* and so on.

Students can discuss the points in pairs or continue talking in the group they were in. Set a time limit of about five minutes and suggest they put the points in order. As feedback, try to get a class consensus as to which purposes are most important. Decide whether the class believes rehabilitation is a realistic goal.

Writing 2

The second part of the lesson presents the Writing task and then concentrates on identifying points that could be made – planning the actual content of the composition. Students have worked through very similar exercises so will know what to do.

A Students will be accustomed to studying Writing task instructions and then discussing them. Refer them to the instructions and give them a minute to read through and check they understand everything. Encourage them to highlight key words or phrases and make notes as they learnt to earlier in the course. Do not allow them to use dictionaries. Get a brief consensus as to whether or not it is a composition students would feel confident about.

B Emphasize that the notes have been made in preparation to write a balanced argument. Note that most of the words required are words learnt in the first part of the lesson.

Students should spend three minutes reading and completing the notes individually, before comparing answers with a partner. Though students will compare their notes with the model notes in a moment, you might prefer to check some of their ideas first.

C Refer students to the completed notes on page 269 at the back of the Course Book to check answers. The notes are provided below for your convenience.

Completed notes:

Yes – agree
More than half of prisoners released reoffend within a year. (I read this!)
Prisoners mix with other criminals in prison – often who have committed more serious crimes.
When released – prisoners have no job / nowhere to live / have lost family.

No – don't agree
Putting offenders in prison protects society.
Prison life is hard – the fear of going to prison deters offenders.
Nowadays, prisons have rehabilitation programmes – inmates learn useful skills.
What is the alternative? Any alternative is softer than prison.

D Give students three minutes to discuss. Monitor to check. Further class feedback is unnecessary.

Writing 3

A By now, students will be confident assessing and commenting on model compositions.

Students should spend four minutes reading the model, highlighting and making notes individually. Then spend another four minutes comparing thoughts with a partner. Monitor to check what points are being made and to guide when necessary. Do not conduct a class feedback stage as the exercise that follows provides further guidance and direction.

B The aim now is to focus students more directly onto features of the writing that need to improve. Show an OHT or other visual medium of the bullet points on the board and use them to provide feedback on A and set up this exercise. Reveal the points one at a time, checking whether students identified each issue in their pair. As you check the first point, emphasize that one major issue is that the composition is too short.

Give students another six minutes to identify an example of each point. Monitor to check and assist. Do not conduct a class feedback stage. Students will go on to discuss an improved version of the composition (see D).

C The aim is to provide a good model, which students should try to emulate. Tell them that they will discuss which features of the original composition have been improved, but first they will work on linking devices. The task should help them to focus on the revised content and prepare them to analyze it in a moment. Tell them to read carefully and fill the spaces they are sure of first.

Students should read and complete the task individually, before comparing answers with a partner. To give clear, concise feedback, show an OHT or other visual medium of the composition on the board. Either you or students can write the linking devices in. Deal with any uncertainties as you go.

Answers:
1. However   2. since   3. because   4. also
5. Despite   6. still   7. Although   8. In any case
9. Of course   10. On the other hand

D Students should work in pairs. Give them five minutes to discuss. Use the copy of the composition on the board to get and give feedback. Use the selected examples as a guide in the answers below.

Answers:
- points could be expanded to make the composition up to 250 words – (in second version) separate introductory paragraph and two middle paragraphs / all paragraphs have been more fully expressed
- language could be expressed in a more appropriately formal style – *make friends with other criminals / socialize with other criminals* and *put in prison for small offences / imprisoned for petty offences*
- different words could be used to avoid repetition – (in second version) *offenders / reoffending / incarcerated*
- grammatical errors should have been checked – *other criminals somewhat are even more dangerous / criminals who have committed more serious offences* and *no hope to find a job / little hope of finding a job*
- sentences need to be properly punctuated – (from first version) *I read that over half of offenders released offend again within a year so of course some people question how useful is imprisonment and ask if another option can be more effective.*

- full forms could be used instead of contractions – (from first version) *I'm not sure / I am not sure.*

Writing task

The Writing tasks are found either in the Workbook or in the Exam Practice Module at the end of the unit. In this unit, the task is in the Exam Practice Module, and teacher's notes for it can be found in the notes for that module.

Consolidation

Instructions are given for Speaking exercises when the procedure is not clear from instructions in the Course Book. Set Vocabulary and Errors exercises either for individual completion and pairwork checking, or as pairwork when you feel immediate interaction is beneficial.

To correct errors in the final exercise, ask students to come and write the correct sentences on the board while other students offer help. You will need to write the corrections on the board to clarify.

Speaking

A The aim is for students to personalize language learnt in the unit and to have an opportunity to express opinions. Give them five minutes to read through the sentences and decide which they want to complete. Encourage them not to choose those that they find easiest. Students should stand up and move around the class to communicate. Every two minutes, clap your hands and tell them to talk to a new partner. Discourage students from talking in groups. Monitor to assess what has been learnt. A feedback stage is unnecessary.

B This should not be a memory test but, at the same time, the aim is not to read what has already been read. Ask students if they feel that they remember enough to compare ideas. If not, tell them to spend two minutes thinking and making notes about what they do remember, and then to spend another two minutes checking key ideas and vocabulary in their passage. Make sure they close books to communicate – they should not read chunks of the text aloud. Monitor to assess what has been learnt and fluency of expression. A feedback stage is unnecessary.

Vocabulary

A Answers:
1. manslaughter 2. blackmail 3. bribery
4. forgery 5. arson 6. fraud 7. vandalism
8. burglary 9. shoplifting 10. assault

B Answers:
crime scene / police patrol / life sentence / petty crime / first-time offender / suspicious behaviour

C Answers:
1. prosecution 2. deterrent 3. rehabilitate
4. surveillance 5. disturbing 6. harassment

Errors

Answers:
1. correct 2. If I hadn't been walking …
3. correct 4. … I wouldn't have told her.

Exam Practice

Writing

This is the fourth time that a discursive writing task has been the subject of the Exam Practice Module, and since this is the final unit of the course, this will be a good opportunity to set the Writing task itself in class time so that you can check timing and monitor to give assistance.

Even if you decide to set the Writing task itself for homework, work through the preparation stage, which involves pairwork discussion, in class time and make sure that students agree to time themselves strictly.

Note that, in this final unit, there is an additional Writing task set in the Workbook. Students can be more independent with that task.

A The aim is to revise and develop themes presented and discussed in the Writing Module and to prepare for and provide content for the Writing task. Students should be aware of this, and not simply talk about the pictures. Students should read the questions and think individually for two minutes before answering them in pairs or groups of three. Note that if students are from various countries, question 3 will allow an exchange of information – if students are from the same country, they will need to discuss and agree.

Monitor to assist, and make a note of observations that can be used during a feedback stage. Use feedback to get ideas on the board that will prepare for and facilitate the writing stage of the lesson. Keep it brief and concise and avoid allowing a lengthy whole-class debate to develop – students will only repeat what they have already said and strong individuals will dominate.

B Students will be accustomed to studying Writing task instructions and then discussing them. Read through the three steps with them and then refer them to the task instructions. Do not allow them to use dictionaries now. Set a time limit of three minutes before students compare ideas. Before they go on to C, you might like to get a class consensus as to whether or not it is a composition students would feel confident about and how many of them plan to agree, disagree or write a balanced composition.

C The aim is to boost confidence and assist weaker students, who may still be finding it difficult to decide what to say. If you feel students are ready to go straight into the writing stage, or should be more independent by now, you can skip this interactive stage.

D Once students start writing their reports, take into account the time already spent preparing. They should need 25–30 minutes. If they write the report at home, tell them to be strict with a time limit – they will not benefit from spending longer on the task than they will have when it comes to the exam.

When students have completed the task, they should compare it with the model composition on page 269. The model is reproduced below.

Model composition:

Whereas at one time prisons were dark and dirty with poor sanitation and no facilities, today many in the developed world are modern, and provide inmates with comfort and a range of recreation and educational facilities. While some people believe that a degree of comfort is humane and increases the likelihood of successful rehabilitation, others feel that institutions are now little more than holiday camps, suggesting even that some criminals may have a better life inside them than they do outside.

For many people, the principal purpose of prison is to punish. Therefore, they believe that imprisonment should be a dreadful experience that makes offenders constantly regret their crimes. They also believe that the fear of imprisonment should deter crime and that if prisons are dark, miserable places, both first-time offending and reoffending will be reduced. They are angry that taxpayers' money is used to make life comfortable for criminals who may have ruined somebody else's life.

Though I do appreciate these concerns, I do not really agree that prison is too easy. The important thing is that offenders lose their freedom and that society is protected. Making prisoners endure terrible conditions does not make the streets safer. Rehabilitation in prison and facilities that enable offenders to learn and improve themselves are vital. Prisoners are far more likely to reoffend if they have no hope of finding work and cannot socialize. While the fear of prison may deter the vast majority of law-abiding people from committing crime, most crime is committed through desperation. Those most likely to commit crime do not think about the consequences.

In conclusion, I would say that I am not convinced anyway that prisons, even in the developed world, are so luxurious. I am from France, which is certainly a developed country. However, there are frequently stories about the poor conditions in prisons. A few years ago, there were protests about the lack of facilities. Newspaper articles about prisoners enjoying themselves all day are hugely exaggerated.

Refer students to the Exam tip and give them time to read and absorb.

Unit 12 Workbook answers

Vocabulary development

A (correct options in phrases)
1. launched a full-scale investigation
2. shown little remorse   3. making enquiries
4. plead guilty   5. reached a unanimous verdict
6. serve their whole sentence   7. taken an oath
8. to give evidence   9. to spread harmful rumours

B 1. f 2. h 3. a 4. i 5. b 6. g 7. d 8. c 9. e

C 1. e 2. a 3. f 4. c 5. d 6. b

D b

E and F 1. d 2. a 3. b 4. e 5. c

Listening

B and C 1. employment 2. friendships
3. mental health 4. in care 5. from school
6. reading skills
7. home 8. job 9. family 10. drugs
11. rent 12. early release

Tapescript 🎧 **135 (2 mins, 55 secs)**

A   Listen and answer the questions.

Voice: Rehabilitating an offender once he or she has become involved in crime, and especially once he or she has served a prison sentence, is a massive challenge. The vast majority of people simply have no idea of the difficulties and disadvantages that most convicted criminals have had to deal with in the past and still have to cope with on a daily basis.

To start with, many prisoners lack the most basic qualifications and have little or no experience of employment. Few have what we all consider to be social contacts or meaningful friendships and most have housing problems of one kind or another. These practical difficulties are often compounded by drug, alcohol and mental health issues. In short, most members of the prison population have experienced a lifetime of social exclusion.

Here are some disturbing statistics. Prisoners are more than ten times as likely to have been in care as a child than the average person and more than ten times as likely to have been a regular truant from school. They're far more likely to be unemployed and far more likely to be or have been a young parent. Prisoners are almost three times as likely as the average person to have had a family member convicted of a criminal offence.

The level of a typical prisoner's basic skills will shock many of you – 80% have the writing skills, 65% the numeracy skills and 50% the reading skills of a child under 11 years old. And the situation is deteriorating – prisoners under 20 years of age have an unemployment rate and school exclusion background far worse than older prisoners.

It's generally now accepted that handing out a prison sentence actually exacerbates the factors associated with offending and reoffending. A third of prisoners, for example, lose their home while in prison. Two-thirds lose their job and a fifth face increased financial problems. Nearly half lose contact with their family. There's also the likelihood of mental and physical health deteriorating further and exposure to drugs – whether already using them or not.

Let me tell you about a real case. Annette lost her accommodation as a result of being in prison. Nobody talked to her when she arrived or during the following months about how she could keep her house or what she could do to ensure that she had somewhere to live on release. Her rent arrears accumulated and she was evicted. Her request for early release was rejected because of the absence of an approved address. When she was finally released, her local authority refused to provide accommodation because of her previous rent arrears. You may find this story incredible but it happens over and over. So, is there a solution? Well, I want to …

Writing

C Model composition:

There is a lot of evidence that shows that rehabilitating offenders in prison is a huge challenge. Despite improved facilities and programmes in prisons that mean inmates can learn to socialize better and acquire new skills, over half reoffend within a year of being released from prison.

There are various reasons for this depressing statistic. Firstly, most people that are sent to prison in the first place are hugely disadvantaged. Many have grown up in care and lack real friendships. Many have had a very poor education and lack appropriate reading, writing and numeracy skills, and most have never been in employment. A high percentage of prisoners come from families where there is a history of criminal activity. All this means that even if opportunities to learn do exist in prison, many prisoners do not know how to access them.

Many prisoners reoffend because of their experience in prison. They socialize with other criminals who have sometimes committed more serious offences than they have and they are likely to be exposed to drugs. While they serve their sentence, they may lose their accommodation or a job, if they have one. Some may lose contact with their family. In short, they are released knowing more about crime and with more reasons to commit crime.

It is very difficult to offer concrete suggestions but, for me, it is clear that the problem must be addressed. Even if it is expensive to help released prisoners pay their rent and find a job, it must be more cost-effective than dealing with more crime. Perhaps programmes could be put in place where accommodation and a job in the community is arranged shortly before the release date.

Reading

B 1. B   2. E   3. F   4. C   5. B   6. D   7. A   8. C
9. NG   10. F   11. T   12. F   13. NG
14. b   15. a thumb print   16. two brothers
17. Lesley Whittle   18. pensioners

Writing task

See notes in the Course Book Writing Module.

Review 3

Speaking and Vocabulary

A Make sure students understand that they are not going to actually talk about the topics again yet. The aim is to discuss whether or not they can. Give them time to read through the topics and think. Tell them to take into consideration whether they have something interesting to say and whether they have the range of vocabulary they need.

B Allow them time to talk in pairs and then get a general class consensus.

C Encourage students to practise exam type interaction – questions and answers rather than random discussion. Students should spend time planning questions individually, but do not need to write them. Students in each pair could select even- and odd-numbered questions so that the process is shortened and they do not ask each other the same questions.

D Give students a moment to look at the web and then read through the headings with them. Start by telling them not to look back at the Course Book units to see what they have retained. After five minutes, allow them to look back, adding words and phrases from the unit. Encourage them to do this in order to store new language rather than simply fulfil a task.

Listening

A Students may or may not need to look back in order to answer the questions. Make sure they know what to do and give them five minutes to work through the questions. Check the answers quickly as a class.

Answers:

1. a matching features task / There are more instructions and it is necessary to keep looking at options at the same time that you listen.
2. You see how the talk is organized and know when the speaker will change topic or move on to a new point.
3. Sections 2 and 4
4. Sections 1 and 3
5. Section 3
6. transfer answers to the answer sheet / 10 minutes
7. spell words wrongly / use too many words

B Give students three minutes to complete the exercise individually and another three minutes to compare thoughts with a partner. Get a general consensus as to whether students feel that their listening skills have improved, but do not go through each point laboriously.

Reading

A   Work through as with the questions about listening skills (Listening A).

Answers:

1. when the speaker passage is largely the author's opinion
2. Students' own answers.
3. references that point forwards and back in a passage – pronouns / adverbs / general nouns and noun phrases / lists of examples
4. cross off those you are sure about so there are fewer options remaining
5. so that you do not spend too long on one passage and have too little time for another / so that you do not spend too long reading without a purpose before you start the tasks
6. because you can copy words from the passage and spell them correctly

B   Work through as with the questions about listening skills (Listening B).

Writing

A   Suggest that students read all questions, think and answer individually before comparing thoughts with a partner. Give them five minutes to read and think and another five to discuss. You might prefer to treat question 5 as a separate exercise. Note that pairwork gives everyone the opportunity to talk about their progress, development and concerns – a quick whole-class feedback stage will not allow that. The benefit here is in identifying strengths and weaknesses and discussing them. No solutions can be offered to each student individually right now.

B   For the process to be beneficial, students must choose reports that clearly show development and improvement. They will need time to select reports carefully and you will need to monitor to assist and give advice. Make sure each individual has selected two appropriate reports before the exchange. Continue to monitor as they give each other feedback.

C   Students should read and think individually before comparing ideas. Read through the instructions and points 1 and 2 with them and make sure they know what to do. Give them five minutes to work individually and then another five minutes to discuss.

D   Work through as with Exercise B. Conclude the discussion by getting a general consensus as to which areas of their writing students have most improved.

What next?

A   Give students time to read through the comments individually and think. Tell them there is no limit to the number of comments they can agree with. Students can either compare with a partner or talk together as a class about how they feel about exams. Write a few of their tips on the board so that they can compare them with the tips they read in a moment.

B   You will know whether your students will benefit from looking at and discussing the tips in class time or if they should read through them in their own time. If you decide to read through them in class time, show an OHT or other visual medium of the tips on the board and reveal them one by one, focusing attention on each in turn.

IELTS Target 5.0
CEF LEVELS A2 TO B1/IELTS 3.5–5.0

Preparation for IELTS General Training – Leading to IELTS Academic

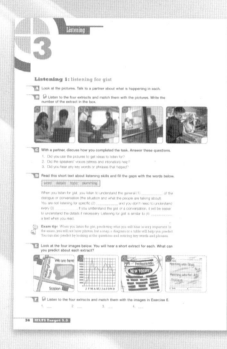
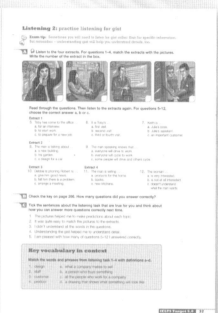

IELTS Target 5.0 is for students who are entering IELTS study between Band 3 (extremely limited user) and Band 4 (limited user). Such students might need to raise their IELTS score to:

- satisfy criteria set by the institution where they study
- work towards a score of 5.0
- lay the foundation for further study of the Academic Module

KEY FEATURES

- Comprehensive 240-hour course
- IELTS General Training ideal for students on lower band scores
- Provides foundation for further General Training or Academic study
- Four sections provide flexibility of use

- Clear, scaffolded activities
- Focus on real student needs
- Interactive Course Book CD-ROM
- Teacher's Book provides vocabulary development

IELTS Target 5.0

Course Book and Workbook, sample tests, audio DVD	978 1 90861 493 3
Teacher's Book	978 1 90861 494 0
Interactive Course Book CD-ROM	978 1 85964 578 9

www.garneteducation.com

Garnet EDUCATION

IELTS Target 7.0

CEF LEVELS B2–C1/IELTS 6.5–7.0

Preparation for IELTS Academic

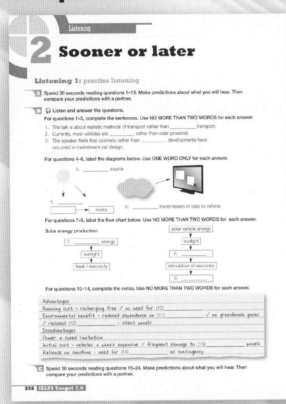

IELTS Target 7.0 addresses the increasing trend of institutions demanding higher language competence from students. This level provides less pre-skills guidance and scaffolding, and more post-skills practice and analysis. It aims to develop core language skills and improve scores through more challenging topics and tasks.

KEY FEATURES

- Live and learn
- Sooner or later
- Haves and have-nots
- Man and beast

IELTS Target 7.0
Course Book and audio DVD 978 1 90861 491 9
Teacher's Book 978 1 90861 492 6

www.garneteducation.com

Garnet EDUCATION

Notes